Suikoden III

幻想水滸伝

............successor of fate............

Vol. 9
by Aki Shimizu

HAMBURG // LONDON // LOS ANGELES // TOKYO

Suikoden III Vol. 9
created by Aki Shimizu

Translation - Patrick Coffman
English Adaptation - Alan Swayze
Associate Editor - Hope Donovan
Retouch and Lettering - Lucas Rivera
Production Artist - Jennifer Carbajal
Cover Design - Gary Shum

Editor - Rob Tokar
Digital Imaging Manager - Chris Buford
Production Managers - Jennifer Miller and Mutsumi Miyazaki
Managing Editor - Lindsey Johnston
VP of Production - Ron Klamert
Publisher and E.I.C. - Mike Kiley
President and C.O.O. - John Parker
C.E.O. and Chief Creative Officer - Stuart Levy

A  Manga

TOKYOPOP Inc.
5900 Wilshire Blvd. Suite 2000
Los Angeles, CA 90036

E-mail: info@TOKYOPOP.com
Come visit us online at www.TOKYOPOP.com

Editor's note: Special thanks to Udi Hoh of suikosource.com
for her invaluable assistance in fact-checking this book.

ISBN: 1-59816-181-4

First TOKYOPOP printing: March 2005
0 9 8 7 6 5 4 3 2 1
Printed in the USA

Zexen

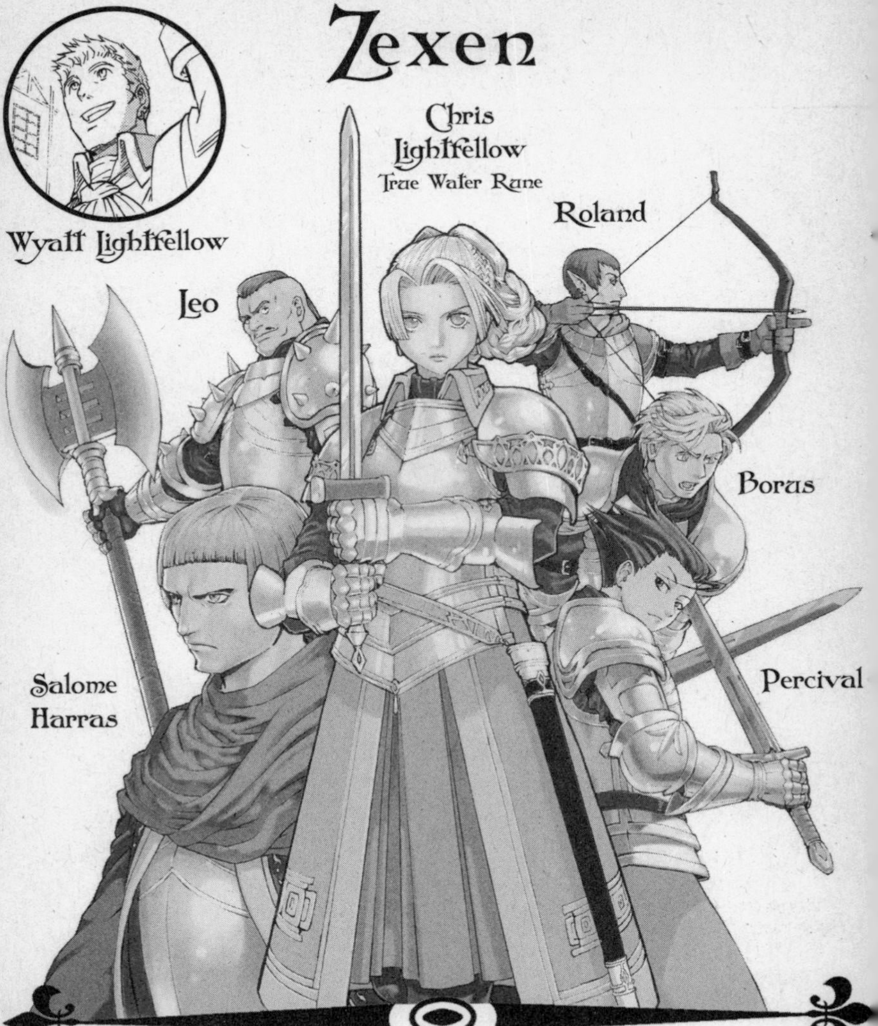

Wyatt Lightfellow
Chris Lightfellow
True Water Rune
Roland
Leo
Borus
Salome Harras
Percival

Suikoden III
幻想水滸伝

Characters

Grasslands

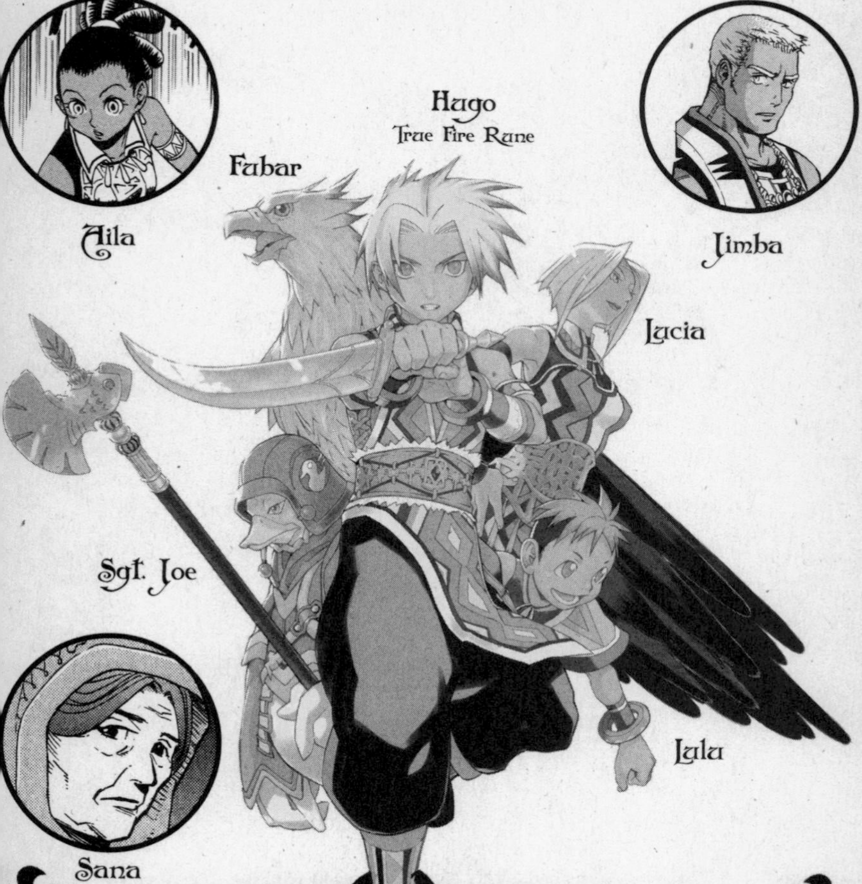

Hugo
True Fire Rune
Fubar
Aila
Jimba
Lucia
Sgt. Joe
Lulu
Sana

Suikoden III
幻想水滸伝
Characters

Mercenaries

Geddoe
True Lightning Rune

Ace

Queen

Joker

Jacques

Suikoden III
幻想水滸伝
Characters

Fire Bringers

Wyatt Lightfellow
(a.k.a. Jimba)
True Water Rune

Flame Champion
True Fire Rune

Geddoe
True Lightning Rune

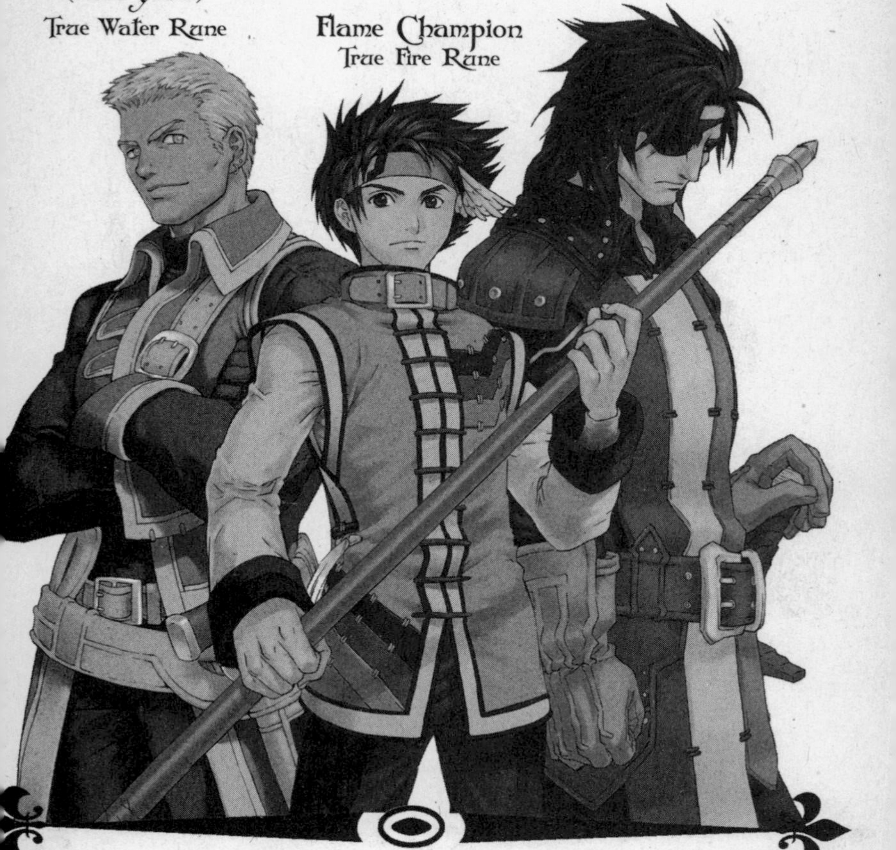

Suikoden III
幻想水滸伝
Characters

Harmonia

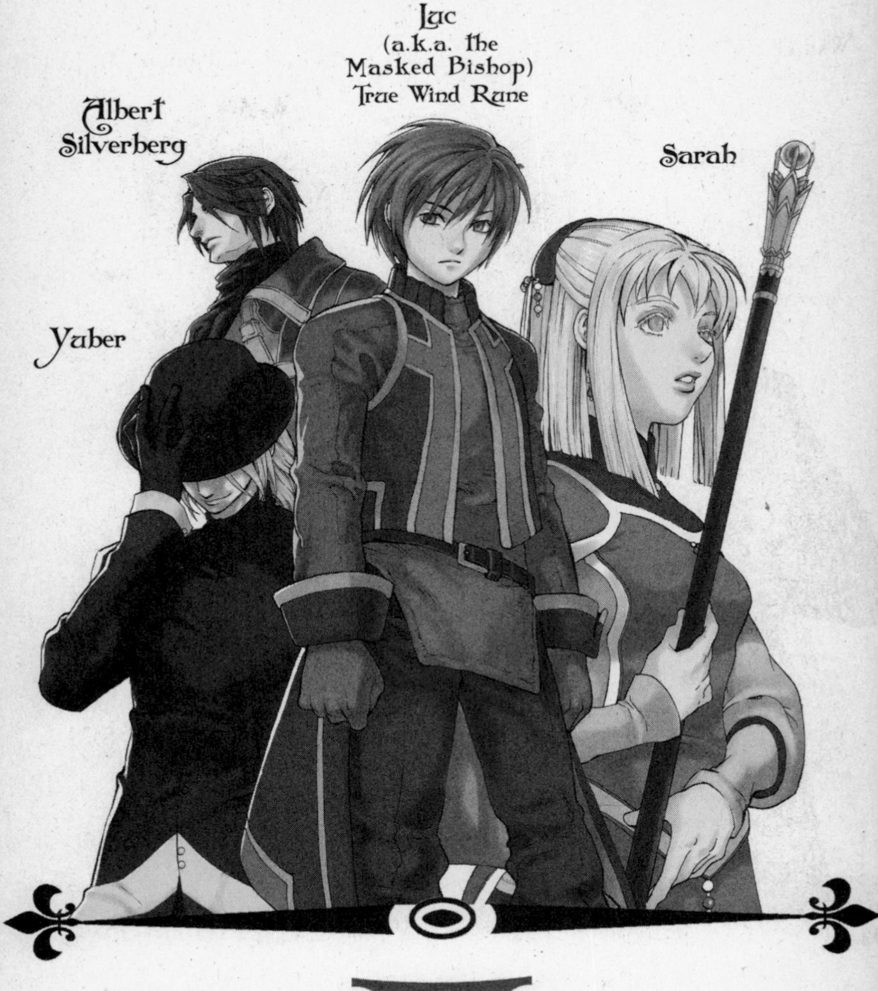
Luc
(a.k.a. the
Masked Bishop)
True Wind Rune
Albert
Silverberg
Sarah
Yuber

Suikoden III
幻想水滸伝
Characters

Budehuc Castle

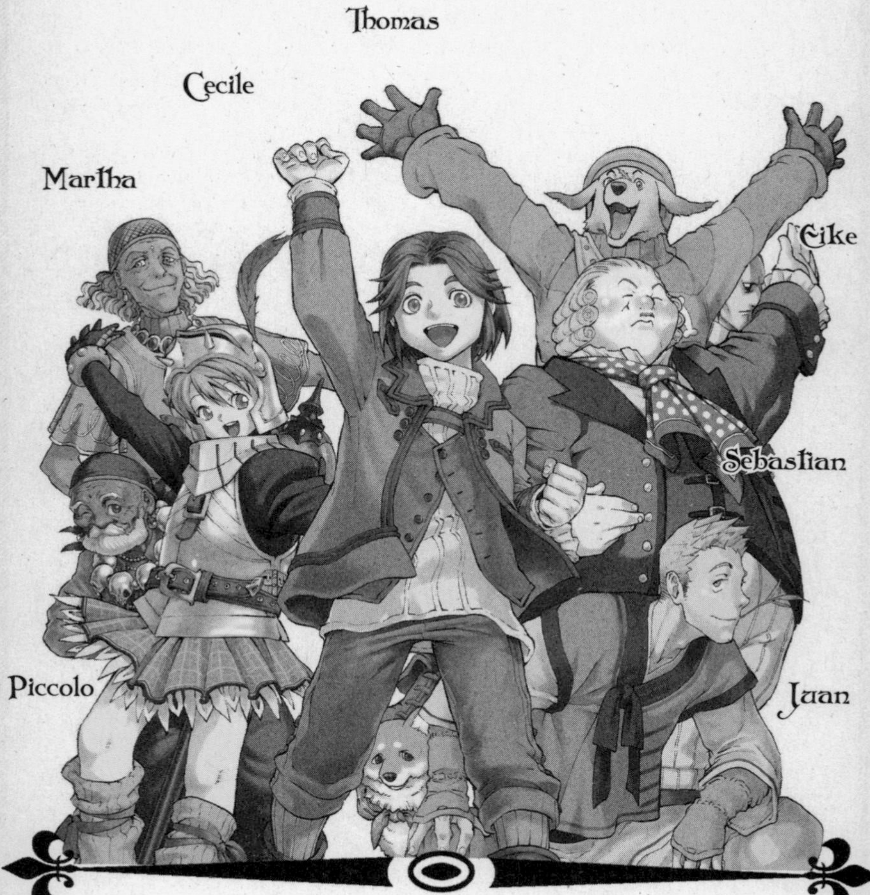
Thomas
Cecile
Martha
Eike
Sebastian
Piccolo
Juan

Suikoden III
幻想水滸伝
Characters

Story Thus Far...

The war between the Six Clans of the Grasslands and the Zexen Commonwealth dragged on far longer than either side expected. Tired of the seemingly pointless conflict, both parties sought a truce.

Lucia, chief of the Karaya Clan, sent her son Hugo to Vinay Del Zexay while the Zexens sent Knight Captain Chris Lightfellow (a.k.a. the Silver Maiden) to the Grasslands. Almost immediately after the truce declarations, both sides appeared to be betrayed by their former enemies. The Lizard Clan reported that their leader had been secretly murdered by the Zexens, while Chris Lightfellow heard reports of the Grasslanders ambushing her forces.

Reluctantly, the Silver Maiden agreed to let her forces set fire to the Karaya village in order to create an escape route for her troops. While the Karaya village burned out of control, Hugo, his best friend Lulu, and the Duck Clan warrior Sgt. Joe returned and discovered Lady Chris in the midst of the chaos.

Enraged, young Lulu attacked Chris and--without thinking--the Knight Captain killed Lulu on the spot. Realizing their vulnerability, Sgt. Joe prevented Hugo from attacking Lady Chris and, in return, Chris spared both of their lives.

Chris' confrontations with Grasslanders were far from over, as she ended up at Budehuc castle, which is owned by Sir Thomas...who was playing host to Hugo! Though Hugo attacked from behind, Chris quickly got the upper hand. Chris avoided killing Hugo, but her young opponent would not stop attacking her until Sir Thomas broke up the fight.

After the battle, Chris left her fellow knights to accompany Nash Clovis on a quest to find her father. According to Nash, Wyatt Lightfellow was not only alive, he was also a "Fire Bringer"--a person in possession of a True Rune that grants him incredible powers and longevity. Nash contends that Chris' father is one of the two men who were always at the side of the Flame Champion, the legendary hero who used the power of the True Fire Rune to end the war between the Grasslands and Holy Harmonia.

Unbeknownst to most of the Zexens or Grasslanders, Chris' father Wyatt Lightfellow and Karaya warrior Jimba were one and the same person. Possessing the True Water Rune, Wyatt/Jimba was also a friend and fellow "Fire Bringer" of Geddoe, a Harmonian mercenary captain who wielded the True Lightning Rune. Geddoe's secret possession of the True Lightning Rune was revealed to his allies and enemies alike when he recently used it in battle against Yuber, an agent of the mysterious Masked Bishop of Holy Harmonia. Despite the revelation, Geddoe's group decided to stay together, and his group of mercs has taken the Firebringers' mission as their own.

In the meantime, aged Sana told Hugo the previous Flame Champion had thrown away the power of his Rune and, over the years, grew old and died. With some slight hesitation, Hugo took on the True Fire Rune that Sana had been keeping hidden. Upon receiving the power, Hugo swore to use it to defend the Grasslands…though he was too far away to save his friends, family and allies from another defeat. Aside from sheer numbers, the Harmonian forces had two distinct advantages: their attack was led by the wielder of the True Earth Rune--Harmonian Lord Sasarai--and it was planned by Albert Silverberg--Caesar Silverberg's older brother!

As the defeated Grasslanders traveled to the Duck Clan's village, Caesar Silverberg tried to convince their leaders to listen to his tactical advice. Realizing the Grasslanders were short on almost everything, his proposals caused an uproar among the chieftans. First, he proposed to flood the Duck Clan village as a way to counter the coming Harmonian attack. Second, he proposed that the Grasslanders form an alliance with the Zexen.

As Chris Lightfellow neared her father's location, Wyatt Lightfellow / Jimba was attacked while trying to fully unseal his True Water Rune. Though a formidable warrior, even Wyatt realized he had no chance against the Masked Bishop when it was revealed that the Bishop wielded the True Wind Rune. Wyatt fought bravely and even managed to shatter the bishop's mask but, in the end, he was defeated. Before the now wounded and unmasked Bishop could acquire the True Water Rune, Chris Lightfellow and Nash Clovis arrived. The Bishop--a.k.a. Luc--escaped and Chris had only moments with her father as he lay dying.

To make matters worse, Wyatt's partially unsealed Rune was building in power as if about to explode. Holding her father's hand, Chris took on the True Water Rune and with it, the memories it held. As Wyatt's memories of their years apart faded into Chris' consciousness, he managed to utter one final apology to his daughter before he died.

With Wyatt dead and their quest together at an end, Nash headed toward Harmonia and Chris returned to Zexen. While Chris agreed to try another truce with the Grasslands, Lord Sasarai was betrayed by Albert and supplanted by Luc. While Luc stole the True Earth Rune from Sasarai, he also revealed that the two of them are merely Rune-created copies of their superior (Hikusaak) and they were created as Rune vessels so Hikusaak can gain ultimate power.

Sasarai's followers freed their weakened leader from his twin, but Luc's power is only growing. Using the power of the True Earth Rune, Sarah, Luc's subordinate, managed to steal Geddoe's True Lightning Rune. Geddoe was attacked while trying to convince Franz, a bug soldier, to get his compatriots to revolt. Since the theft of his True Rune, Geddoe's survival--and the survival of his allies--is increasingly unlikely.

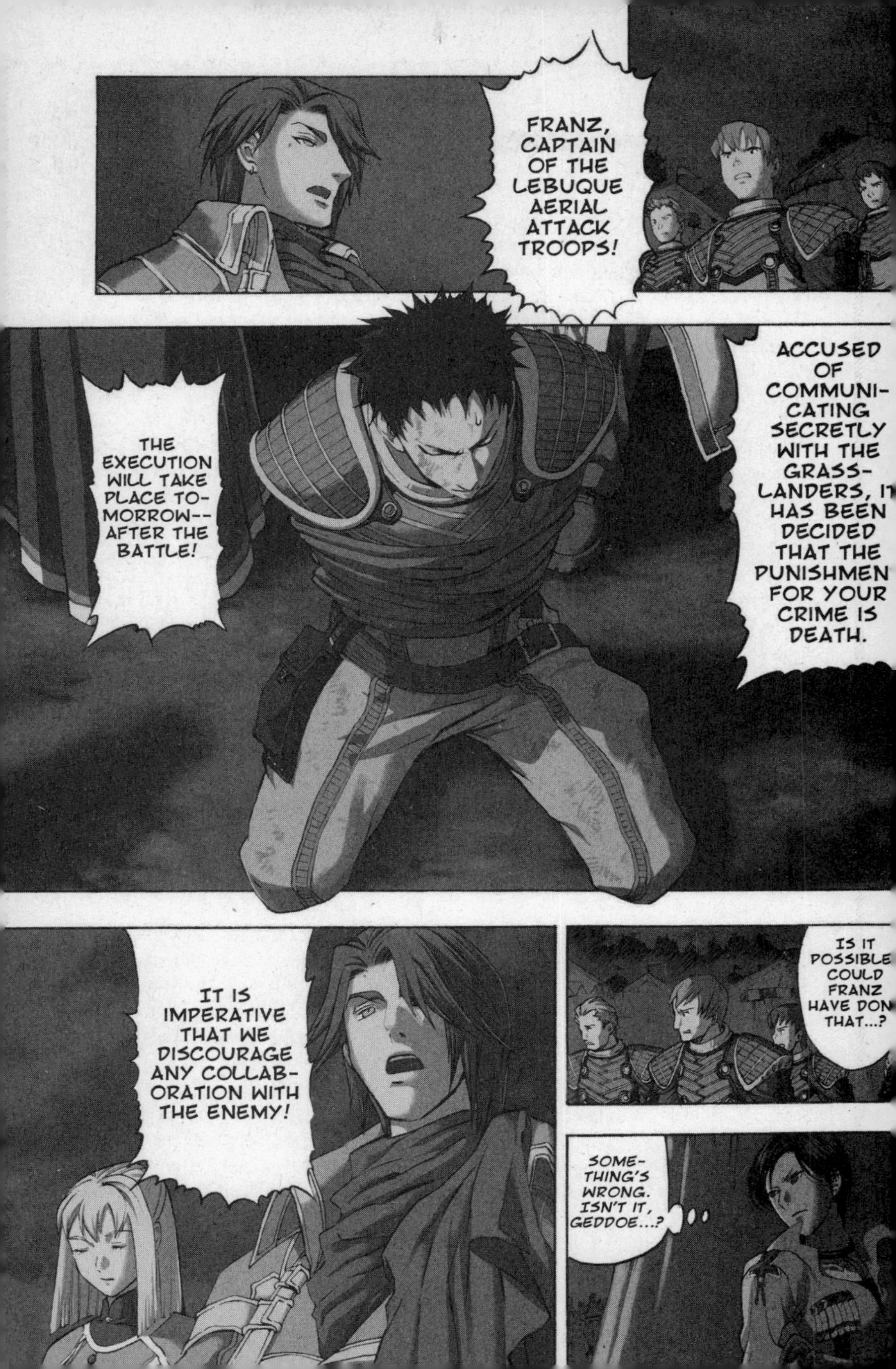
FRANZ, CAPTAIN OF THE LEBUQUE AERIAL ATTACK TROOPS!
ACCUSED OF COMMUNICATING SECRETLY WITH THE GRASSLANDERS, IT HAS BEEN DECIDED THAT THE PUNISHMEN FOR YOUR CRIME IS DEATH.
THE EXECUTION WILL TAKE PLACE TOMORROW--AFTER THE BATTLE!
IS IT POSSIBLE COULD FRANZ HAVE DON THAT...?
SOMETHING'S WRONG. ISN'T IT, GEDDOE...?
...
IT IS IMPERATIVE THAT WE DISCOURAGE ANY COLLABORATION WITH THE ENEMY!

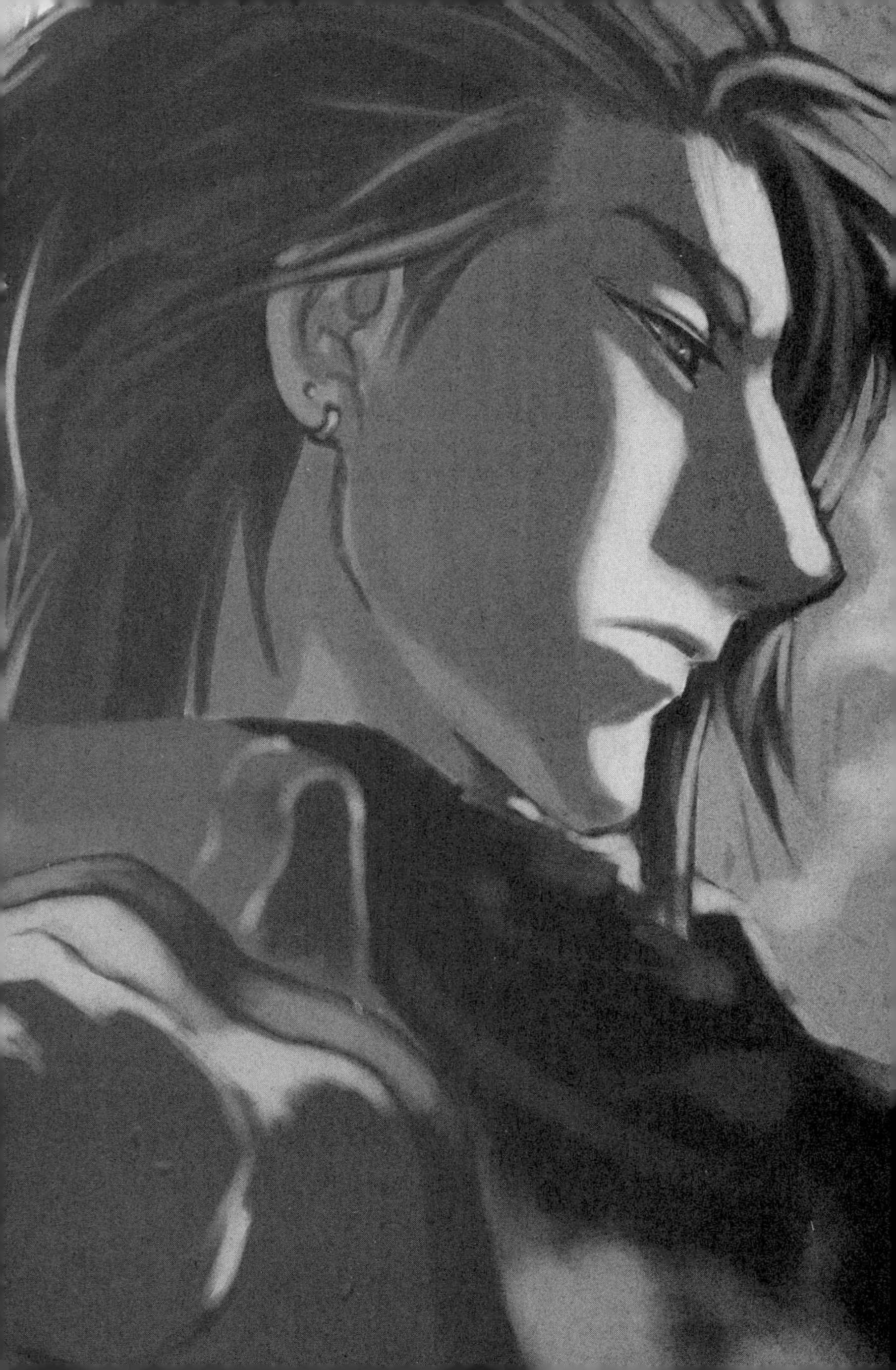

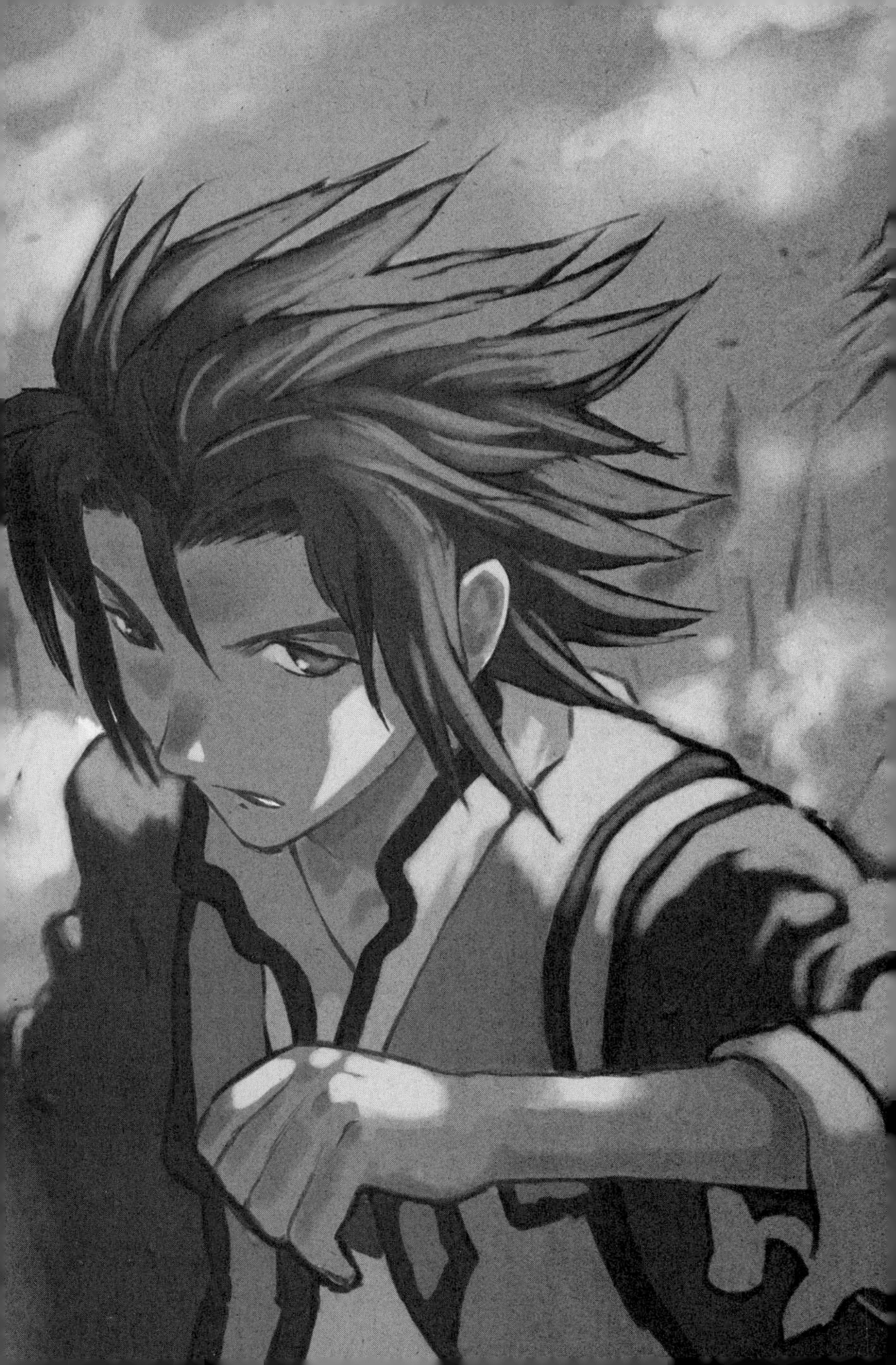

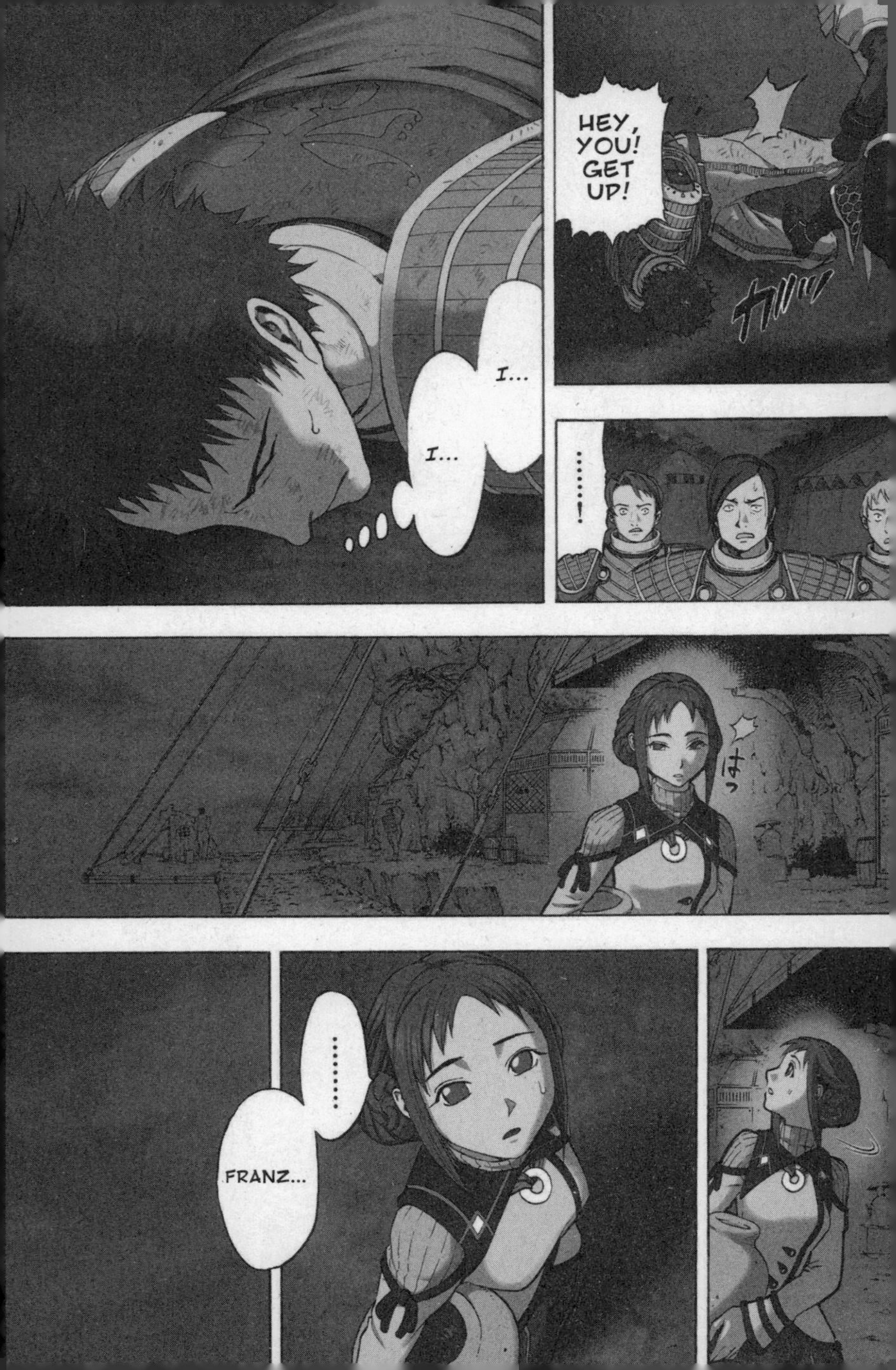
HEY, YOU! GET UP!
......!
I...
I...
はっ
......
FRANZ...

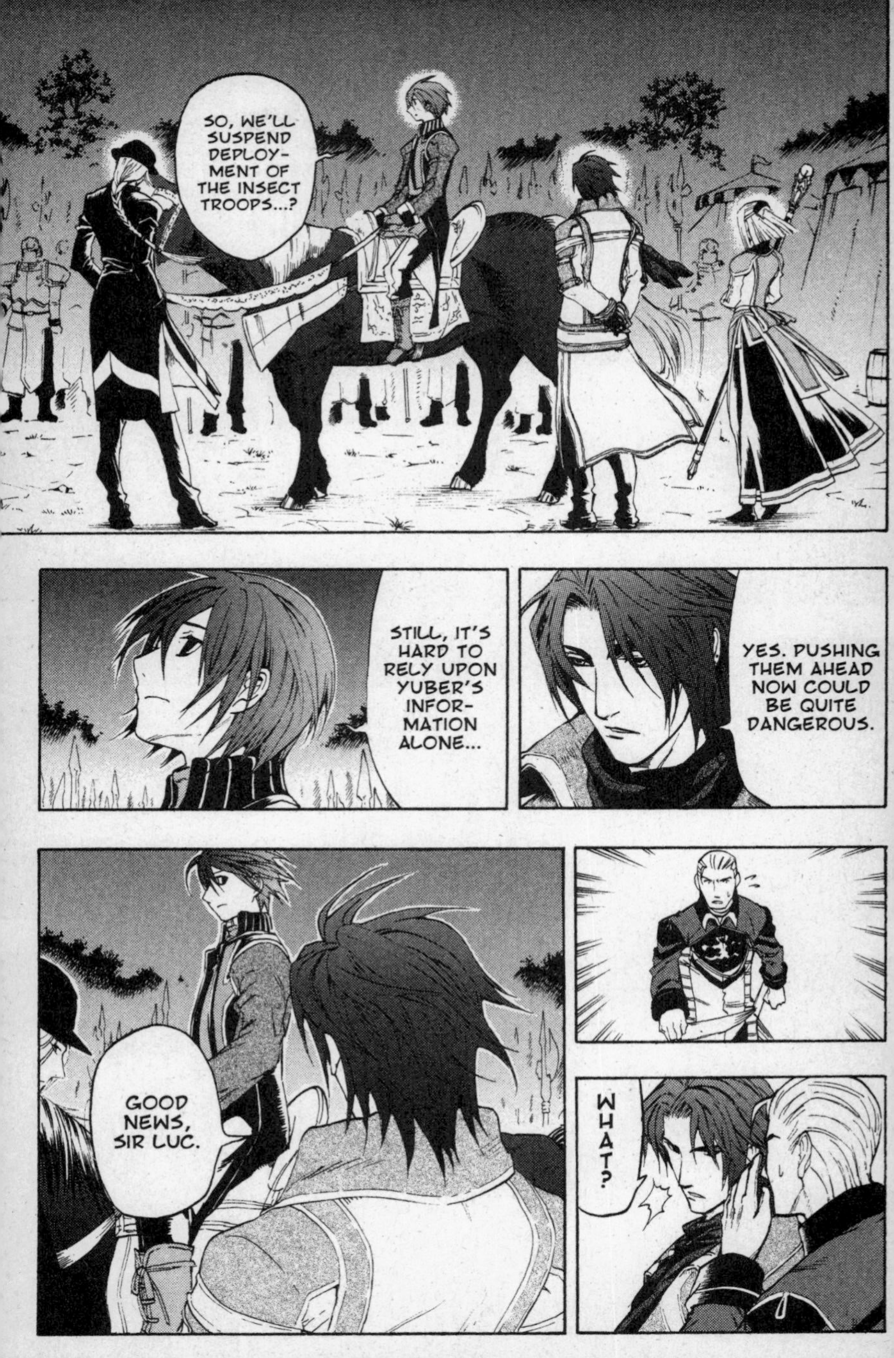
SO, WE'LL SUSPEND DEPLOY-MENT OF THE INSECT TROOPS...?
YES. PUSHING THEM AHEAD NOW COULD BE QUITE DANGEROUS.
STILL, IT'S HARD TO RELY UPON YUBER'S INFOR-MATION ALONE...
WHAT?
GOOD NEWS, SIR LUC.

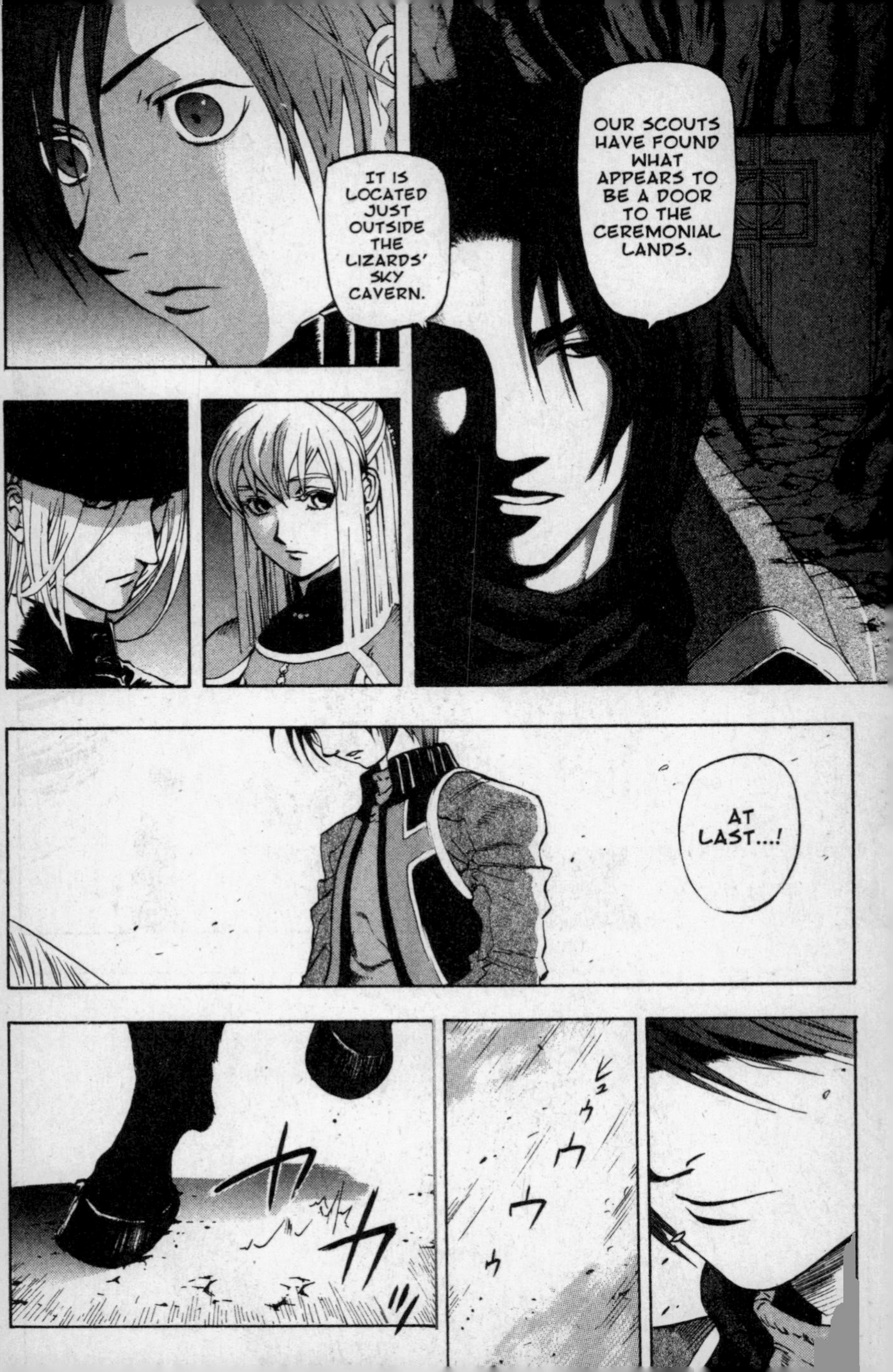
OUR SCOUTS HAVE FOUND WHAT APPEARS TO BE A DOOR TO THE CEREMONIAL LANDS.
IT IS LOCATED JUST OUTSIDE THE LIZARDS' SKY CAVERN.
AT LAST...!
ヒュウウウゥ
カカッ

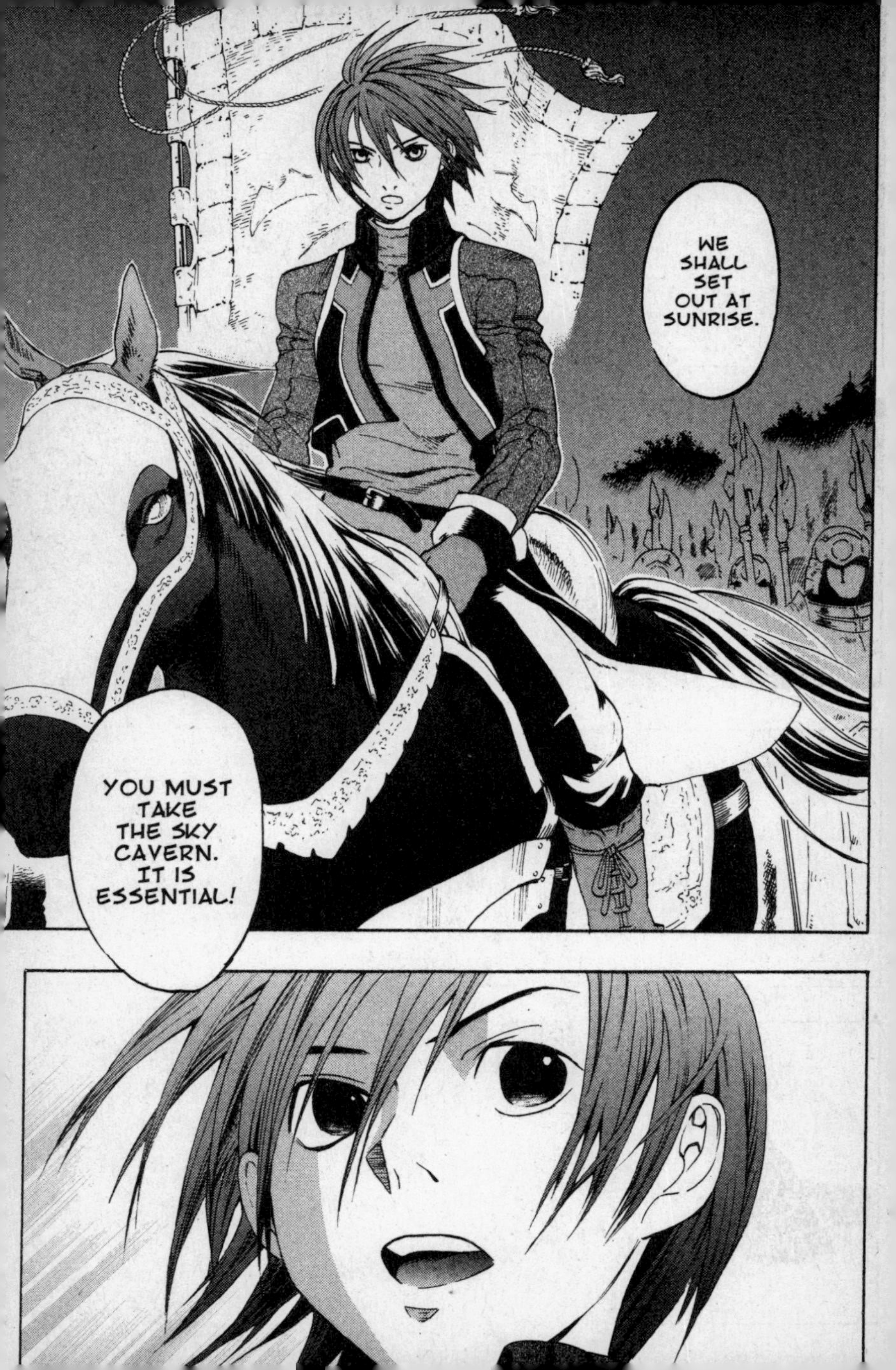
WE SHALL SET OUT AT SUNRISE.
YOU MUST TAKE THE SKY CAVERN. IT IS ESSENTIAL!

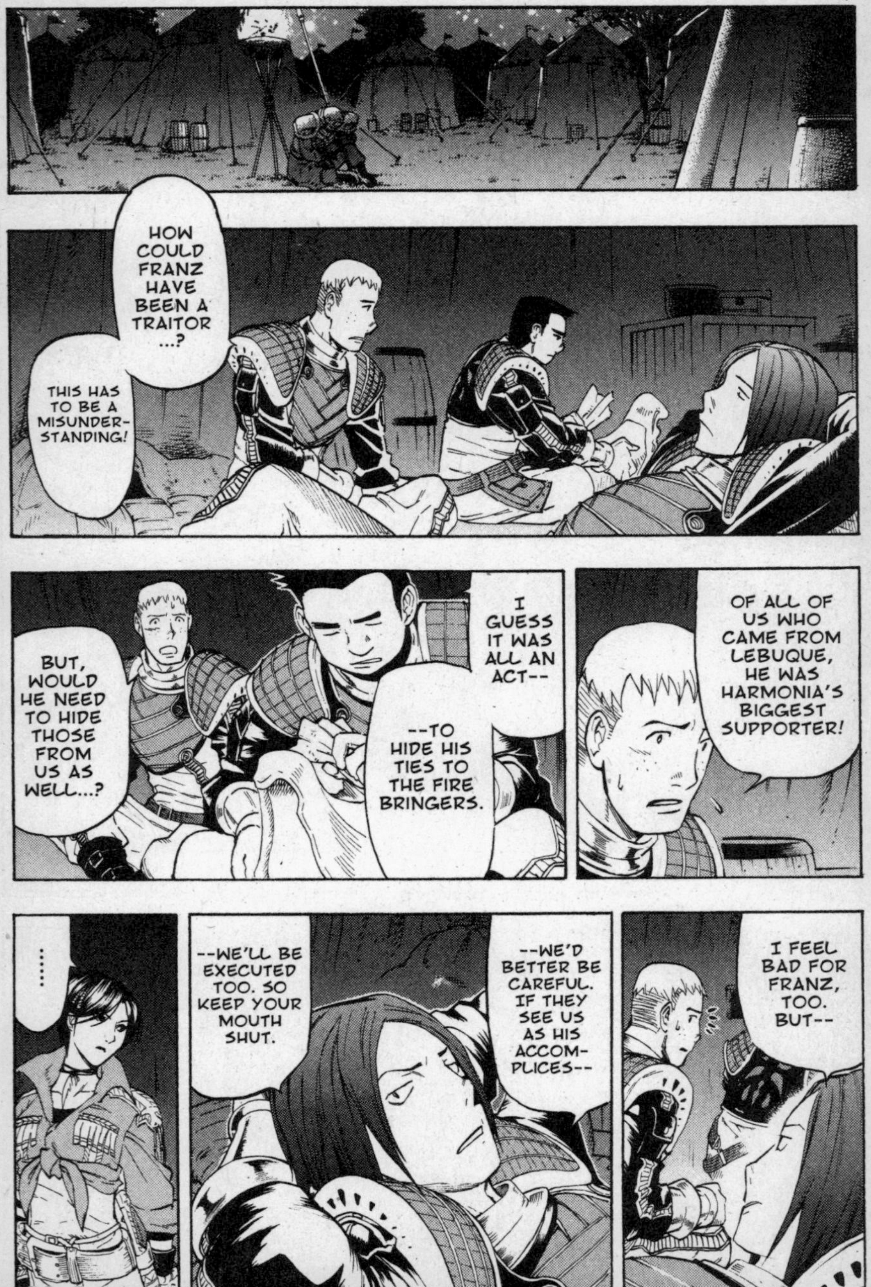
HOW COULD FRANZ HAVE BEEN A TRAITOR...?
THIS HAS TO BE A MISUNDERSTANDING!
OF ALL OF US WHO CAME FROM LEBUQUE, HE WAS HARMONIA'S BIGGEST SUPPORTER!
I GUESS IT WAS ALL AN ACT--
--TO HIDE HIS TIES TO THE FIRE BRINGERS.
BUT, WOULD HE NEED TO HIDE THOSE FROM US AS WELL...?
I FEEL BAD FOR FRANZ, TOO. BUT--
--WE'D BETTER BE CAREFUL. IF THEY SEE US AS HIS ACCOMPLICES--
--WE'LL BE EXECUTED TOO. SO KEEP YOUR MOUTH SHUT.
......

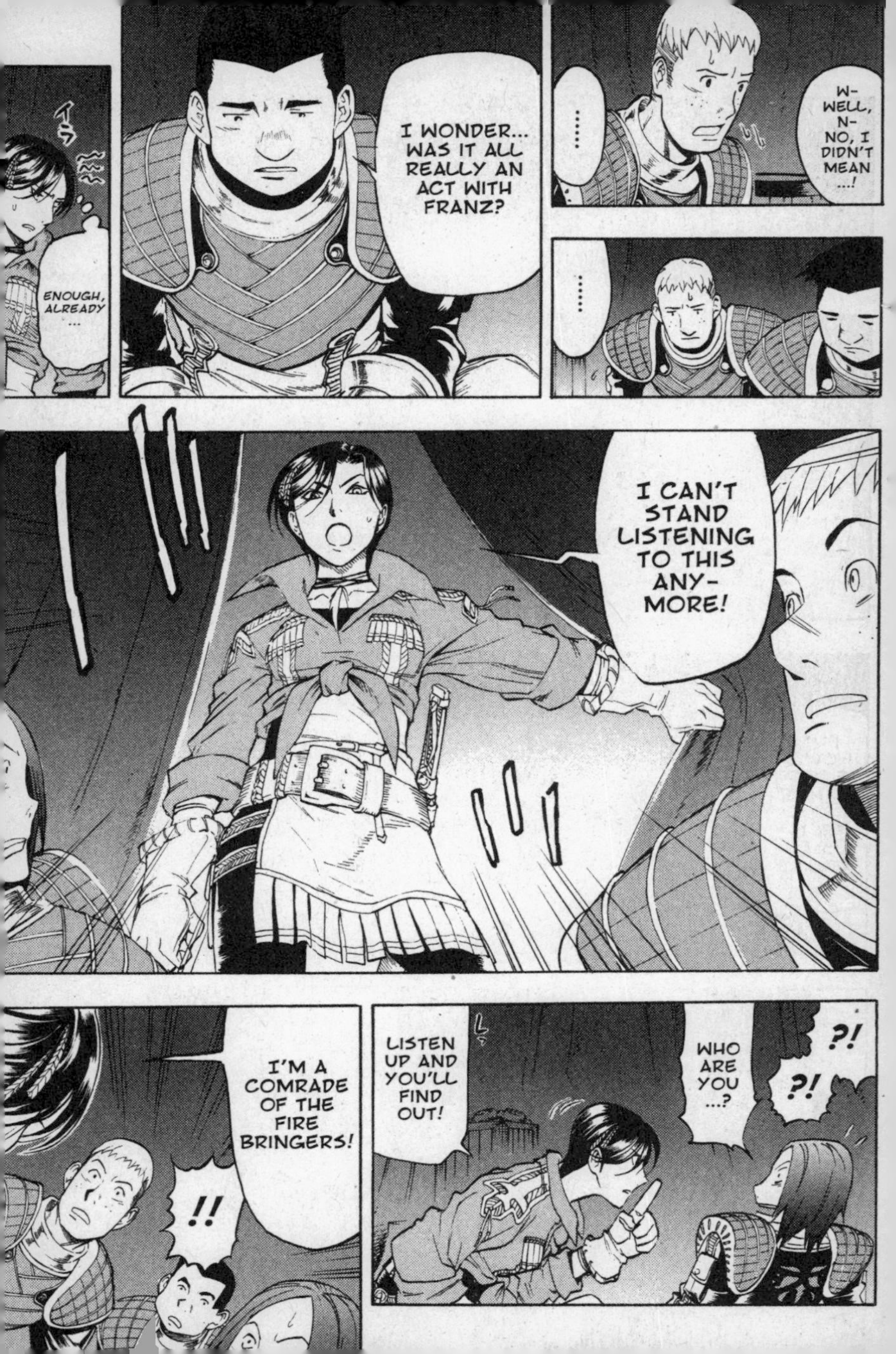

W-WELL, N-NO, I DIDN'T MEAN ....!
......
......
I WONDER... WAS IT ALL REALLY AN ACT WITH FRANZ?
イラ
ENOUGH, ALREADY ...
I CAN'T STAND LISTENING TO THIS ANY-MORE!
?!
?!
WHO ARE YOU ...?
LISTEN UP AND YOU'LL FIND OUT!
I'M A COMRADE OF THE FIRE BRINGERS!
!!

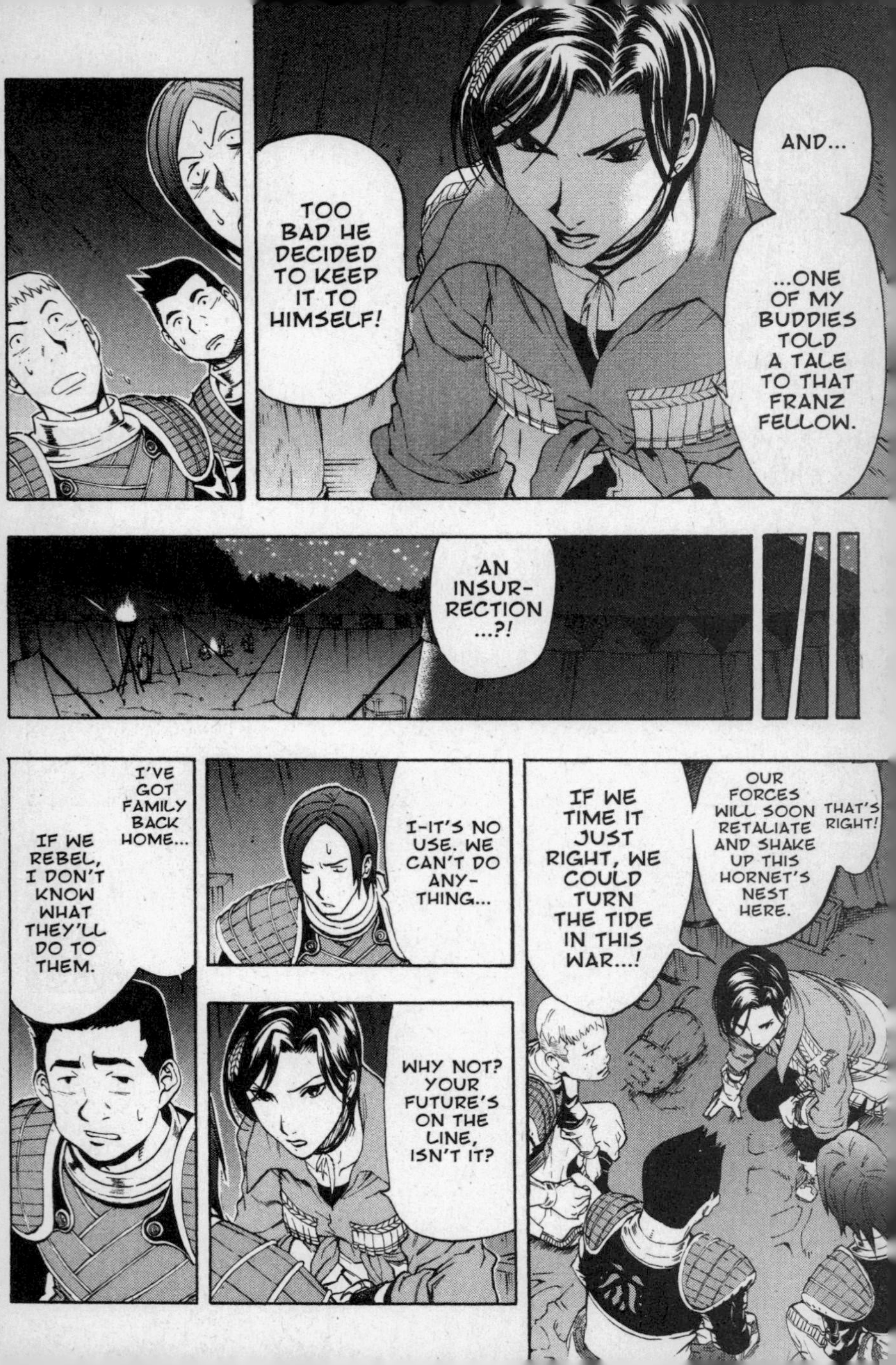
AND...
...ONE OF MY BUDDIES TOLD A TALE TO THAT FRANZ FELLOW.
TOO BAD HE DECIDED TO KEEP IT TO HIMSELF!
AN INSURREC-TION ...?!
THAT'S RIGHT!
OUR FORCES WILL SOON RETALIATE AND SHAKE UP THIS HORNET'S NEST HERE.
IF WE TIME IT JUST RIGHT, WE COULD TURN THE TIDE IN THIS WAR...!
I-IT'S NO USE. WE CAN'T DO ANY-THING...
WHY NOT? YOUR FUTURE'S ON THE LINE, ISN'T IT?
I'VE GOT FAMILY BACK HOME...
IF WE REBEL, I DON'T KNOW WHAT THEY'LL DO TO THEM.

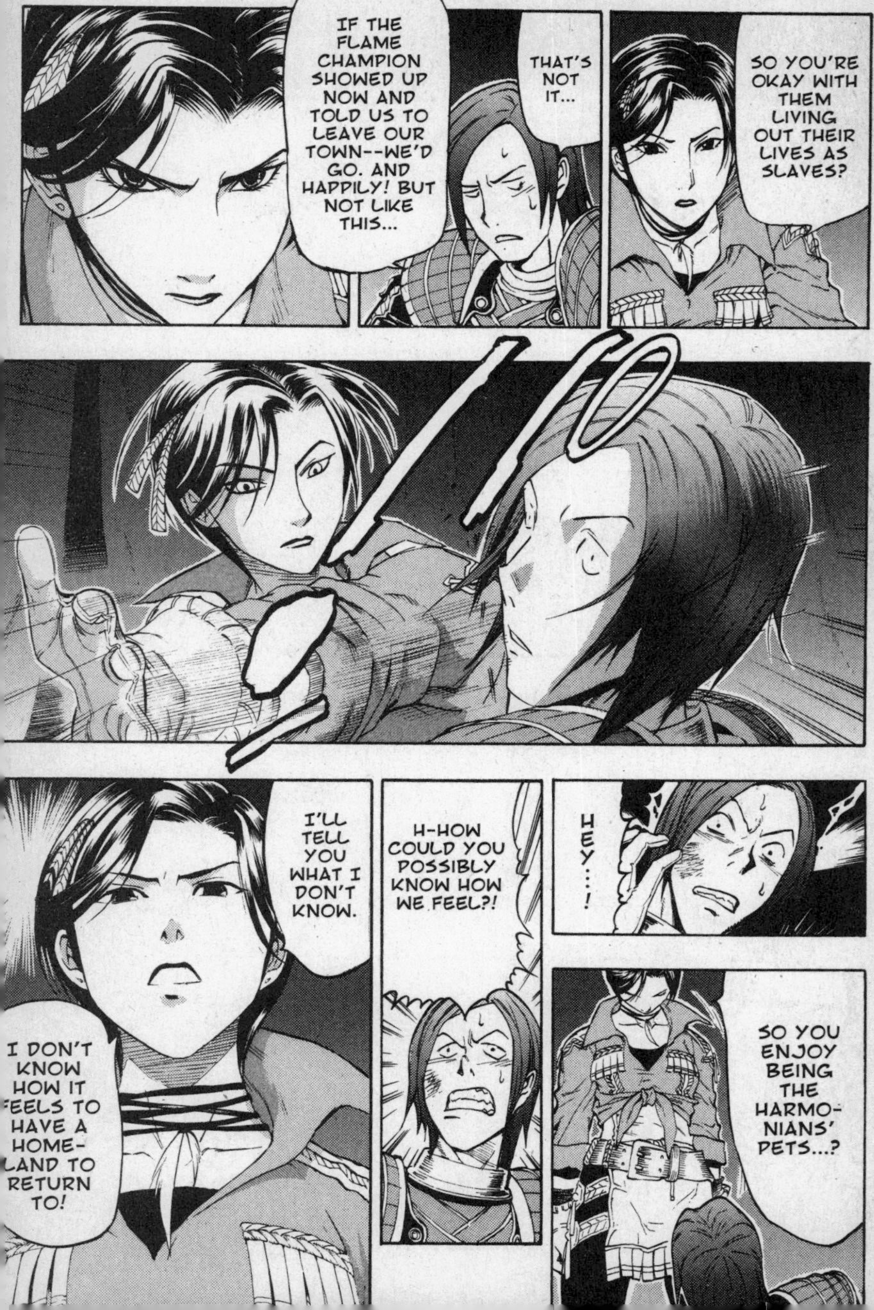
SO YOU'RE OKAY WITH THEM LIVING OUT THEIR LIVES AS SLAVES?
THAT'S NOT IT...
IF THE FLAME CHAMPION SHOWED UP NOW AND TOLD US TO LEAVE OUR TOWN--WE'D GO. AND HAPPILY! BUT NOT LIKE THIS...
HEY...!
SO YOU ENJOY BEING THE HARMONIANS' PETS...?
H-HOW COULD YOU POSSIBLY KNOW HOW WE FEEL?!
I'LL TELL YOU WHAT I DON'T KNOW.
I DON'T KNOW HOW IT FEELS TO HAVE A HOMELAND TO RETURN TO!

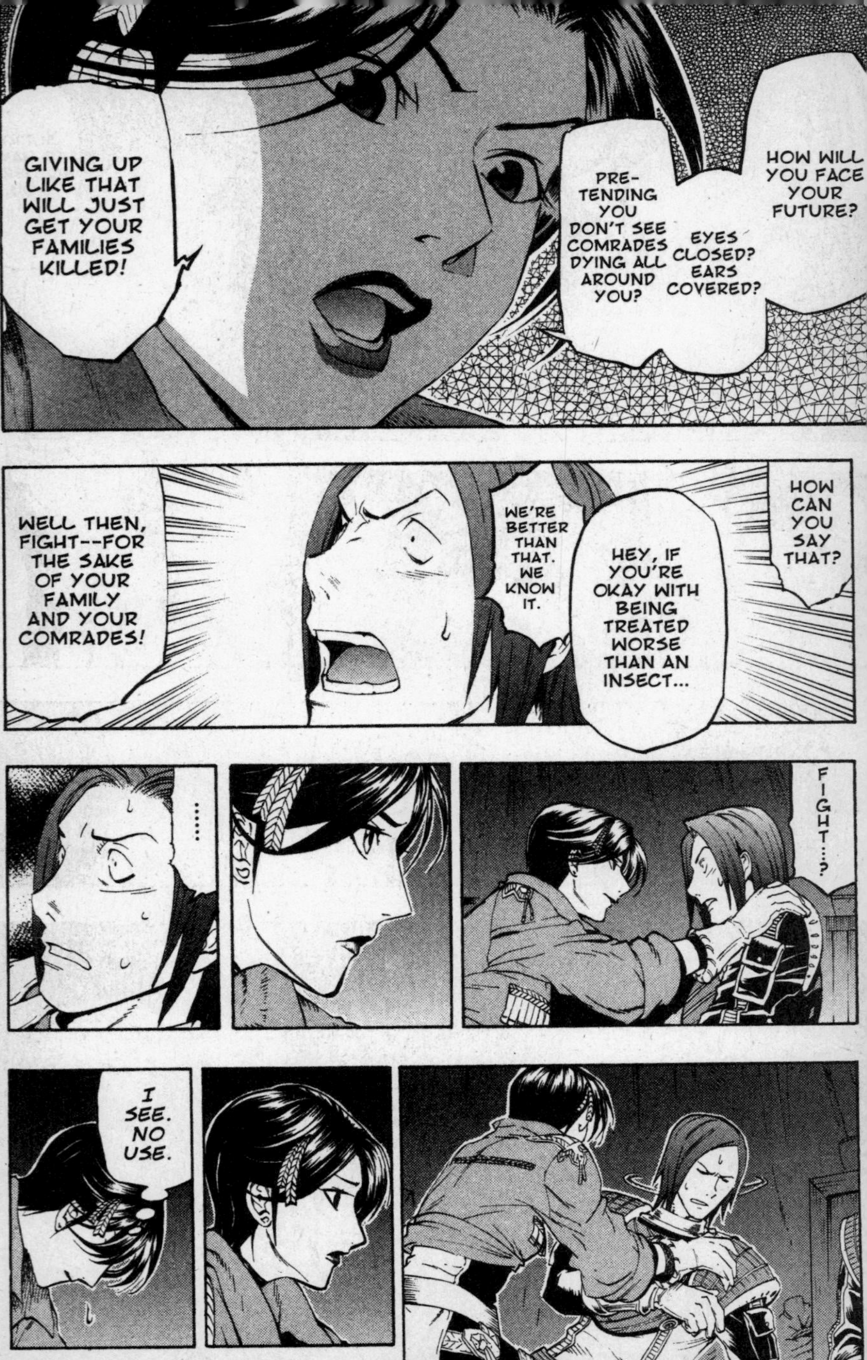
HOW WILL YOU FACE YOUR FUTURE?
EYES CLOSED? EARS COVERED?
PRE-TENDING YOU DON'T SEE COMRADES DYING ALL AROUND YOU?
GIVING UP LIKE THAT WILL JUST GET YOUR FAMILIES KILLED!
HOW CAN YOU SAY THAT?
HEY, IF YOU'RE OKAY WITH BEING TREATED WORSE THAN AN INSECT...
WE'RE BETTER THAN THAT. WE KNOW IT.
WELL THEN, FIGHT--FOR THE SAKE OF YOUR FAMILY AND YOUR COMRADES!
FIGHT...?
......
I SEE. NO USE.

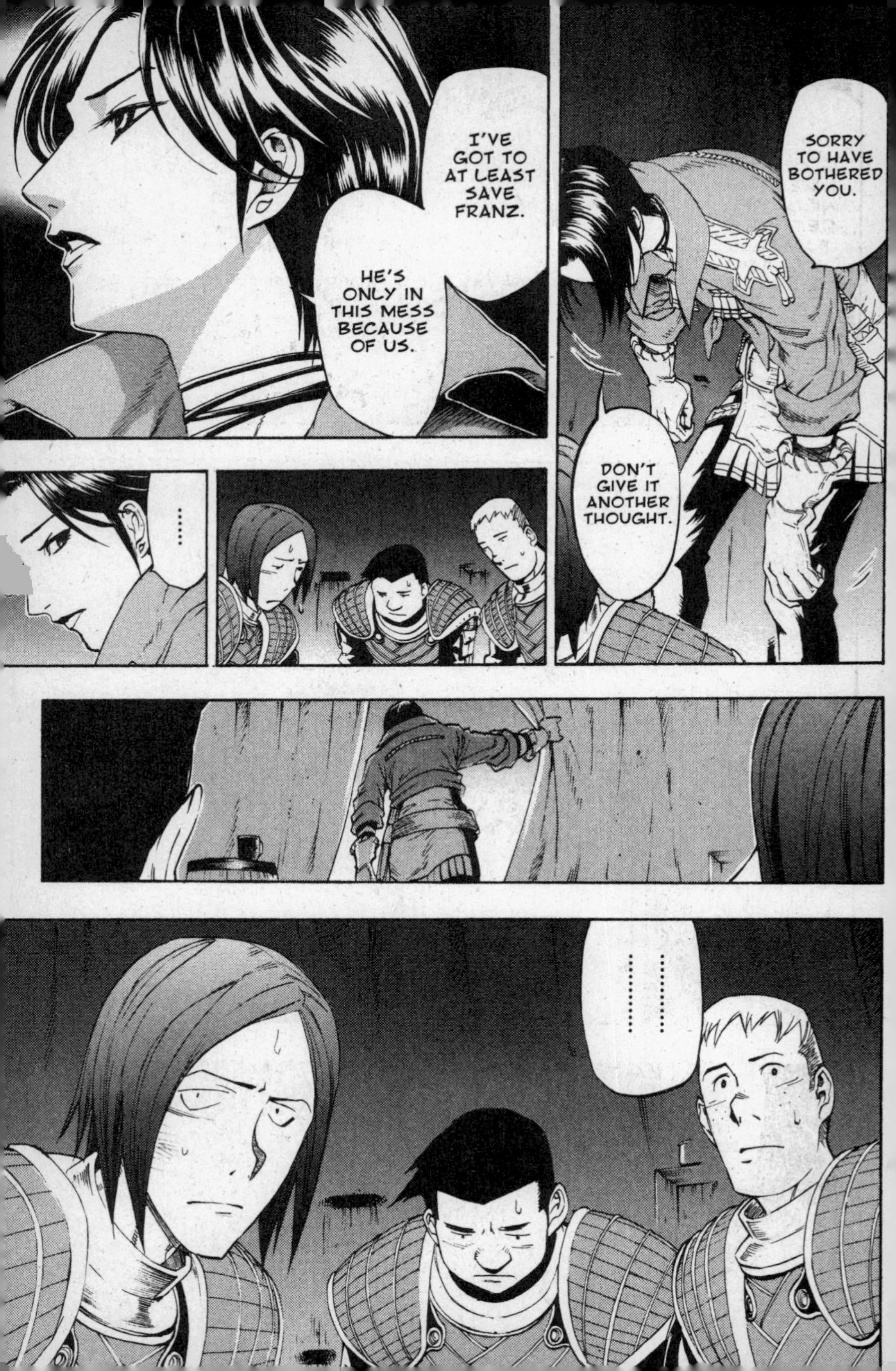
SORRY TO HAVE BOTHERED YOU.
DON'T GIVE IT ANOTHER THOUGHT.
I'VE GOT TO AT LEAST SAVE FRANZ.
HE'S ONLY IN THIS MESS BECAUSE OF US.
......
....

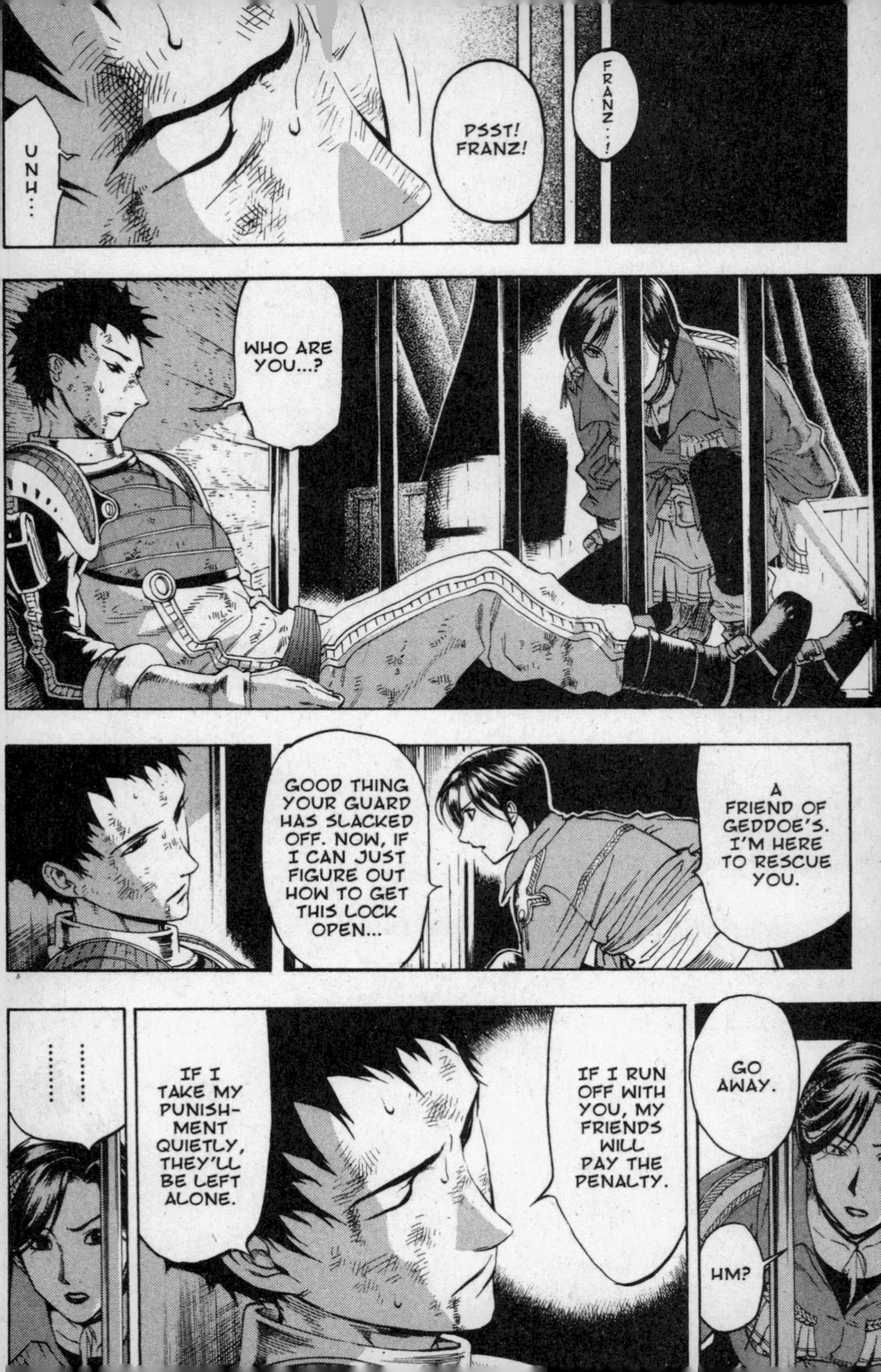
FRANZ...!
PSSST! FRANZ!
UNH...
WHO ARE YOU...?
A FRIEND OF GEDDOE'S. I'M HERE TO RESCUE YOU.
GOOD THING YOUR GUARD HAS SLACKED OFF. NOW, IF I CAN JUST FIGURE OUT HOW TO GET THIS LOCK OPEN...
GO AWAY.
HM?
IF I RUN OFF WITH YOU, MY FRIENDS WILL PAY THE PENALTY.
IF I TAKE MY PUNISH-MENT QUIETLY, THEY'LL BE LEFT ALONE.
......

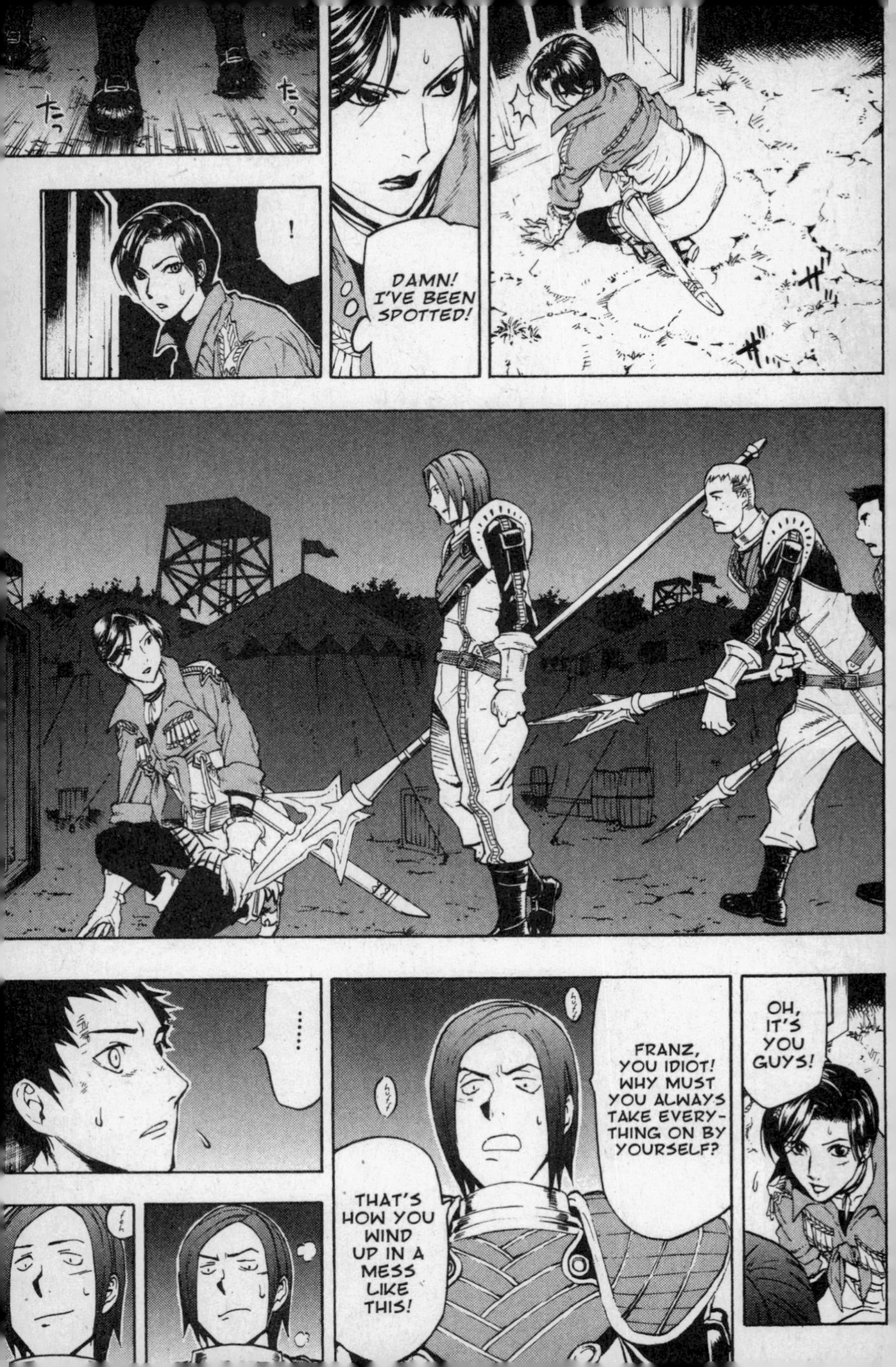
DAMN! I'VE BEEN SPOTTED!
たっ
たっ
!
OH, IT'S YOU GUYS!
FRANZ, YOU IDIOT! WHY MUST YOU ALWAYS TAKE EVERY-THING ON BY YOURSELF?
THAT'S HOW YOU WIND UP IN A MESS LIKE THIS!
......

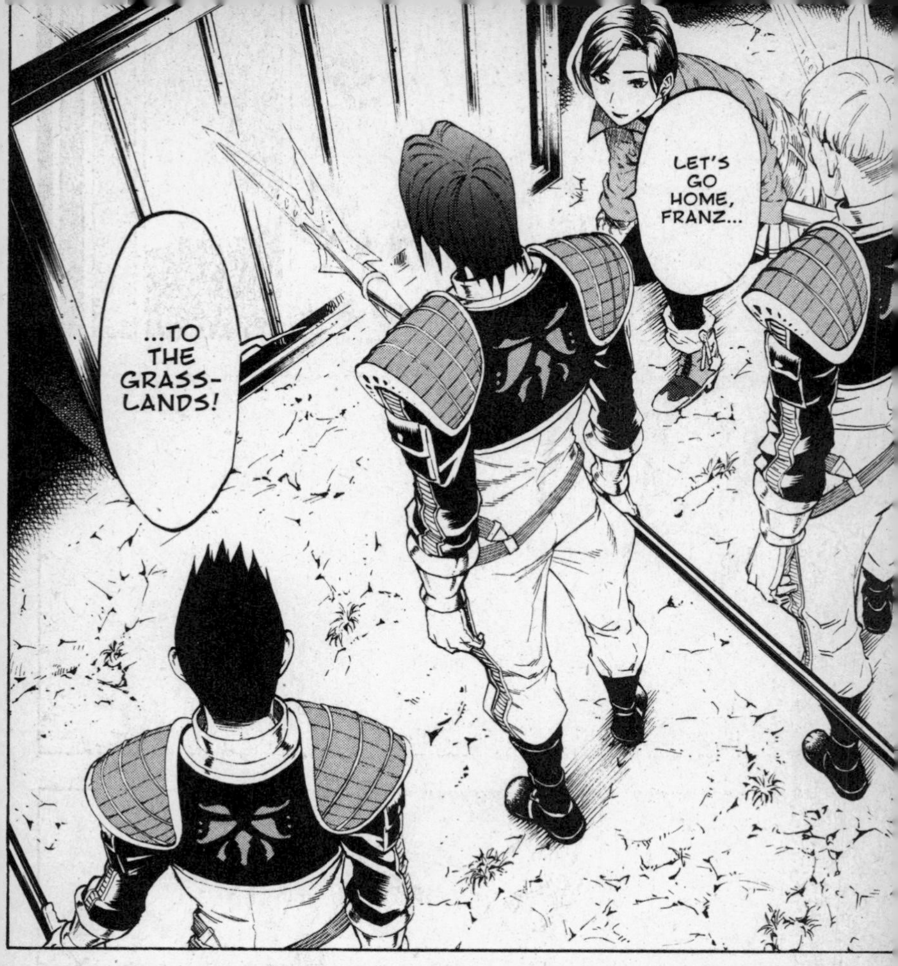
LET'S GO HOME, FRANZ...
...TO THE GRASSLANDS!
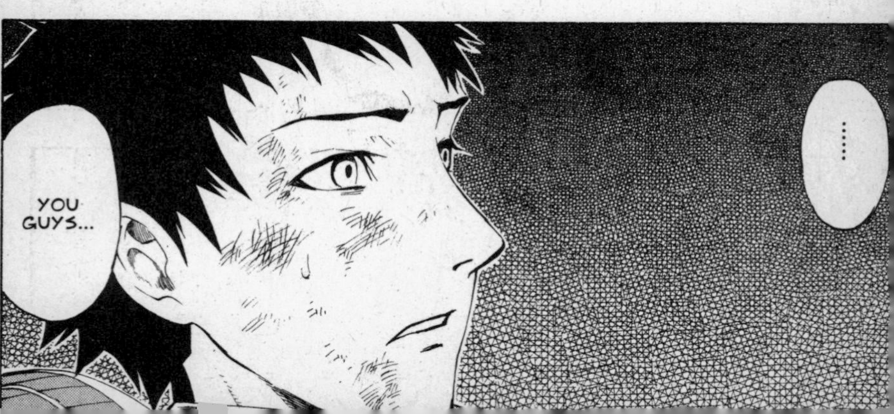
......
YOU GUYS...

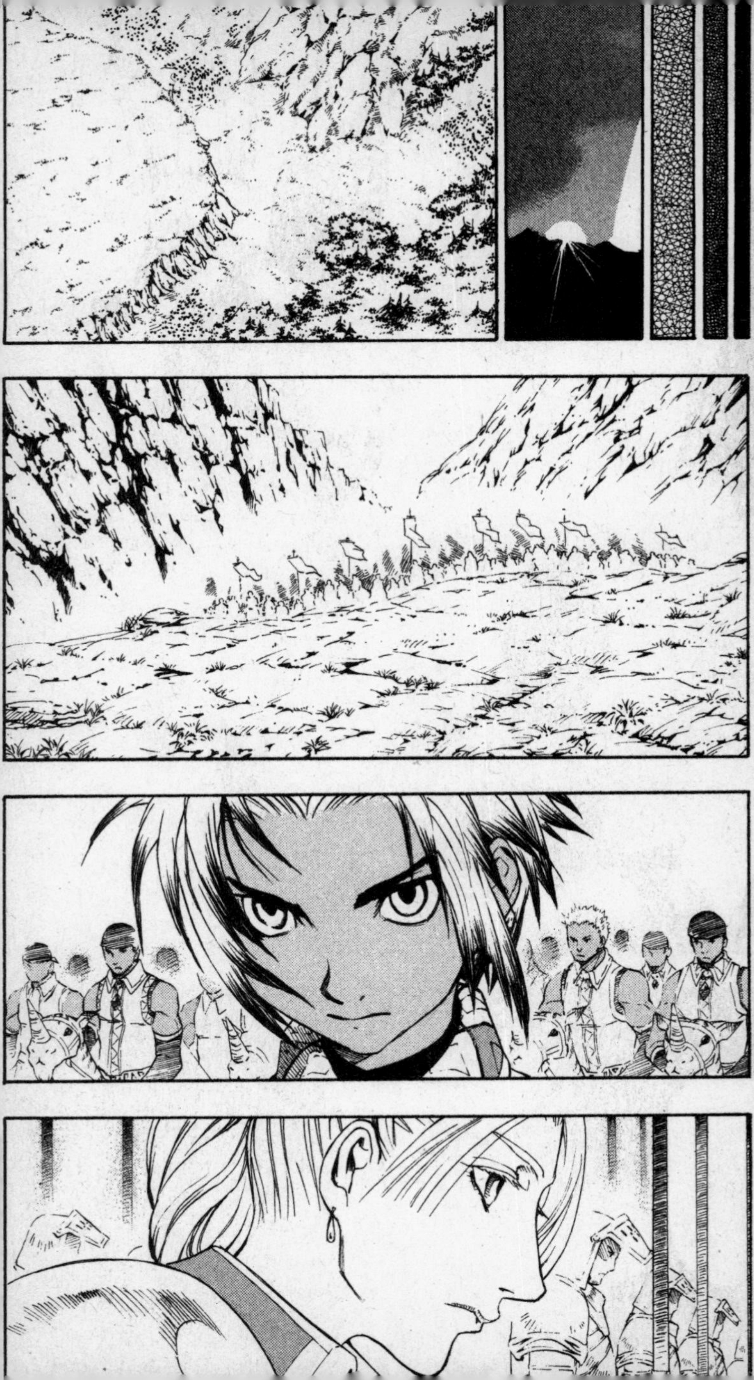

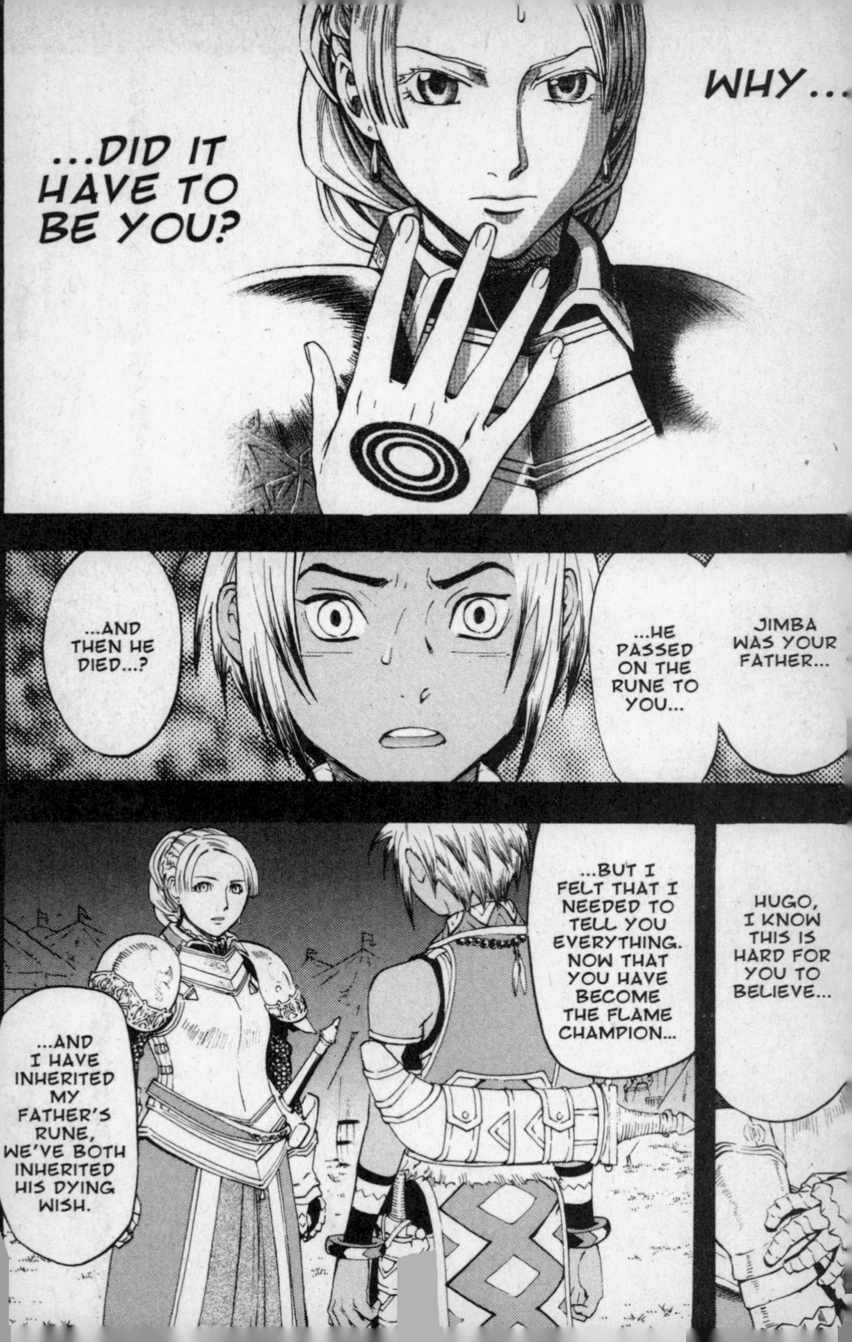
WHY...
...DID IT HAVE TO BE YOU?
JIMBA WAS YOUR FATHER...
...HE PASSED ON THE RUNE TO YOU...
...AND THEN HE DIED...?
HUGO, I KNOW THIS IS HARD FOR YOU TO BELIEVE...
...BUT I FELT THAT I NEEDED TO TELL YOU EVERYTHING. NOW THAT YOU HAVE BECOME THE FLAME CHAMPION...
...AND I HAVE INHERITED MY FATHER'S RUNE, WE'VE BOTH INHERITED HIS DYING WISH.

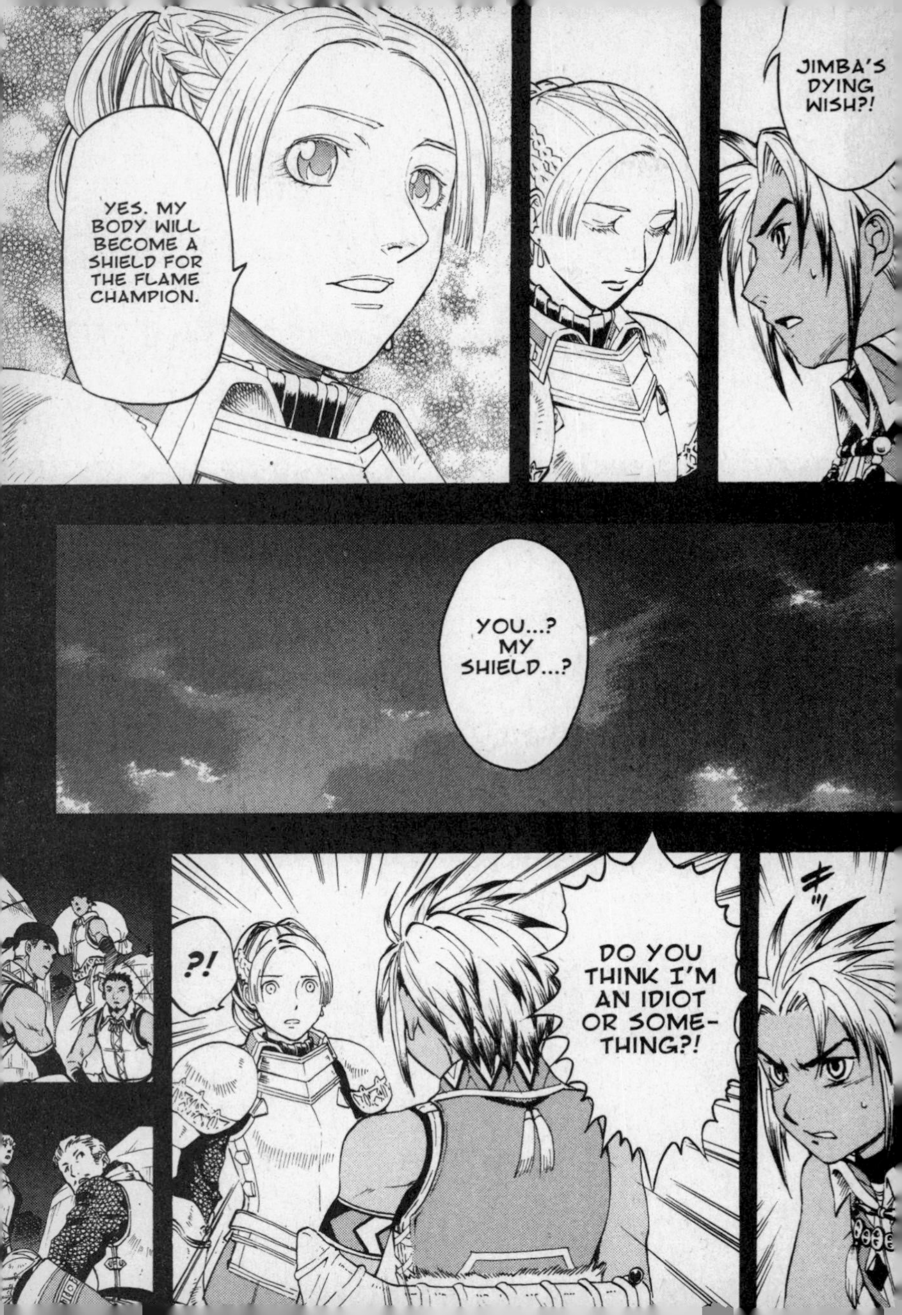
JIMBA'S DYING WISH?!
YES. MY BODY WILL BECOME A SHIELD FOR THE FLAME CHAMPION.
YOU...? MY SHIELD...?
DO YOU THINK I'M AN IDIOT OR SOME-THING?!
?!

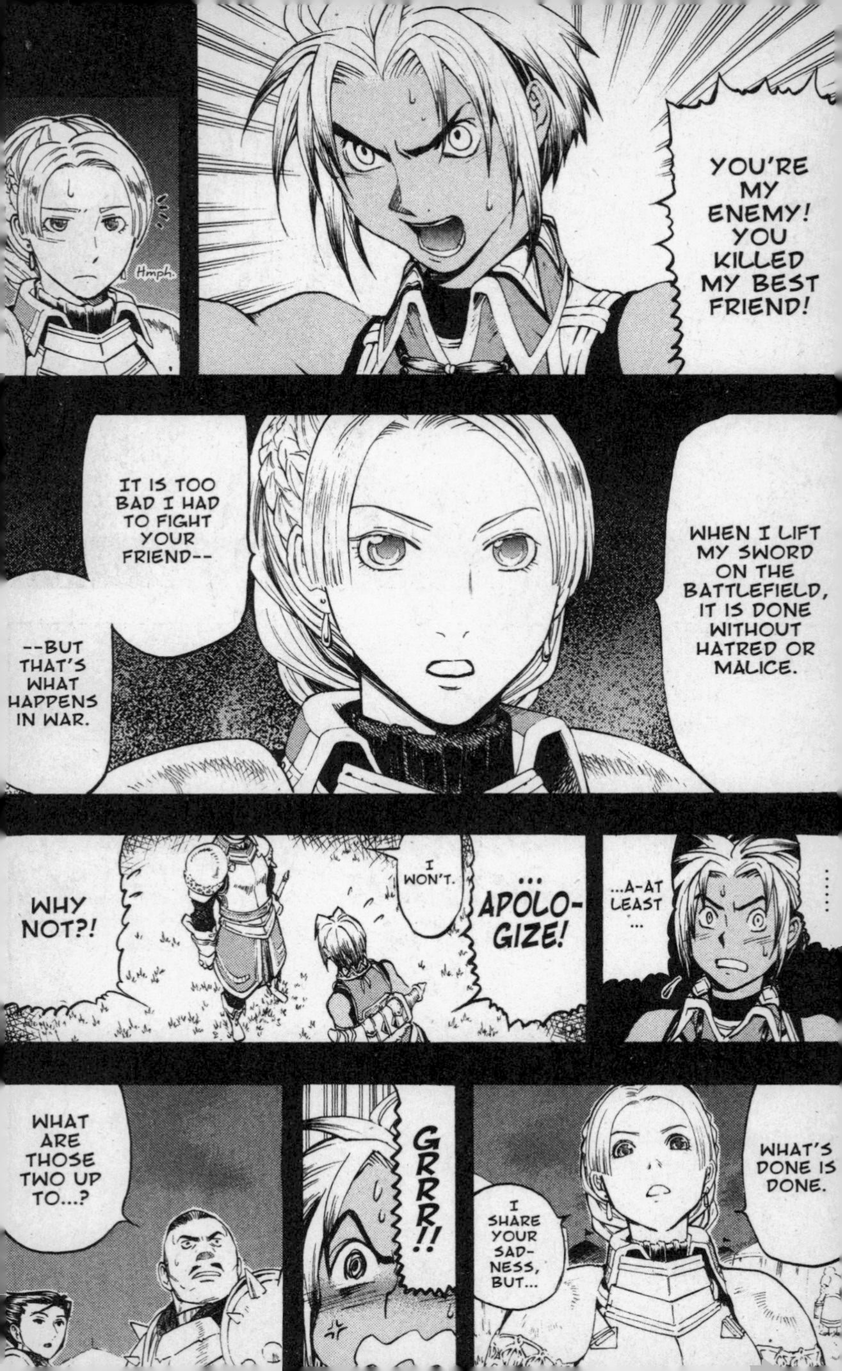
YOU'RE MY ENEMY! YOU KILLED MY BEST FRIEND!
Hmph.
WHEN I LIFT MY SWORD ON THE BATTLEFIELD, IT IS DONE WITHOUT HATRED OR MALICE.
IT IS TOO BAD I HAD TO FIGHT YOUR FRIEND--
--BUT THAT'S WHAT HAPPENS IN WAR.
......
...A-AT LEAST ...
... APOLO-GIZE!
I WON'T.
WHY NOT?!
WHAT'S DONE IS DONE.
I SHARE YOUR SAD-NESS, BUT...
GRRR!!
WHAT ARE THOSE TWO UP TO...?

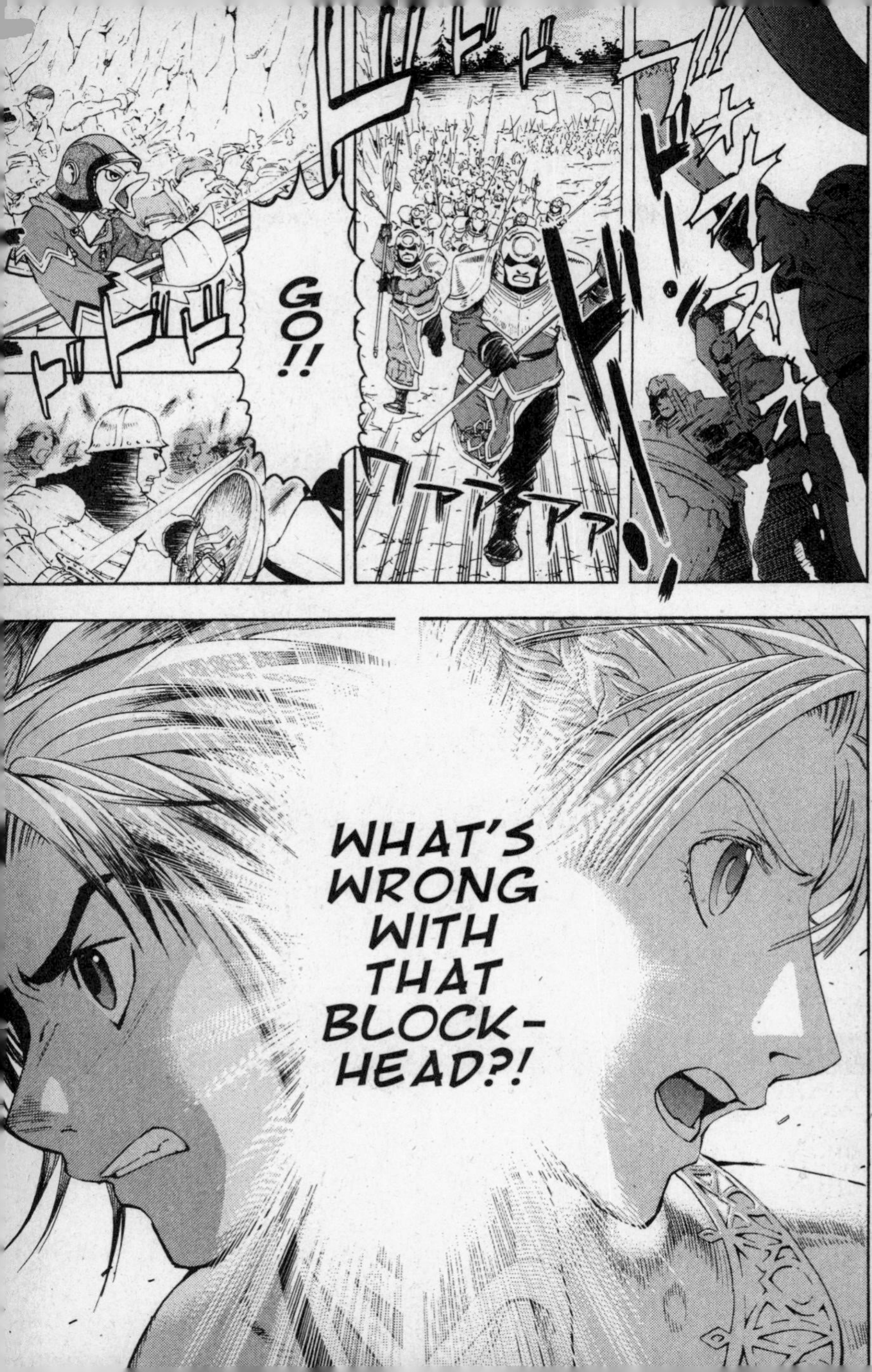
GO!!
WHAT'S WRONG WITH THAT BLOCK-HEAD?!

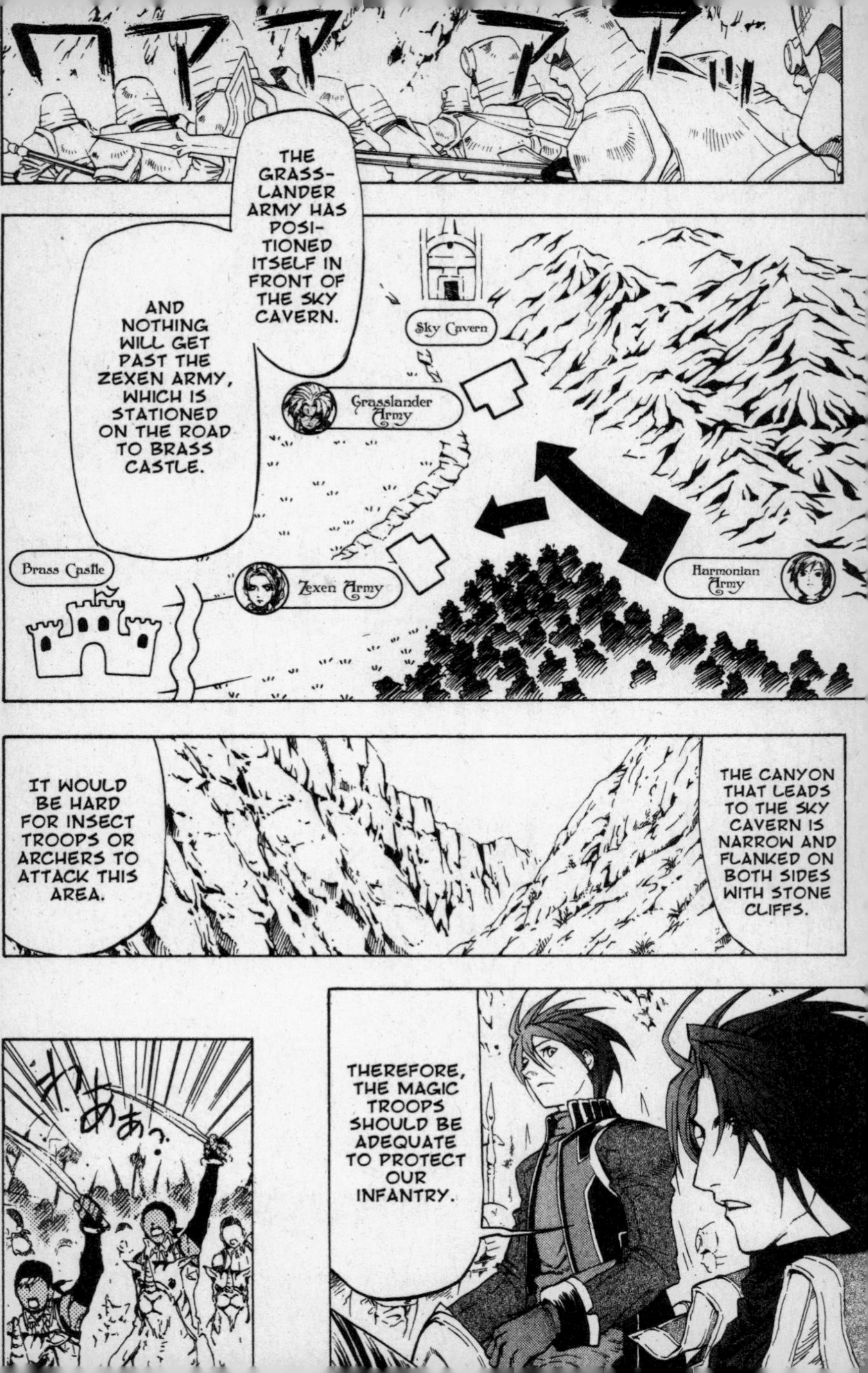

THE GRASS-LANDER ARMY HAS POSI-TIONED ITSELF IN FRONT OF THE SKY CAVERN.
AND NOTHING WILL GET PAST THE ZEXEN ARMY, WHICH IS STATIONED ON THE ROAD TO BRASS CASTLE.
Sky Cavern
Grasslander Army
Harmonian Army
Zexen Army
Brass Castle
THE CANYON THAT LEADS TO THE SKY CAVERN IS NARROW AND FLANKED ON BOTH SIDES WITH STONE CLIFFS.
IT WOULD BE HARD FOR INSECT TROOPS OR ARCHERS TO ATTACK THIS AREA.
THEREFORE, THE MAGIC TROOPS SHOULD BE ADEQUATE TO PROTECT OUR INFANTRY.
わああっ

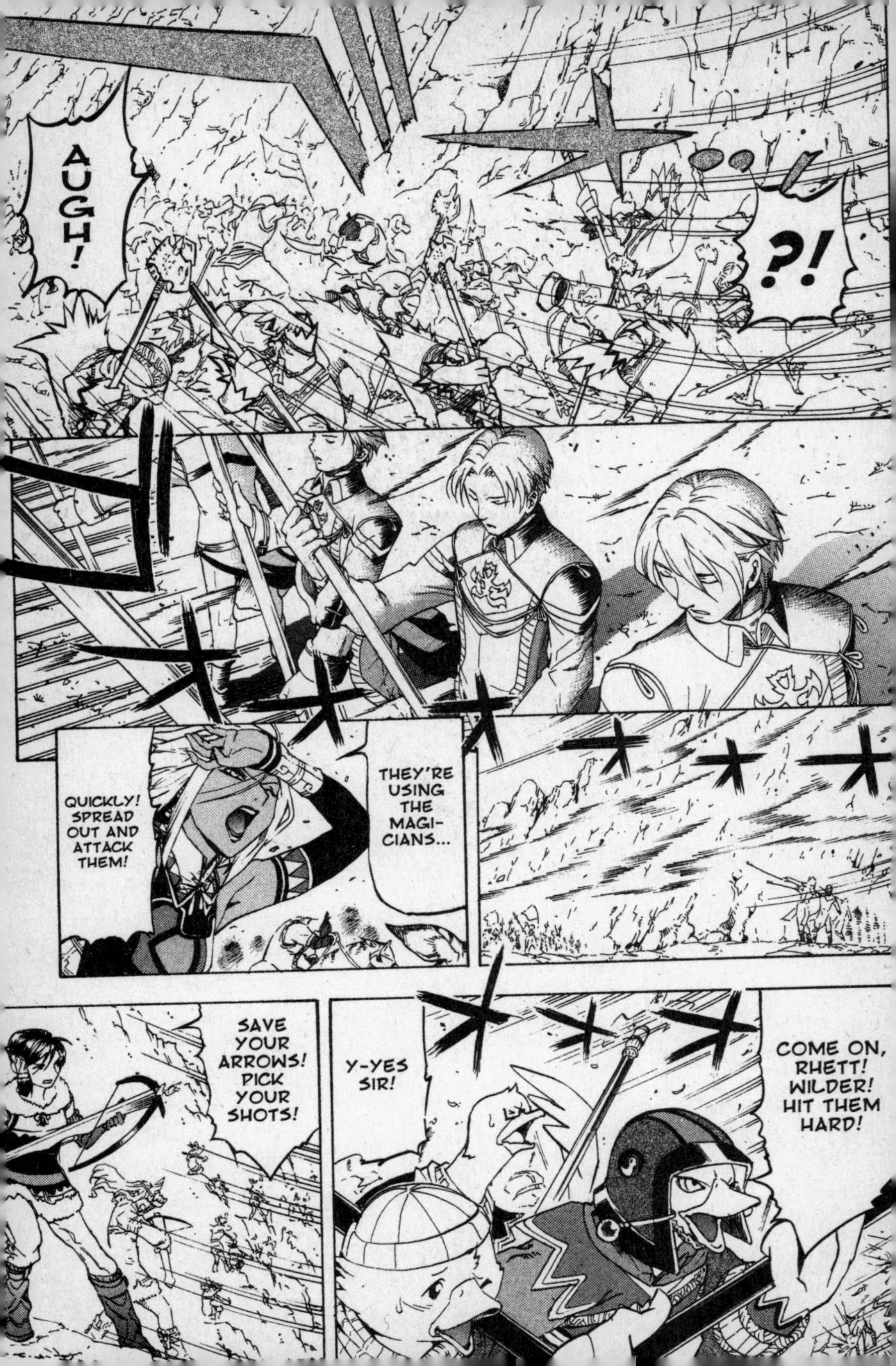
?!
AUGH!
THEY'RE USING THE MAGICIANS...
QUICKLY! SPREAD OUT AND ATTACK THEM!
COME ON, RHETT! WILDER! HIT THEM HARD!
Y-YES SIR!
SAVE YOUR ARROWS! PICK YOUR SHOTS!

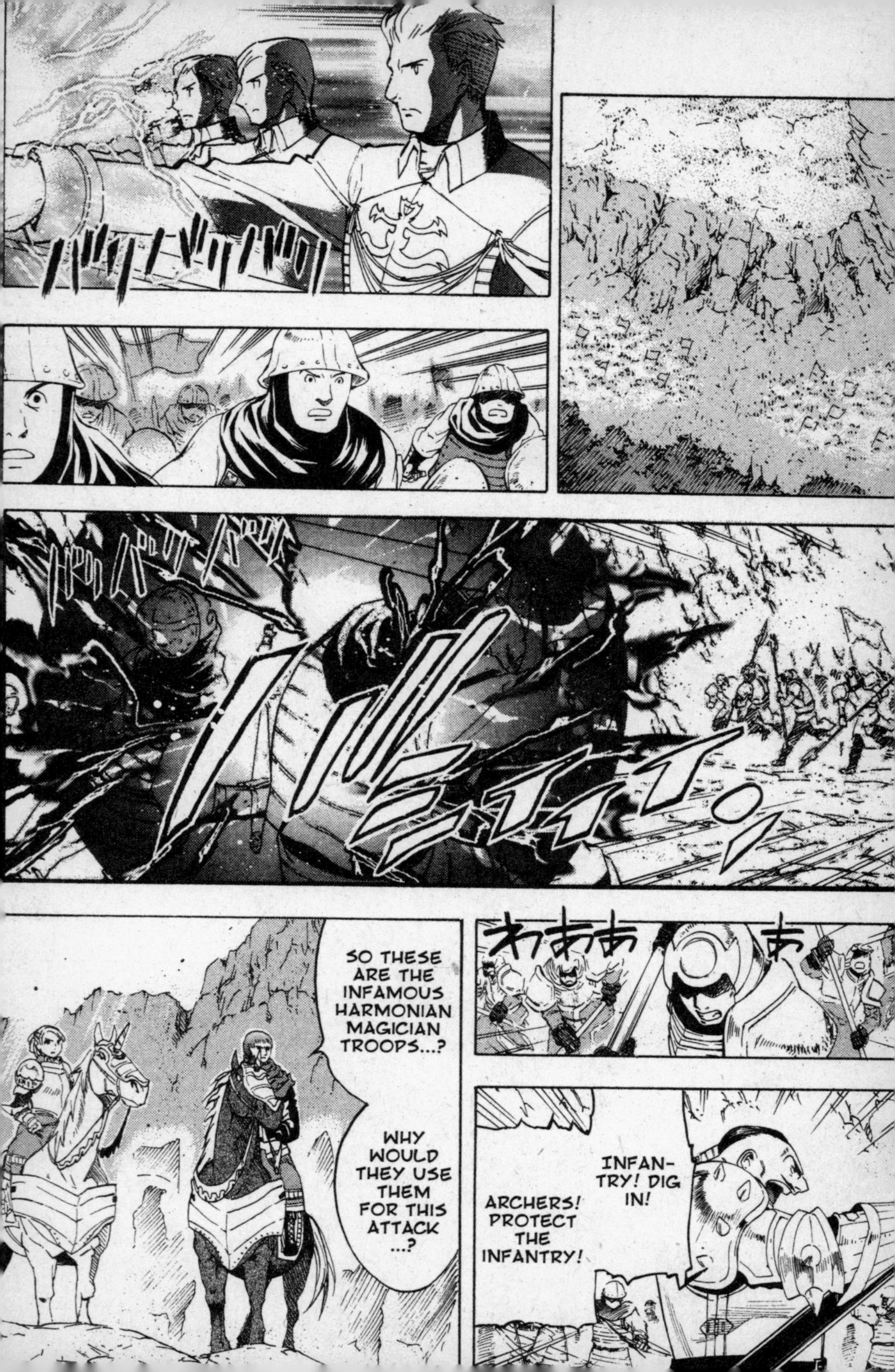

わあああ
INFANTRY! DIG IN!
ARCHERS! PROTECT THE INFANTRY!
SO THESE ARE THE INFAMOUS HARMONIAN MAGICIAN TROOPS...?
WHY WOULD THEY USE THEM FOR THIS ATTACK ...?

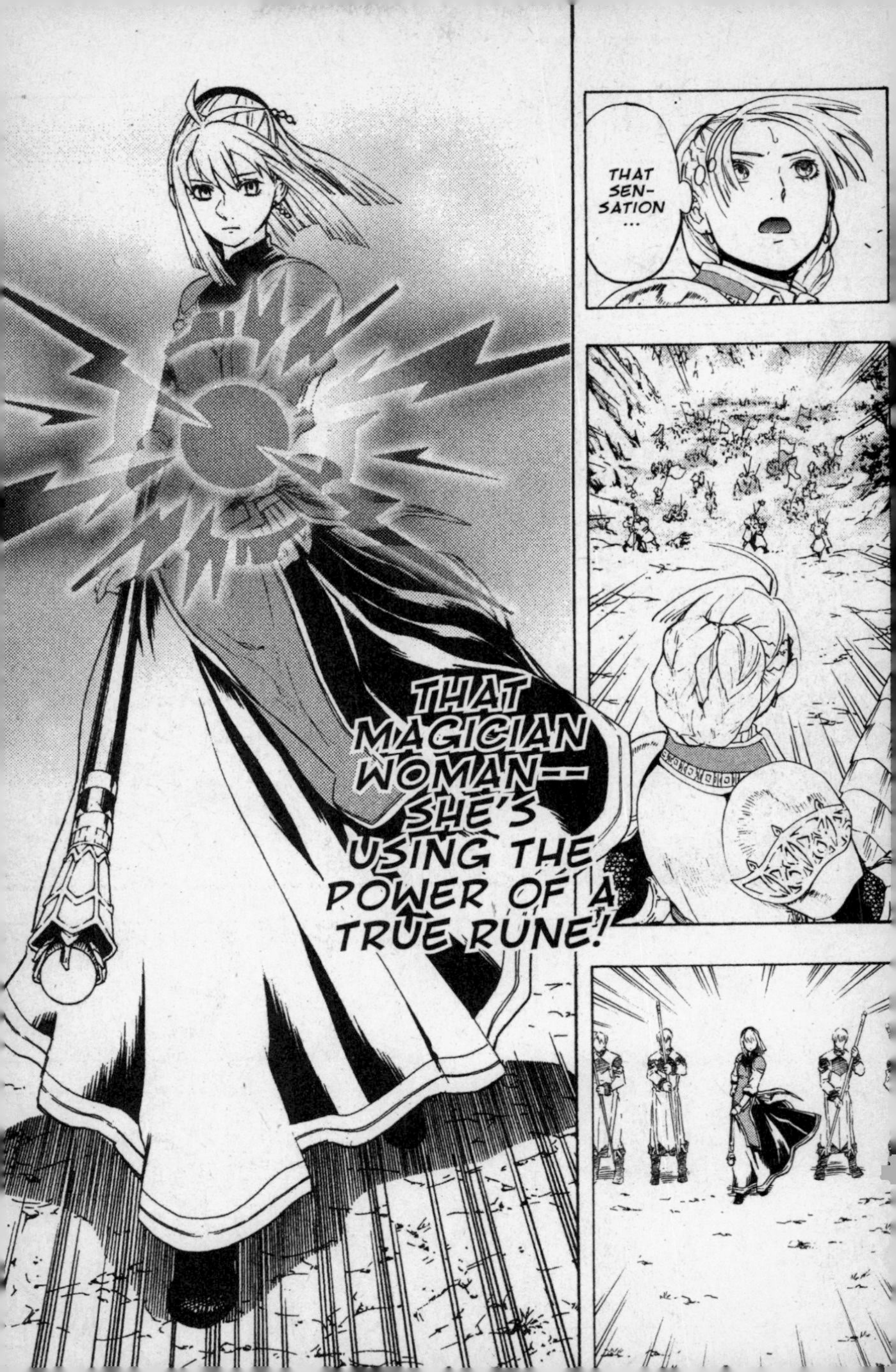
THAT SEN-SATION ...
THAT MAGICIAN WOMAN-- SHE'S USING THE POWER OF A TRUE RUNE!

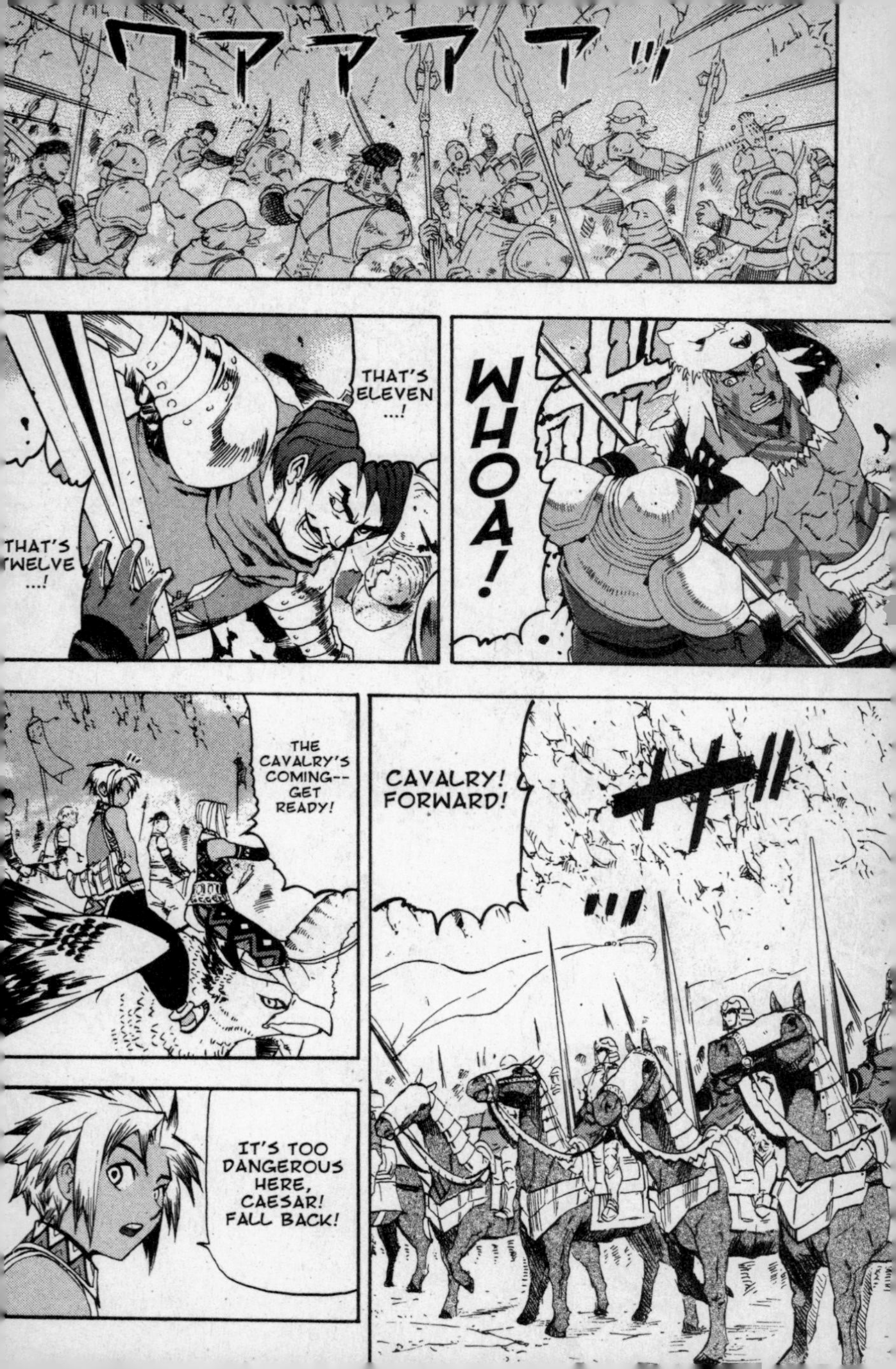
ワァァァァッ!!
WHOA!
THAT'S ELEVEN ...!
THAT'S TWELVE ...!
CAVALRY! FORWARD!
ザッ
THE CAVALRY'S COMING-- GET READY!
IT'S TOO DANGEROUS HERE, CAESAR! FALL BACK!

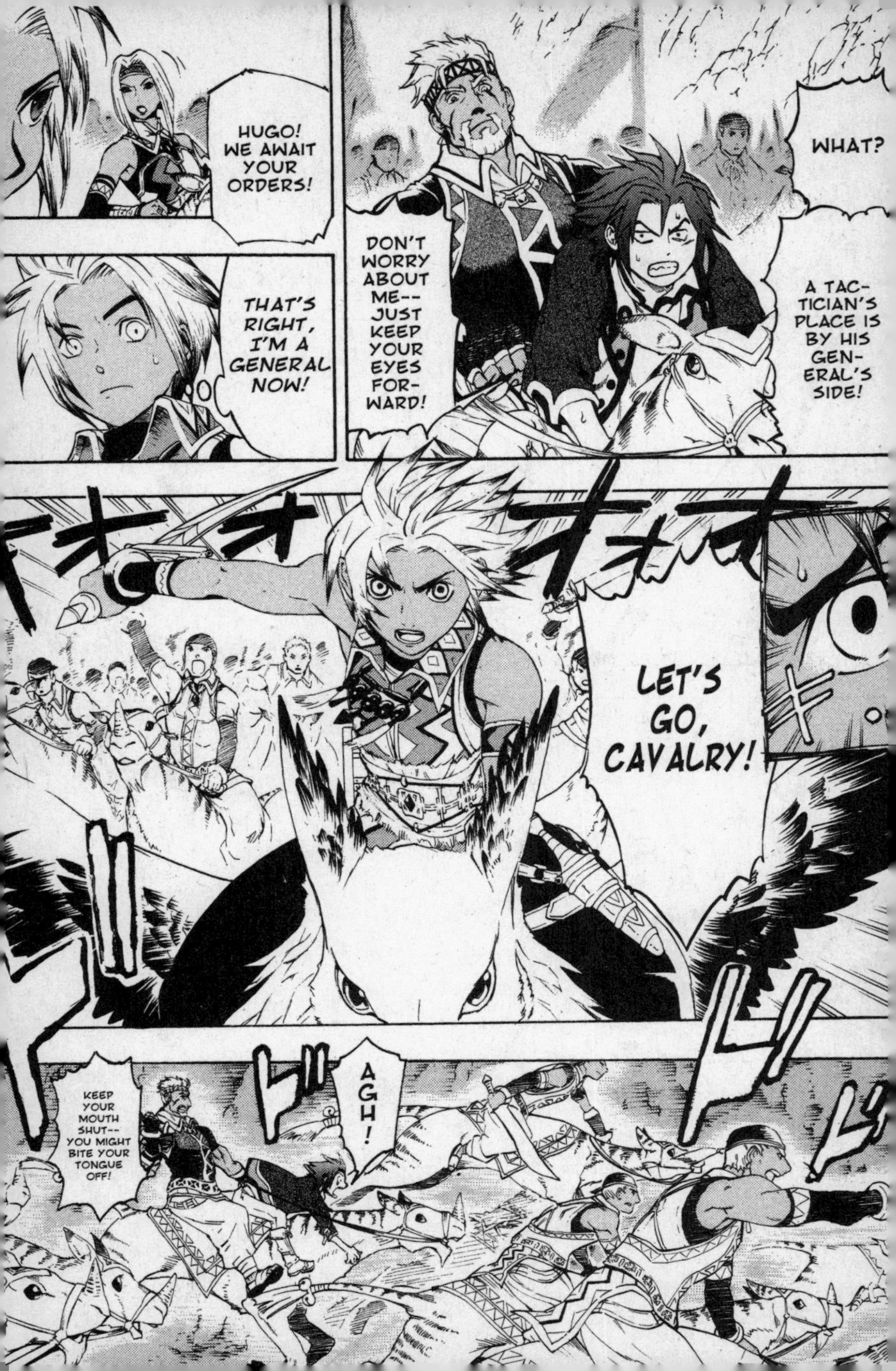
WHAT?
A TAC-TICIAN'S PLACE IS BY HIS GEN-ERAL'S SIDE!
DON'T WORRY ABOUT ME--JUST KEEP YOUR EYES FOR-WARD!
HUGO! WE AWAIT YOUR ORDERS!
THAT'S RIGHT, I'M A GENERAL NOW!
LET'S GO, CAVALRY!
AGH!
KEEP YOUR MOUTH SHUT--YOU MIGHT BITE YOUR TONGUE OFF!

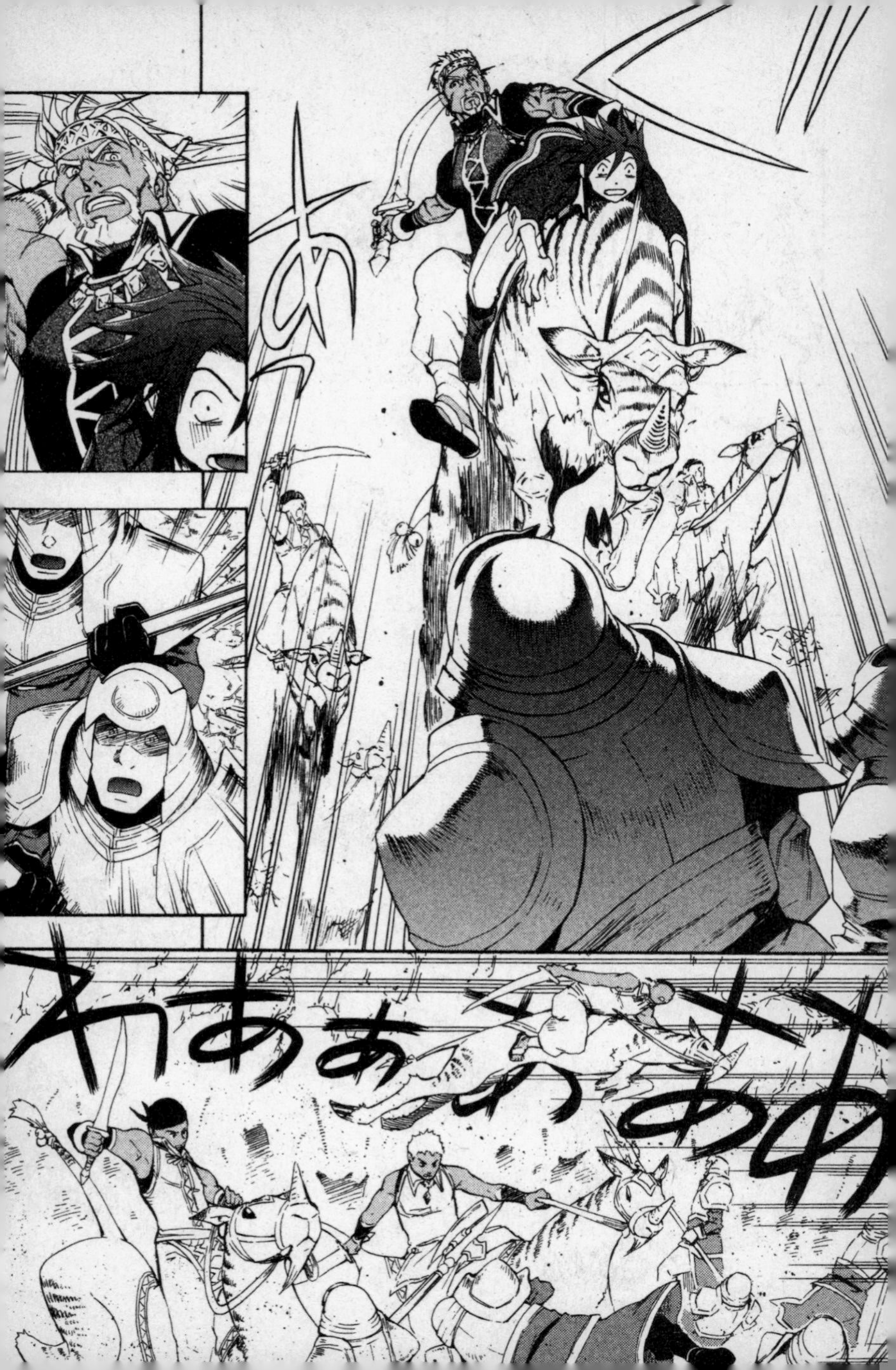
わあああああ

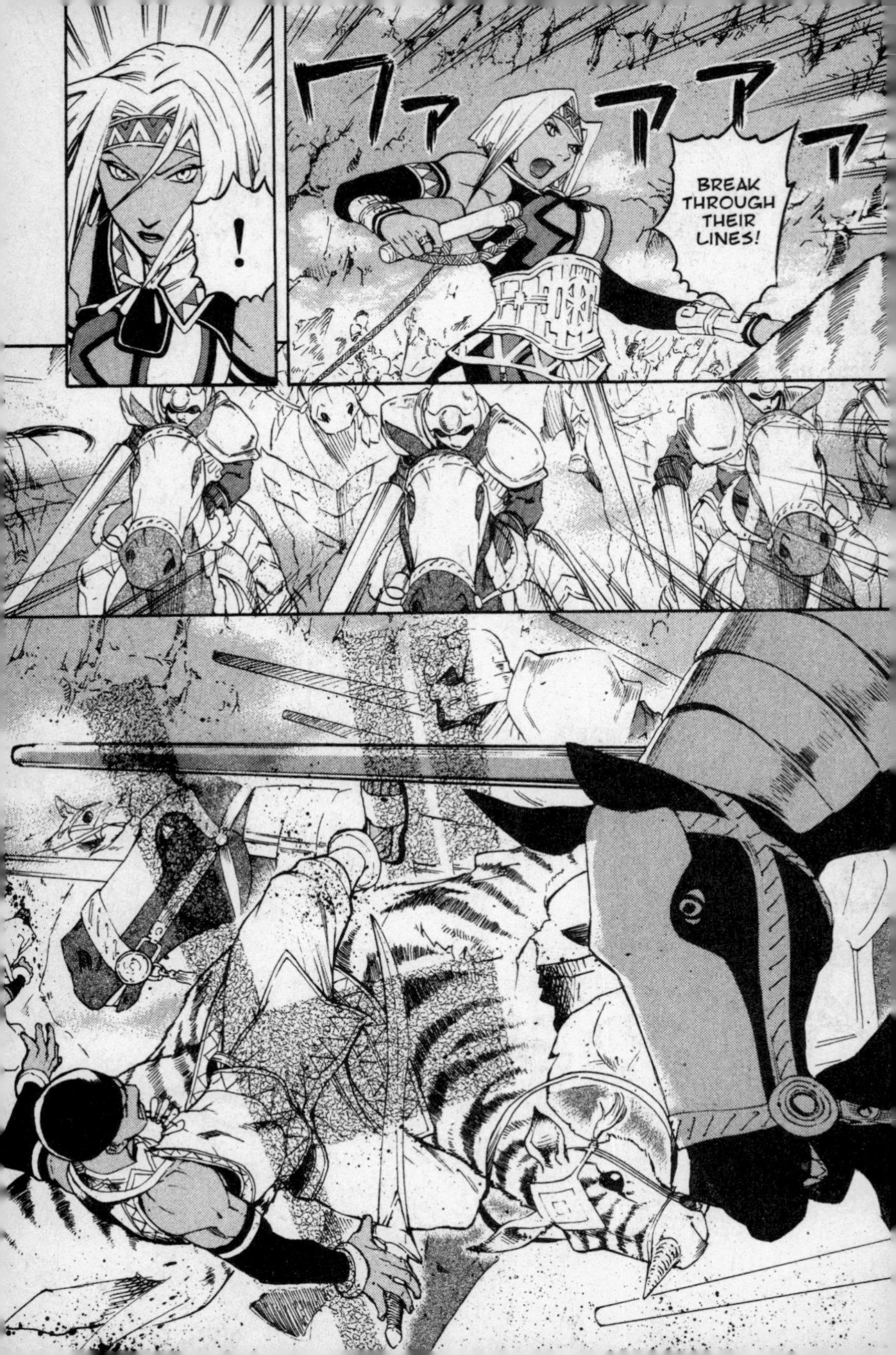
ワァアアア
BREAK THROUGH THEIR LINES!
!

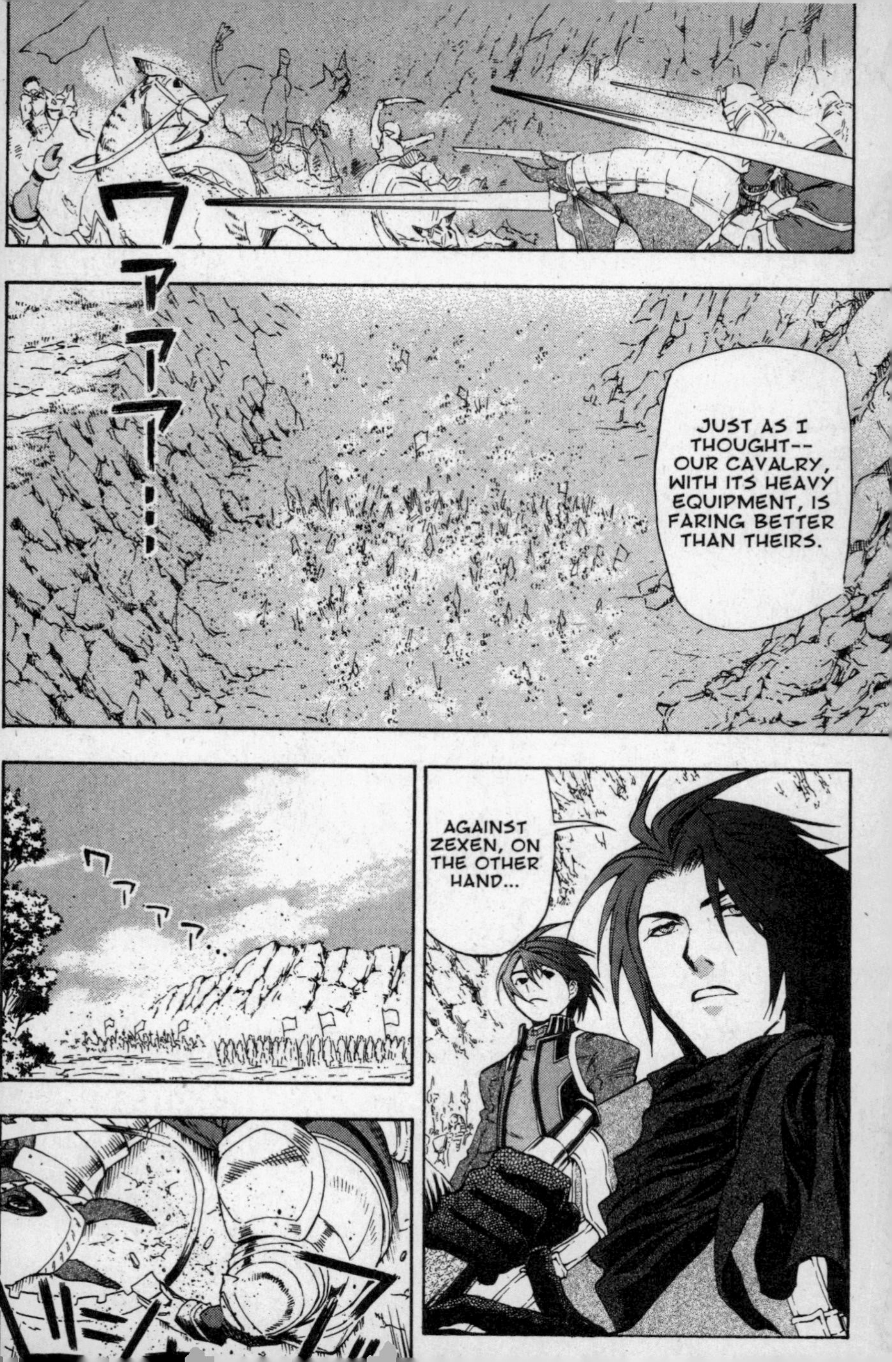
JUST AS I THOUGHT-- OUR CAVALRY, WITH ITS HEAVY EQUIPMENT, IS FARING BETTER THAN THEIRS.
AGAINST ZEXEN, ON THE OTHER HAND...

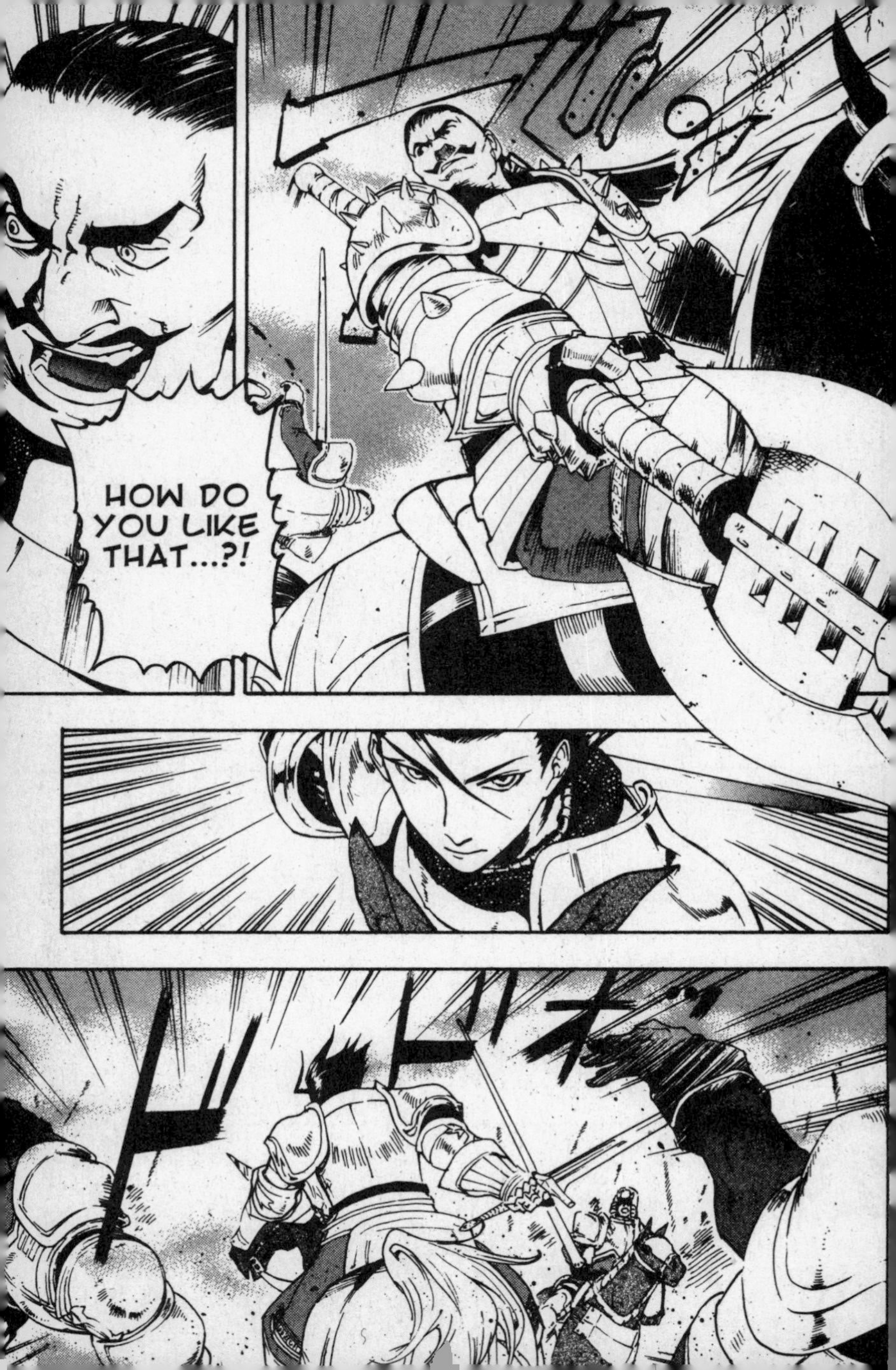
HOW DO YOU LIKE THAT...?!

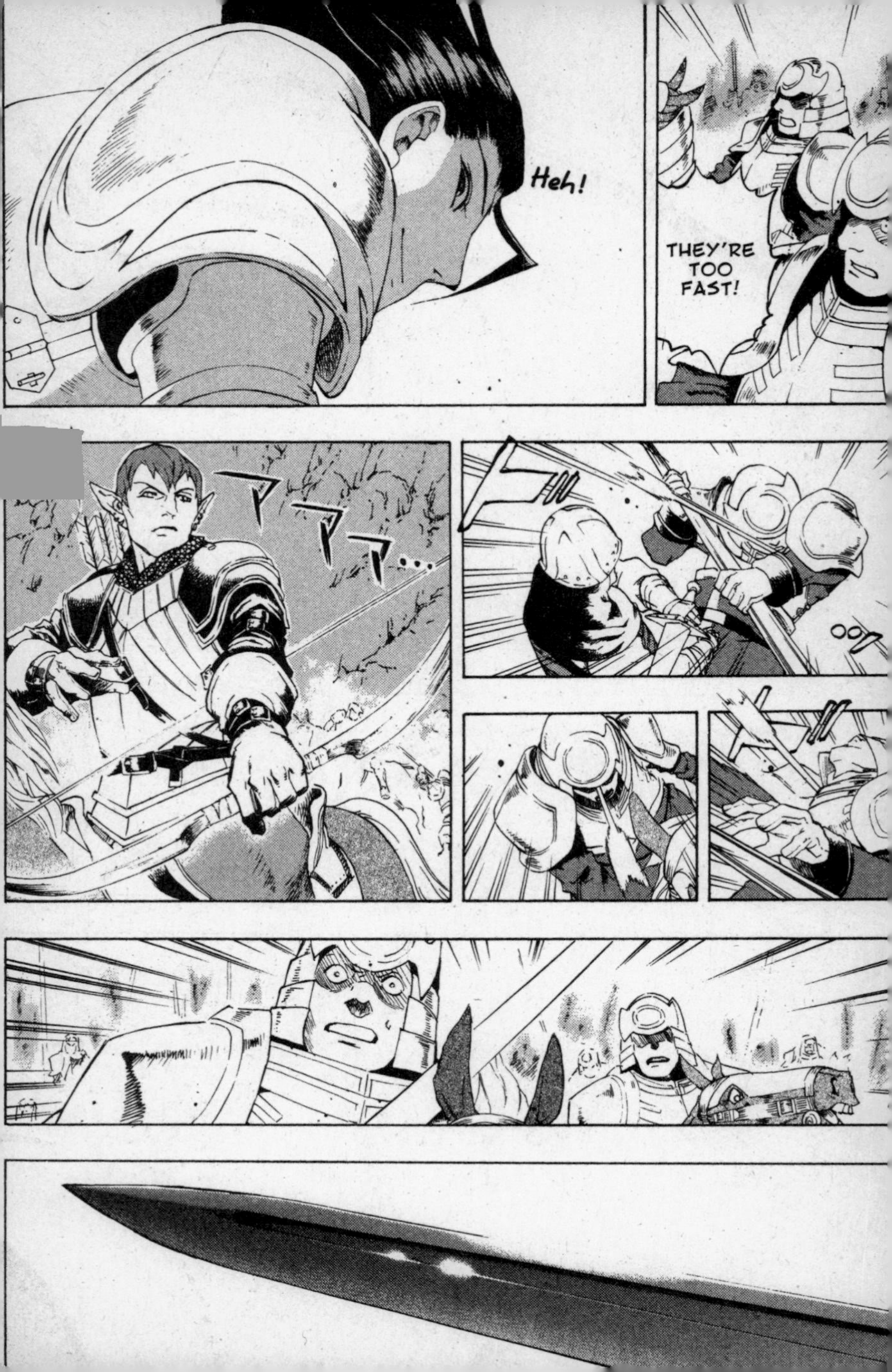
THEY'RE TOO FAST!
Heh!
アアア...

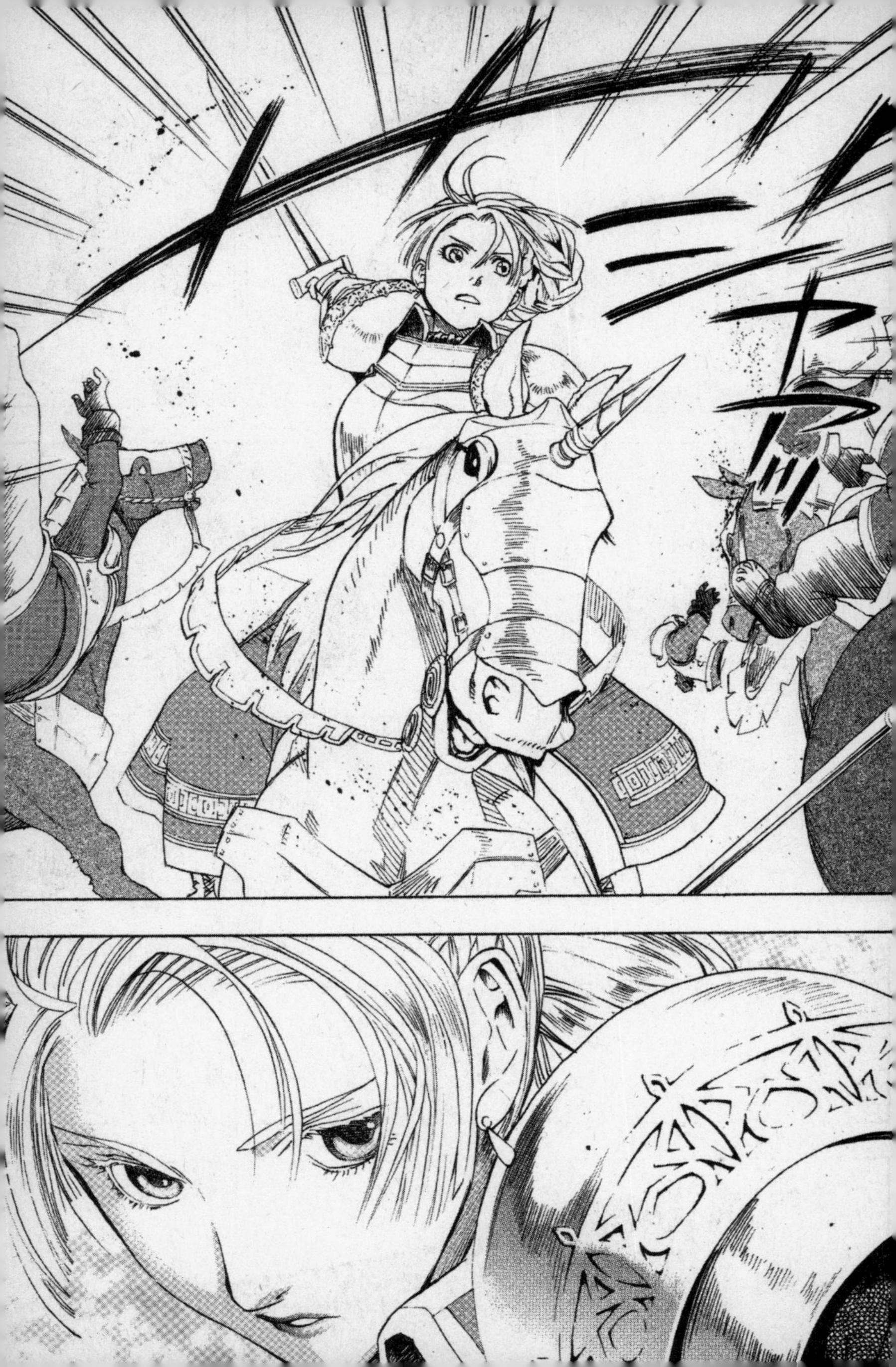

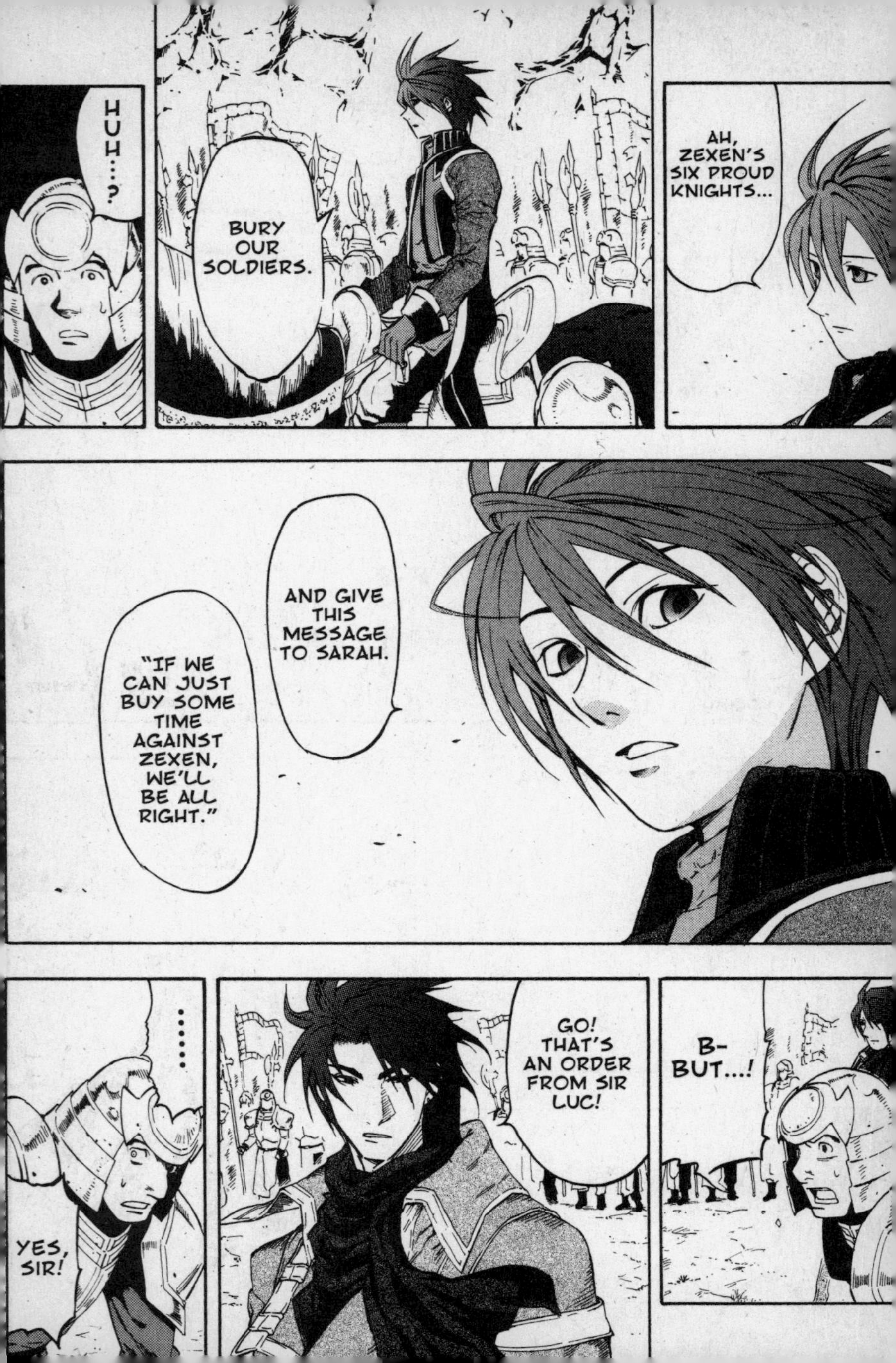
AH, ZEXEN'S SIX PROUD KNIGHTS...
BURY OUR SOLDIERS.
HUH...?
AND GIVE THIS MESSAGE TO SARAH.
"IF WE CAN JUST BUY SOME TIME AGAINST ZEXEN, WE'LL BE ALL RIGHT."
B-BUT...!
GO! THAT'S AN ORDER FROM SIR LUC!
......
YES, SIR!

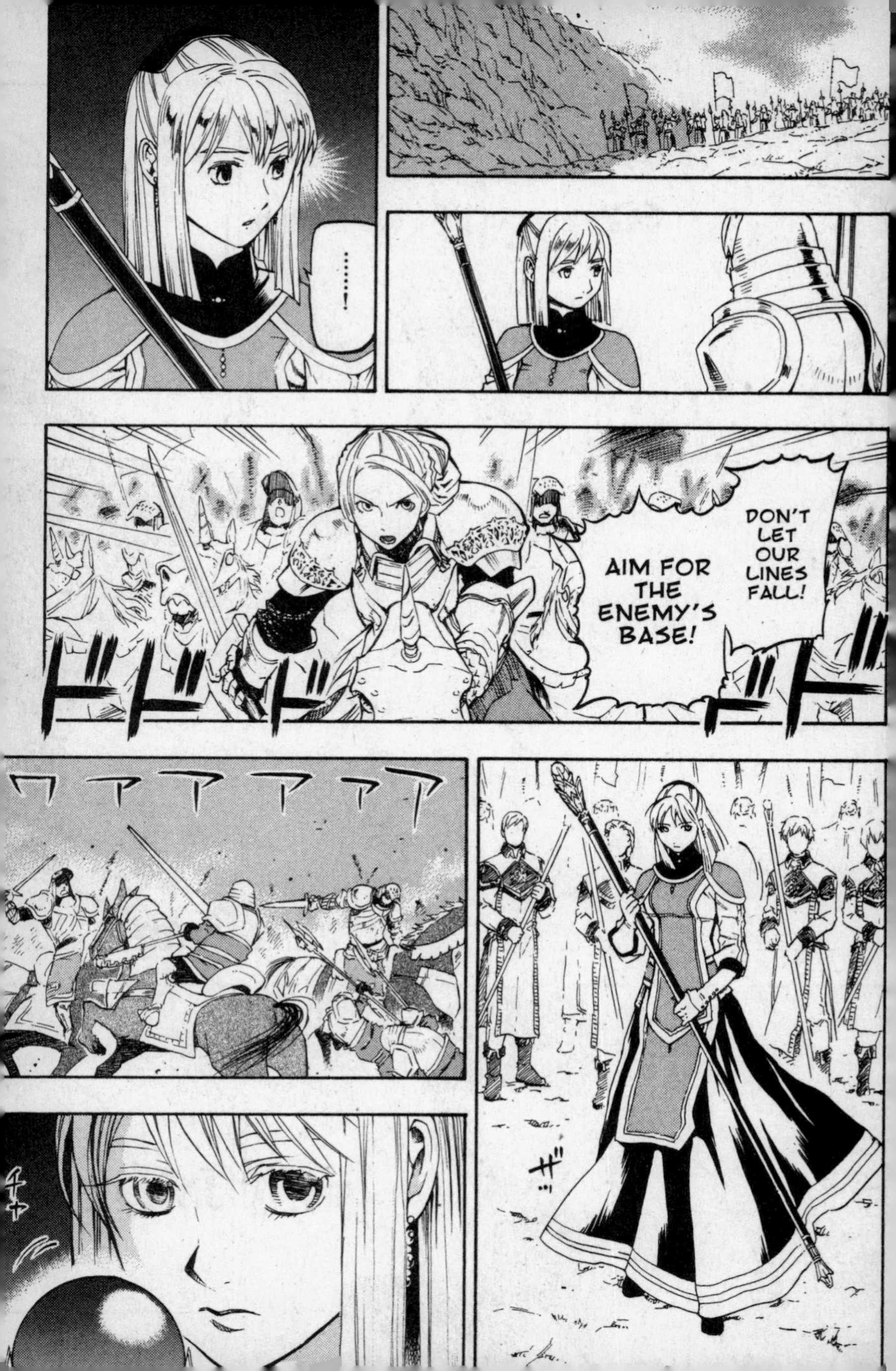

......!
DON'T LET OUR LINES FALL!
AIM FOR THE ENEMY'S BASE!
ドドド
ドドドド
ザッ
ワァァァァァ

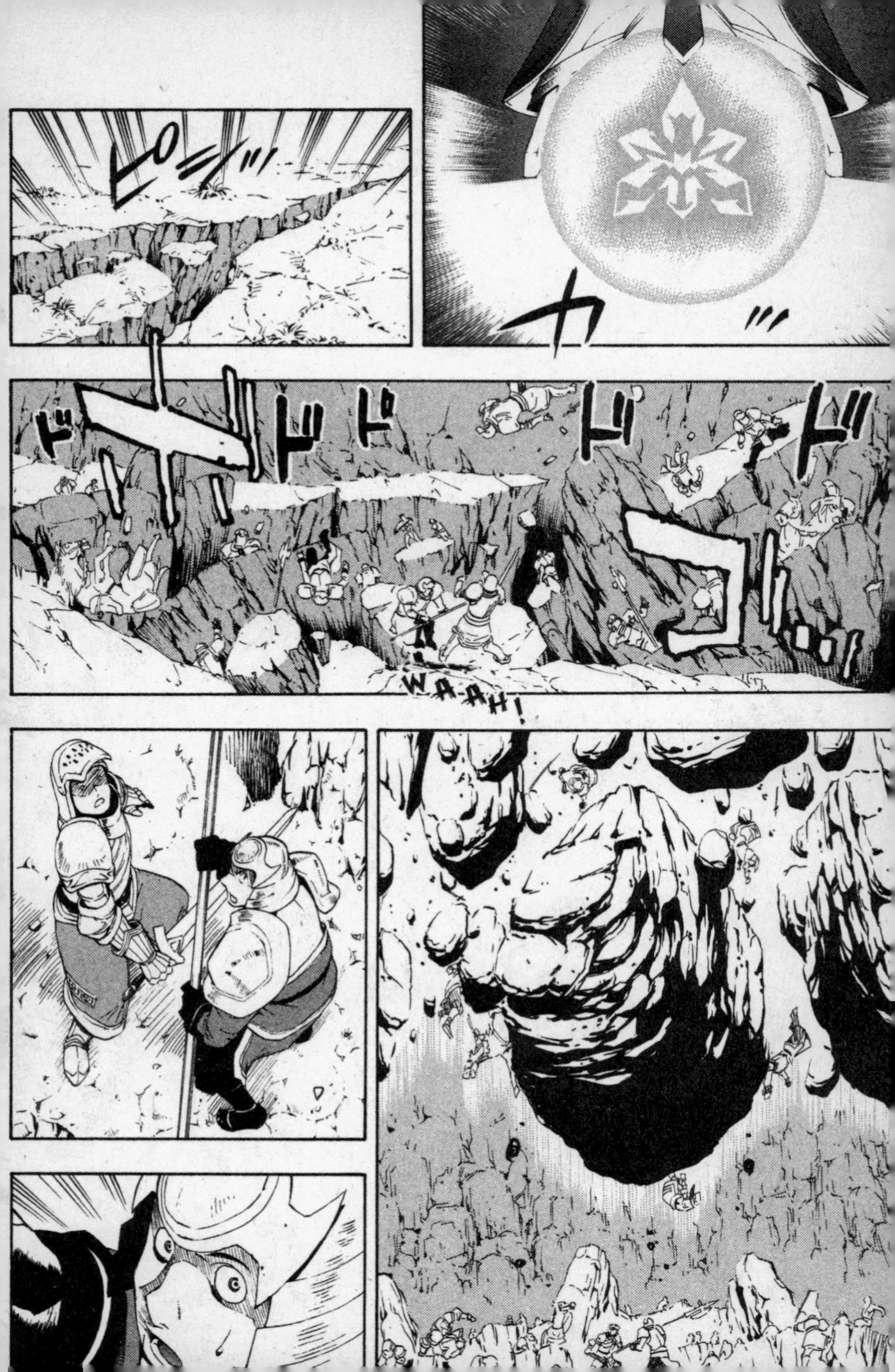
WAAH!

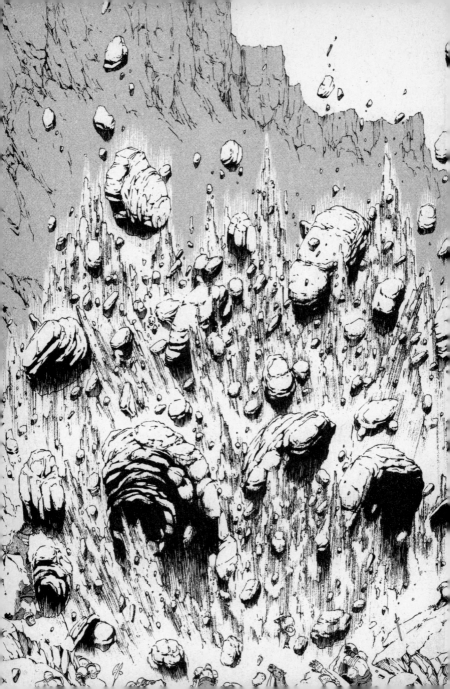

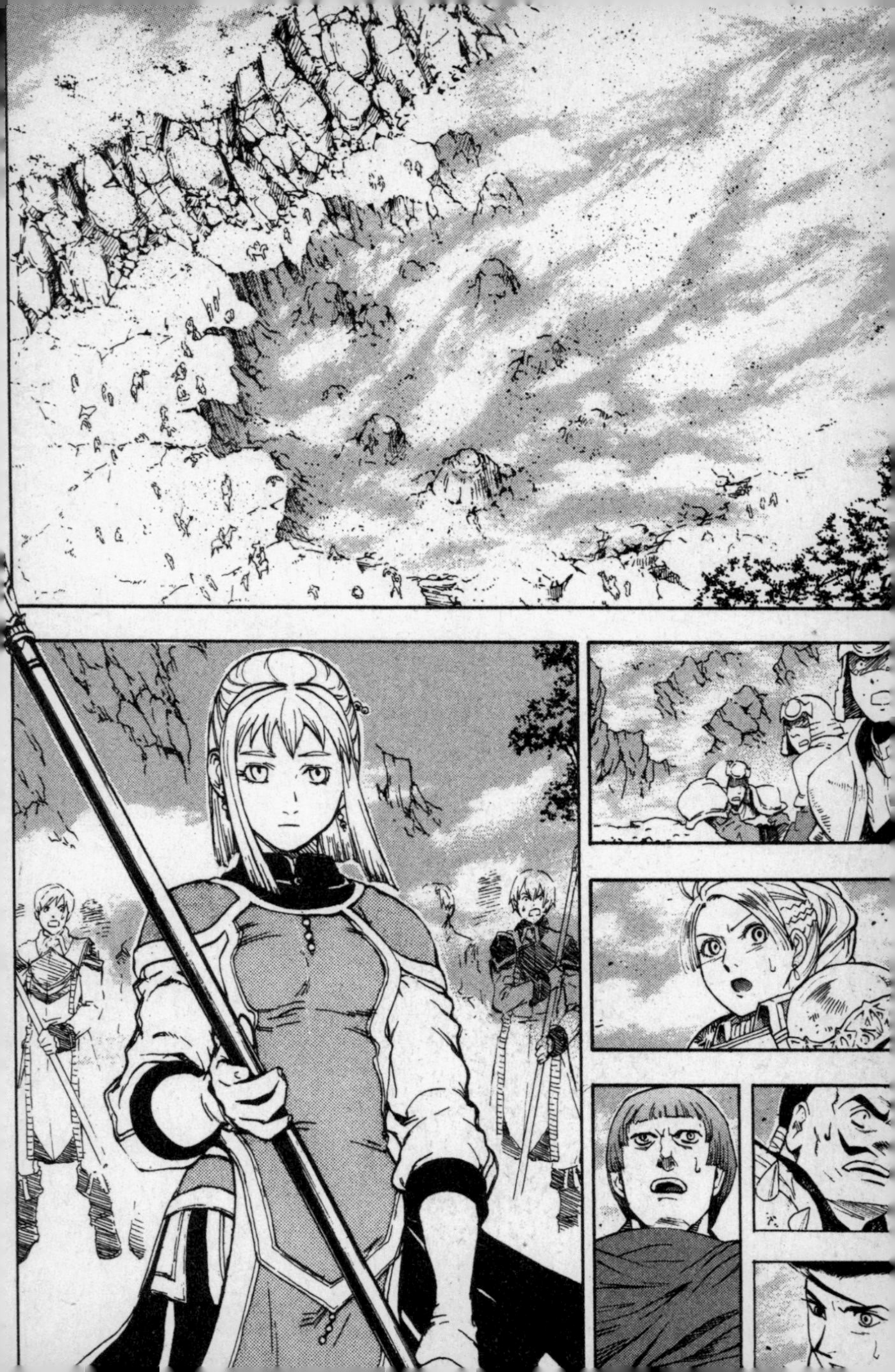

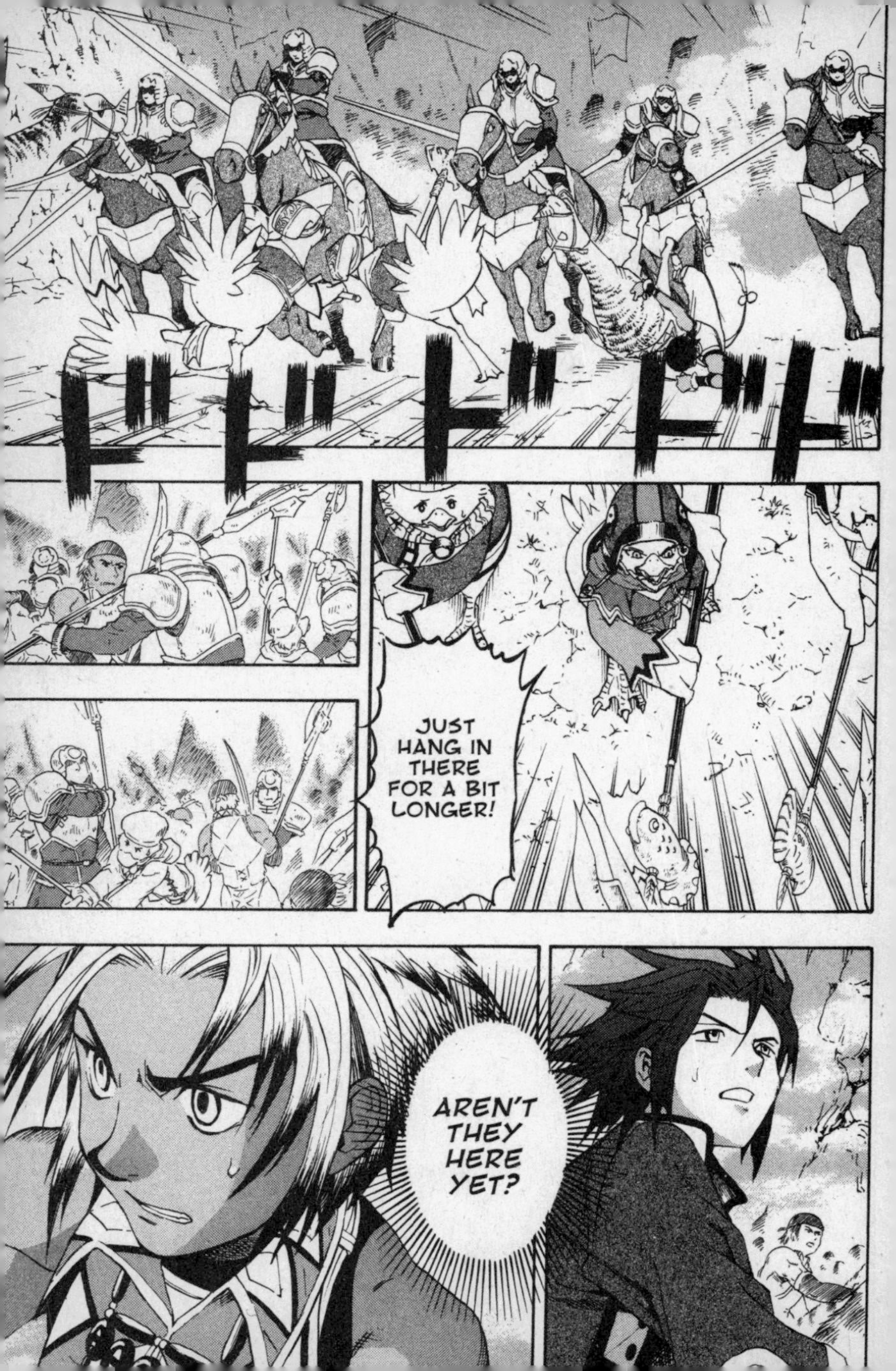

ドドドドド
JUST HANG IN THERE FOR A BIT LONGER!
AREN'T THEY HERE YET?

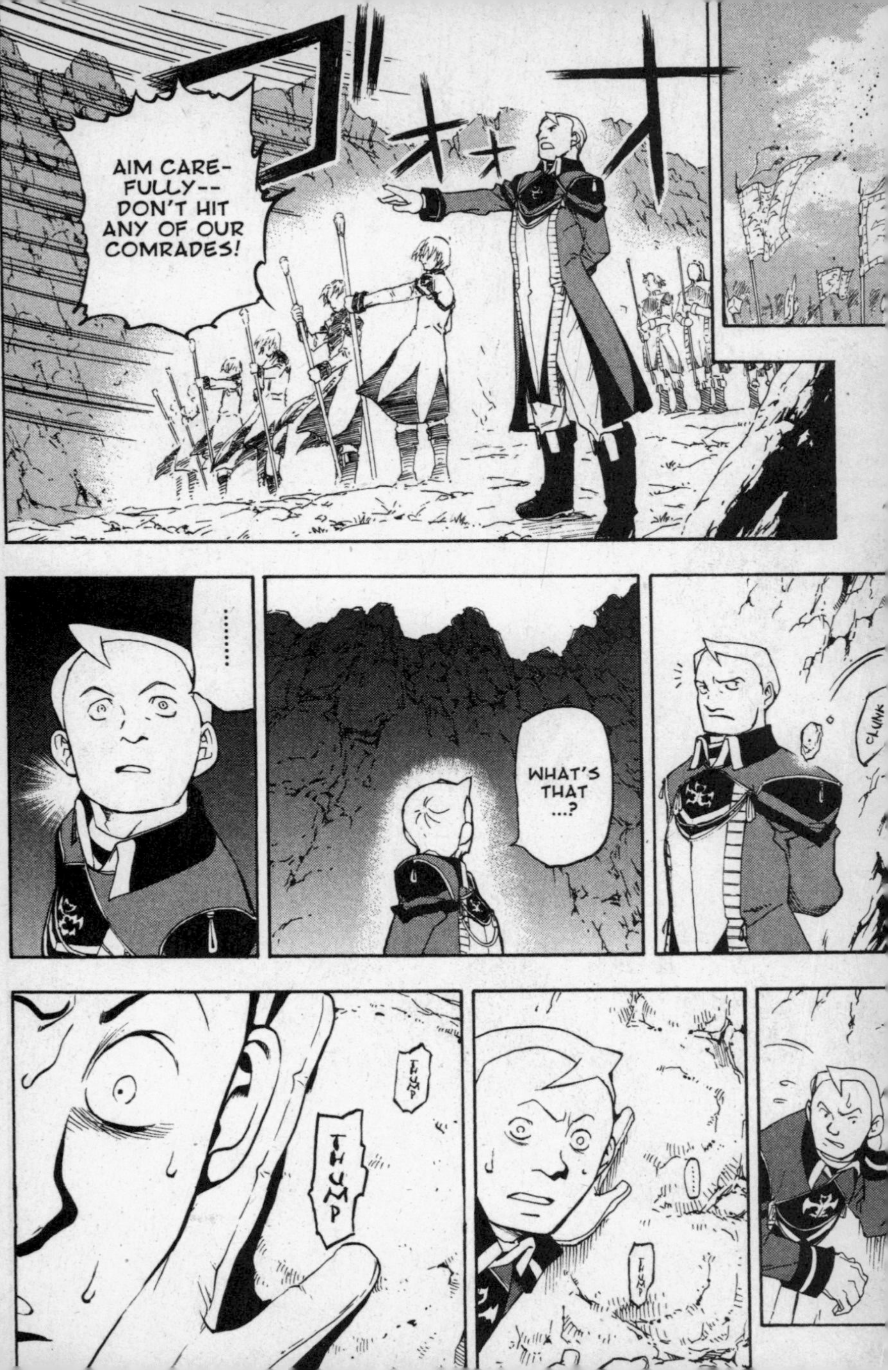
AIM CARE-FULLY-- DON'T HIT ANY OF OUR COMRADES!
CLUNK
WHAT'S THAT ...?
....
......
THUMP
THUMP
THUMP

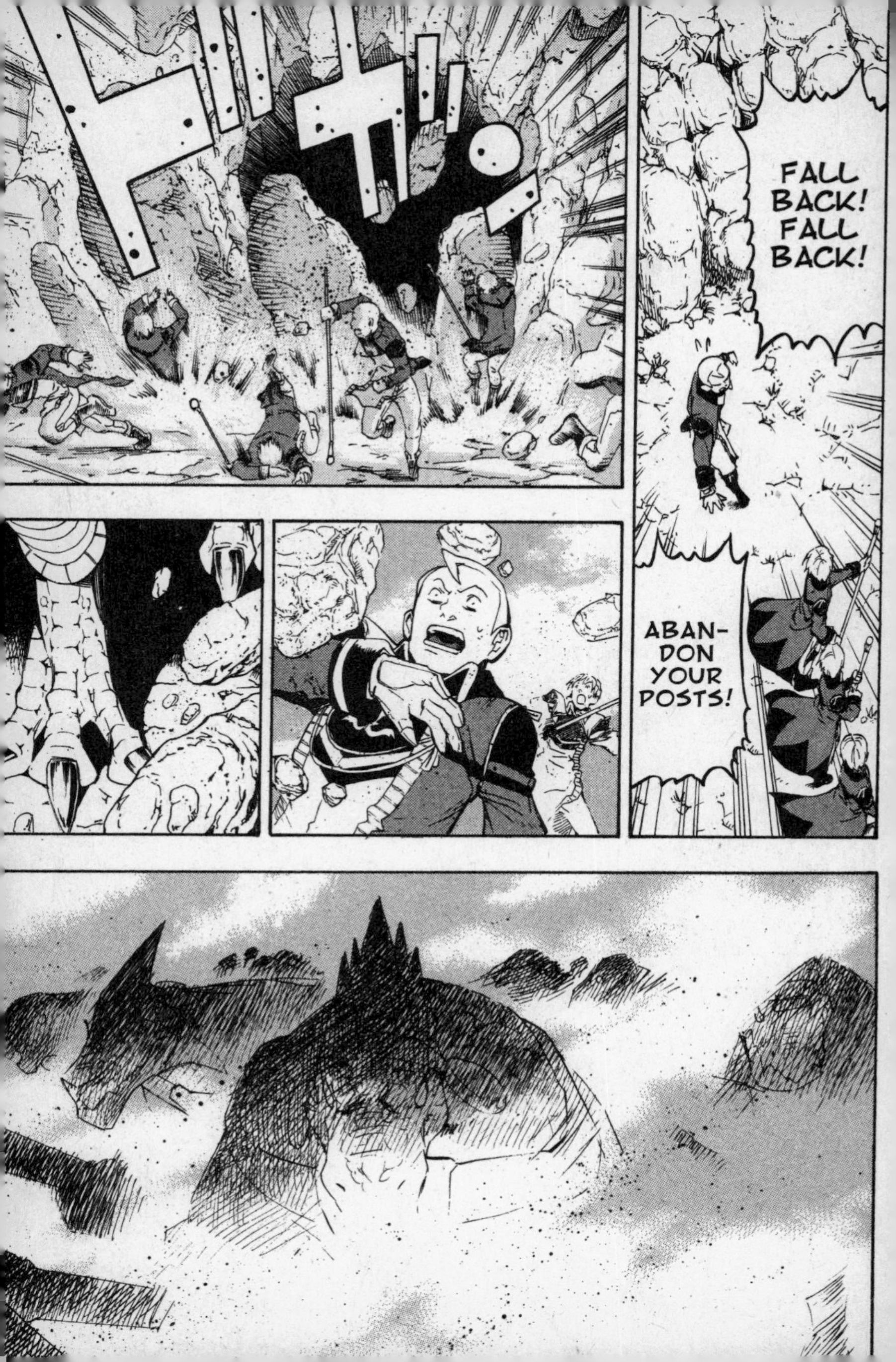
FALL BACK! FALL BACK!
ABAN-
DON
YOUR
POSTS!

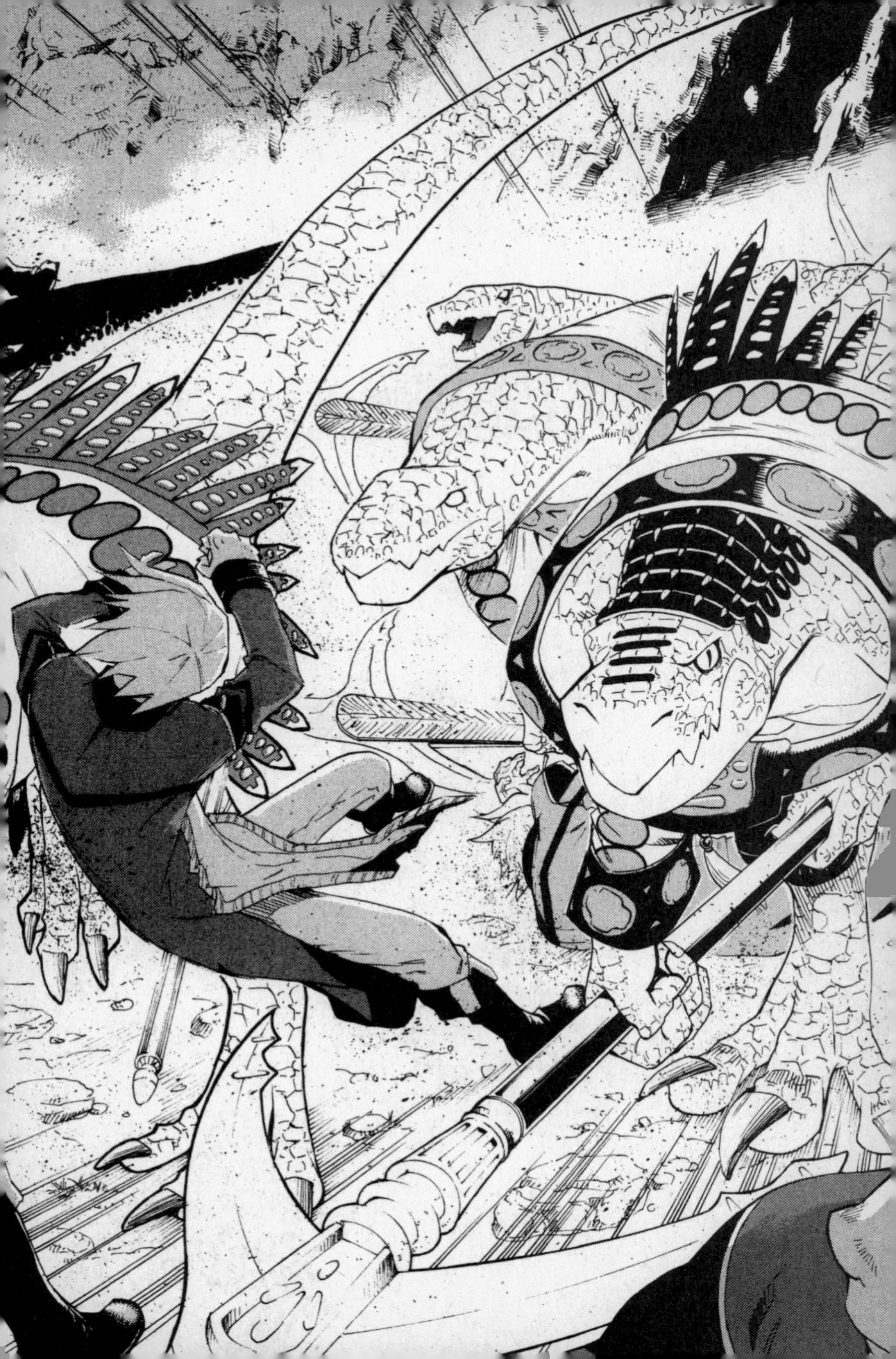

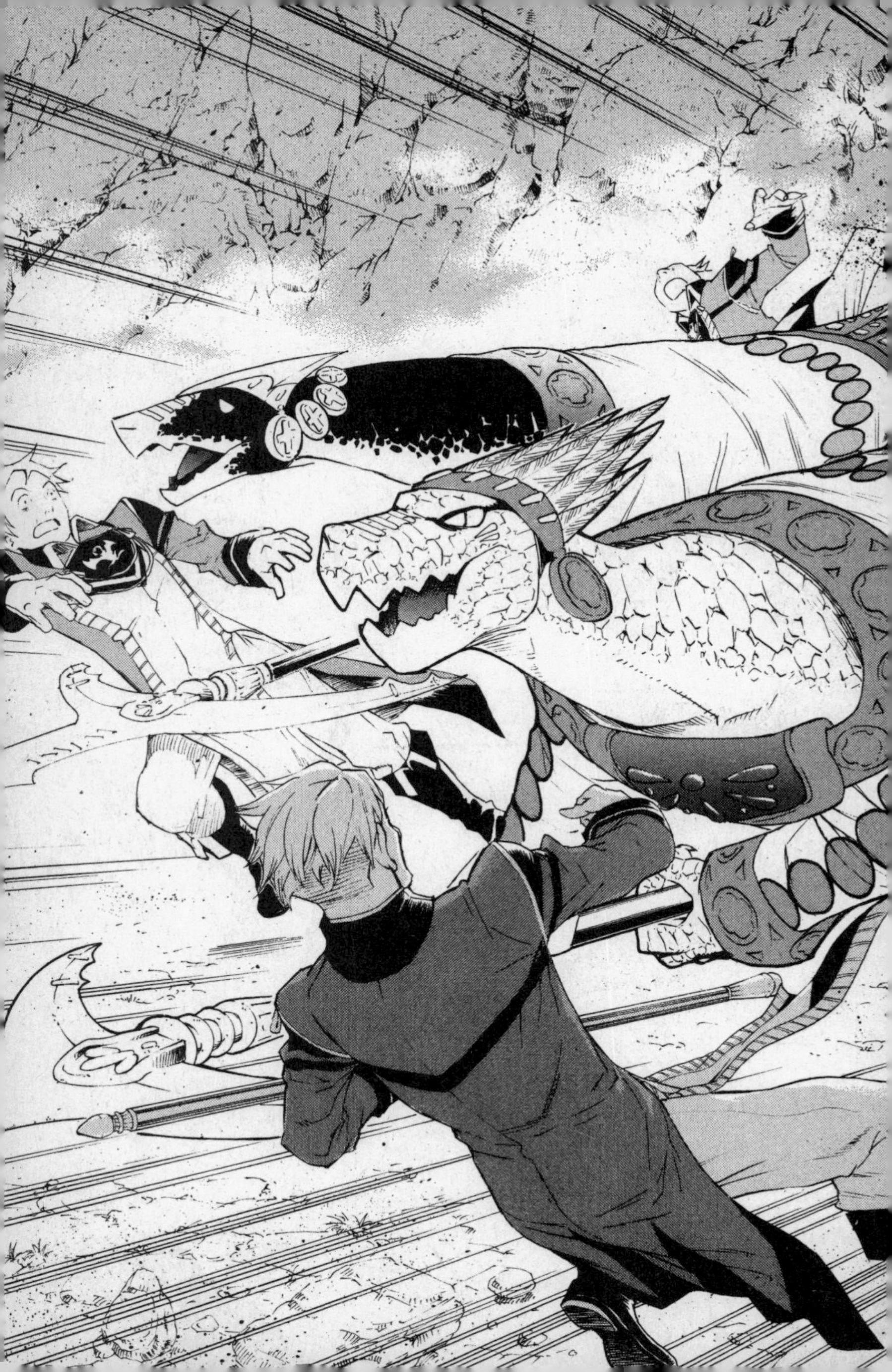

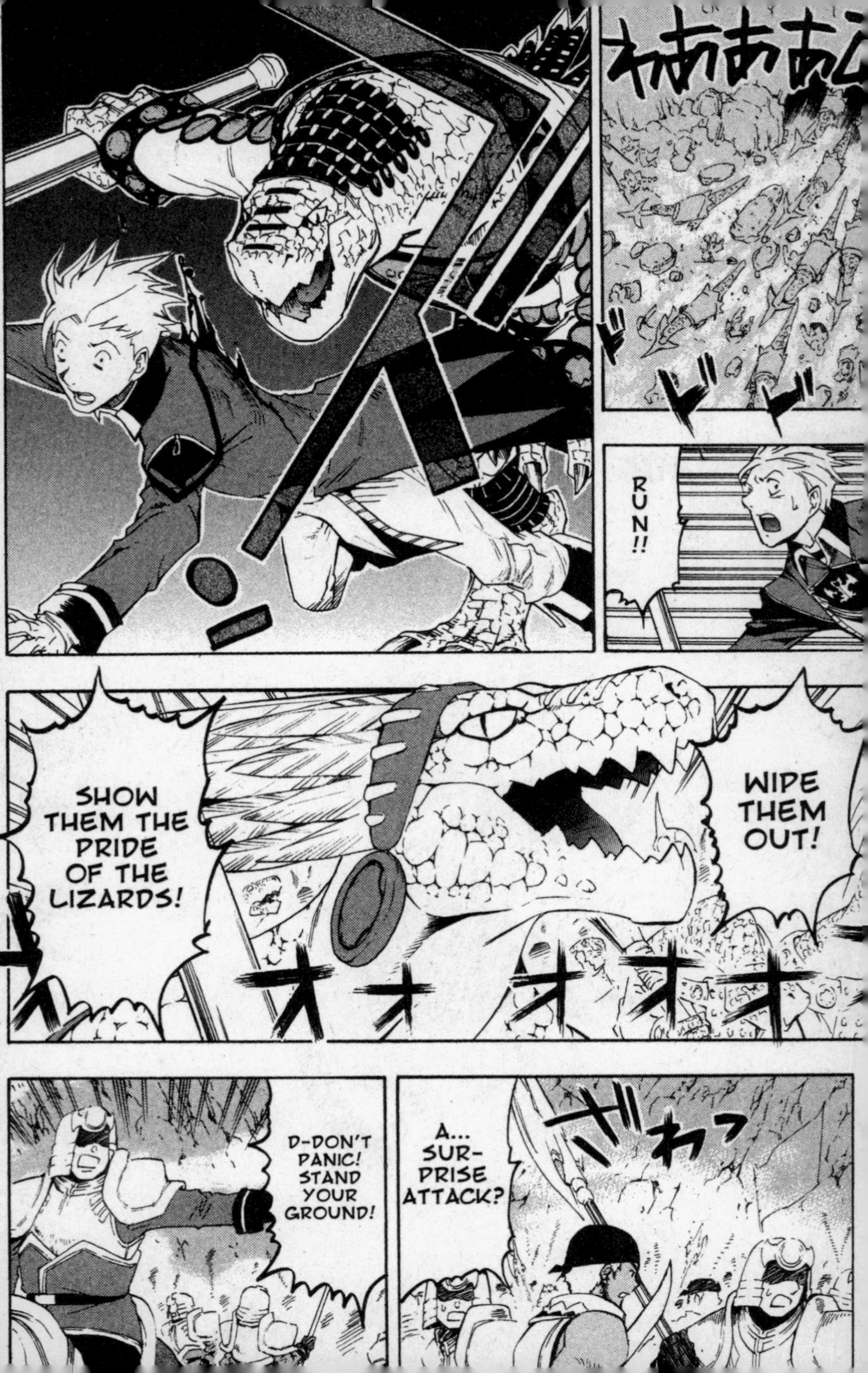
わあああ
RUN!!
WIPE THEM OUT!
SHOW THEM THE PRIDE OF THE LIZARDS!
ざわっ
A... SUR-PRISE ATTACK?
D-DON'T PANIC! STAND YOUR GROUND!

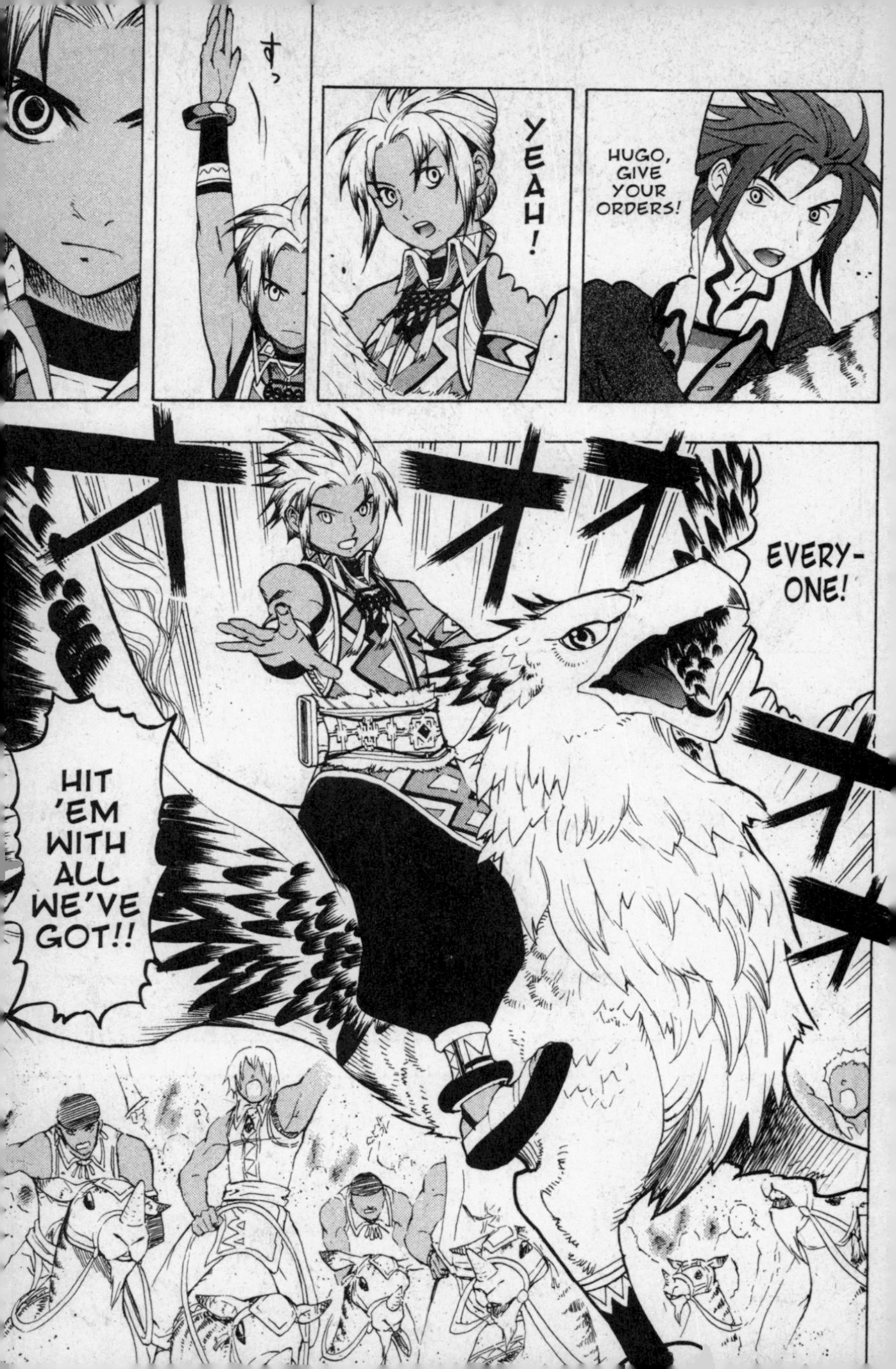
HUGO, GIVE YOUR ORDERS!
YEAH!
すっ
EVERY-ONE!
HIT 'EM WITH ALL WE'VE GOT!!

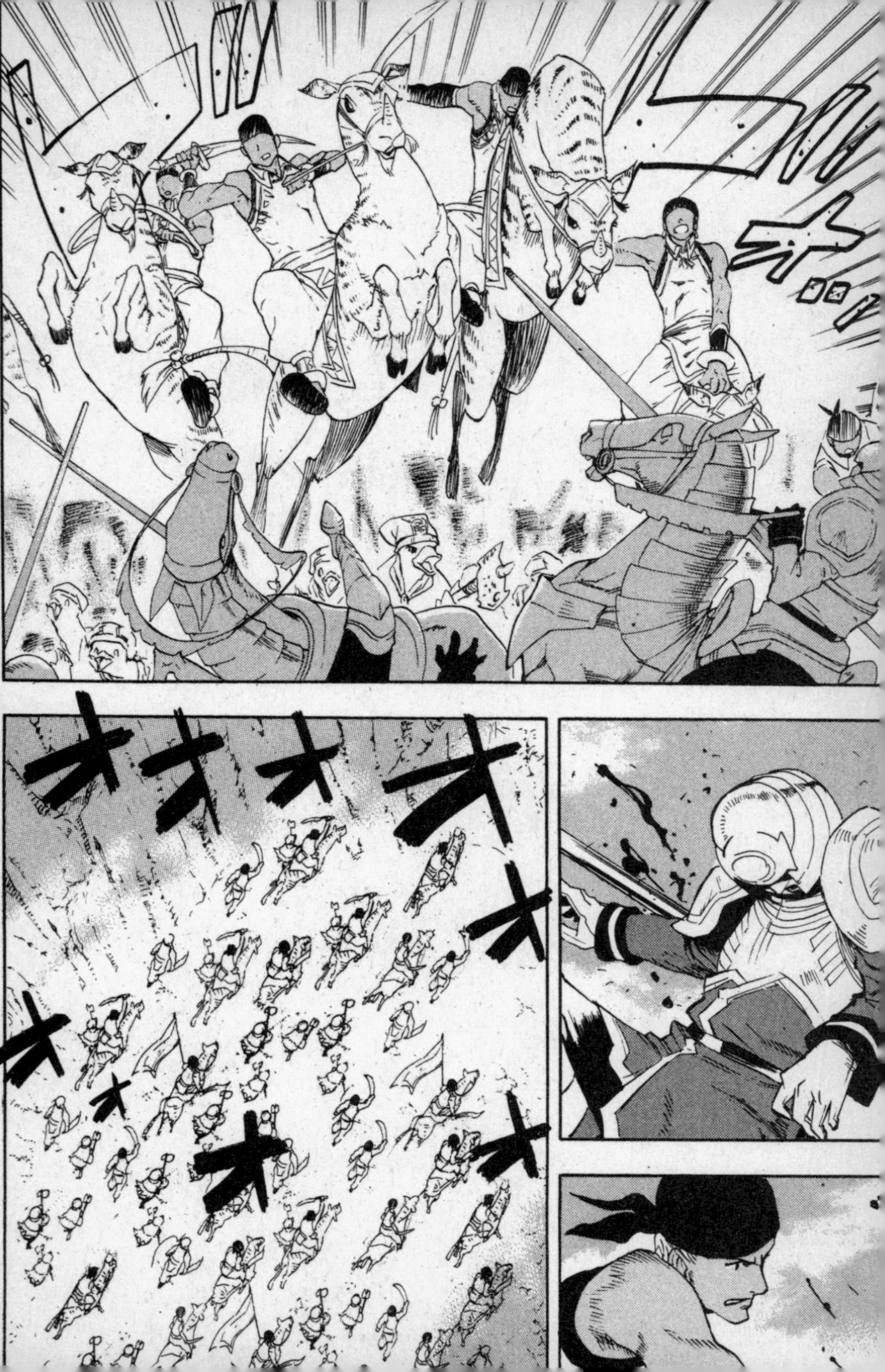
オオオオオオオオオオ

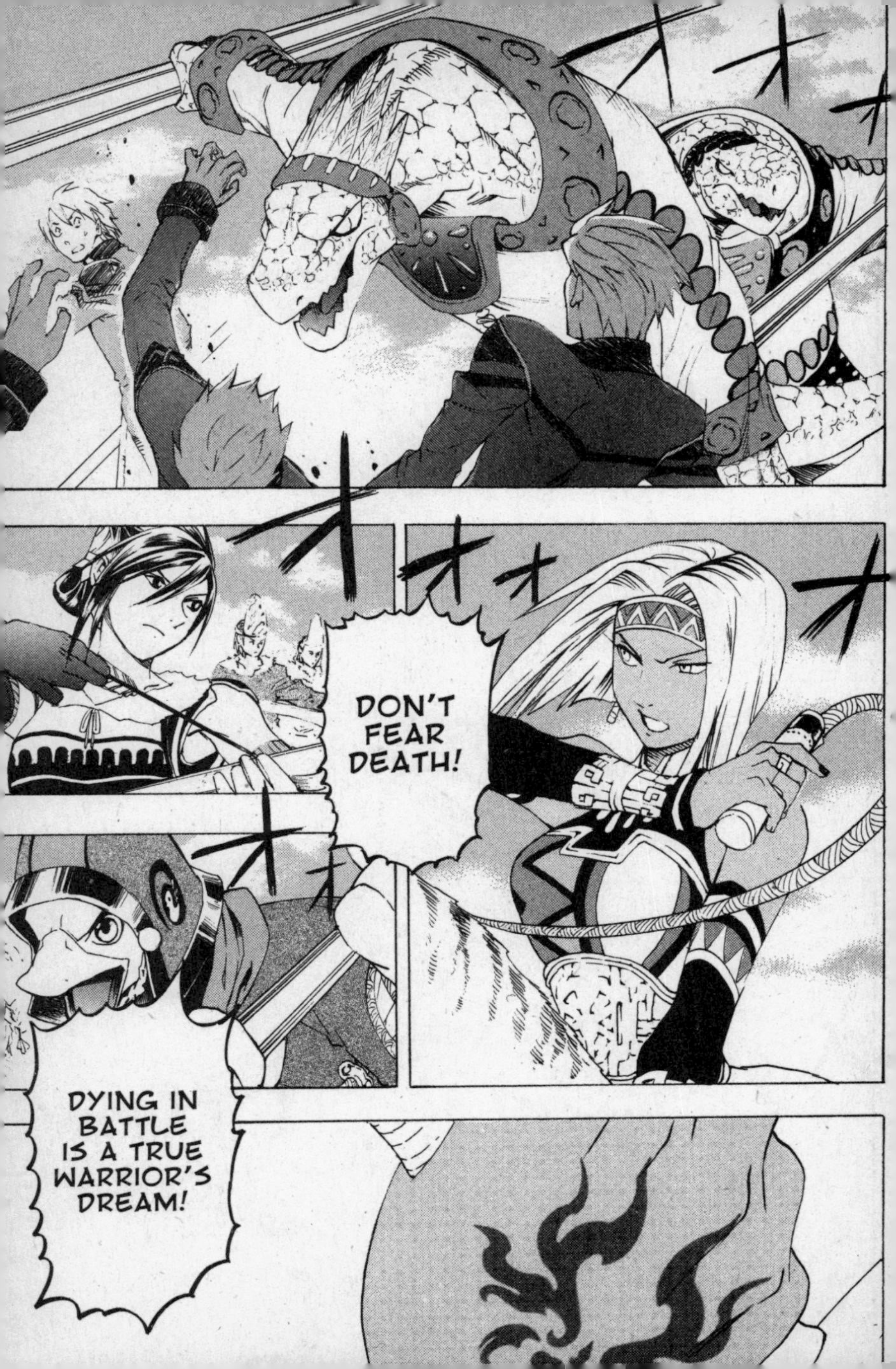

DON'T FEAR DEATH!
DYING IN BATTLE IS A TRUE WARRIOR'S DREAM!

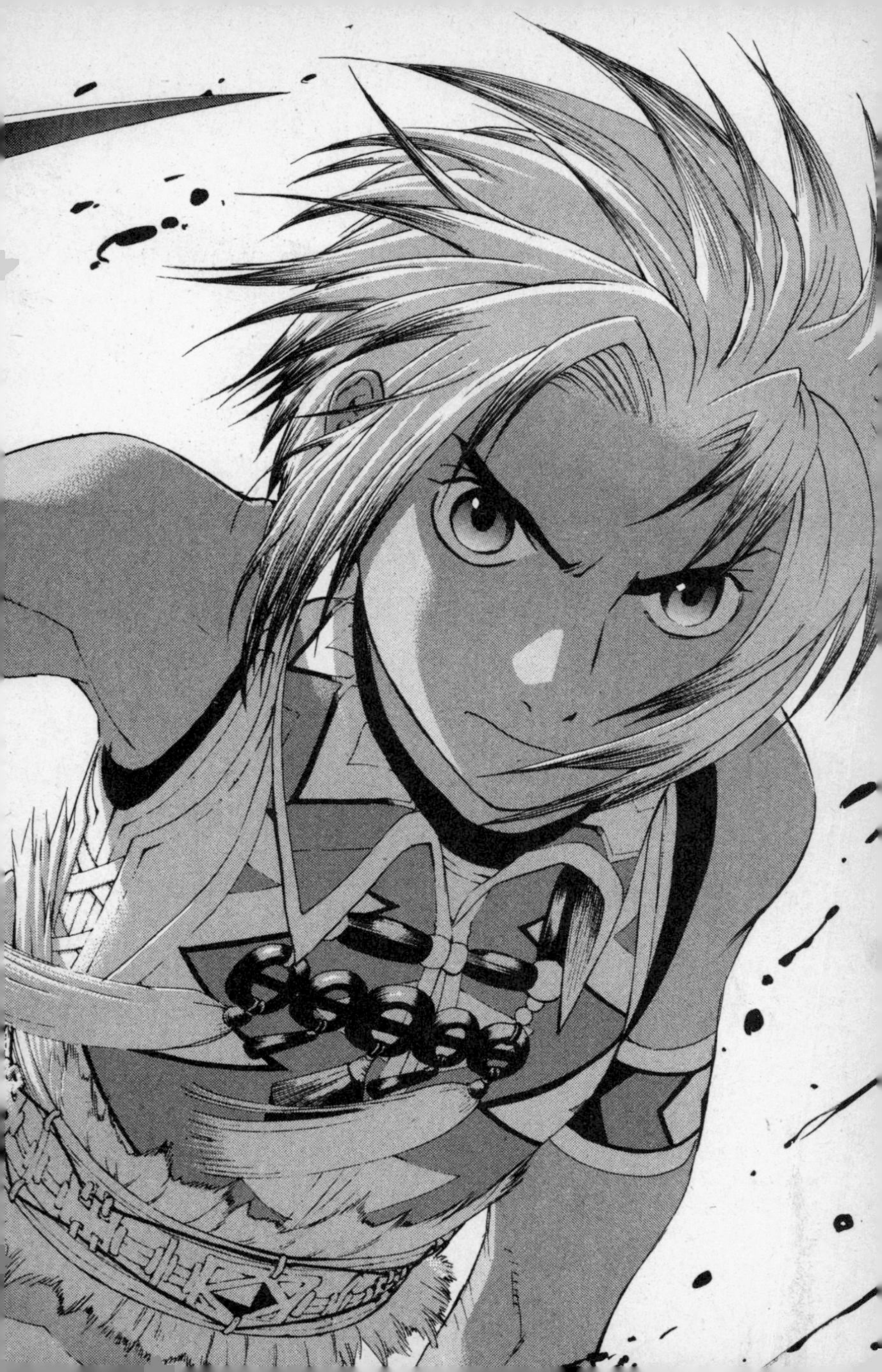

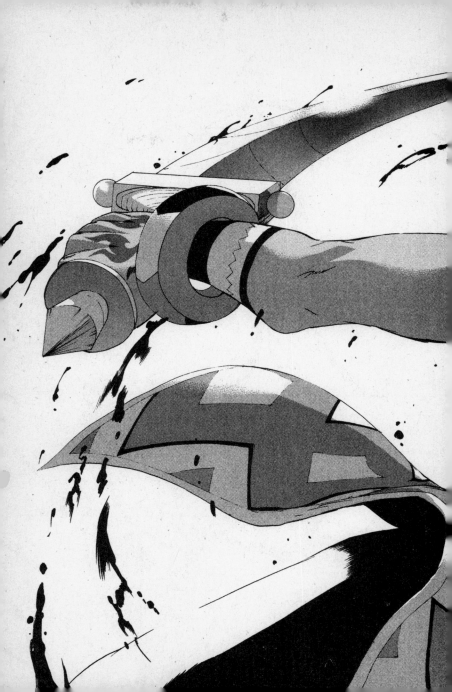

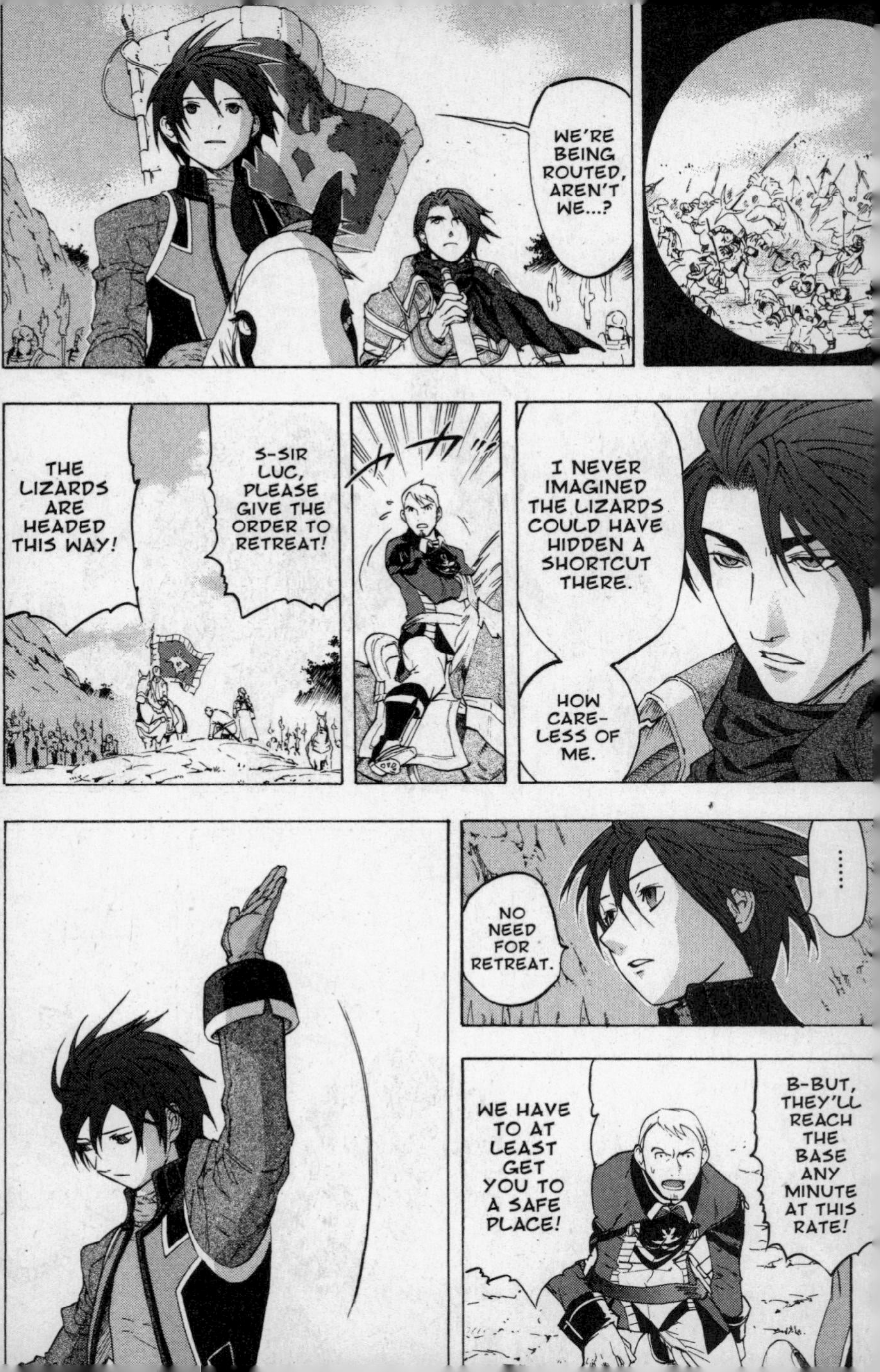
WE'RE BEING ROUTED, AREN'T WE...?
I NEVER IMAGINED THE LIZARDS COULD HAVE HIDDEN A SHORTCUT THERE.
HOW CARE-LESS OF ME.
S-SIR LUC, PLEASE GIVE THE ORDER TO RETREAT!
THE LIZARDS ARE HEADED THIS WAY!
......
NO NEED FOR RETREAT.
B-BUT, THEY'LL REACH THE BASE ANY MINUTE AT THIS RATE!
WE HAVE TO AT LEAST GET YOU TO A SAFE PLACE!

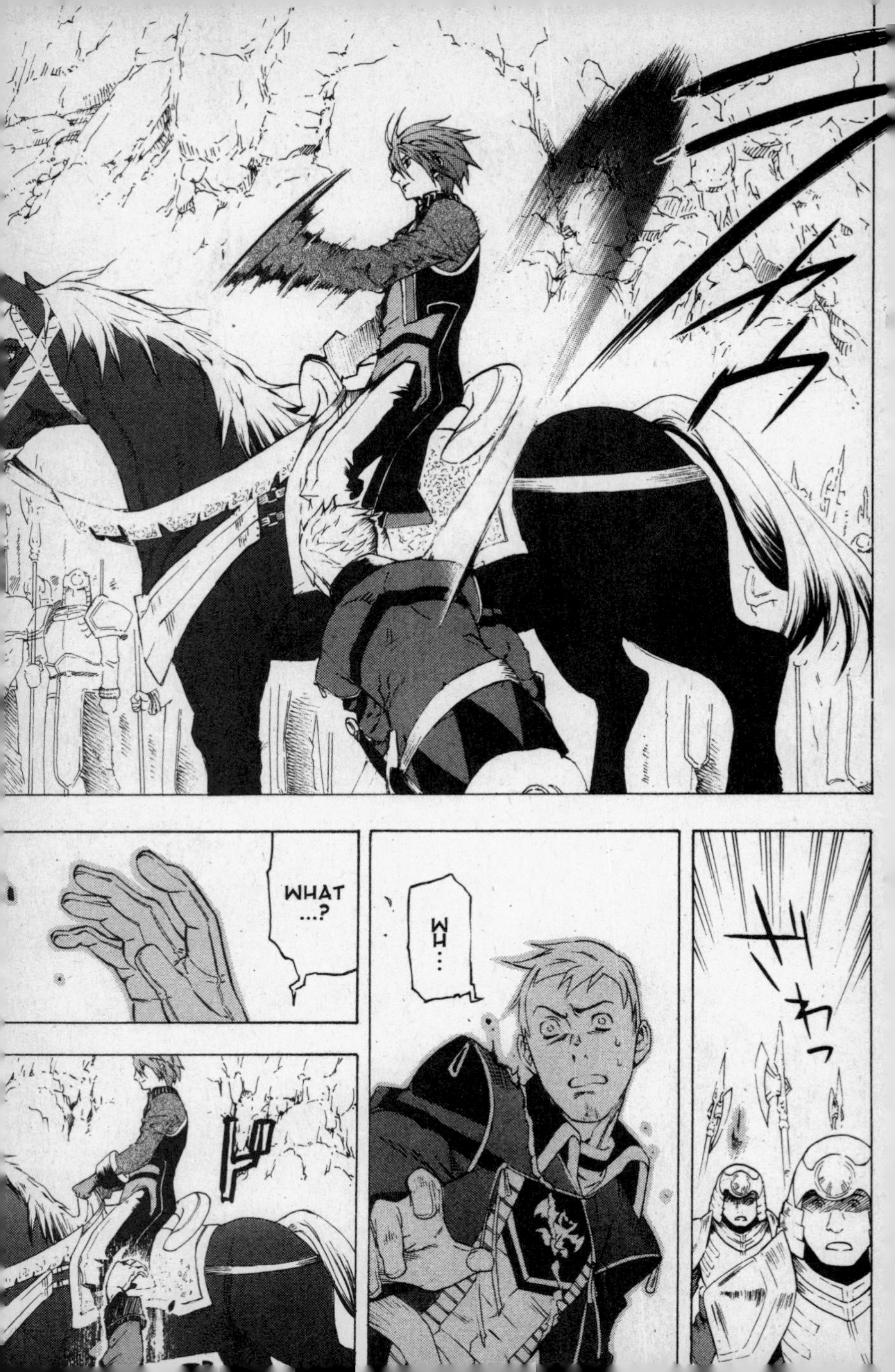
WH...
WHAT ...?

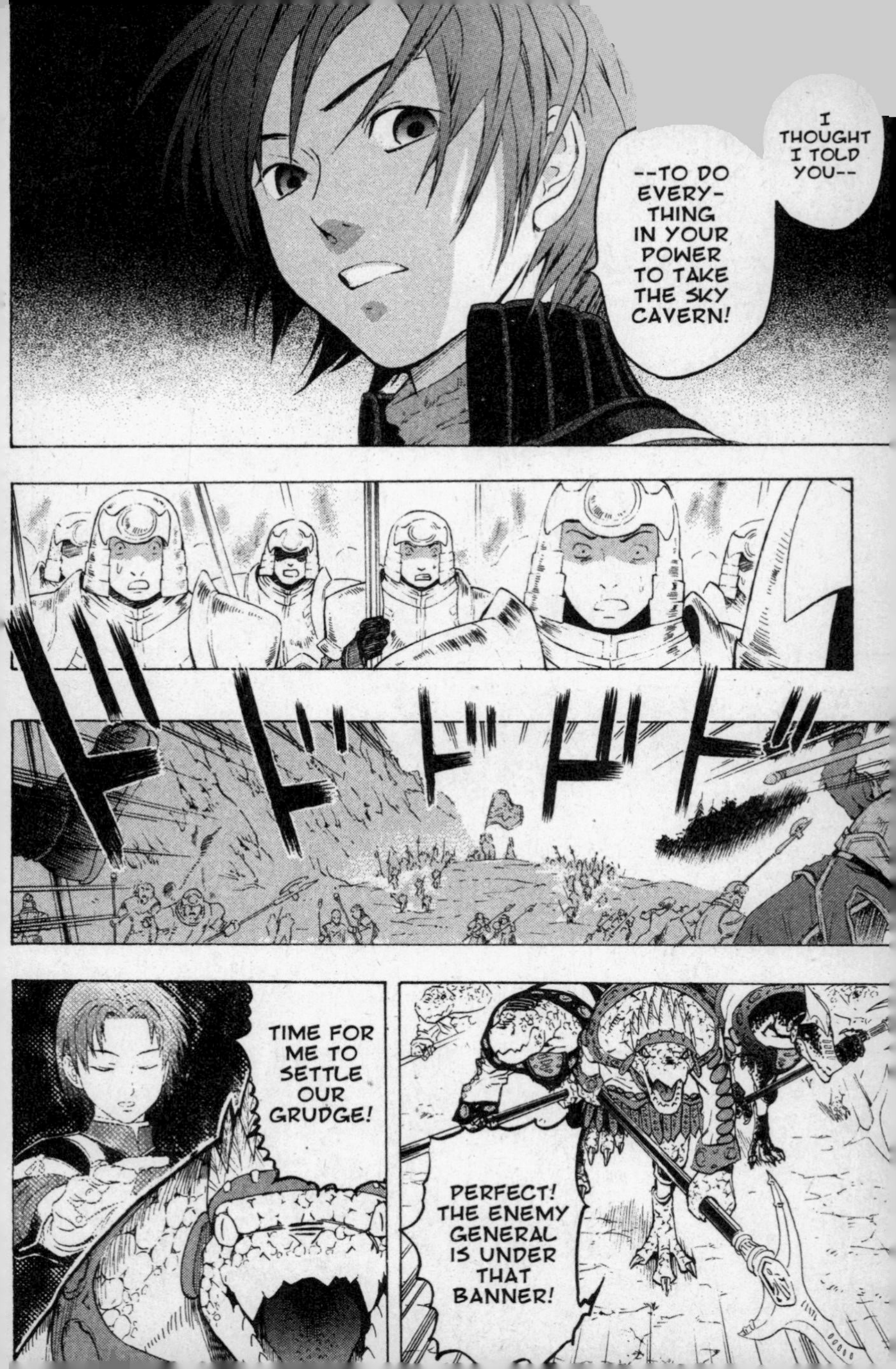
I THOUGHT I TOLD YOU--
--TO DO EVERYTHING IN YOUR POWER TO TAKE THE SKY CAVERN!
PERFECT! THE ENEMY GENERAL IS UNDER THAT BANNER!
TIME FOR ME TO SETTLE OUR GRUDGE!

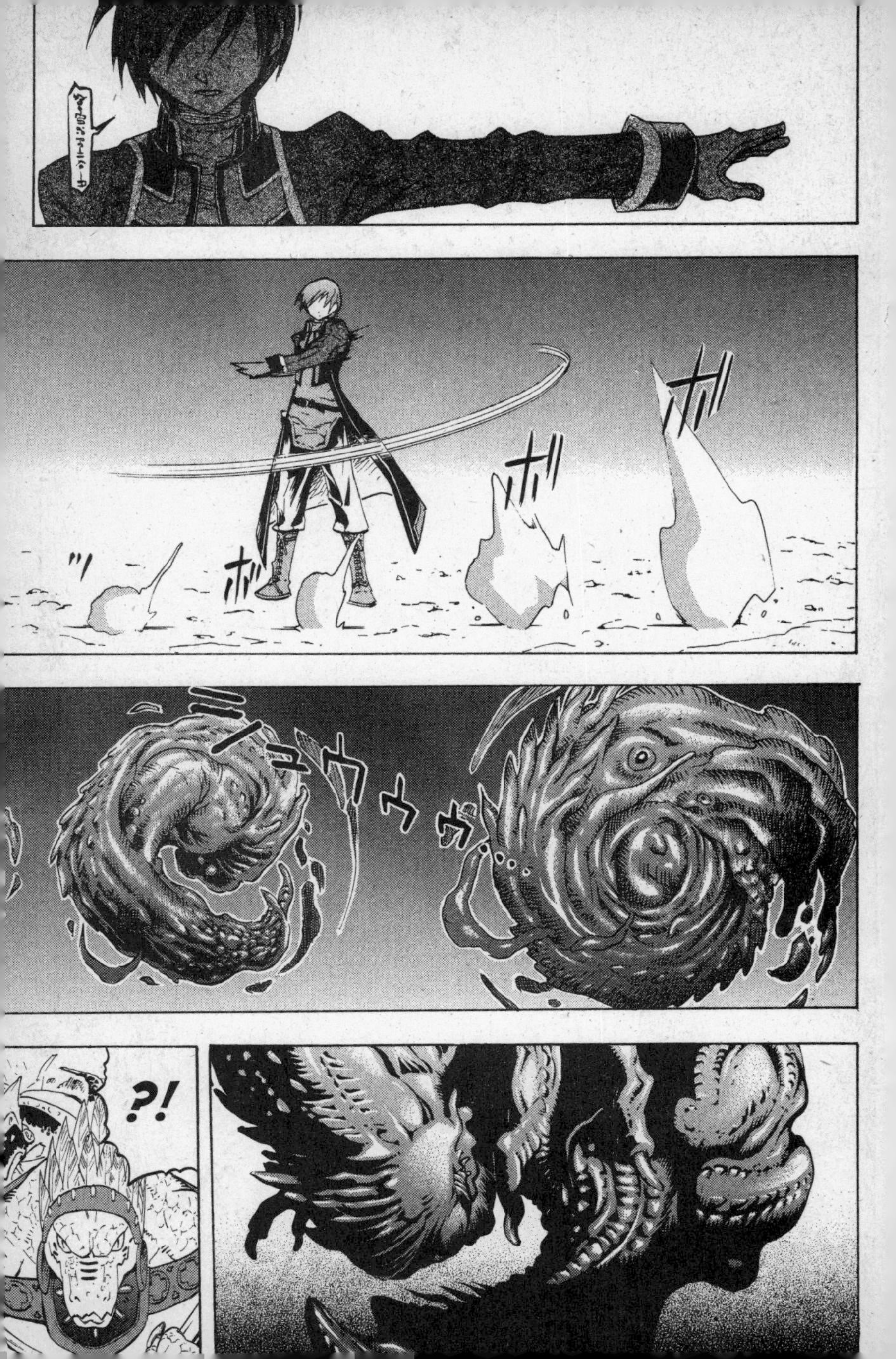
?!

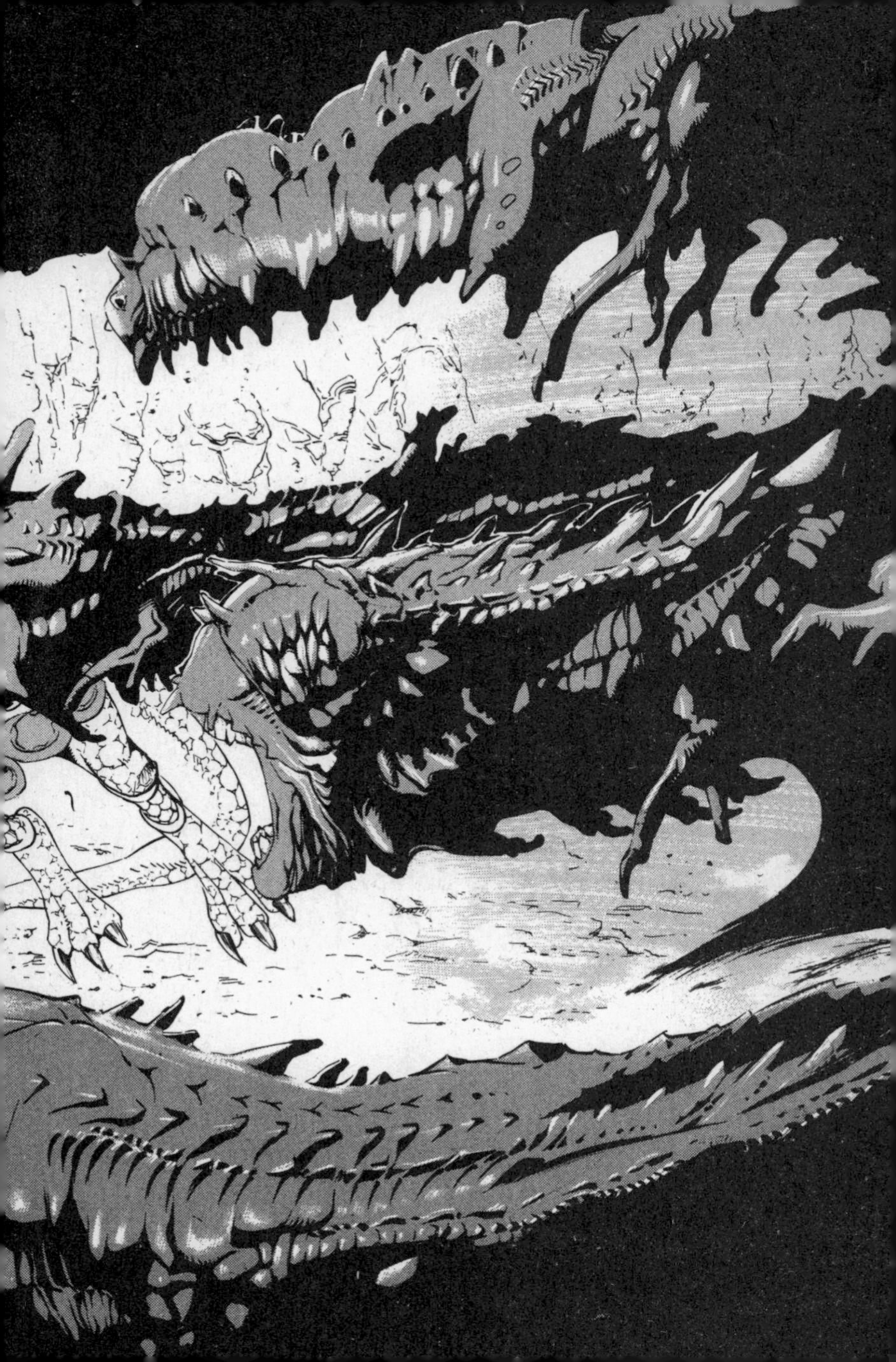

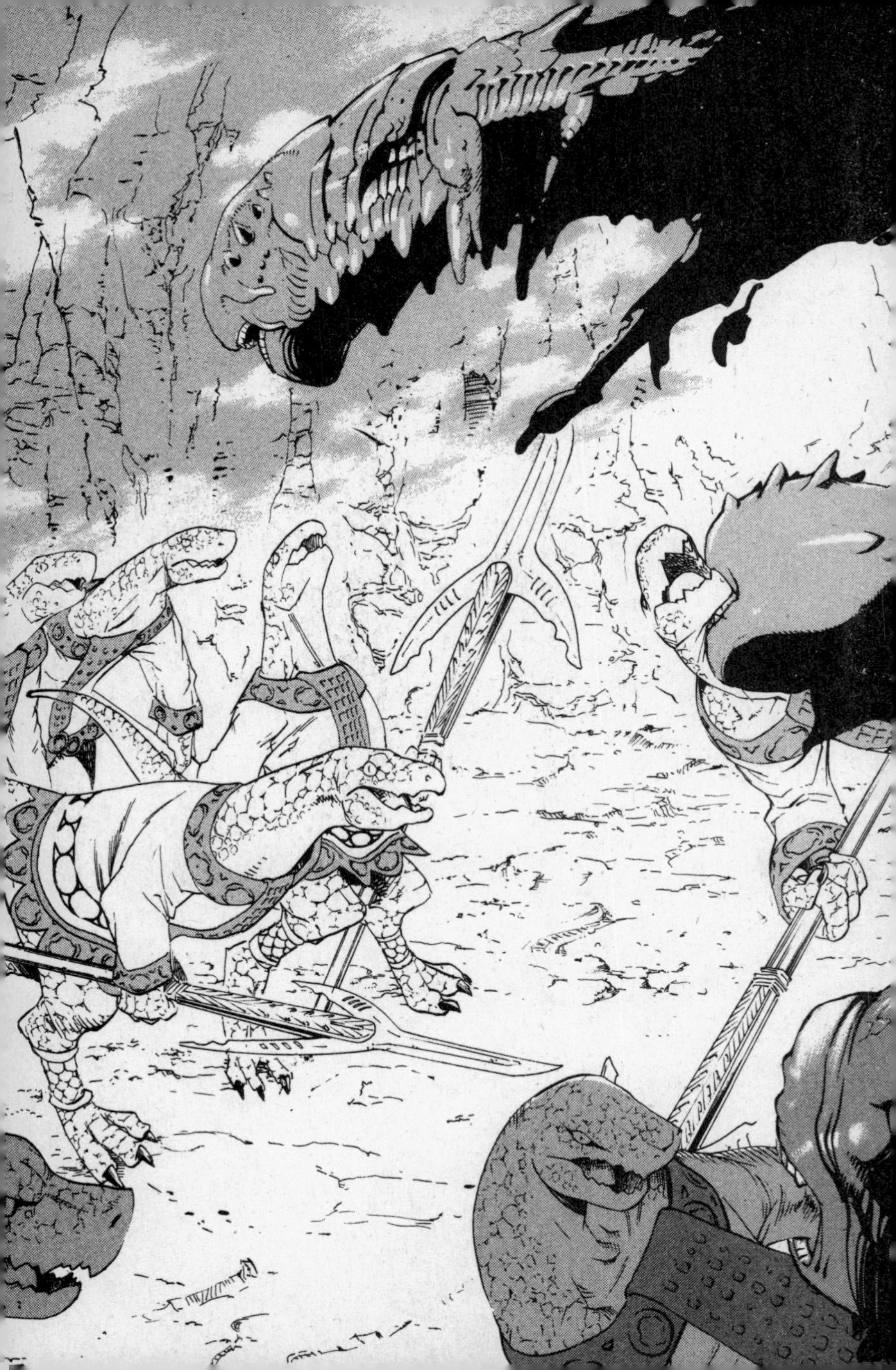

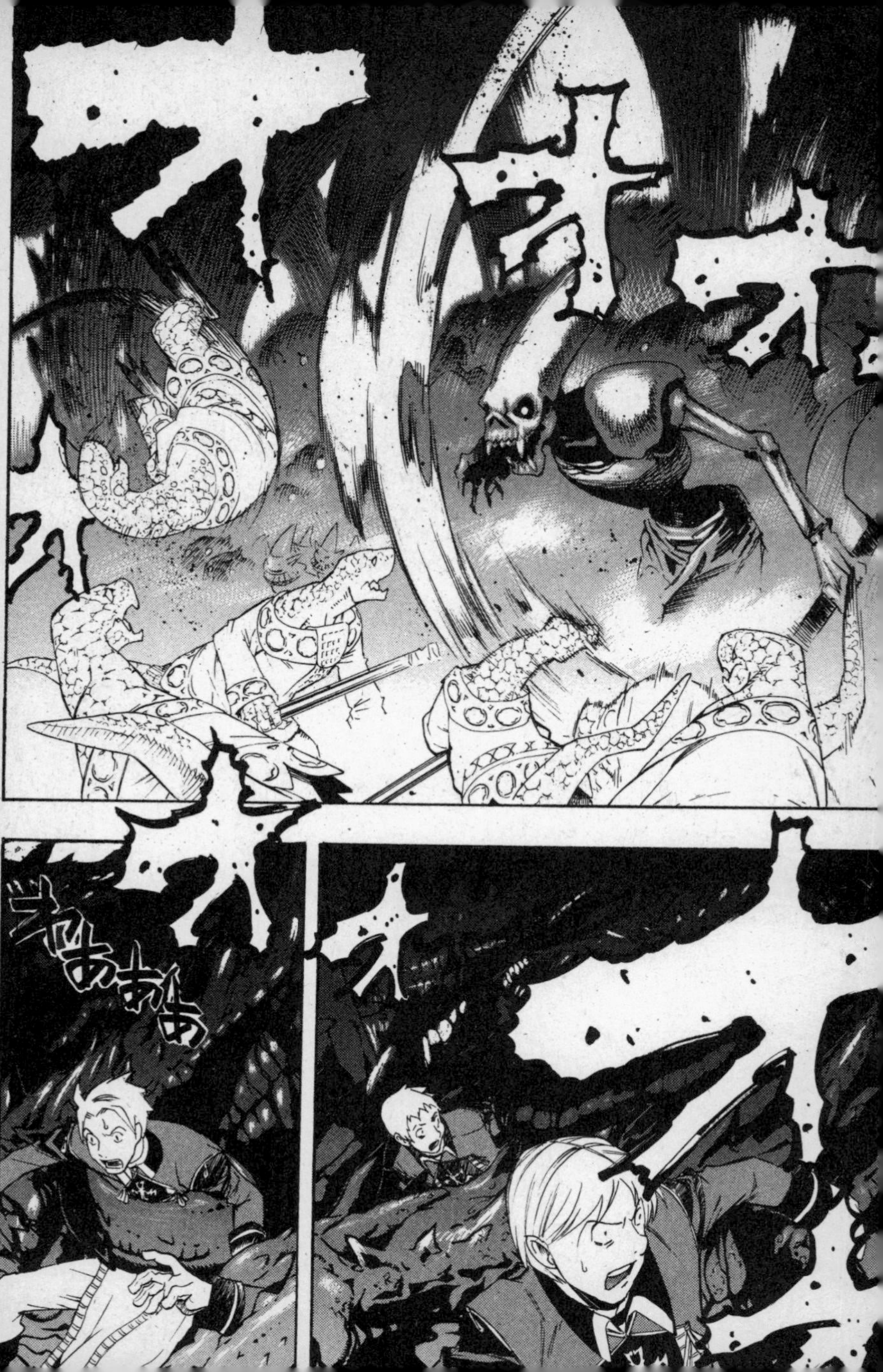
ぎあああ

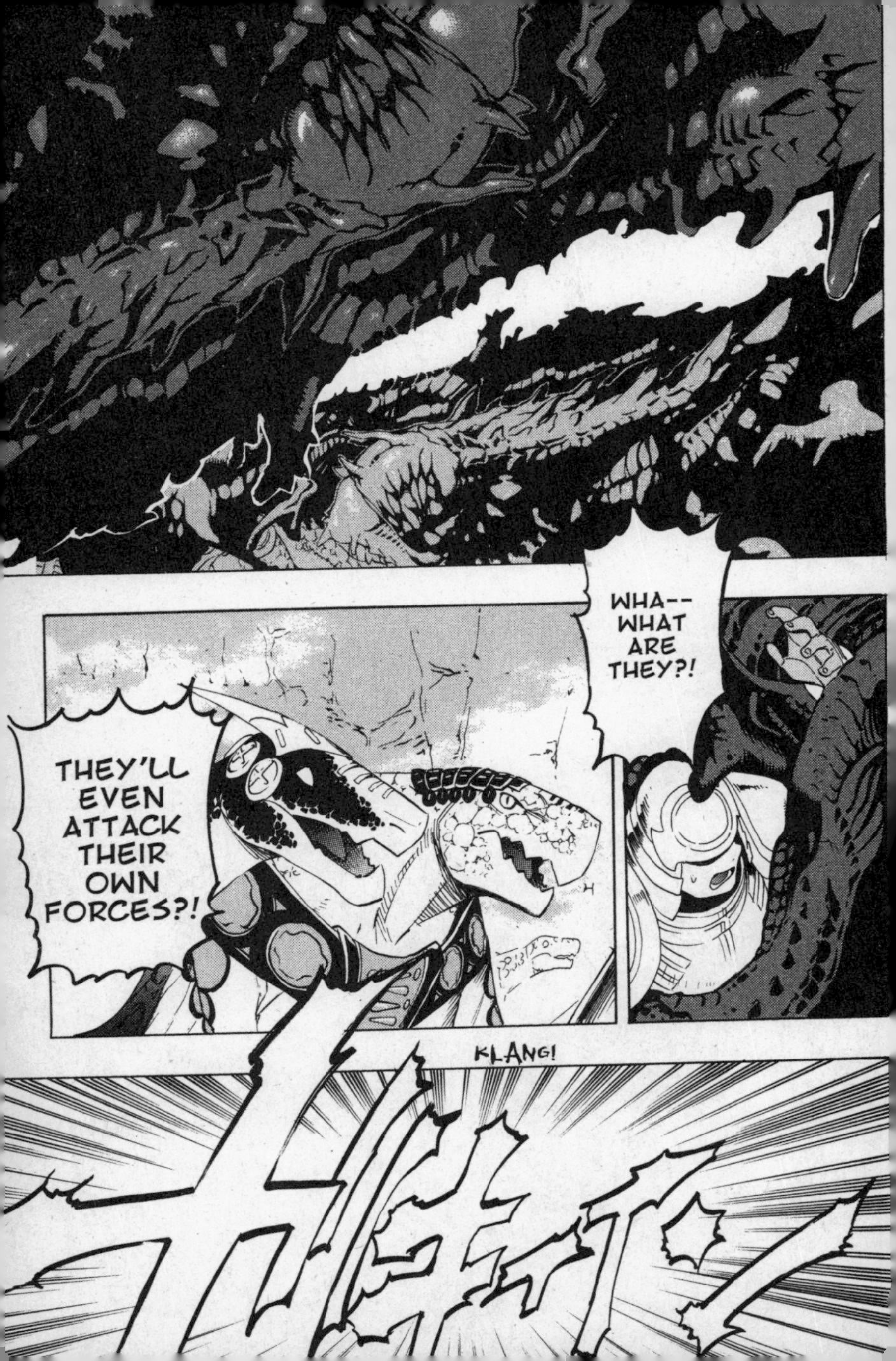
WHA-- WHAT ARE THEY?!
THEY'LL EVEN ATTACK THEIR OWN FORCES?!
KLANG!

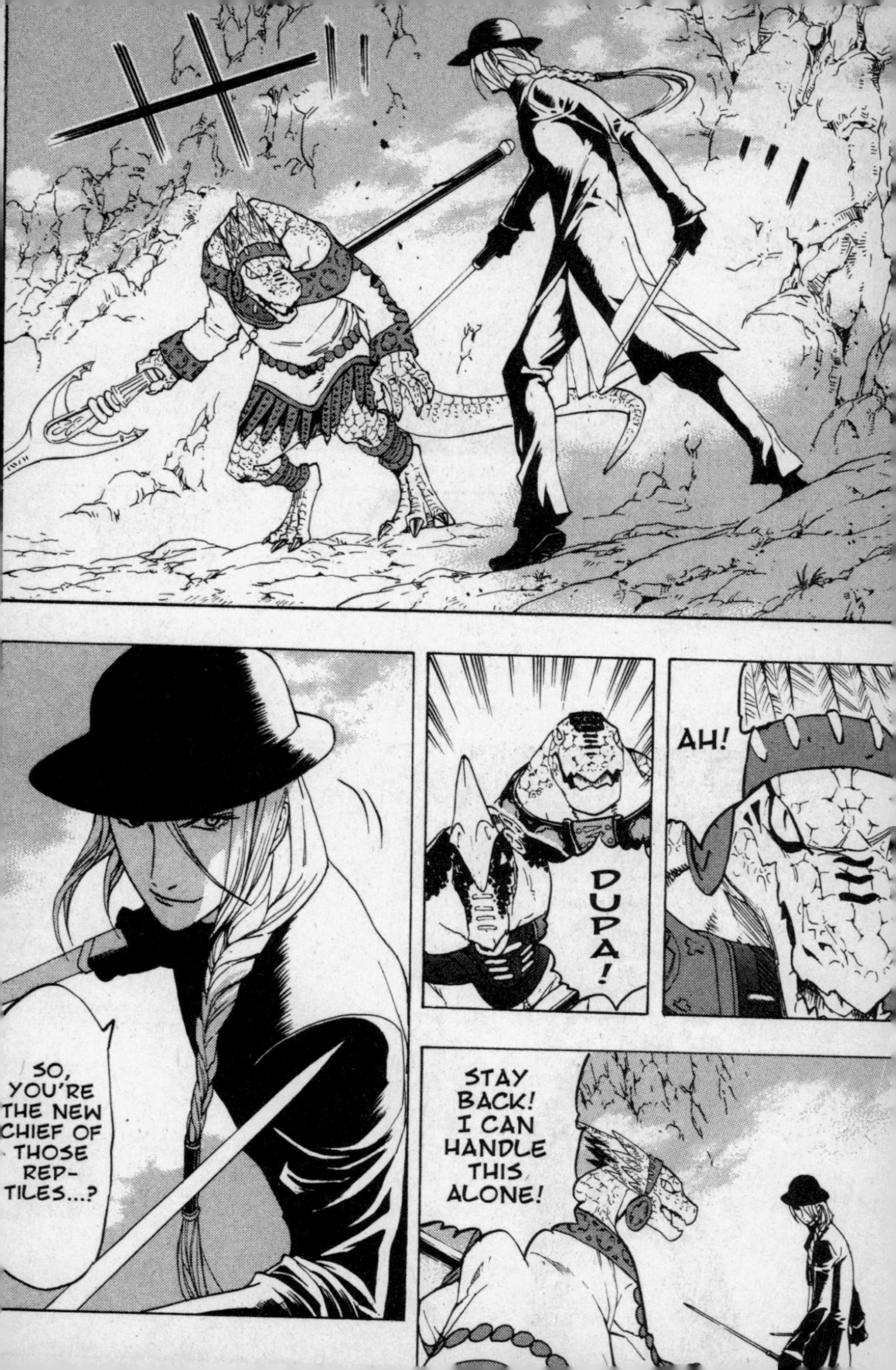
AH!
DUPA!
STAY BACK! I CAN HANDLE THIS ALONE!
SO, YOU'RE THE NEW CHIEF OF THOSE REP-TILES...?

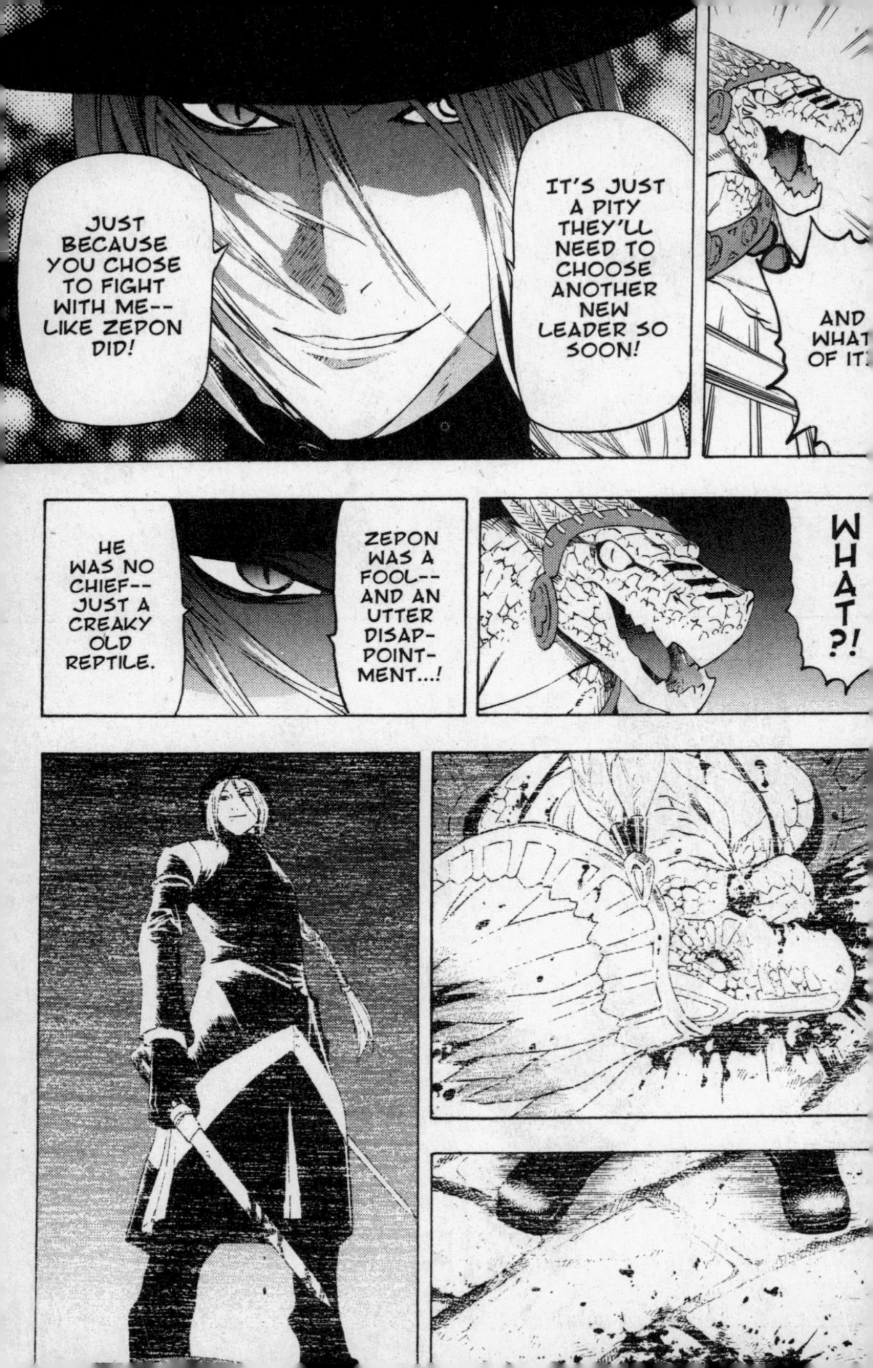
AND WHAT OF IT
IT'S JUST A PITY THEY'LL NEED TO CHOOSE ANOTHER NEW LEADER SO SOON!
JUST BECAUSE YOU CHOSE TO FIGHT WITH ME-- LIKE ZEPON DID!
WHAT?!
ZEPON WAS A FOOL-- AND AN UTTER DISAP-POINT-MENT...!
HE WAS NO CHIEF-- JUST A CREAKY OLD REPTILE.

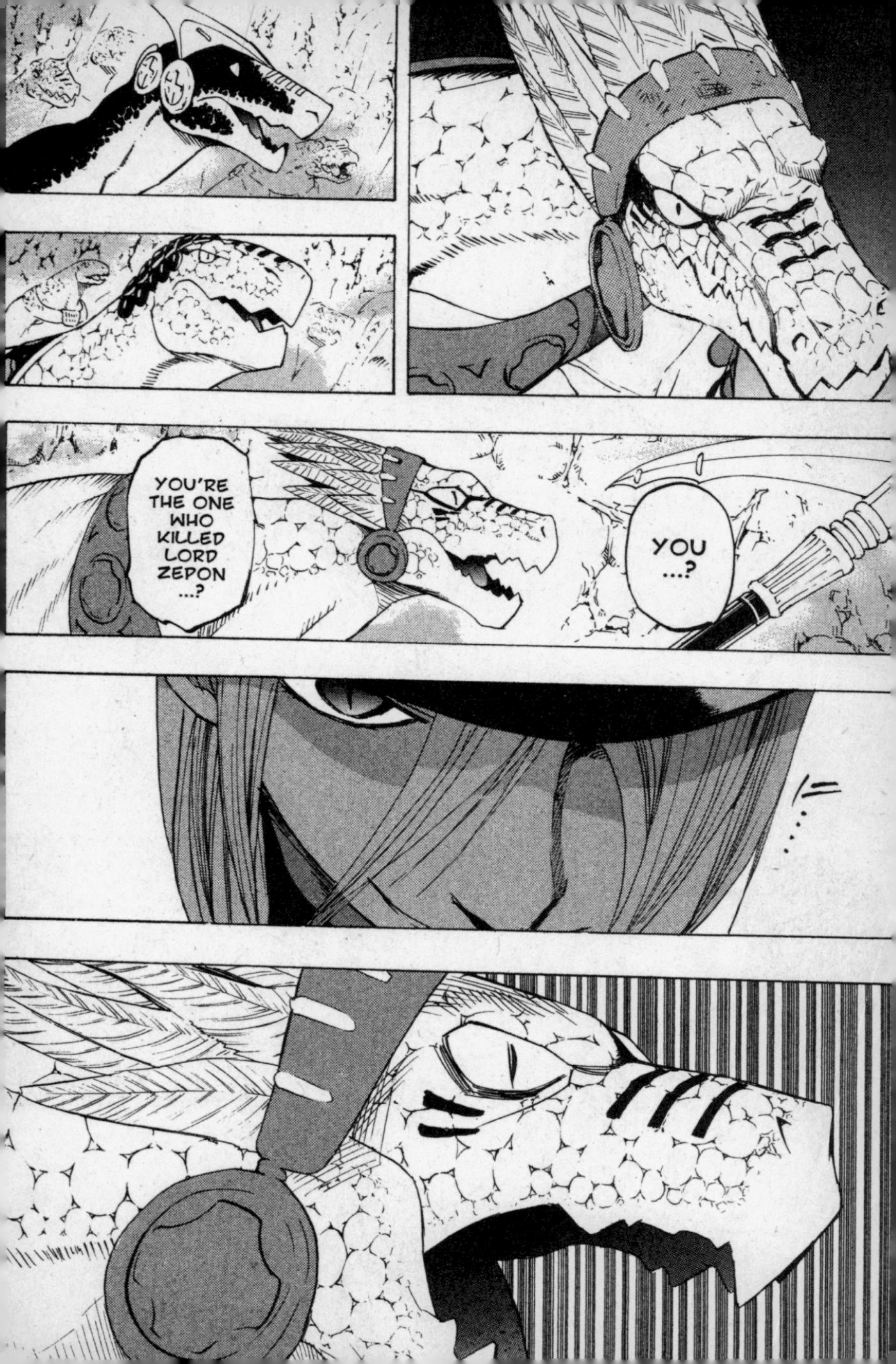
YOU ...?
YOU'RE THE ONE WHO KILLED LORD ZEPON ...?
...

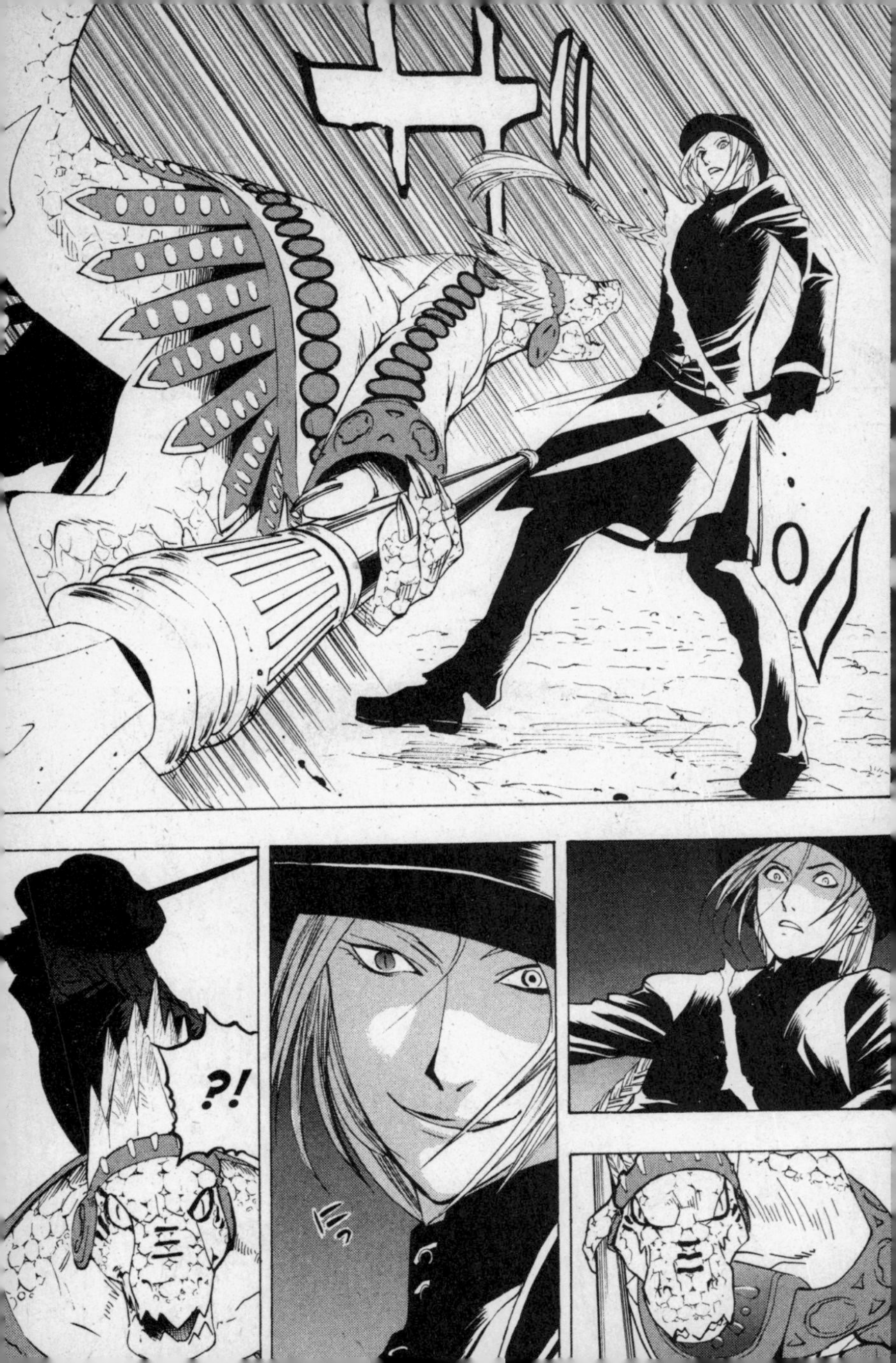
?!

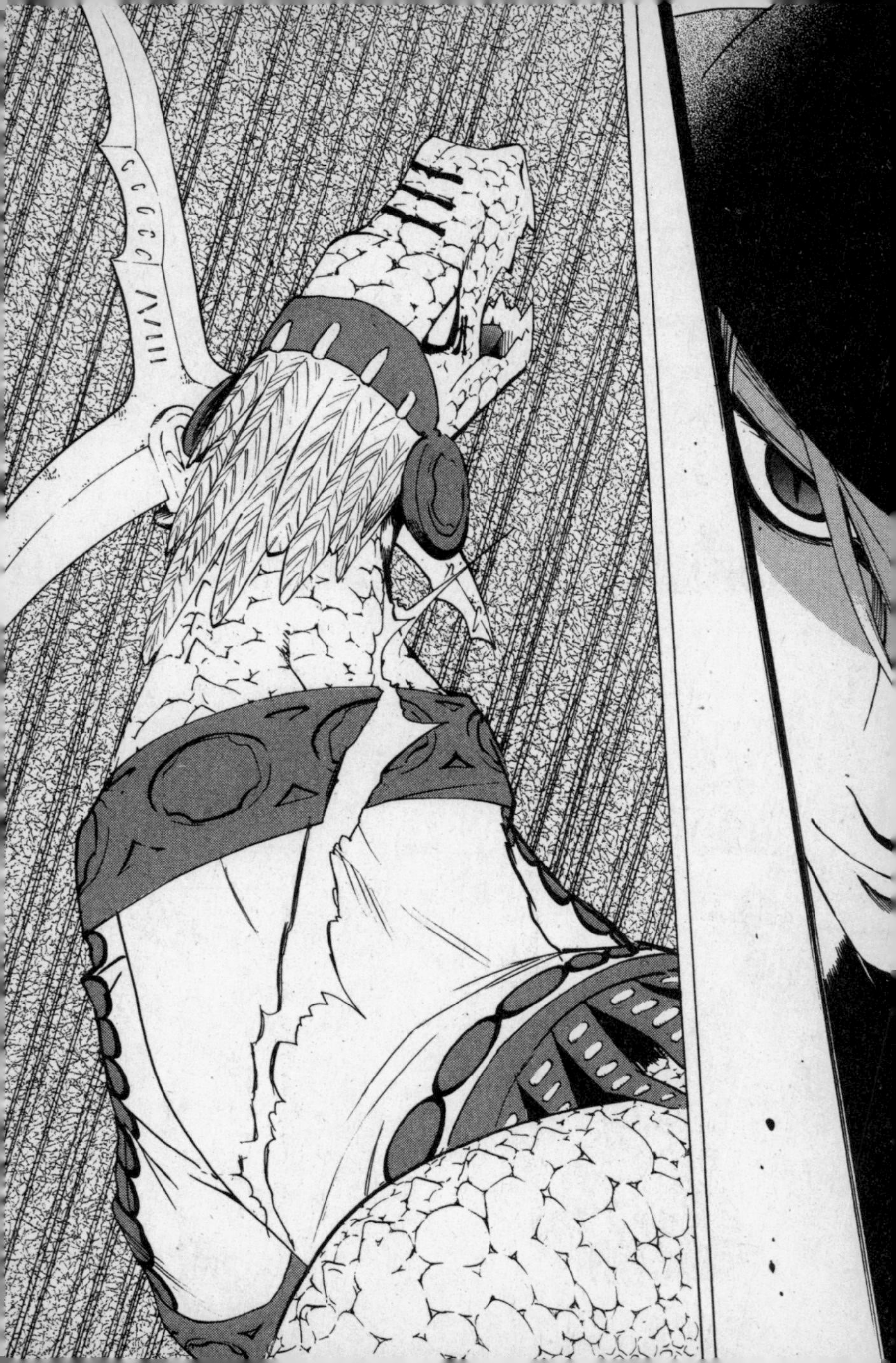

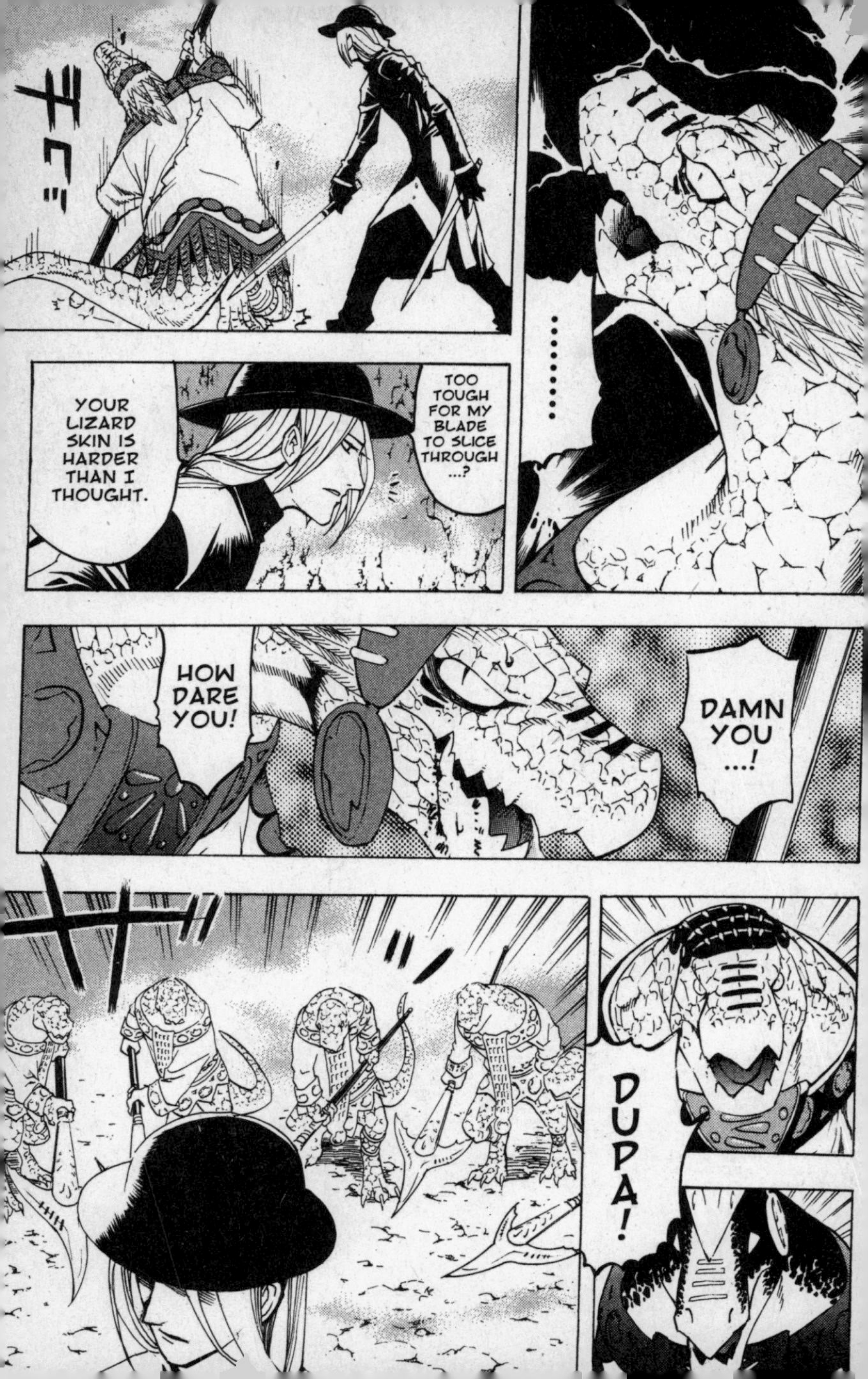
......
TOO TOUGH FOR MY BLADE TO SLICE THROUGH ...?
YOUR LIZARD SKIN IS HARDER THAN I THOUGHT.
DAMN YOU ...!
HOW DARE YOU!
DUPA!

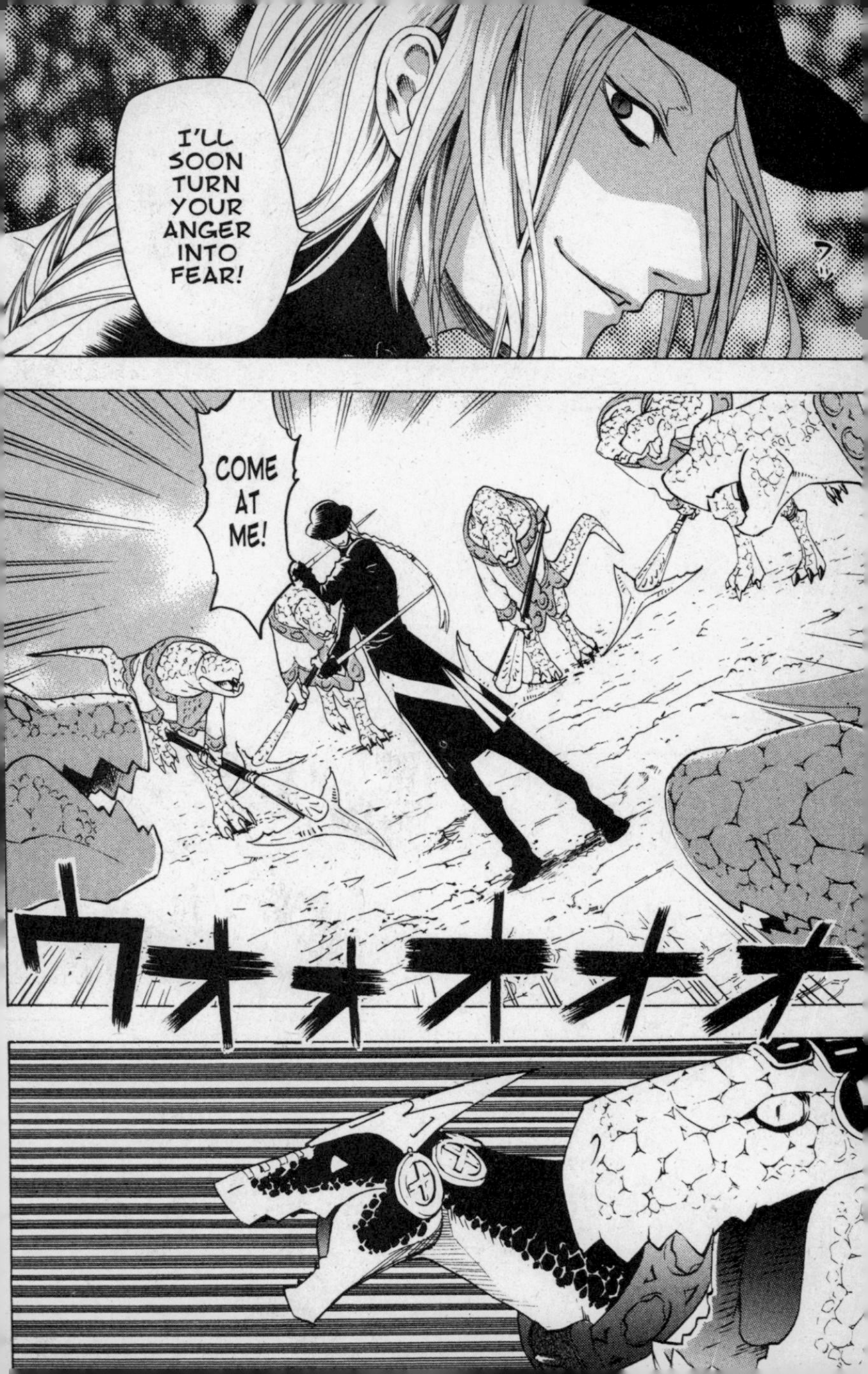
I'LL SOON TURN YOUR ANGER INTO FEAR!
?!
COME AT ME!
ウオォオオオ

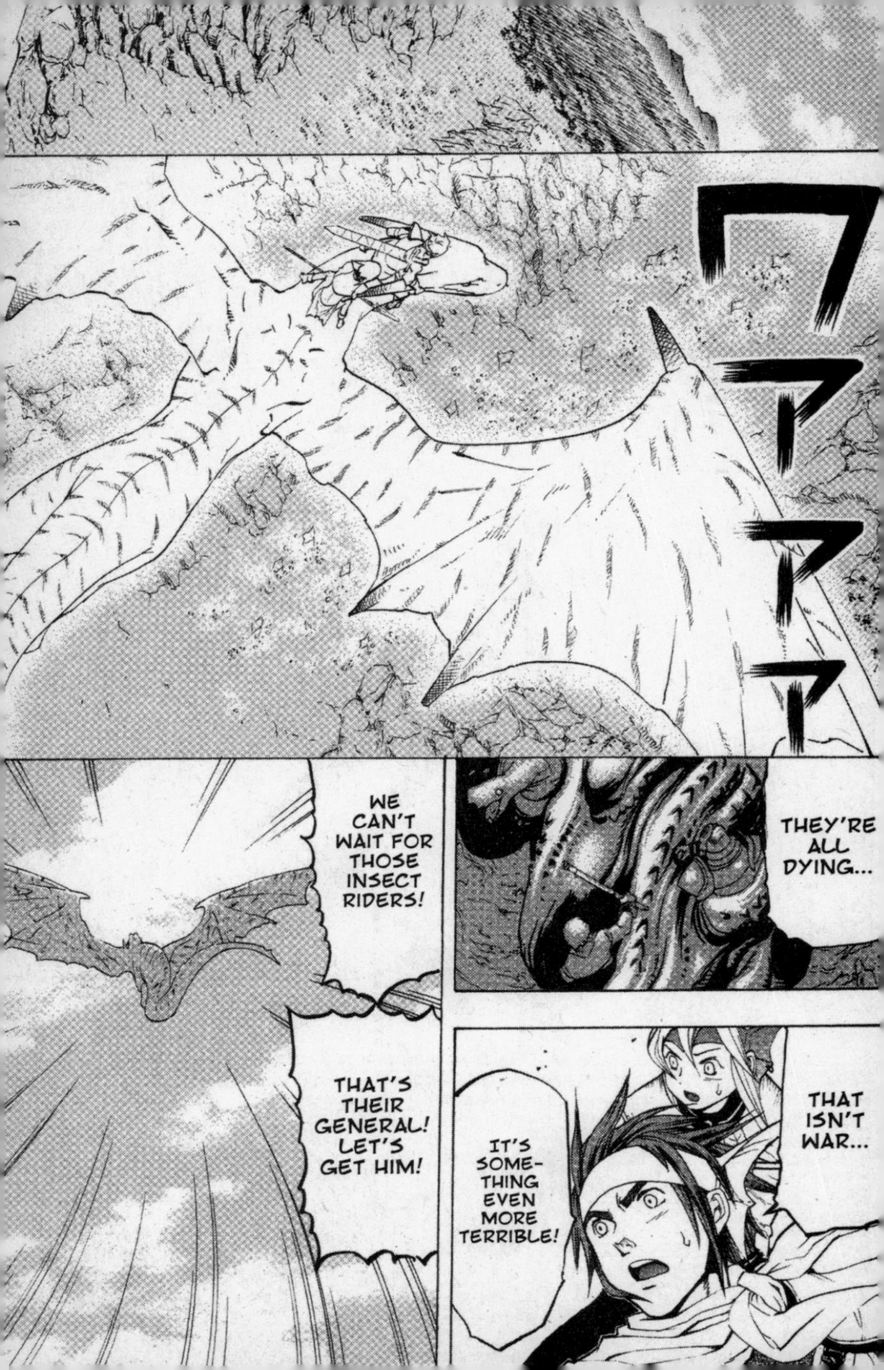
ワアアア
THEY'RE ALL DYING...
THAT ISN'T WAR...
IT'S SOMETHING EVEN MORE TERRIBLE!
WE CAN'T WAIT FOR THOSE INSECT RIDERS!
THAT'S THEIR GENERAL! LET'S GET HIM!

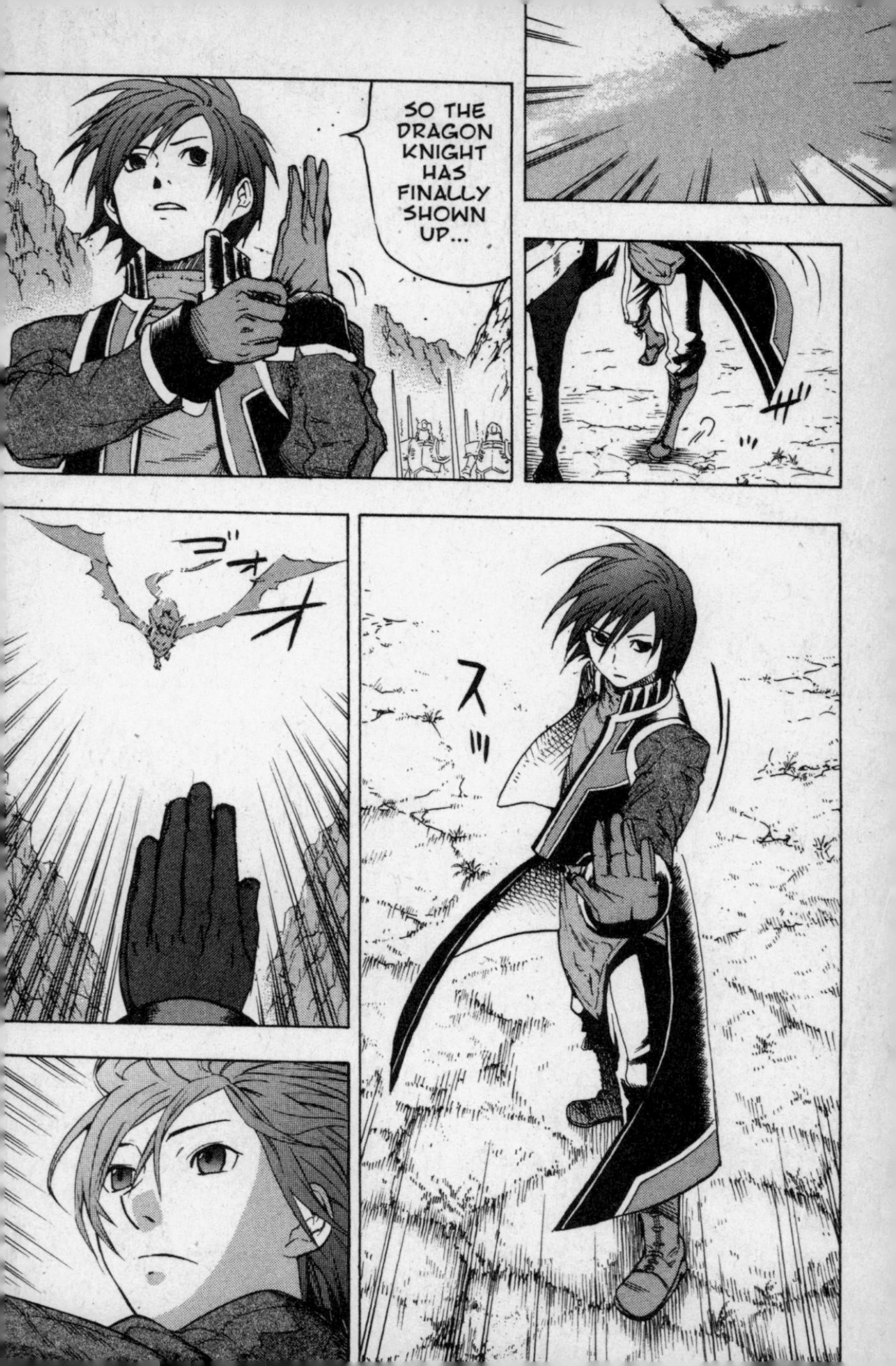
SO THE DRAGON KNIGHT HAS FINALLY SHOWN UP...
ゴォオ
スッ

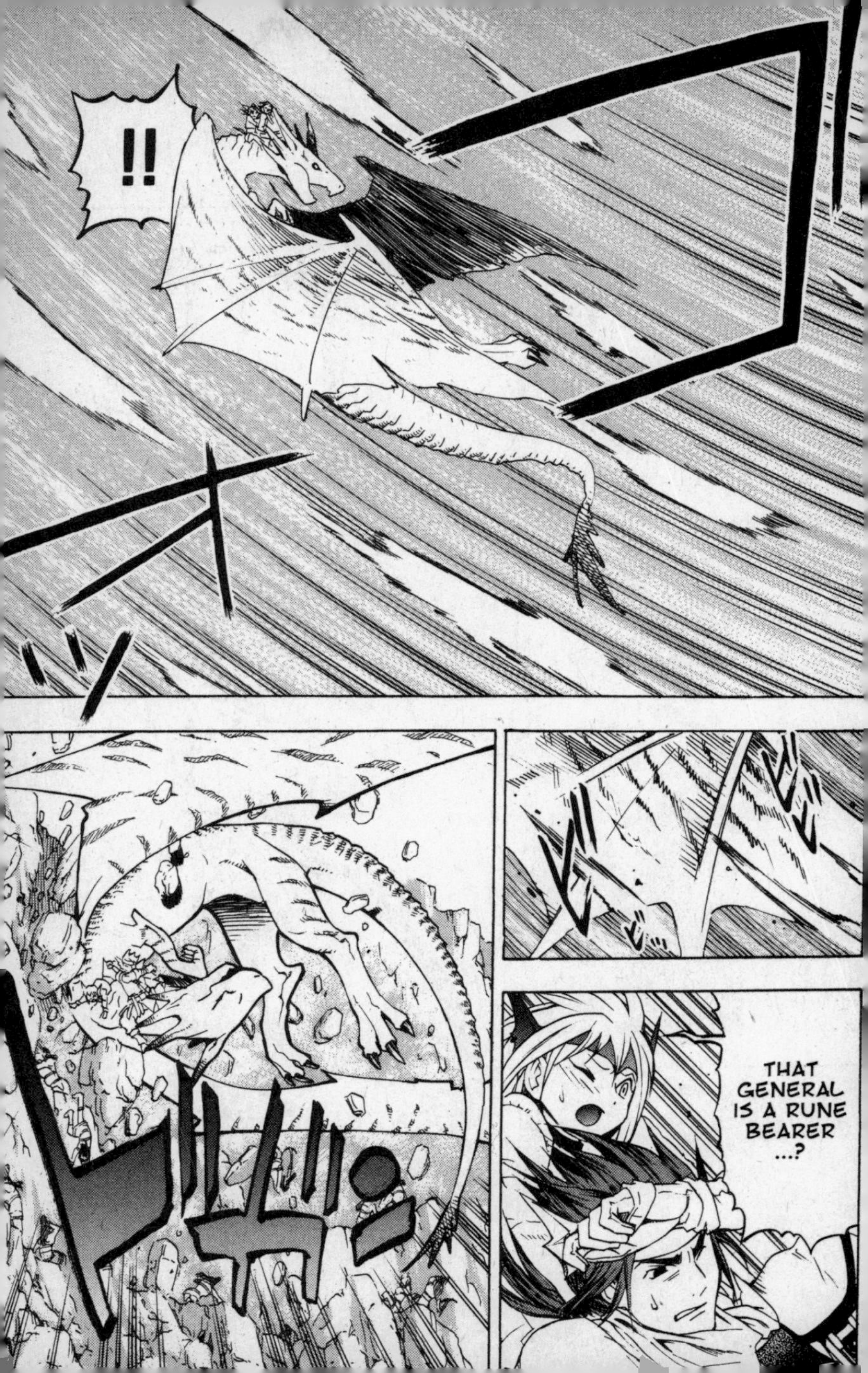
!!
THAT GENERAL IS A RUNE BEARER ...?

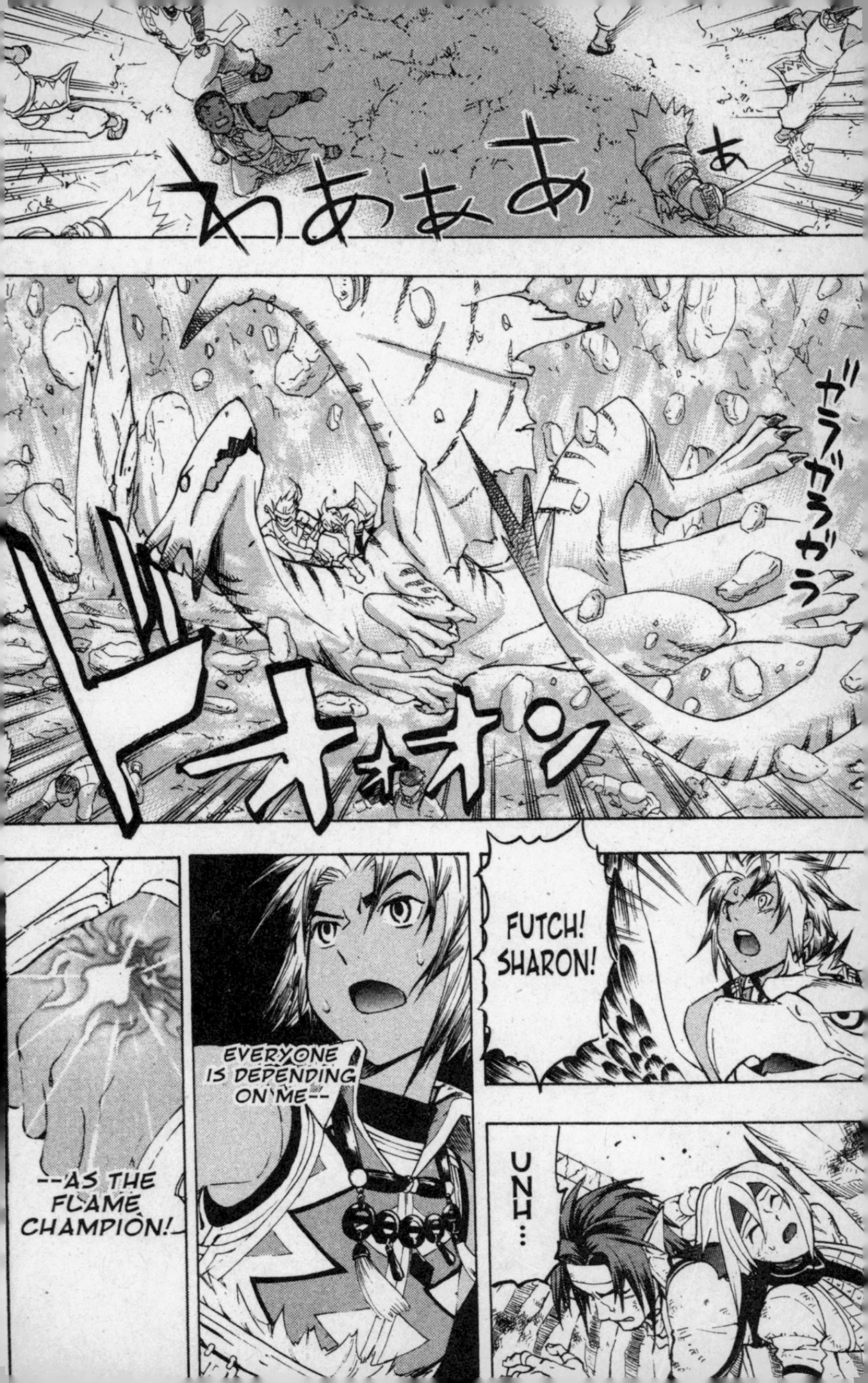
わあぁあぁ
ガラガラガラ
ドオォオン
FUTCH! SHARON!
UNH...
EVERYONE IS DEPENDING ON ME--
--AS THE FLAME CHAMPION!

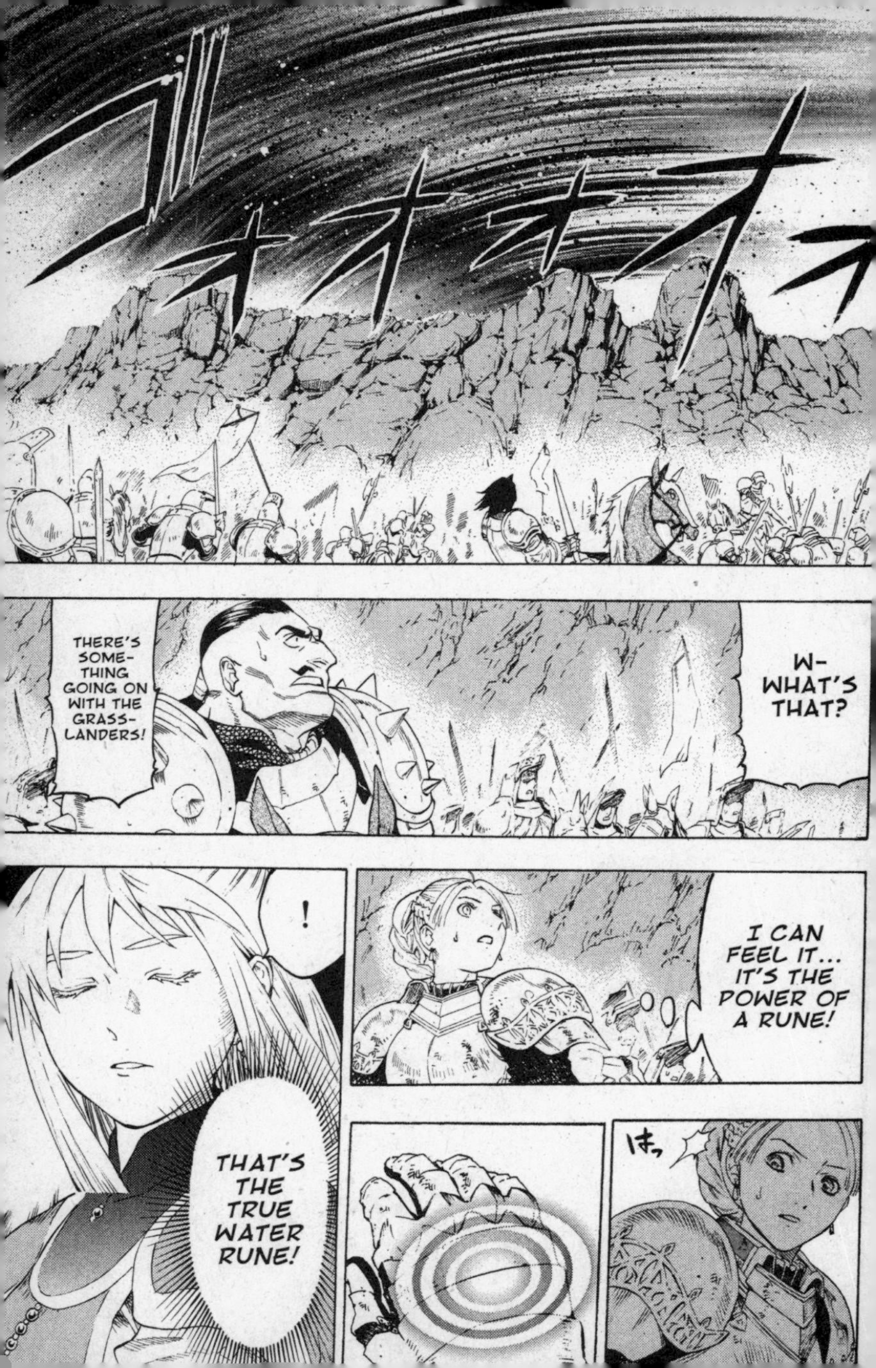
ゴオオオオオ
W-WHAT'S THAT?
THERE'S SOMETHING GOING ON WITH THE GRASSLANDERS!
I CAN FEEL IT... IT'S THE POWER OF A RUNE!
はっ
!
THAT'S THE TRUE WATER RUNE!

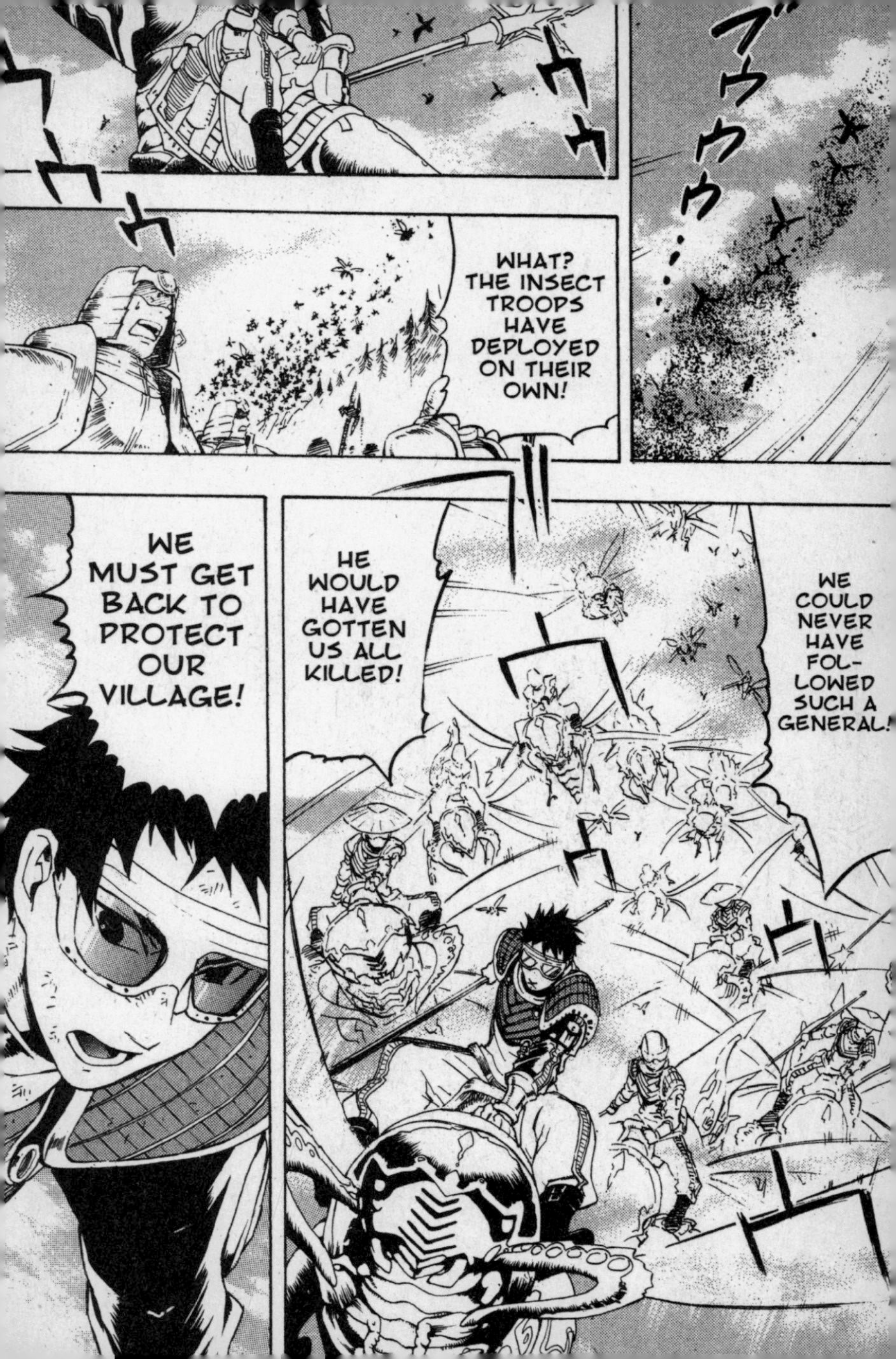
ブウウウ…
WHAT? THE INSECT TROOPS HAVE DEPLOYED ON THEIR OWN!
WE COULD NEVER HAVE FOL-LOWED SUCH A GENERAL!
HE WOULD HAVE GOTTEN US ALL KILLED!
WE MUST GET BACK TO PROTECT OUR VILLAGE!

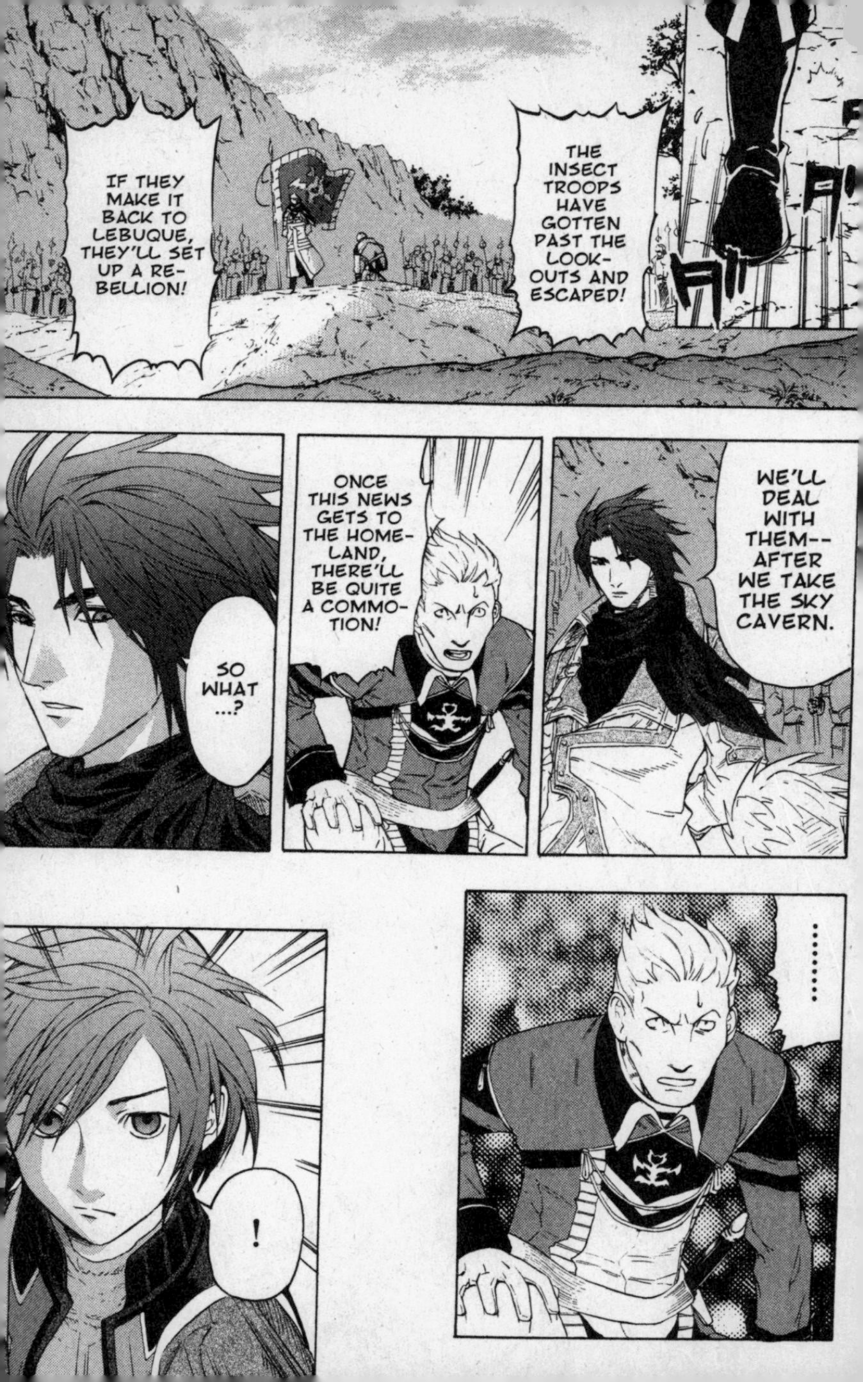
THE INSECT TROOPS HAVE GOTTEN PAST THE LOOKOUTS AND ESCAPED!
IF THEY MAKE IT BACK TO LEBUQUE, THEY'LL SET UP A REBELLION!
WE'LL DEAL WITH THEM-- AFTER WE TAKE THE SKY CAVERN.
ONCE THIS NEWS GETS TO THE HOMELAND, THERE'LL BE QUITE A COMMOTION!
SO WHAT ...?
....
!

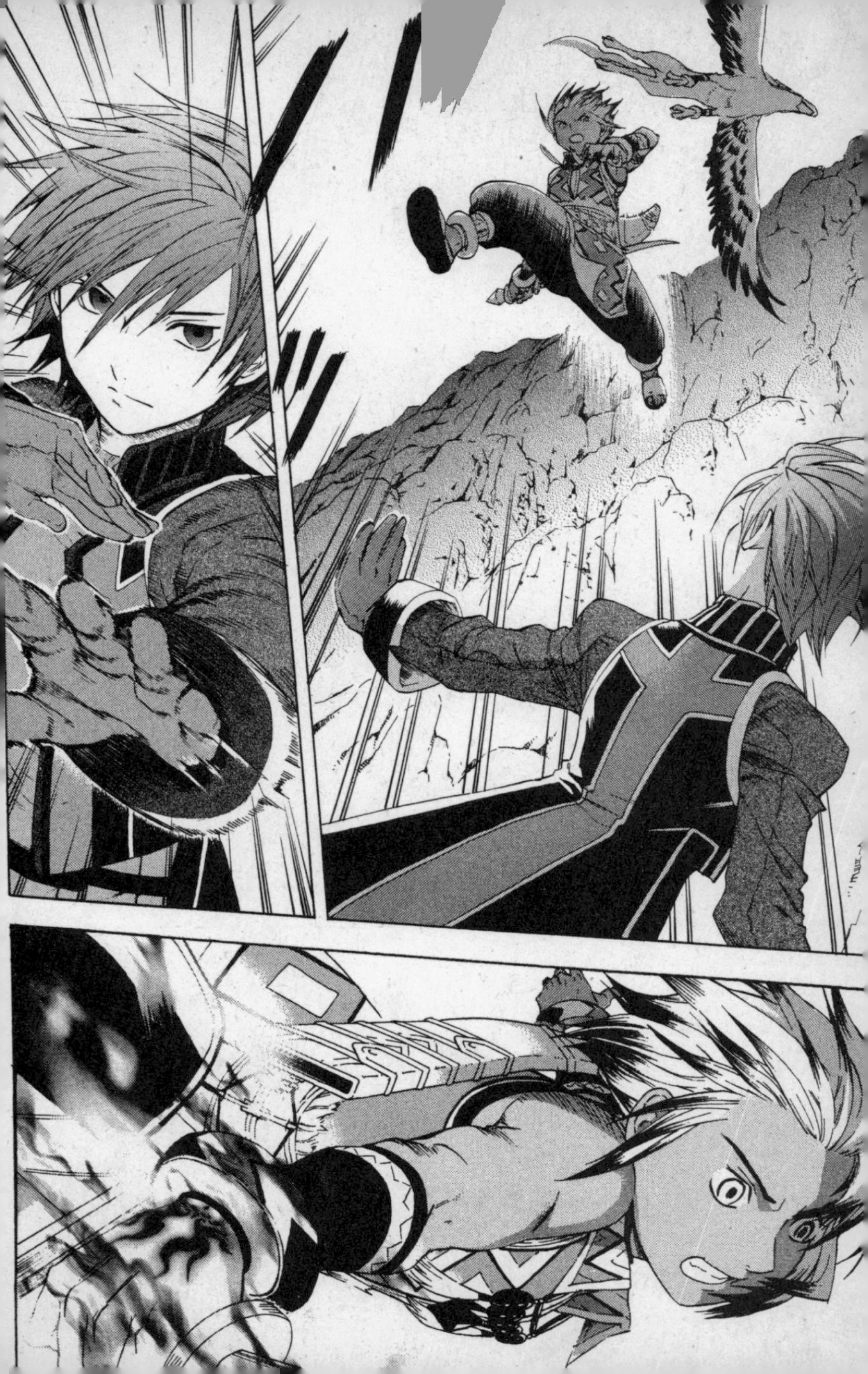

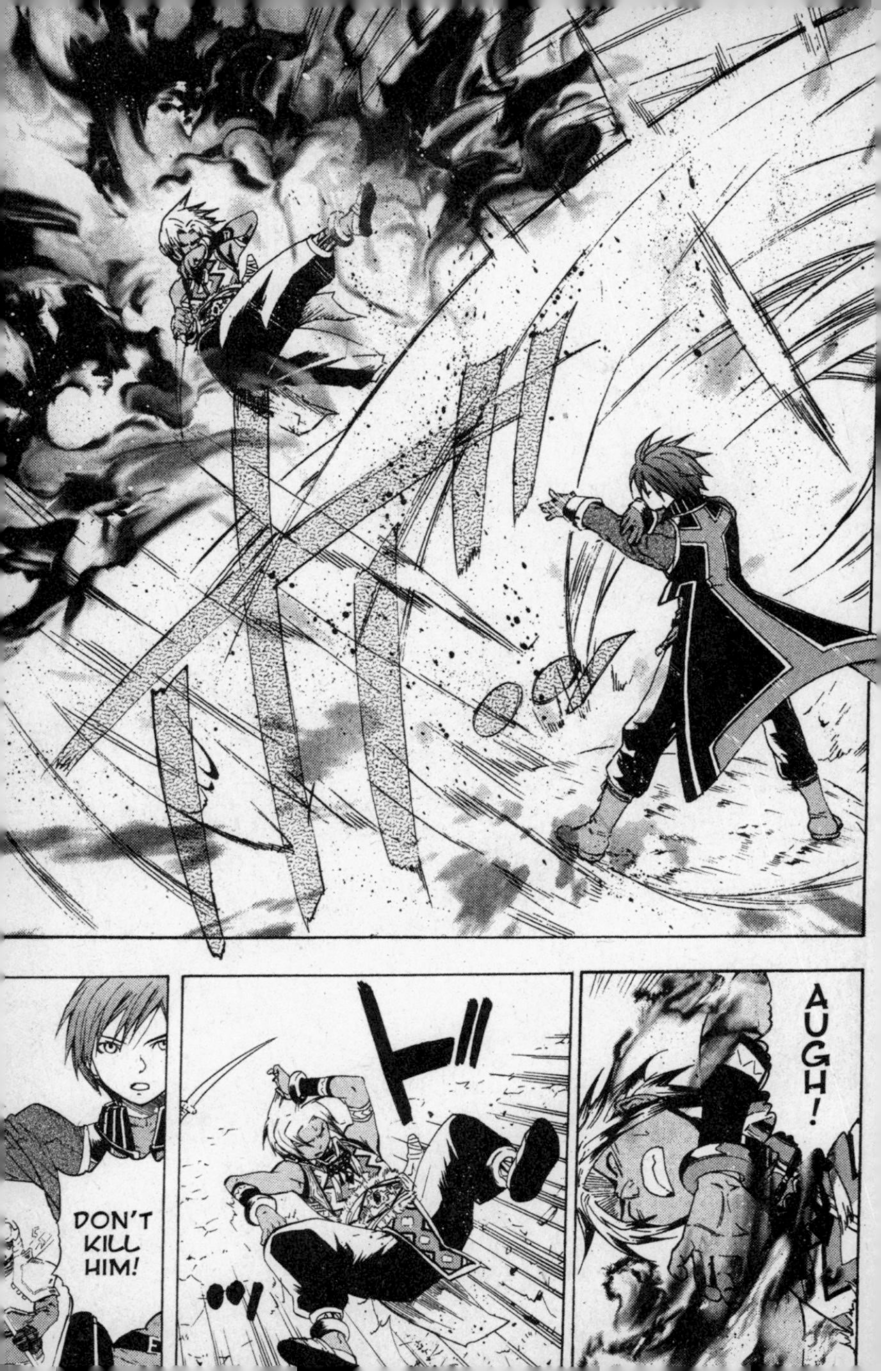
AUGH!
DON'T KILL HIM!

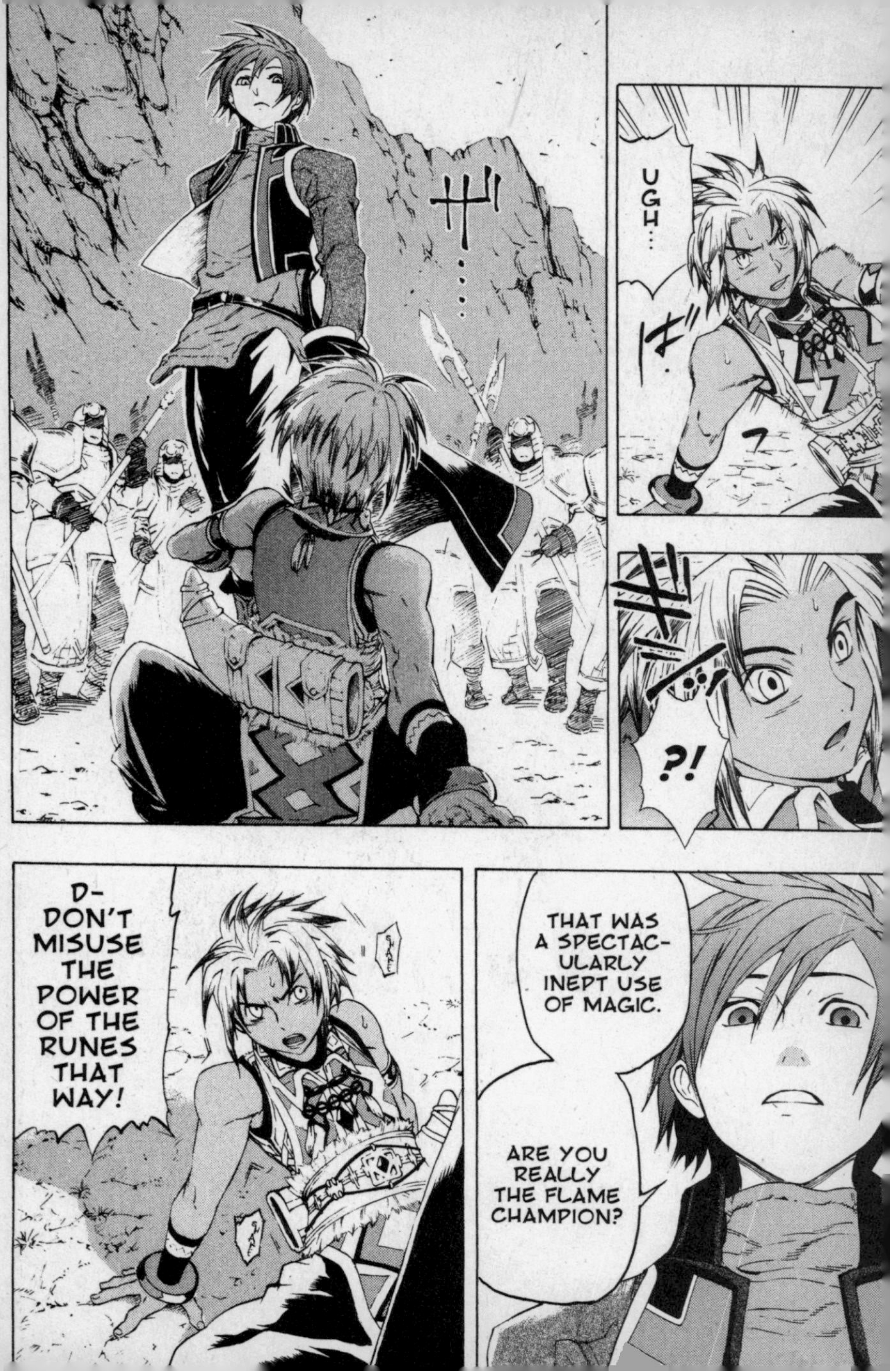
UGH...
?!
THAT WAS A SPECTACULARLY INEPT USE OF MAGIC.
ARE YOU REALLY THE FLAME CHAMPION?
D-DON'T MISUSE THE POWER OF THE RUNES THAT WAY!
SHAKE
SHAKE

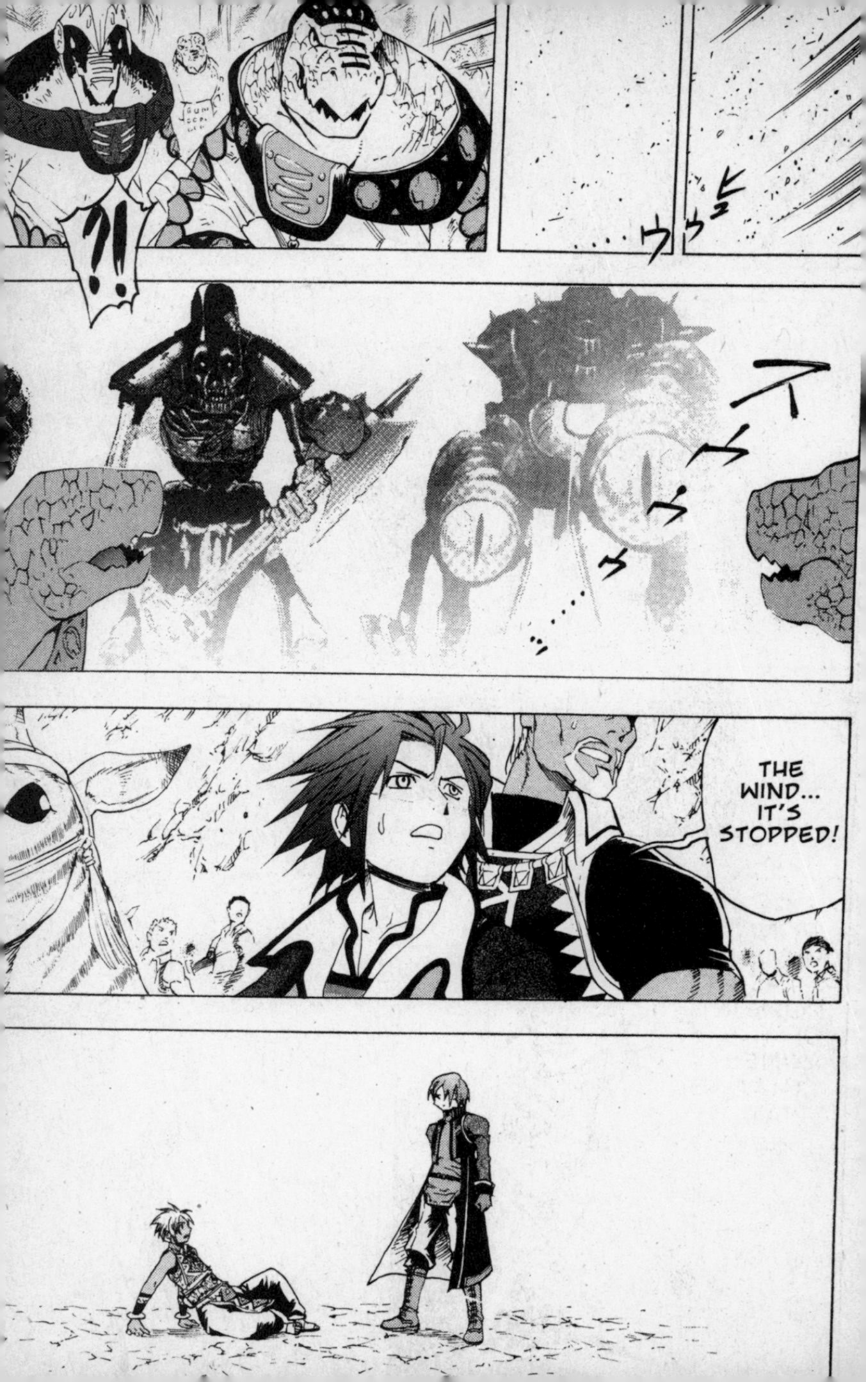

?!!
THE WIND... IT'S STOPPED!

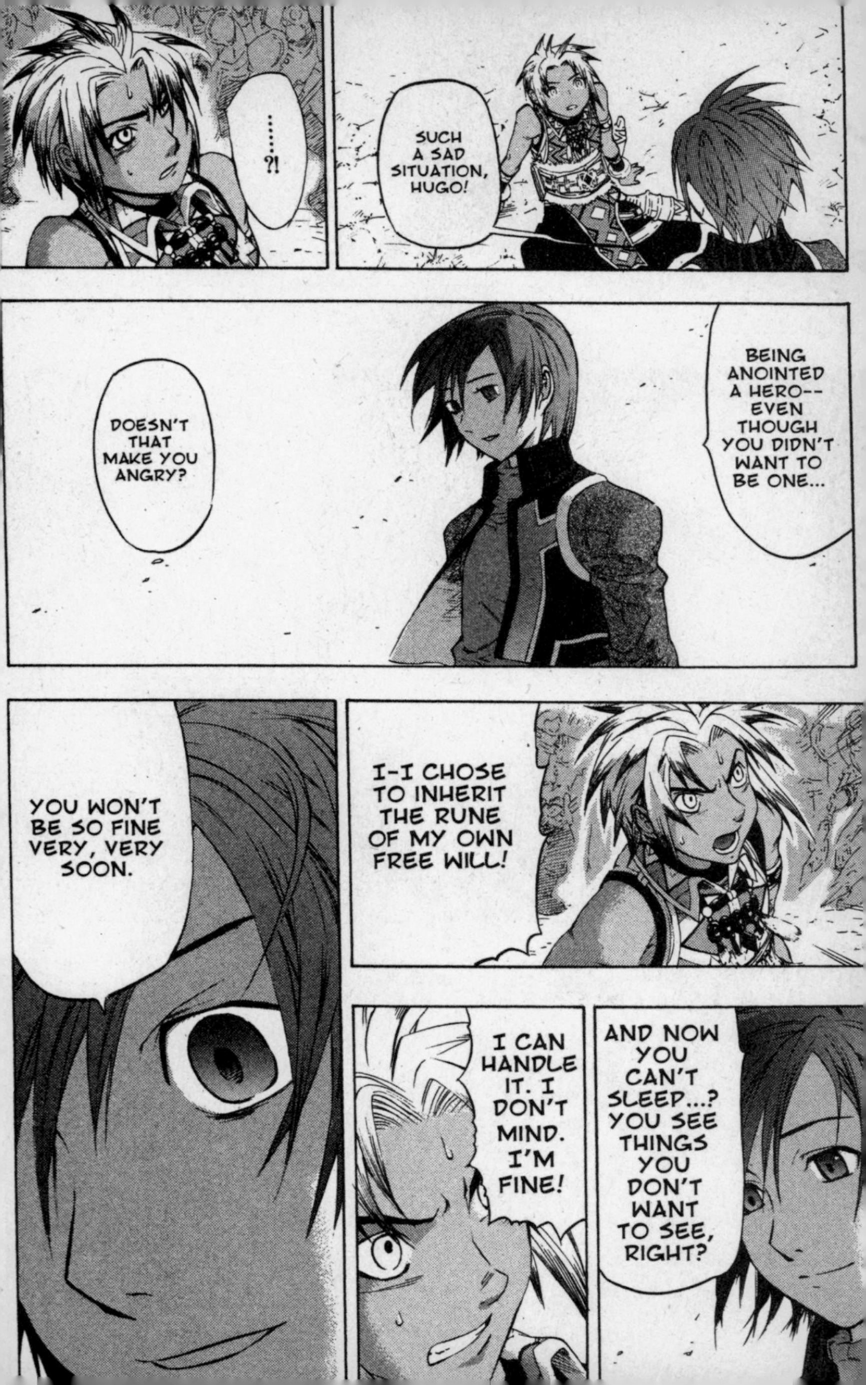
SUCH A SAD SITUATION, HUGO!
......?!
BEING ANOINTED A HERO-- EVEN THOUGH YOU DIDN'T WANT TO BE ONE...
DOESN'T THAT MAKE YOU ANGRY?
I-I CHOSE TO INHERIT THE RUNE OF MY OWN FREE WILL!
AND NOW YOU CAN'T SLEEP...? YOU SEE THINGS YOU DON'T WANT TO SEE, RIGHT?
I CAN HANDLE IT. I DON'T MIND. I'M FINE!
YOU WON'T BE SO FINE VERY, VERY SOON.

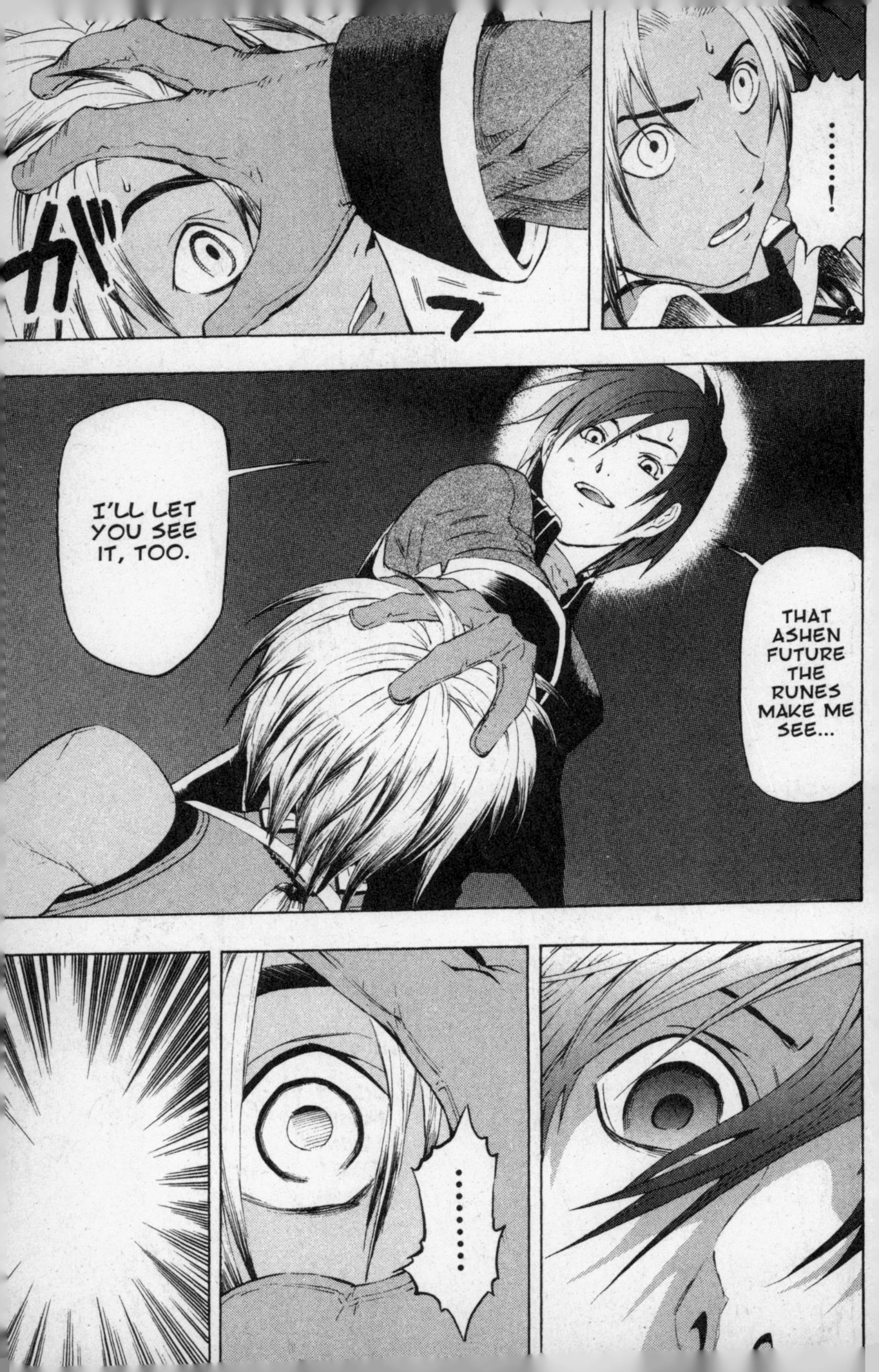
......!
ガッ
THAT ASHEN FUTURE THE RUNES MAKE ME SEE...
I'LL LET YOU SEE IT, TOO.
......

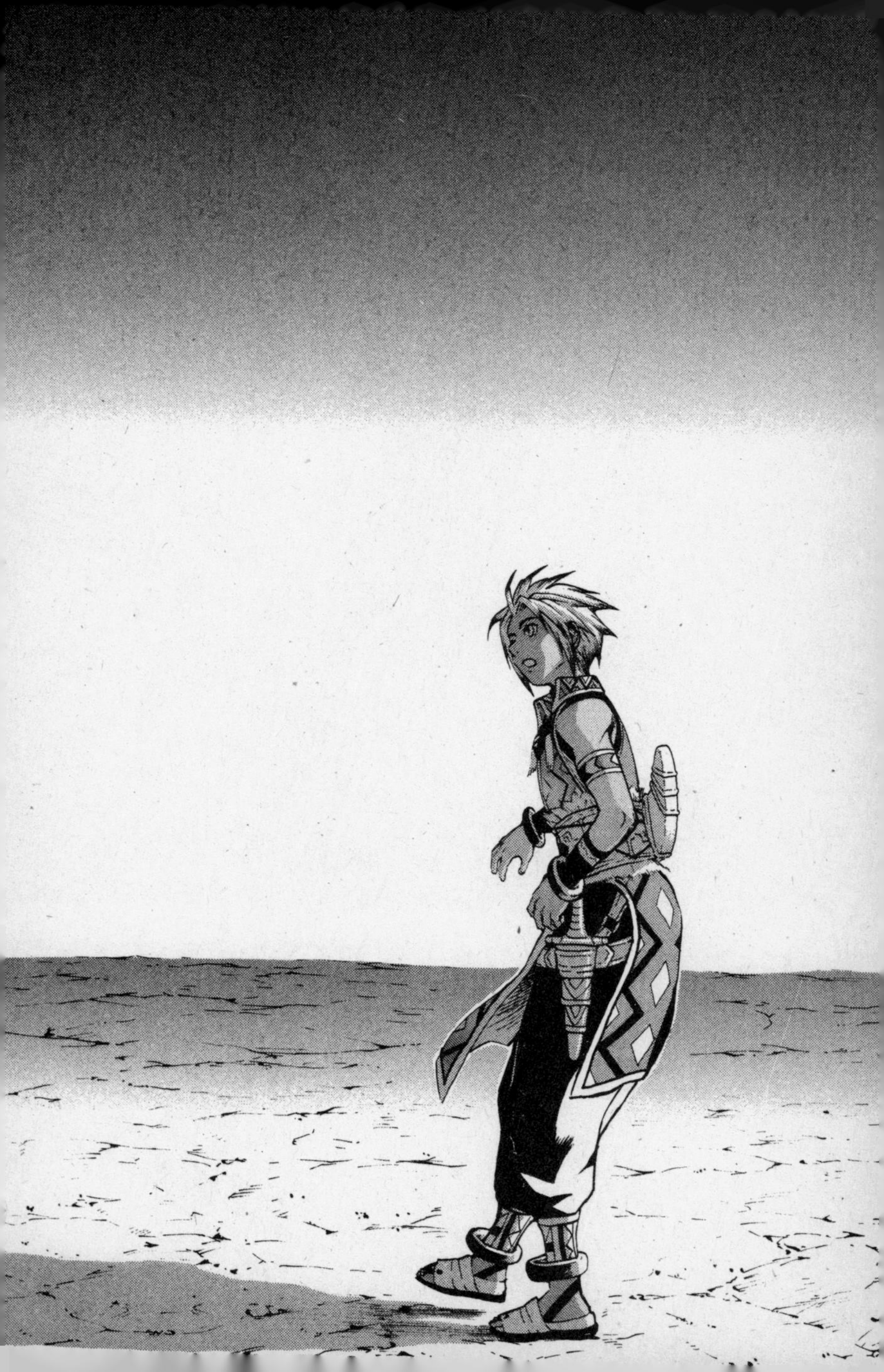

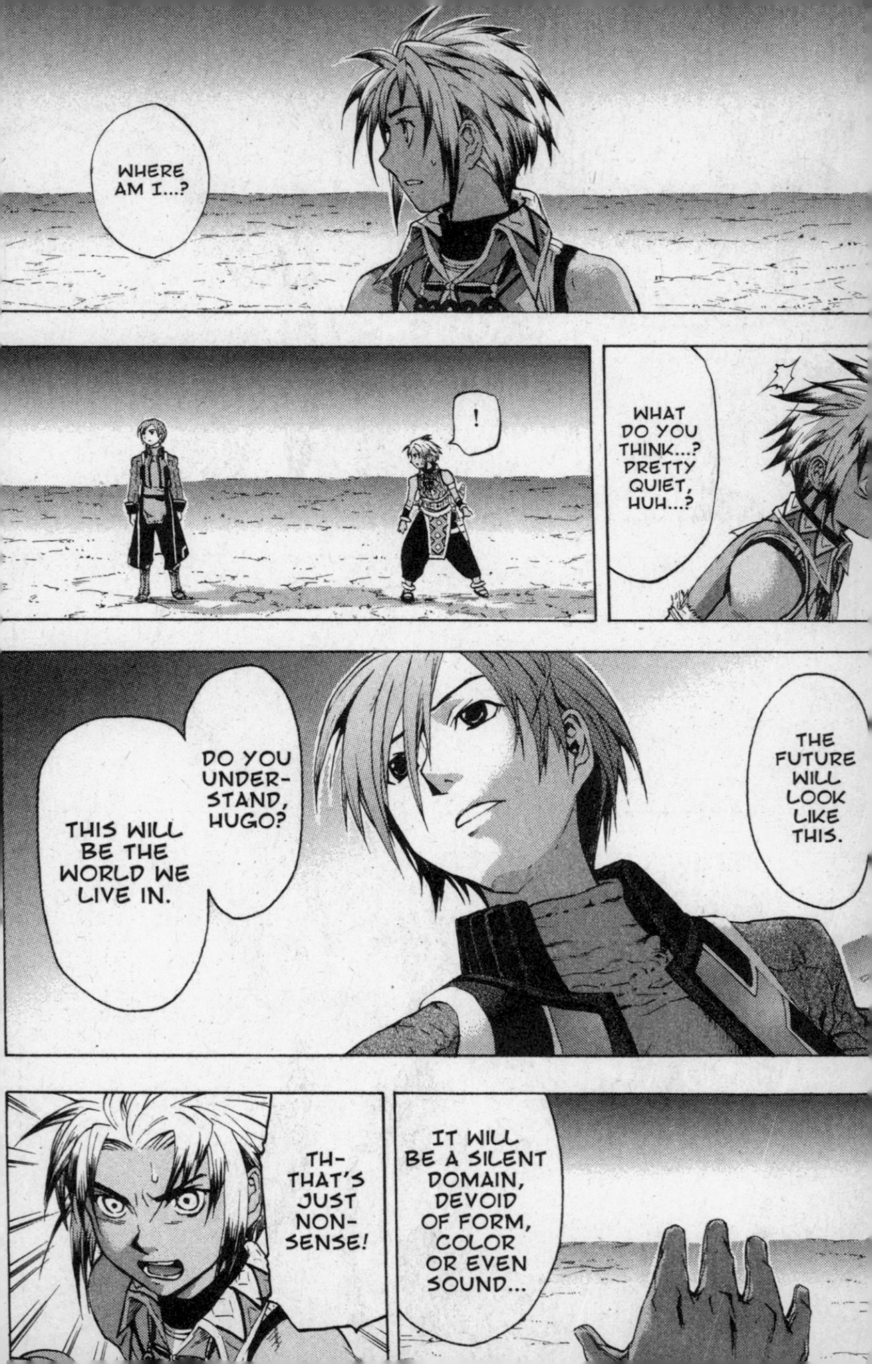
WHERE AM I...?
WHAT DO YOU THINK...? PRETTY QUIET, HUH...?
!
THE FUTURE WILL LOOK LIKE THIS.
DO YOU UNDER-STAND, HUGO?
THIS WILL BE THE WORLD WE LIVE IN.
IT WILL BE A SILENT DOMAIN, DEVOID OF FORM, COLOR OR EVEN SOUND...
TH-THAT'S JUST NON-SENSE!

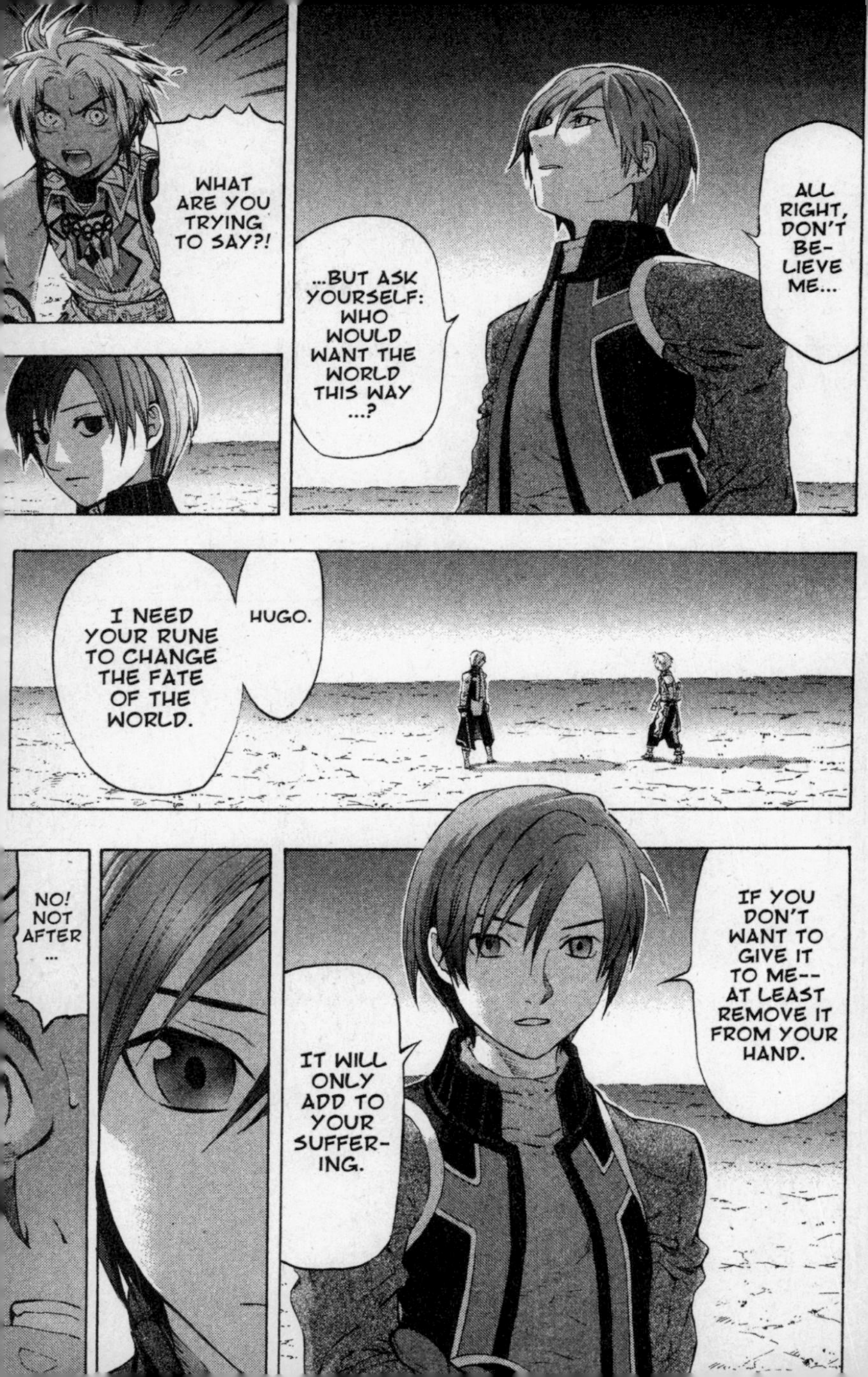
ALL RIGHT, DON'T BE-LIEVE ME...
...BUT ASK YOURSELF: WHO WOULD WANT THE WORLD THIS WAY ...?
WHAT ARE YOU TRYING TO SAY?!
HUGO.
I NEED YOUR RUNE TO CHANGE THE FATE OF THE WORLD.
IF YOU DON'T WANT TO GIVE IT TO ME-- AT LEAST REMOVE IT FROM YOUR HAND.
IT WILL ONLY ADD TO YOUR SUFFER-ING.
NO! NOT AFTER ...

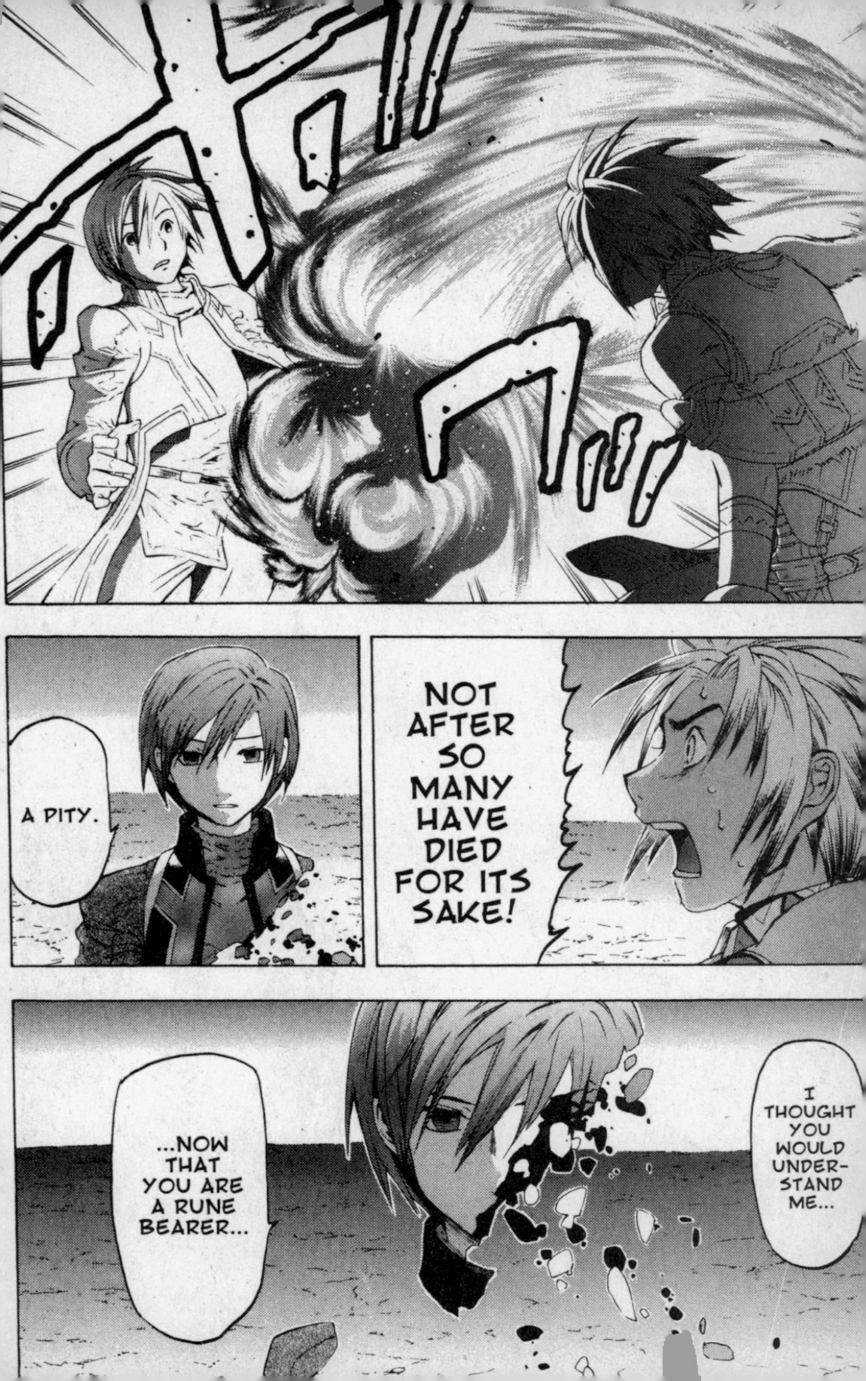
NOT AFTER SO MANY HAVE DIED FOR ITS SAKE!
A PITY.
I THOUGHT YOU WOULD UNDER-STAND ME...
...NOW THAT YOU ARE A RUNE BEARER...

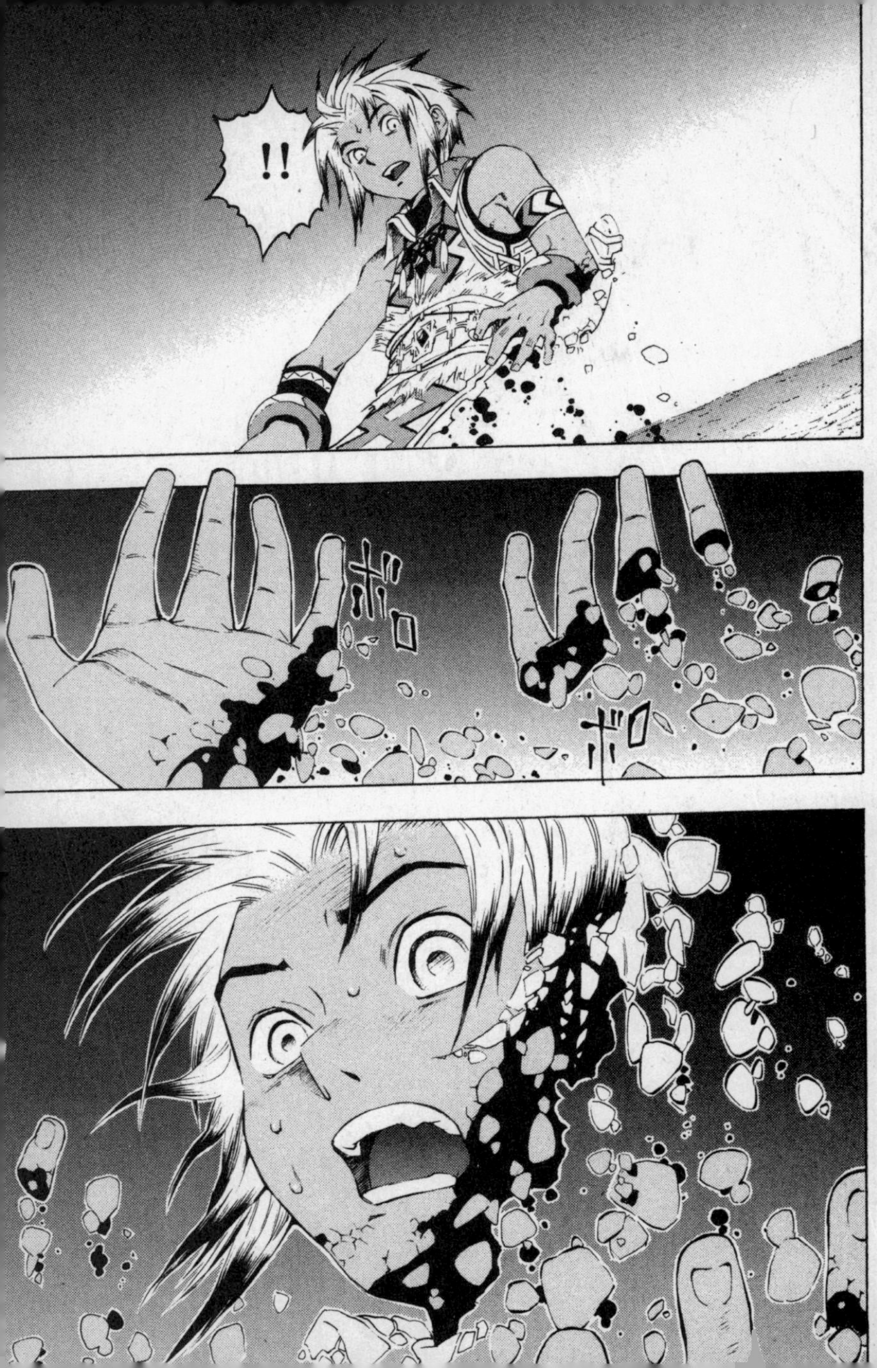
!!
ボロ
ボロ

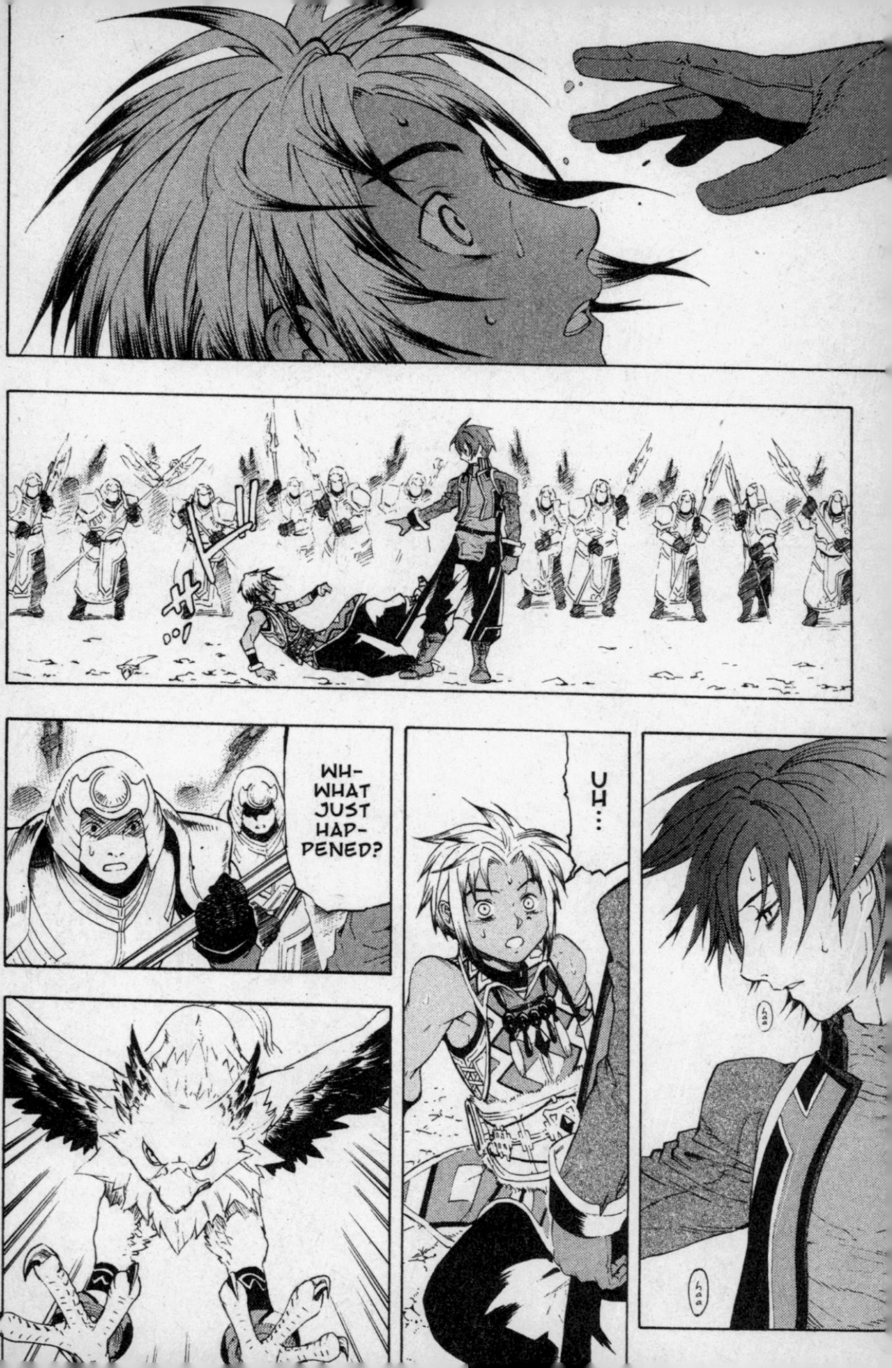
DO!
haa
haa
UH...
WH-WHAT JUST HAP-PENED?

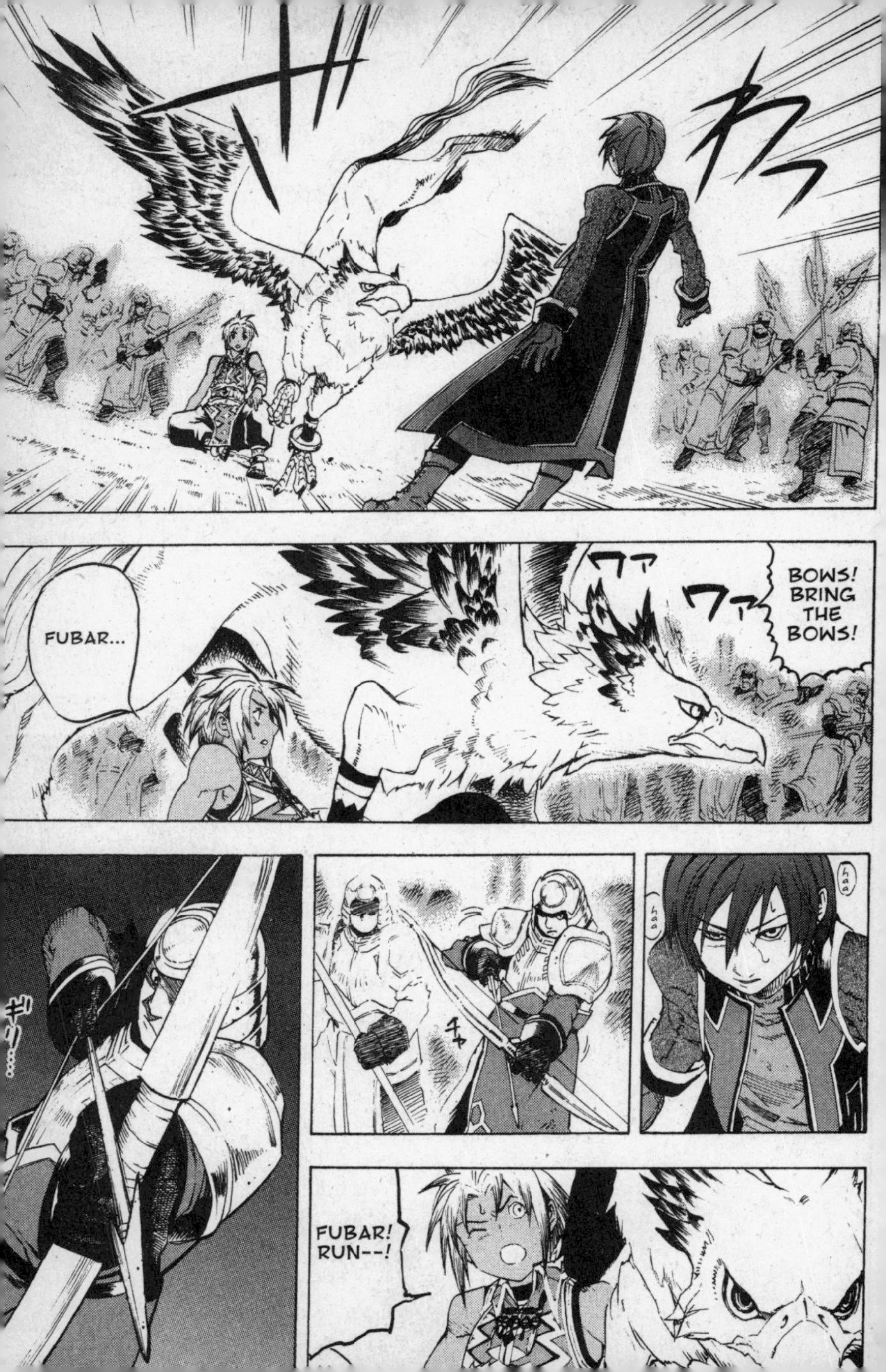

BOWS! BRING THE BOWS!
FUBAR...
haa
haa
FUBAR! RUN--!

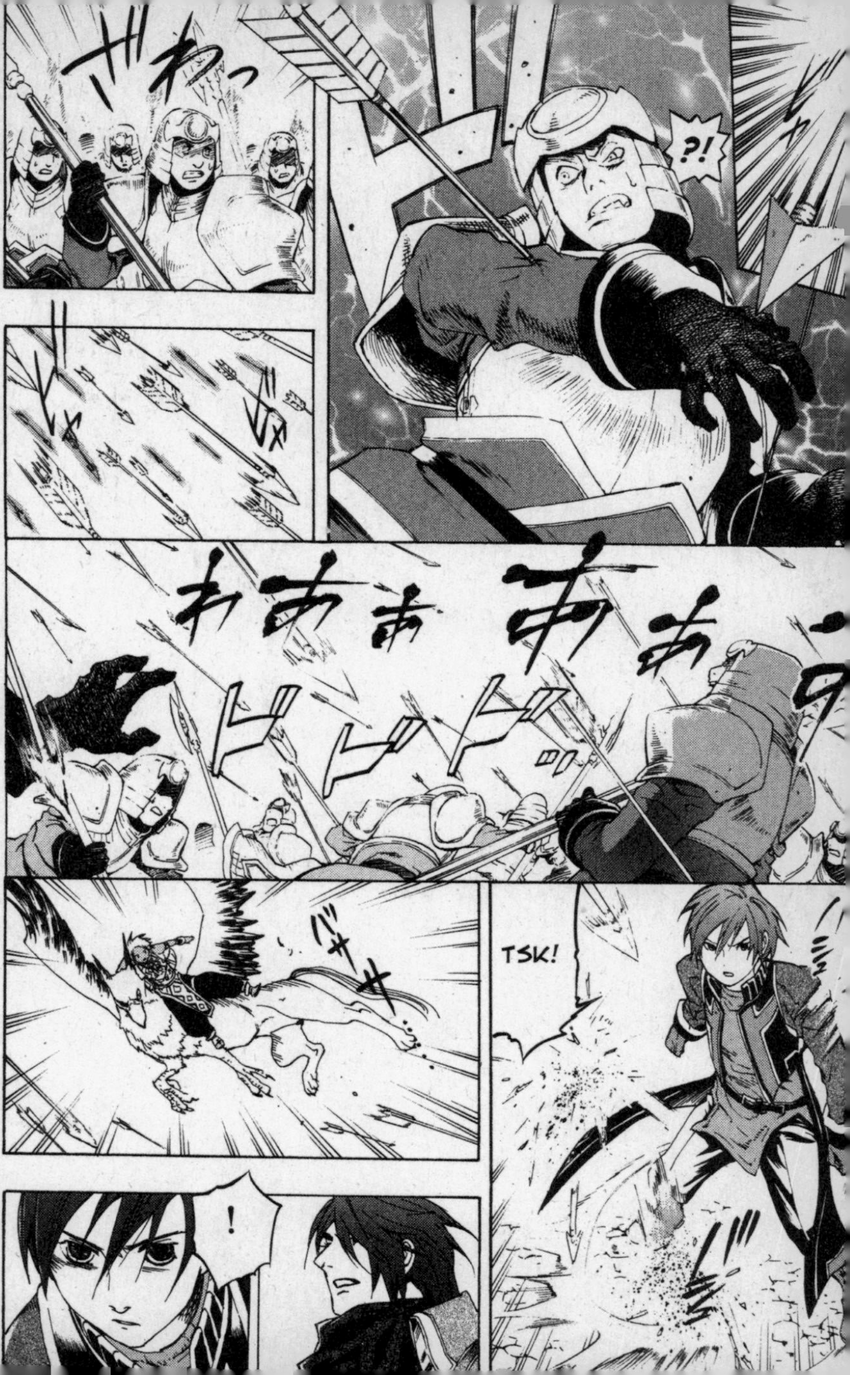
?!
ざわっ
わああ あああっ
ドドドッ
TSK!
バサッ
!

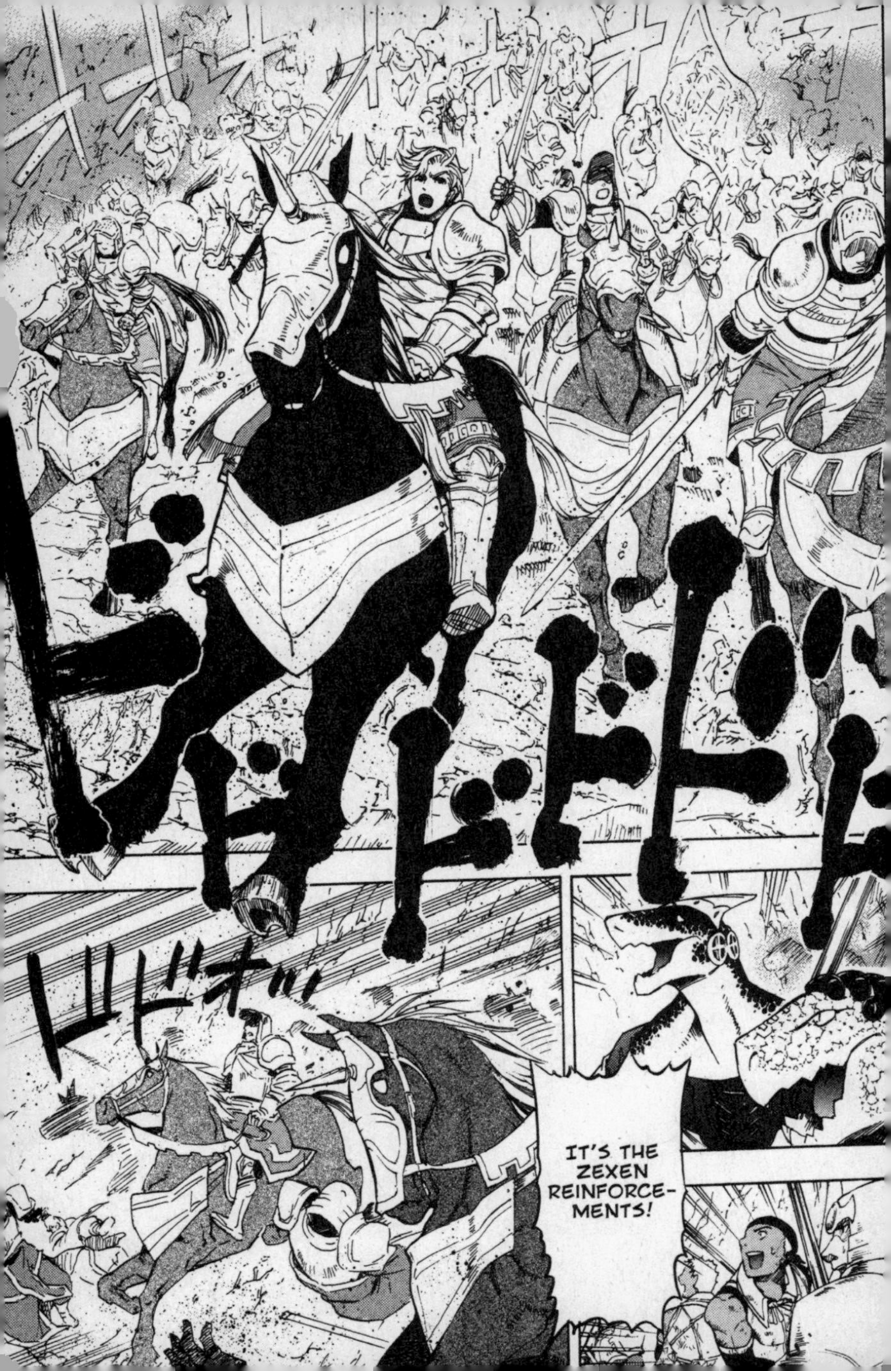
IT'S THE ZEXEN REINFORCE-MENTS!

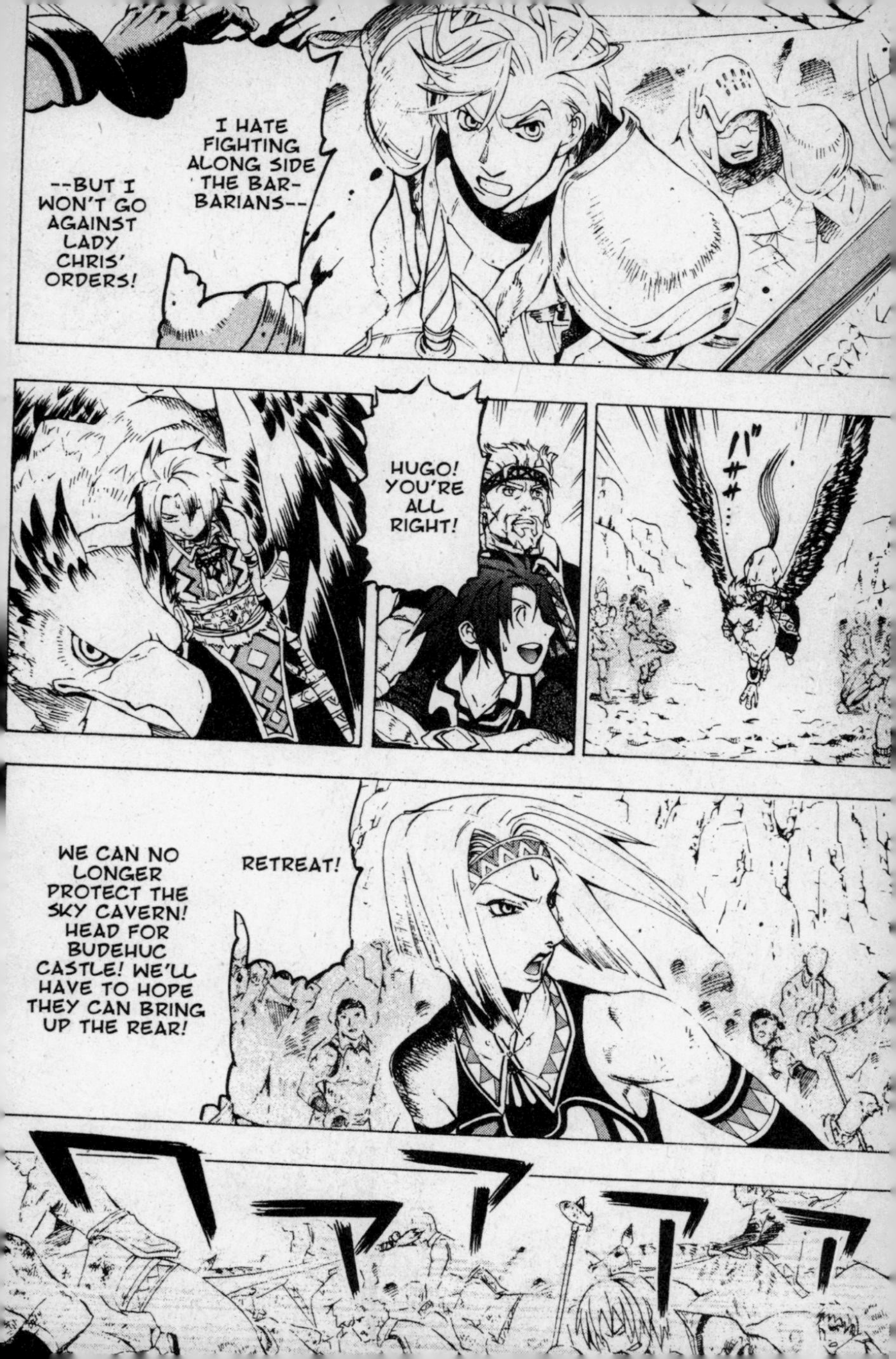
I HATE FIGHTING ALONG SIDE THE BAR-BARIANS--
--BUT I WON'T GO AGAINST LADY CHRIS' ORDERS!
バササ……
HUGO! YOU'RE ALL RIGHT!
RETREAT!
WE CAN NO LONGER PROTECT THE SKY CAVERN! HEAD FOR BUDEHUC CASTLE! WE'LL HAVE TO HOPE THEY CAN BRING UP THE REAR!

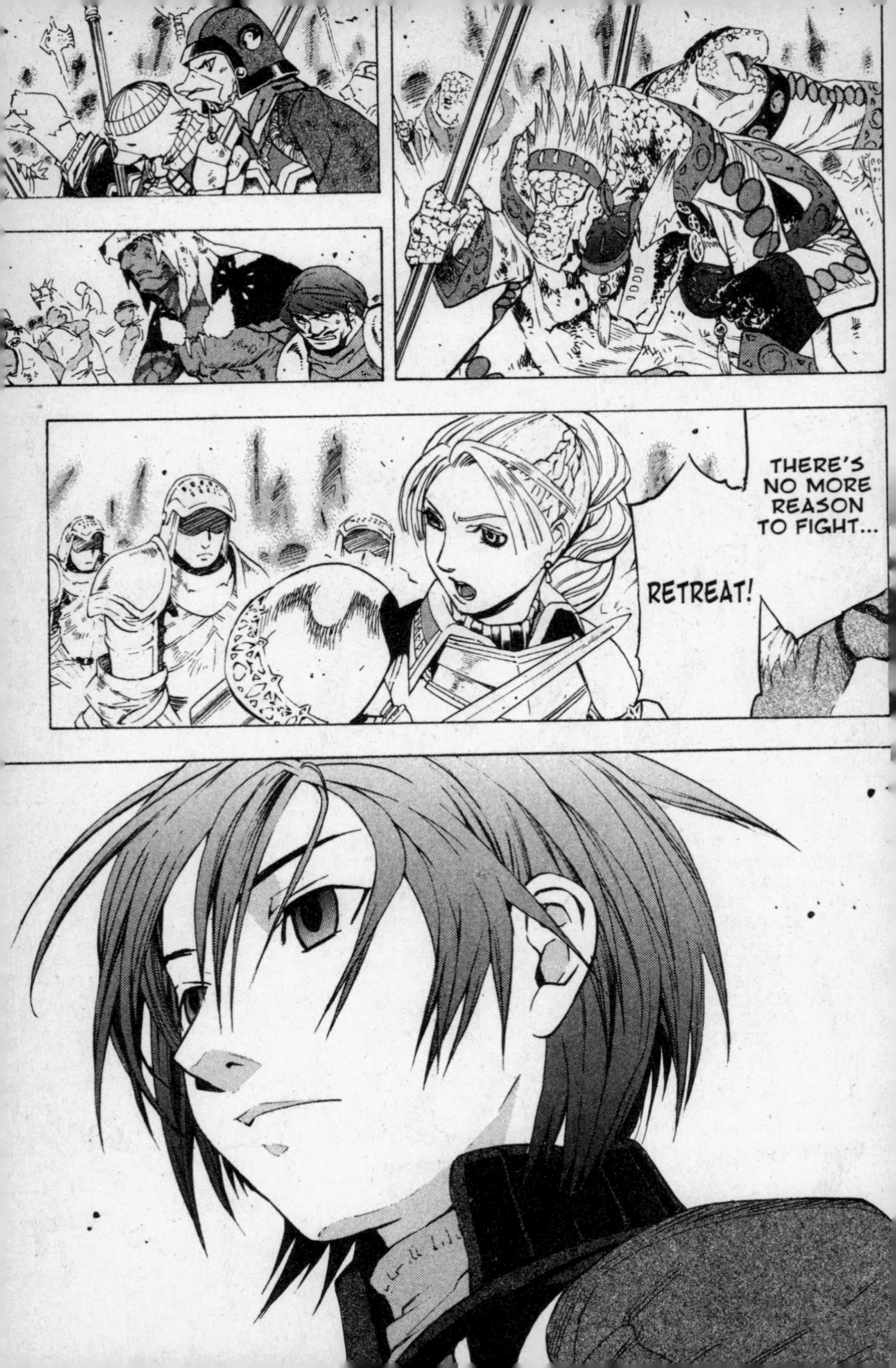
THERE'S NO MORE REASON TO FIGHT...
RETREAT!

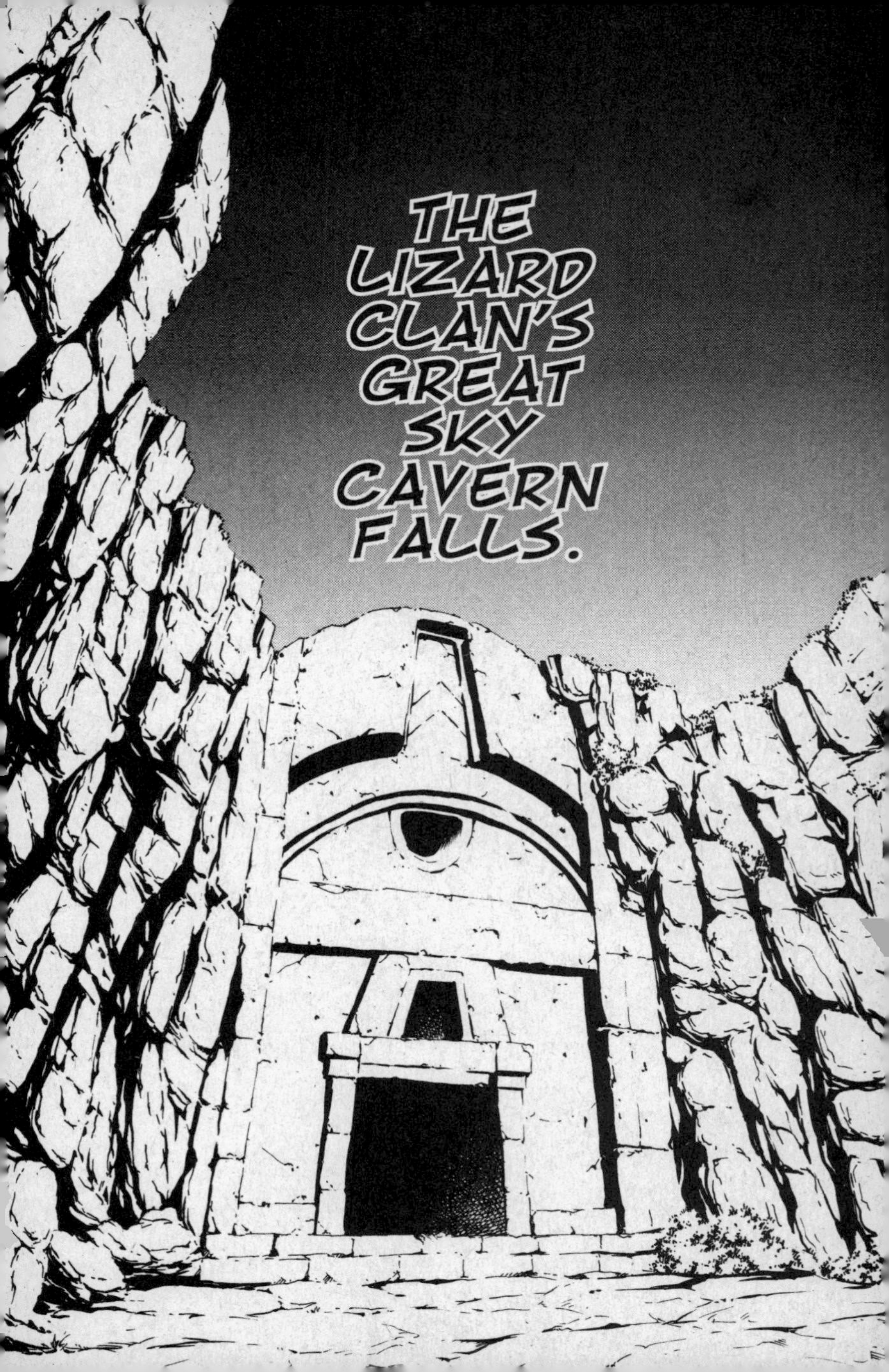
THE LIZARD CLAN'S GREAT SKY CAVERN FALLS.

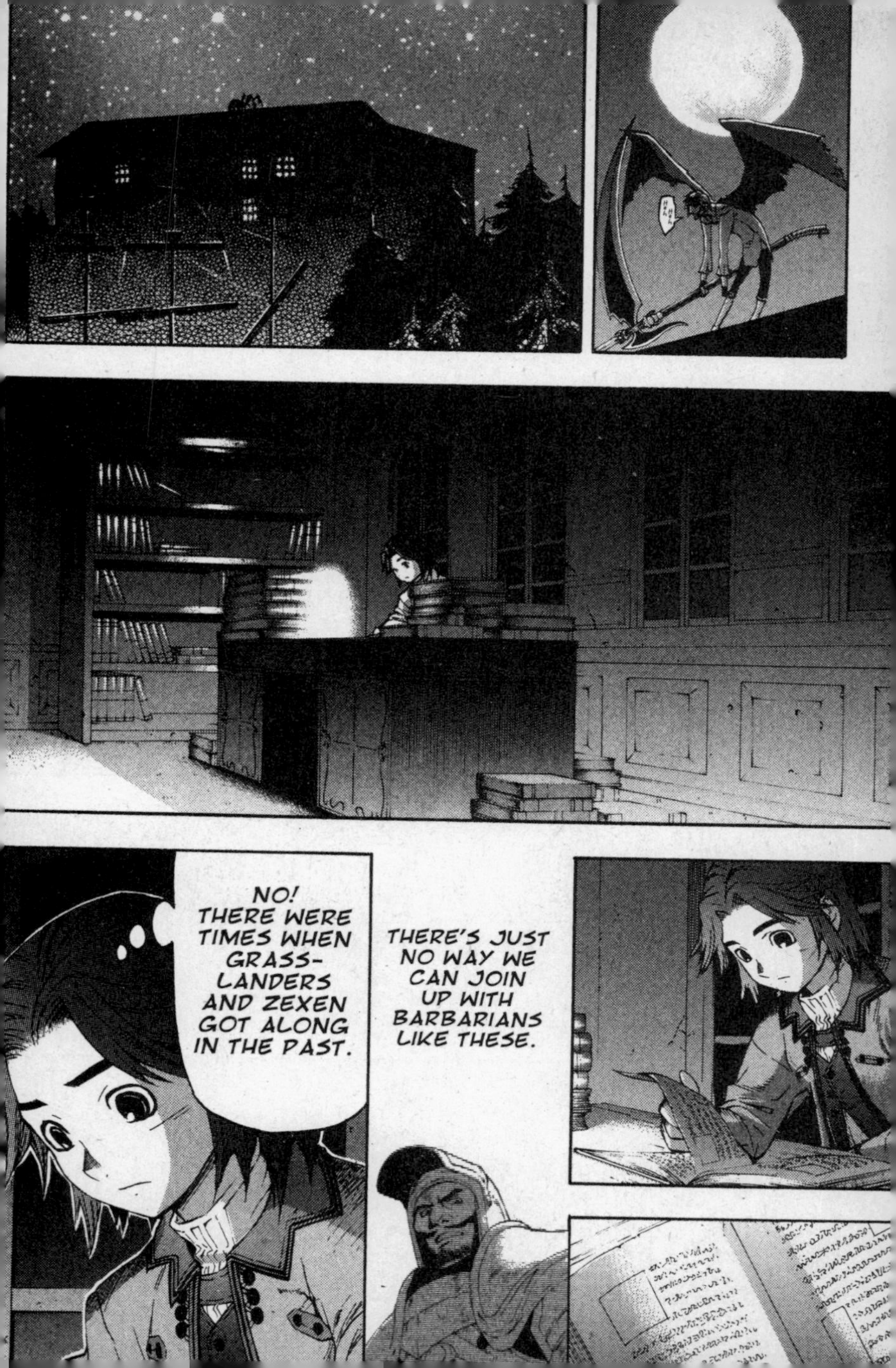
THERE'S JUST NO WAY WE CAN JOIN UP WITH BARBARIANS LIKE THESE.
NO! THERE WERE TIMES WHEN GRASS-LANDERS AND ZEXEN GOT ALONG IN THE PAST.

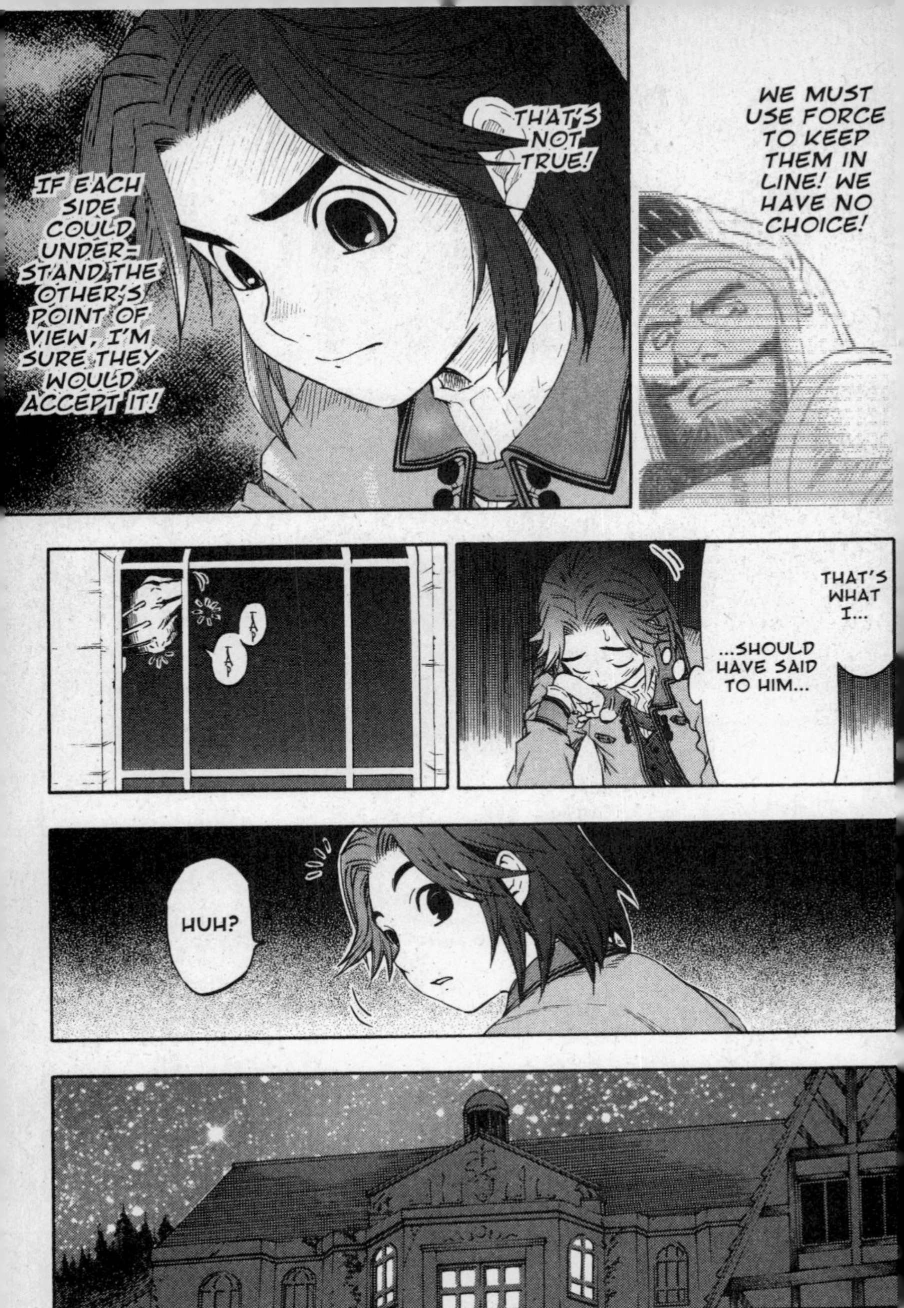

WE MUST USE FORCE TO KEEP THEM IN LINE! WE HAVE NO CHOICE!
THAT'S NOT TRUE!
IF EACH SIDE COULD UNDER-STAND THE OTHER'S POINT OF VIEW, I'M SURE THEY WOULD ACCEPT IT!
THAT'S WHAT I...
...SHOULD HAVE SAID TO HIM...
TAP
TAP
HUH?

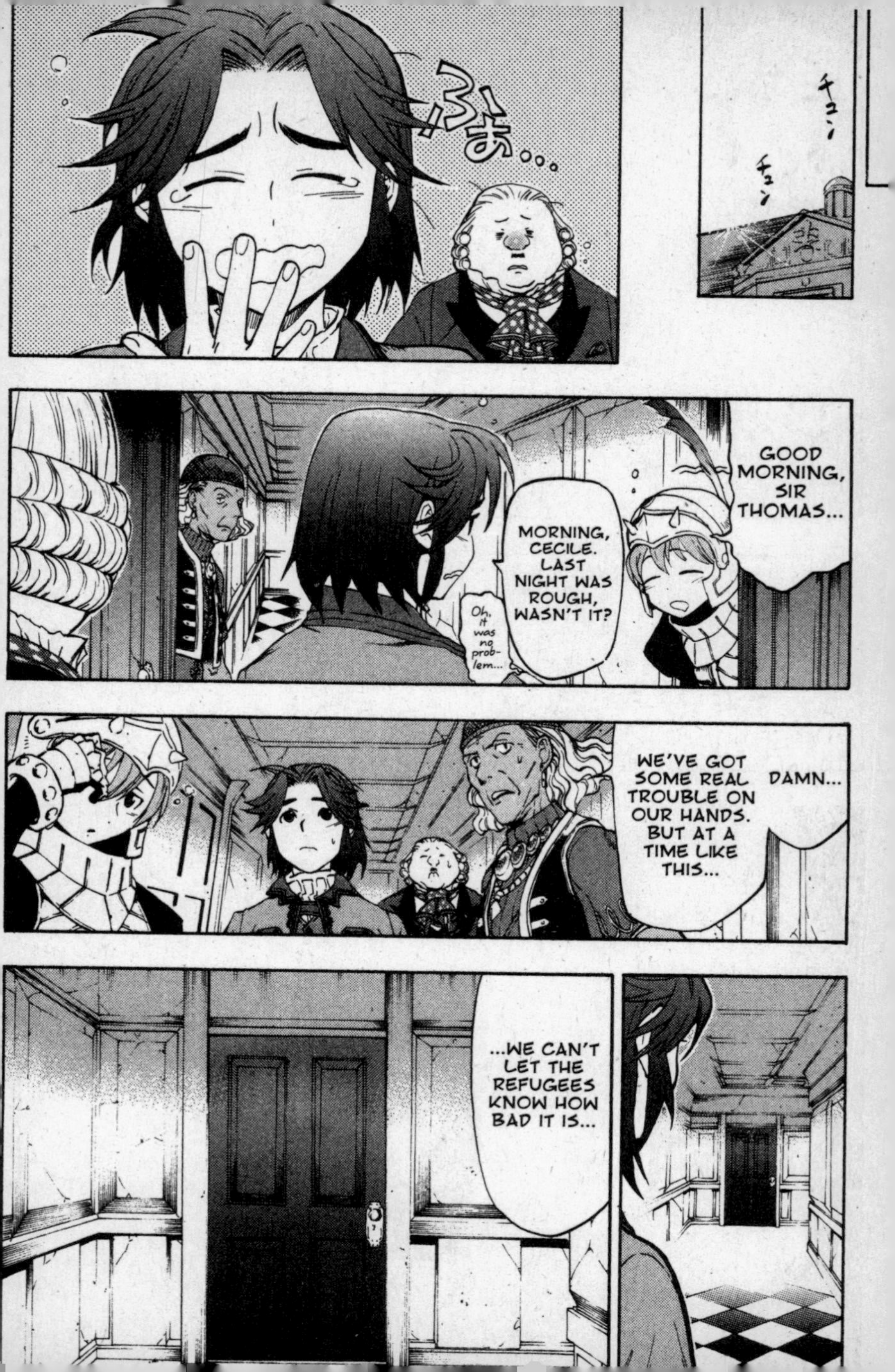
チュン
チュン
ふぁ。。。
GOOD MORNING, SIR THOMAS...
MORNING, CECILE. LAST NIGHT WAS ROUGH, WASN'T IT?
Oh, it was no prob-lem...
DAMN...
WE'VE GOT SOME REAL TROUBLE ON OUR HANDS. BUT AT A TIME LIKE THIS...
...WE CAN'T LET THE REFUGEES KNOW HOW BAD IT IS...

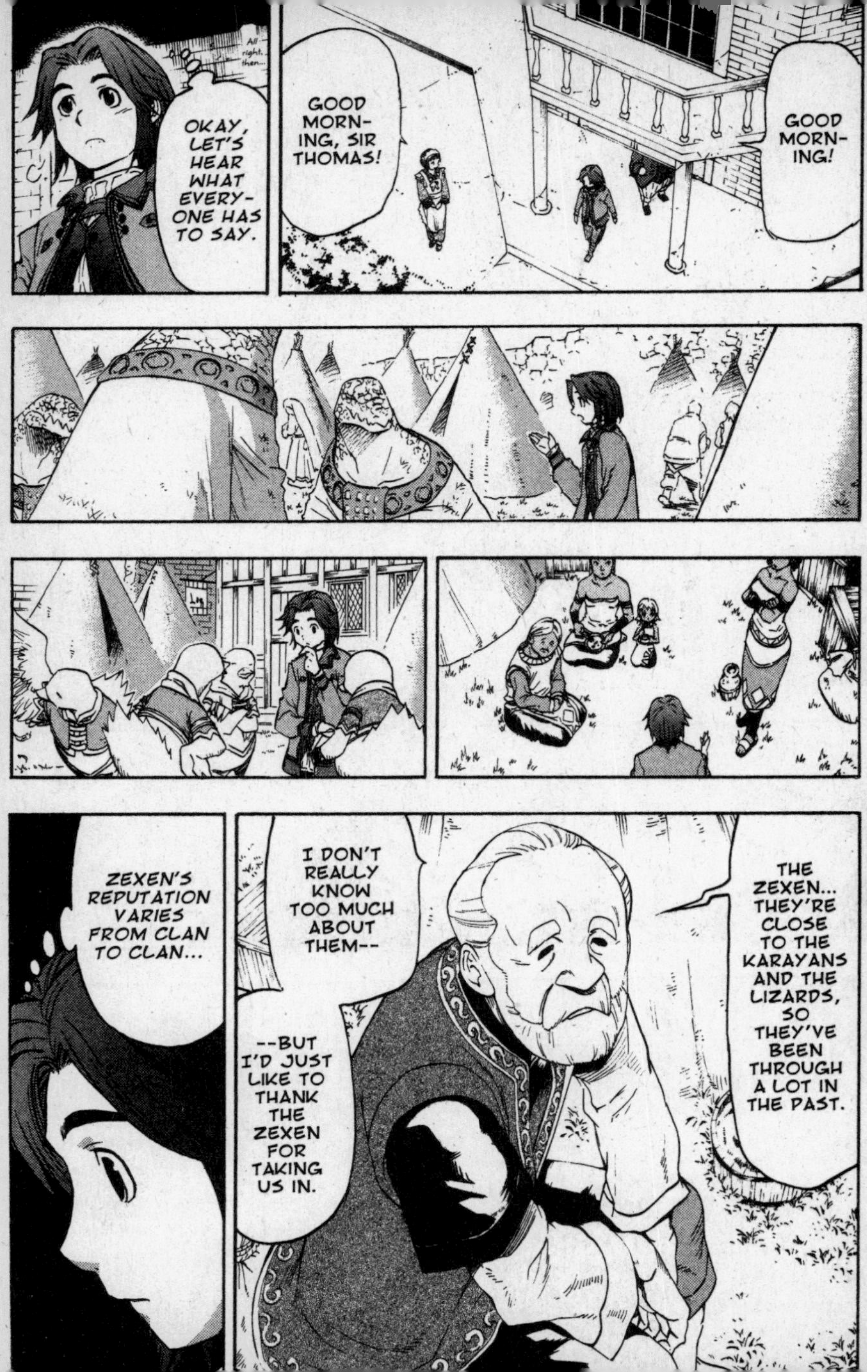

GOOD MORNING!
GOOD MORNING, SIR THOMAS!
All right, then...
OKAY, LET'S HEAR WHAT EVERYONE HAS TO SAY.
THE ZEXEN... THEY'RE CLOSE TO THE KARAYANS AND THE LIZARDS, SO THEY'VE BEEN THROUGH A LOT IN THE PAST.
I DON'T REALLY KNOW TOO MUCH ABOUT THEM--
--BUT I'D JUST LIKE TO THANK THE ZEXEN FOR TAKING US IN.
ZEXEN'S REPUTATION VARIES FROM CLAN TO CLAN...

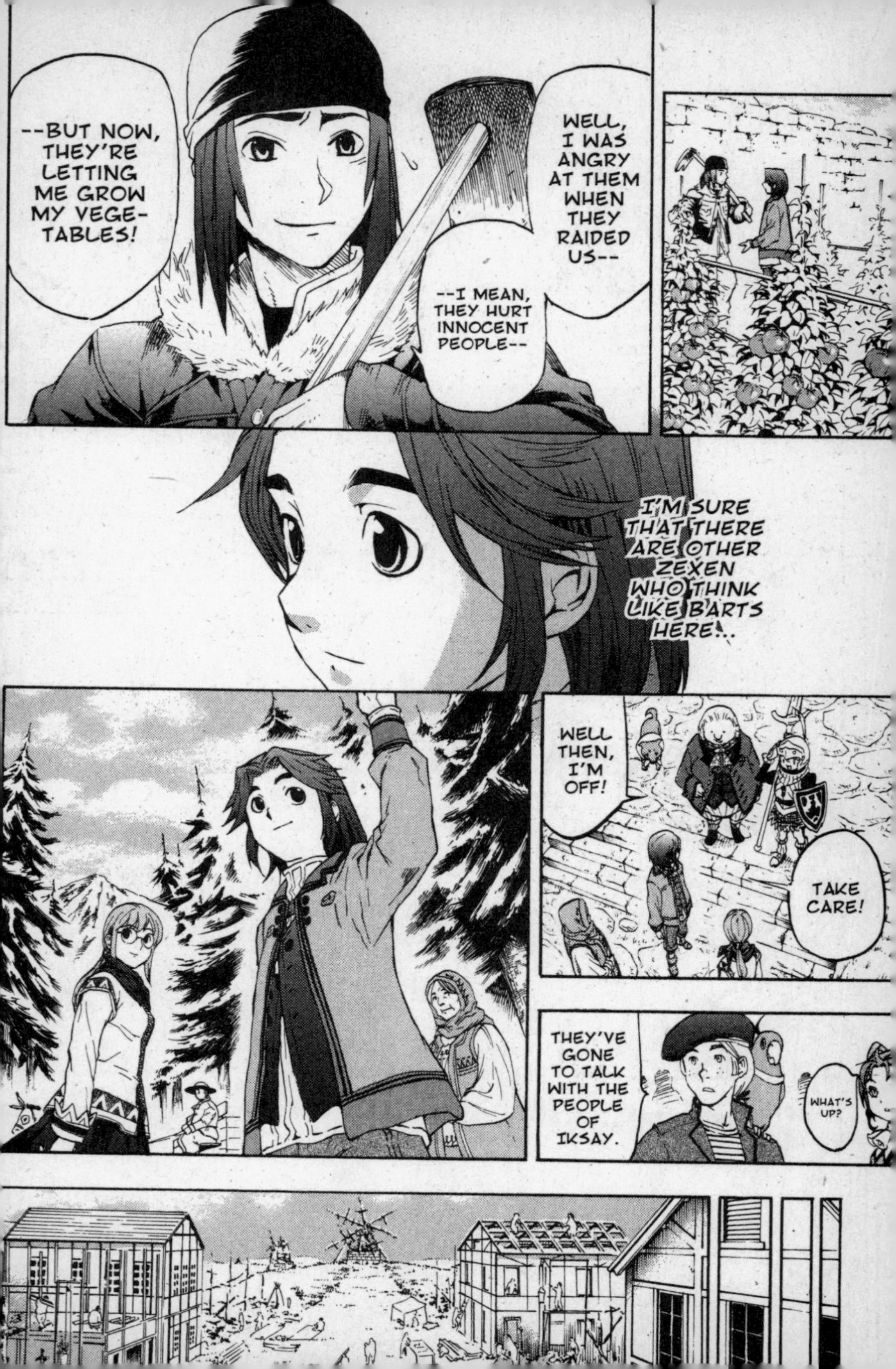

WELL, I WAS ANGRY AT THEM WHEN THEY RAIDED US--
--I MEAN, THEY HURT INNOCENT PEOPLE--
--BUT NOW, THEY'RE LETTING ME GROW MY VEGE-TABLES!
I'M SURE THAT THERE ARE OTHER ZEXEN WHO THINK LIKE BARTS HERE...
WELL THEN, I'M OFF!
TAKE CARE!
WHAT'S UP?
THEY'VE GONE TO TALK WITH THE PEOPLE OF IKSAY.

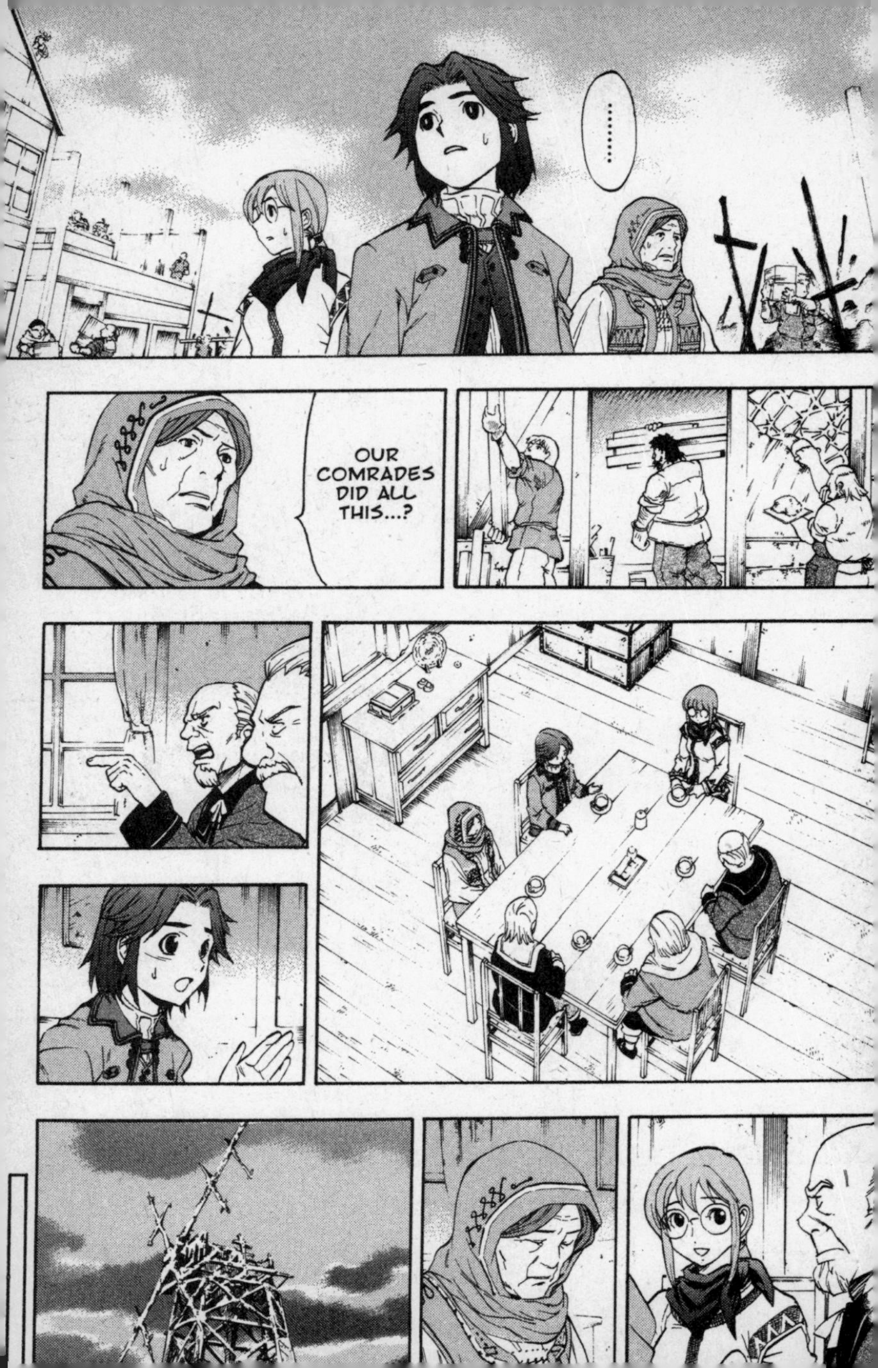
......
OUR COMRADES DID ALL THIS...?

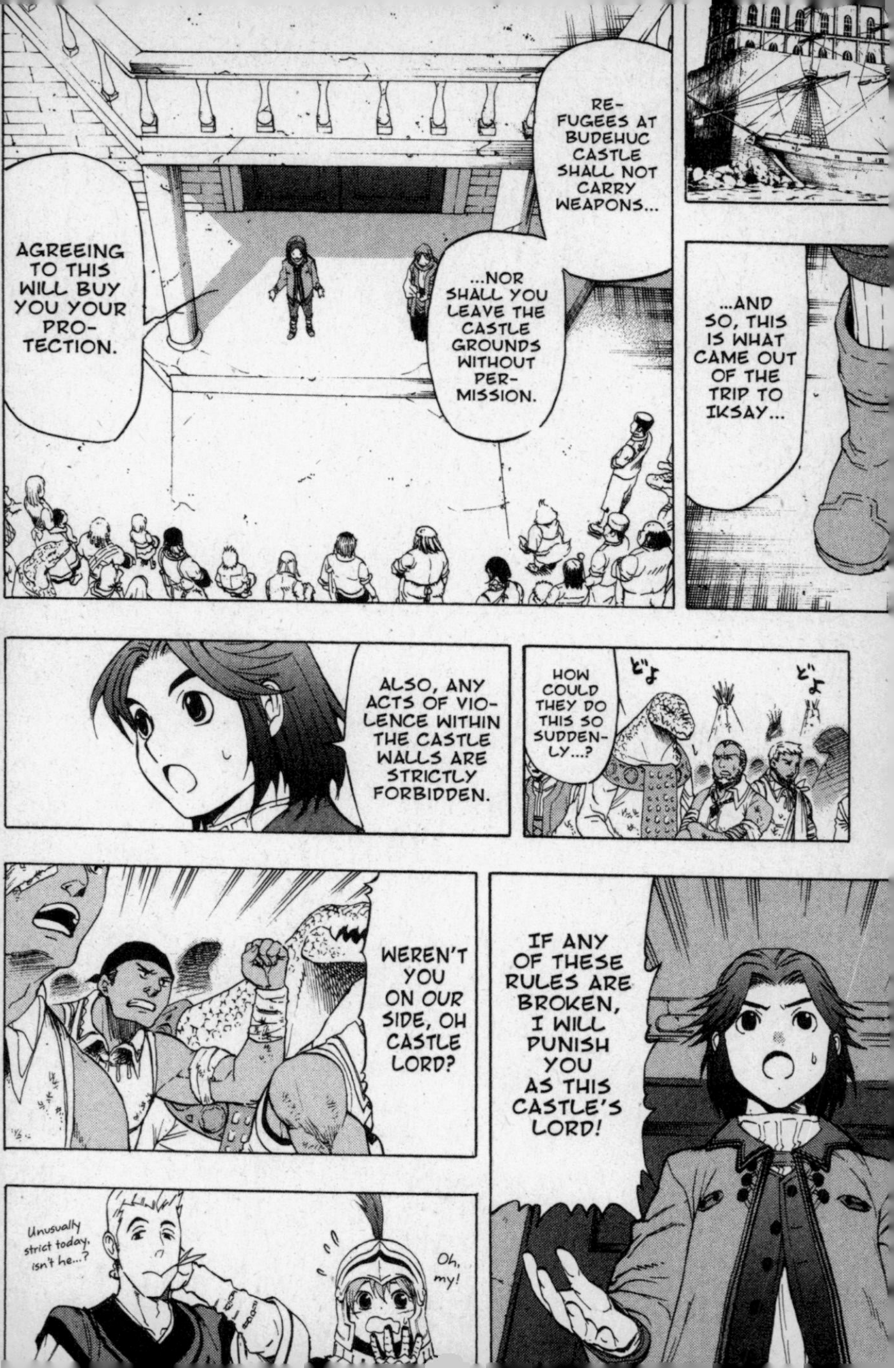
...AND SO, THIS IS WHAT CAME OUT OF THE TRIP TO IKSAY...
RE-FUGEES AT BUDEHUC CASTLE SHALL NOT CARRY WEAPONS...
...NOR SHALL YOU LEAVE THE CASTLE GROUNDS WITHOUT PER-MISSION.
AGREEING TO THIS WILL BUY YOU YOUR PRO-TECTION.
どよ
どよ
HOW COULD THEY DO THIS SO SUDDEN-LY...?
ALSO, ANY ACTS OF VIO-LENCE WITHIN THE CASTLE WALLS ARE STRICTLY FORBIDDEN.
IF ANY OF THESE RULES ARE BROKEN, I WILL PUNISH YOU AS THIS CASTLE'S LORD!
WEREN'T YOU ON OUR SIDE, OH CASTLE LORD?
Oh, my!
Unusually strict today, isn't he...?

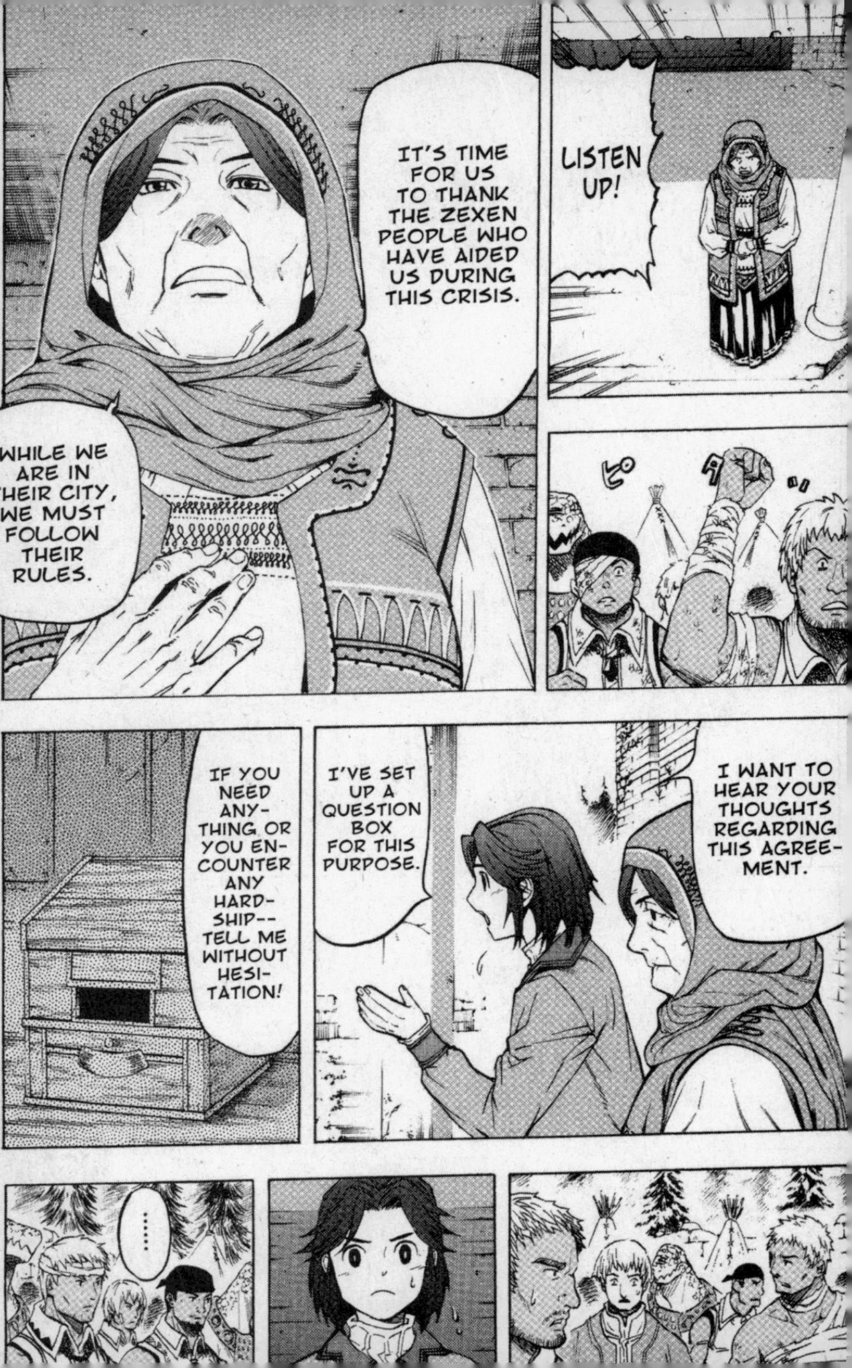

LISTEN UP!
IT'S TIME FOR US TO THANK THE ZEXEN PEOPLE WHO HAVE AIDED US DURING THIS CRISIS.
WHILE WE ARE IN THEIR CITY, WE MUST FOLLOW THEIR RULES.
I WANT TO HEAR YOUR THOUGHTS REGARDING THIS AGREEMENT.
I'VE SET UP A QUESTION BOX FOR THIS PURPOSE.
IF YOU NEED ANYTHING OR YOU ENCOUNTER ANY HARDSHIP-- TELL ME WITHOUT HESITATION!
......

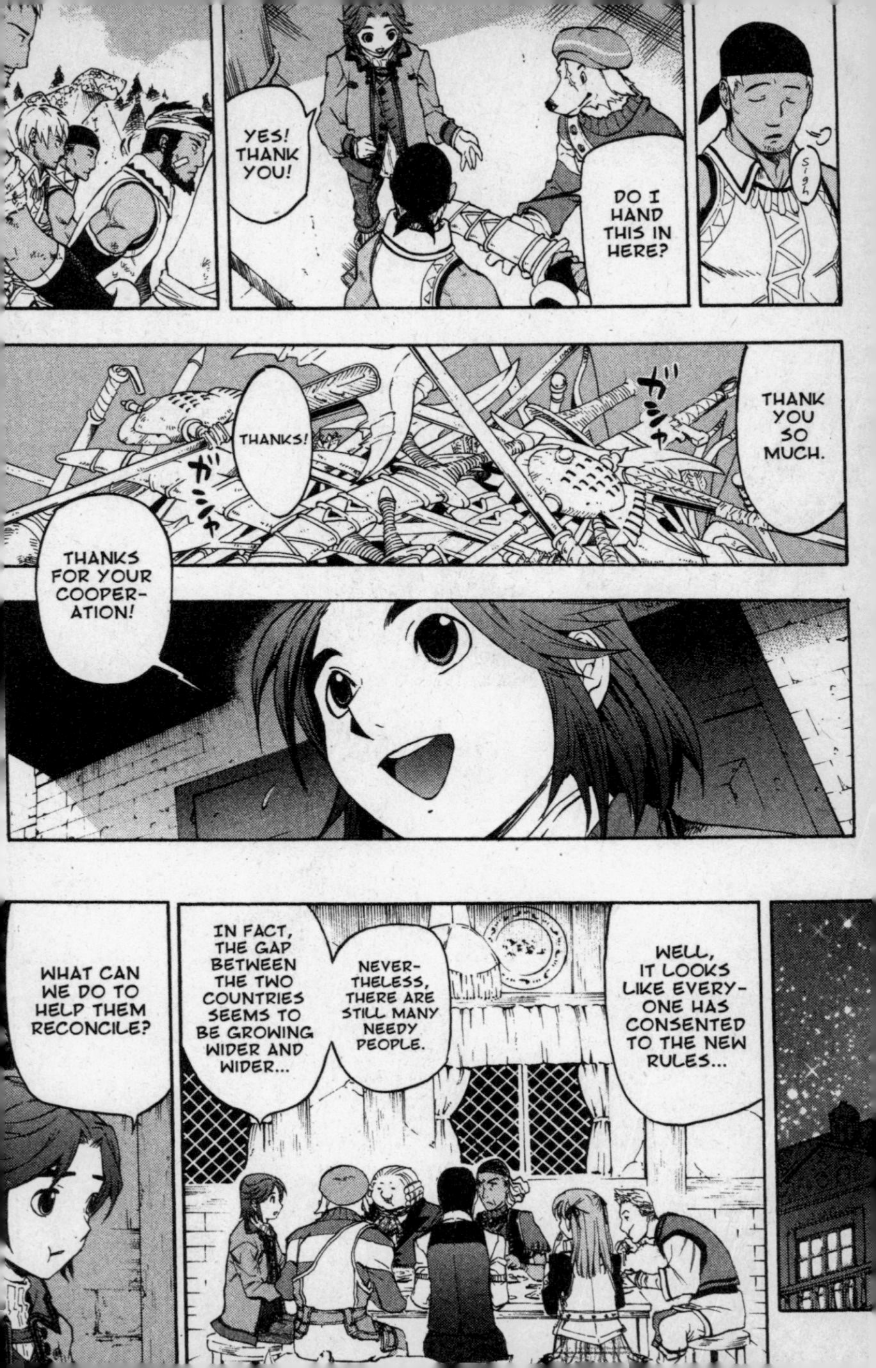
Sigh
DO I HAND THIS IN HERE?
YES! THANK YOU!
THANK YOU SO MUCH.
ガシャ
THANKS!
ガシャ
THANKS FOR YOUR COOPERATION!
WELL, IT LOOKS LIKE EVERYONE HAS CONSENTED TO THE NEW RULES...
NEVERTHELESS, THERE ARE STILL MANY NEEDY PEOPLE.
IN FACT, THE GAP BETWEEN THE TWO COUNTRIES SEEMS TO BE GROWING WIDER AND WIDER...
WHAT CAN WE DO TO HELP THEM RECONCILE?

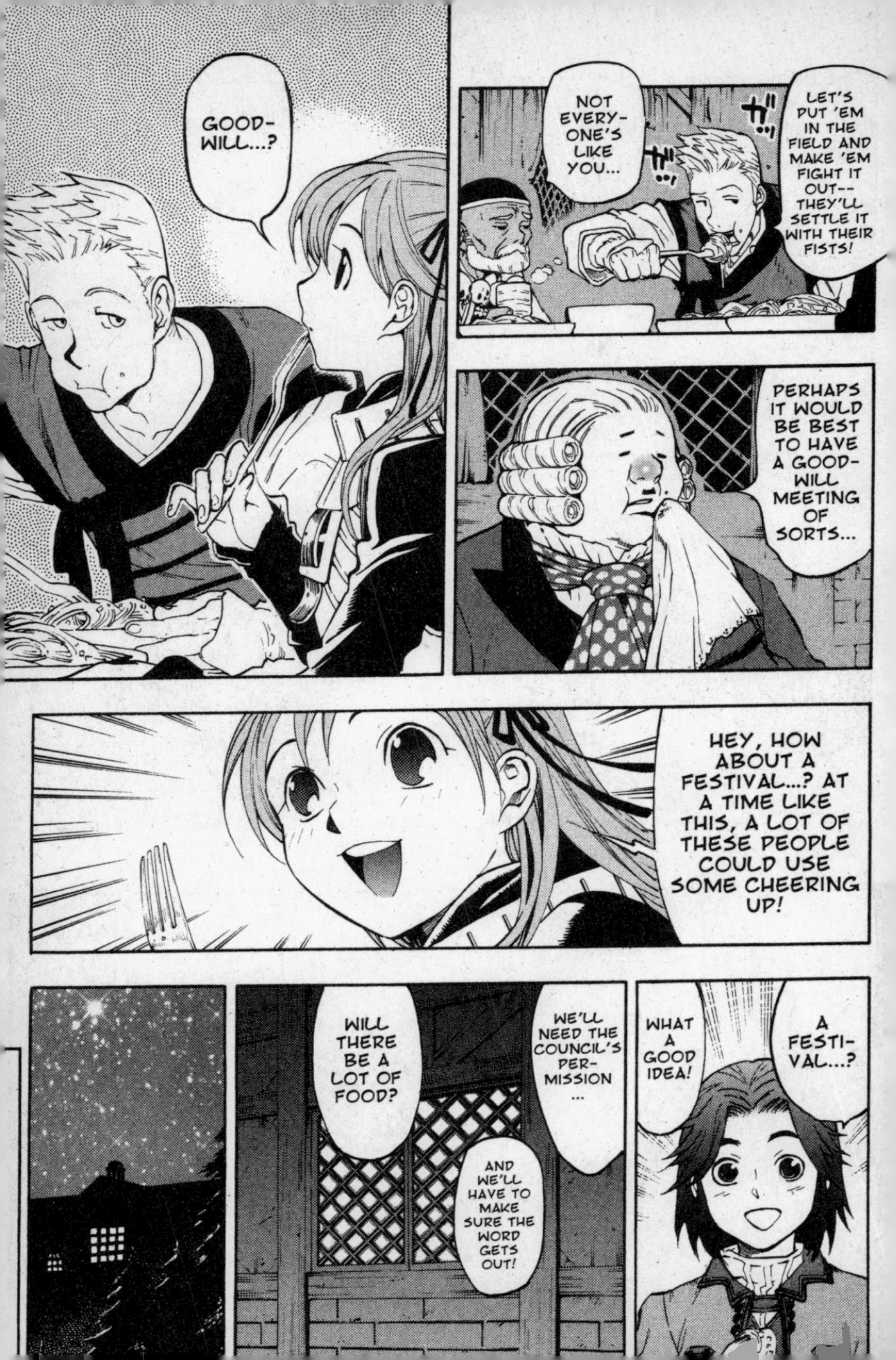
LET'S PUT 'EM IN THE FIELD AND MAKE 'EM FIGHT IT OUT-- THEY'LL SETTLE IT WITH THEIR FISTS!
ガッ
ガッ
NOT EVERY-ONE'S LIKE YOU...
PERHAPS IT WOULD BE BEST TO HAVE A GOOD-WILL MEETING OF SORTS...
GOOD-WILL...?
HEY, HOW ABOUT A FESTIVAL...? AT A TIME LIKE THIS, A LOT OF THESE PEOPLE COULD USE SOME CHEERING UP!
A FESTI-VAL...?
WHAT A GOOD IDEA!
WE'LL NEED THE COUNCIL'S PER-MISSION ...
WILL THERE BE A LOT OF FOOD?
AND WE'LL HAVE TO MAKE SURE THE WORD GETS OUT!

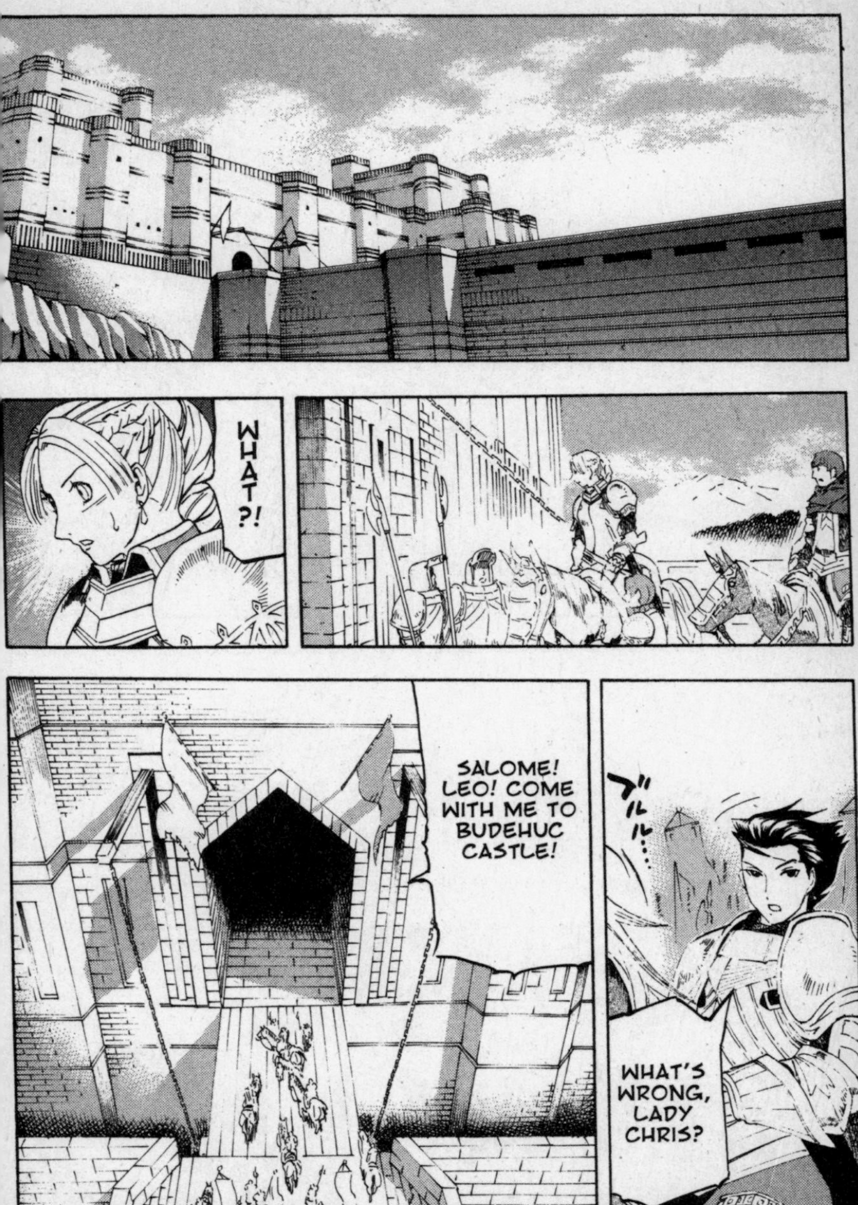
WHAT?!
ブルル…
WHAT'S WRONG, LADY CHRIS?
SALOME! LEO! COME WITH ME TO BUDEHUC CASTLE!

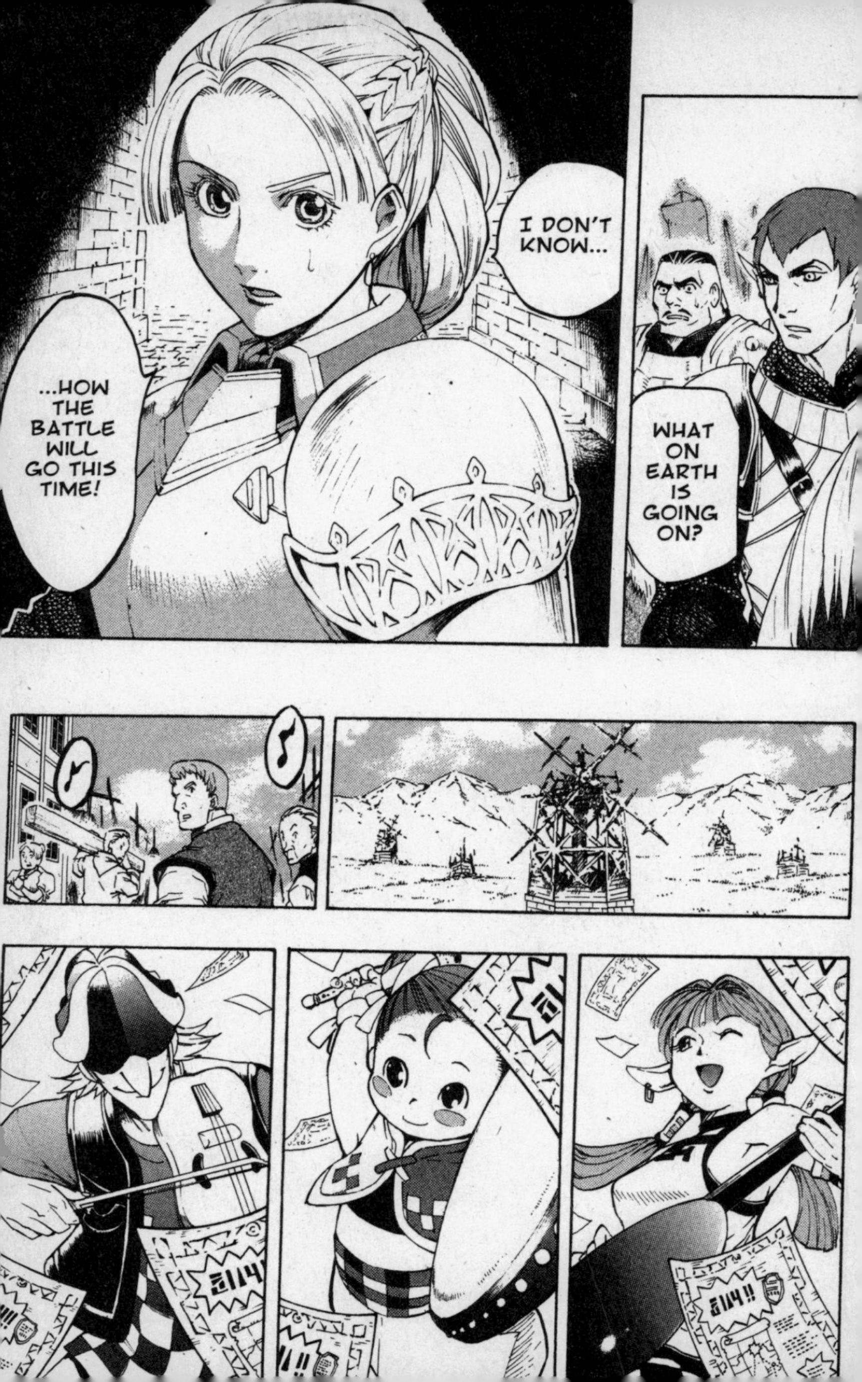
WHAT ON EARTH IS GOING ON?
I DON'T KNOW...
...HOW THE BATTLE WILL GO THIS TIME!

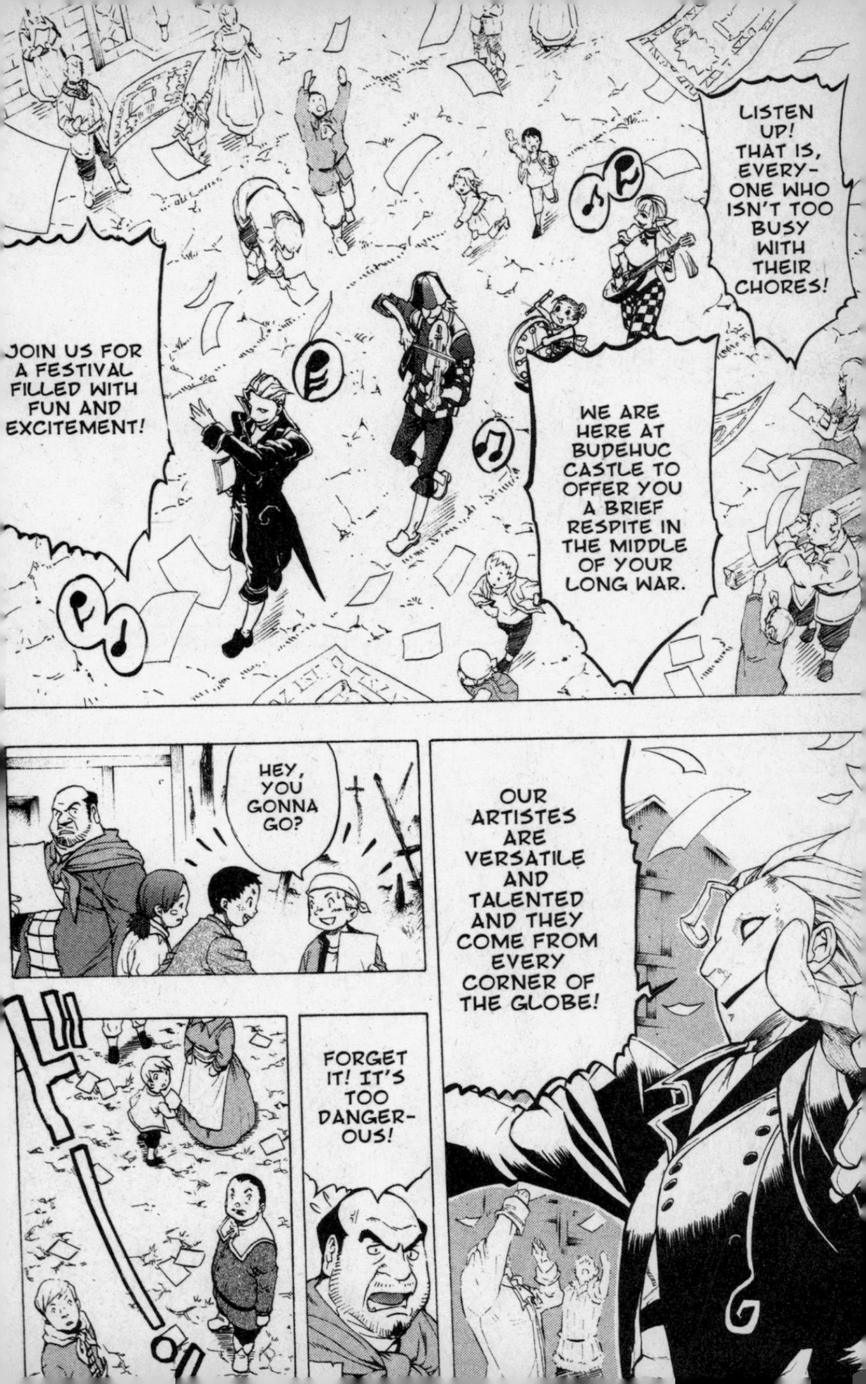
LISTEN UP! THAT IS, EVERY-ONE WHO ISN'T TOO BUSY WITH THEIR CHORES!
WE ARE HERE AT BUDEHUC CASTLE TO OFFER YOU A BRIEF RESPITE IN THE MIDDLE OF YOUR LONG WAR.
JOIN US FOR A FESTIVAL FILLED WITH FUN AND EXCITEMENT!
OUR ARTISTES ARE VERSATILE AND TALENTED AND THEY COME FROM EVERY CORNER OF THE GLOBE!
HEY, YOU GONNA GO?
FORGET IT! IT'S TOO DANGER-OUS!

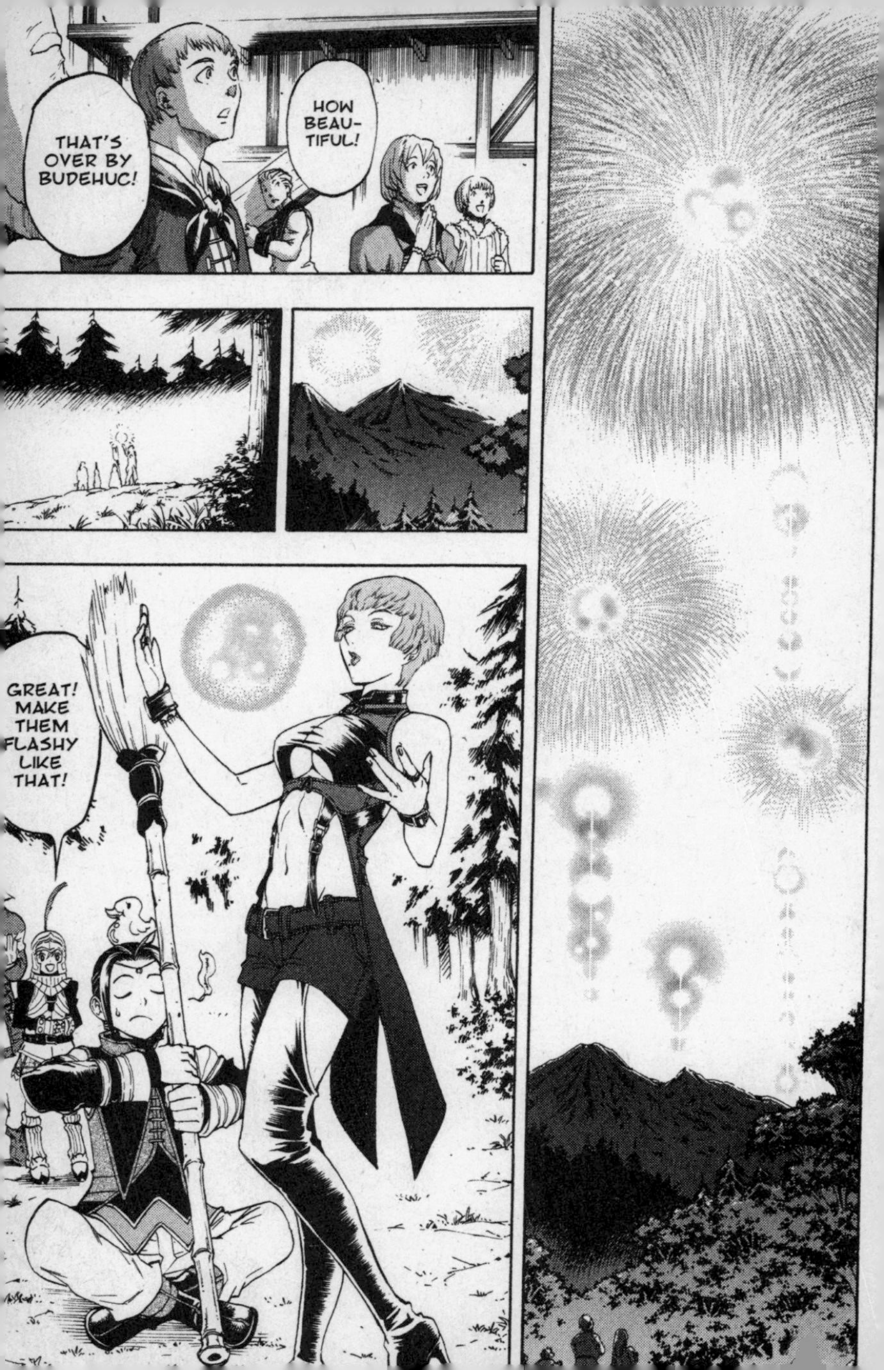
HOW BEAU-TIFUL!
THAT'S OVER BY BUDEHUC!
GREAT! MAKE THEM FLASHY LIKE THAT!

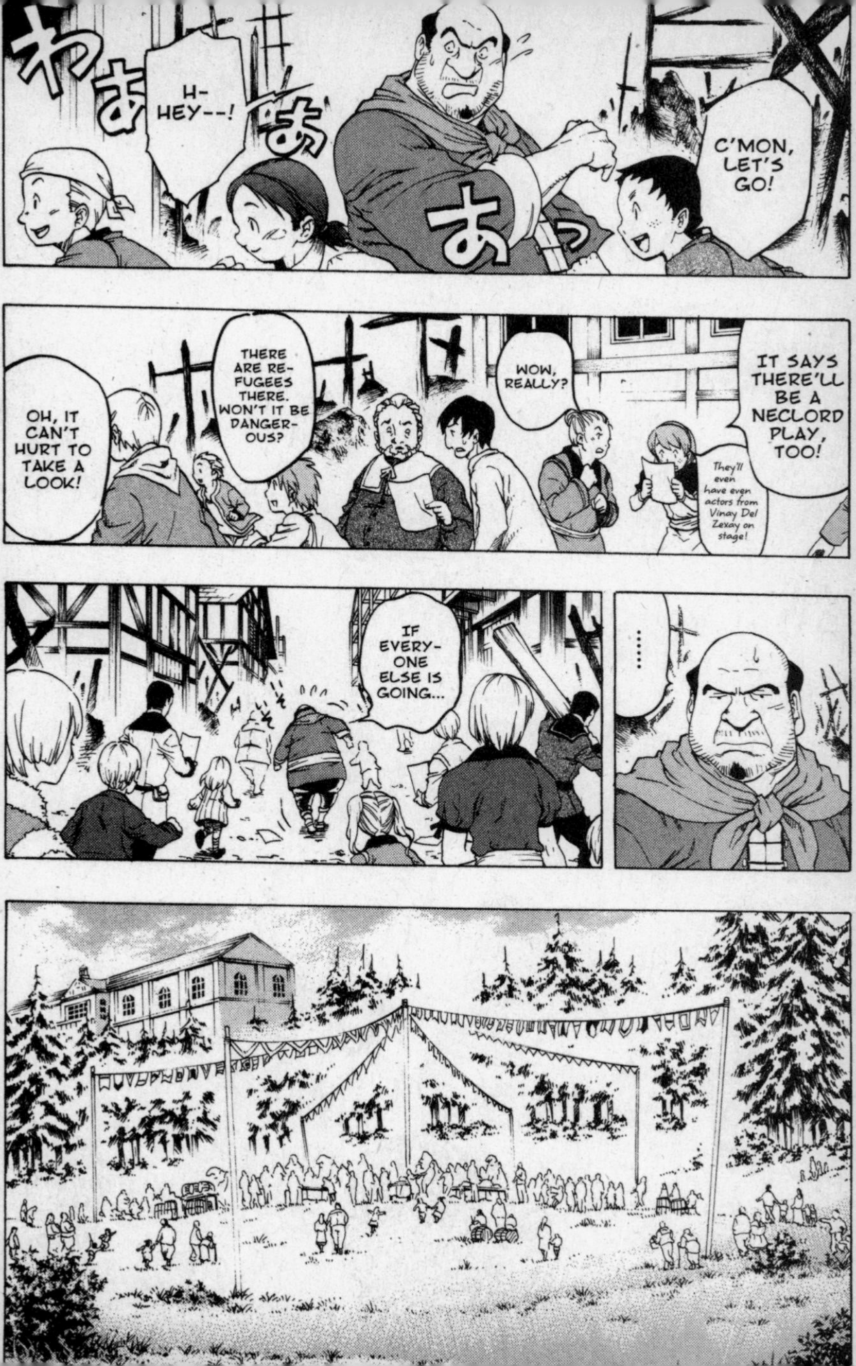
C'MON, LET'S GO!
あっ
H-HEY--!
わぁ
IT SAYS THERE'LL BE A NECLORD PLAY, TOO!
They'll even have even actors from Vinay Del Zexay on stage!
WOW, REALLY?
THERE ARE REFUGEES THERE. WON'T IT BE DANGEROUS?
OH, IT CAN'T HURT TO TAKE A LOOK!
......
IF EVERYONE ELSE IS GOING...

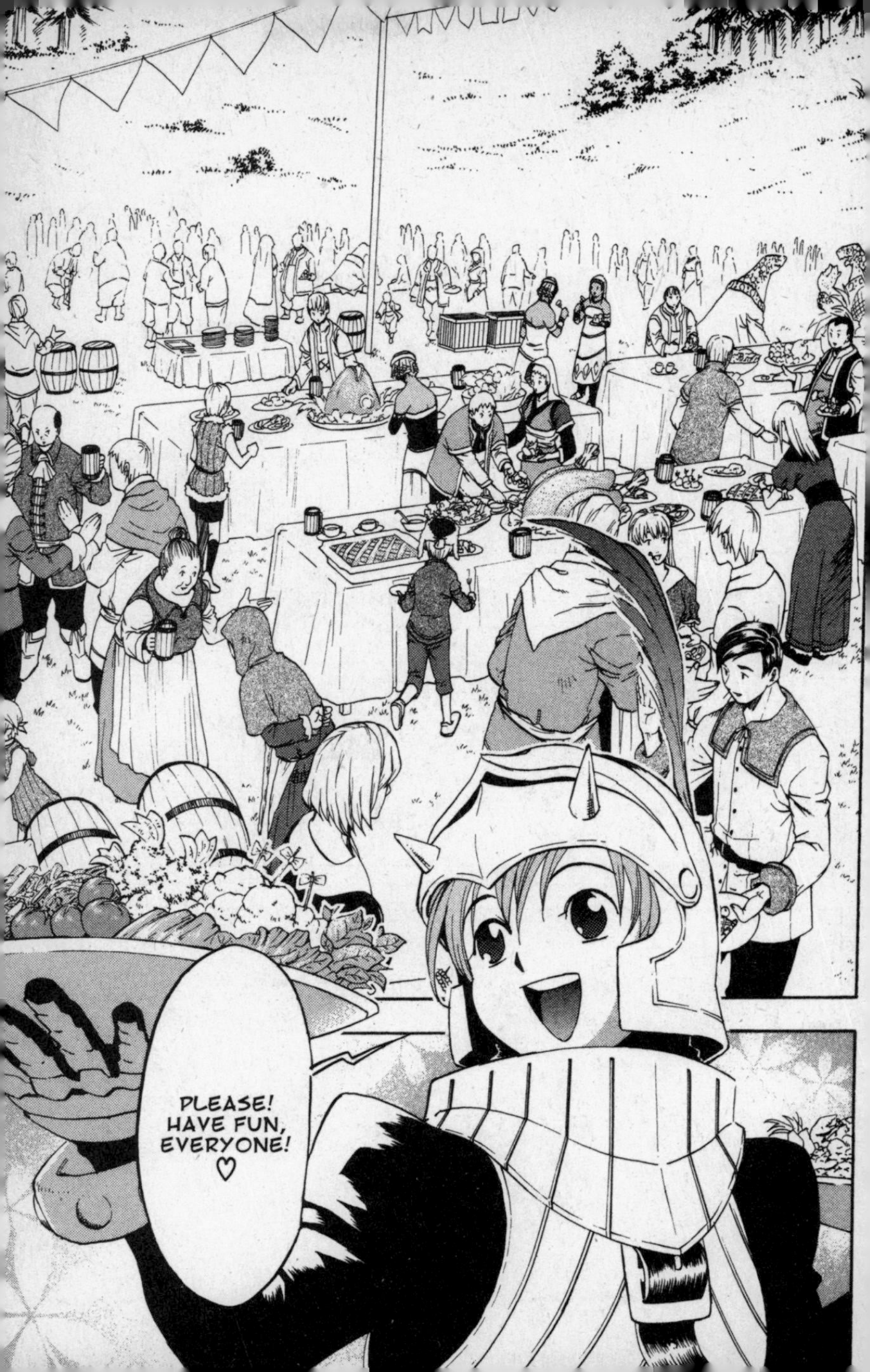
PLEASE! HAVE FUN, EVERYONE! ♡

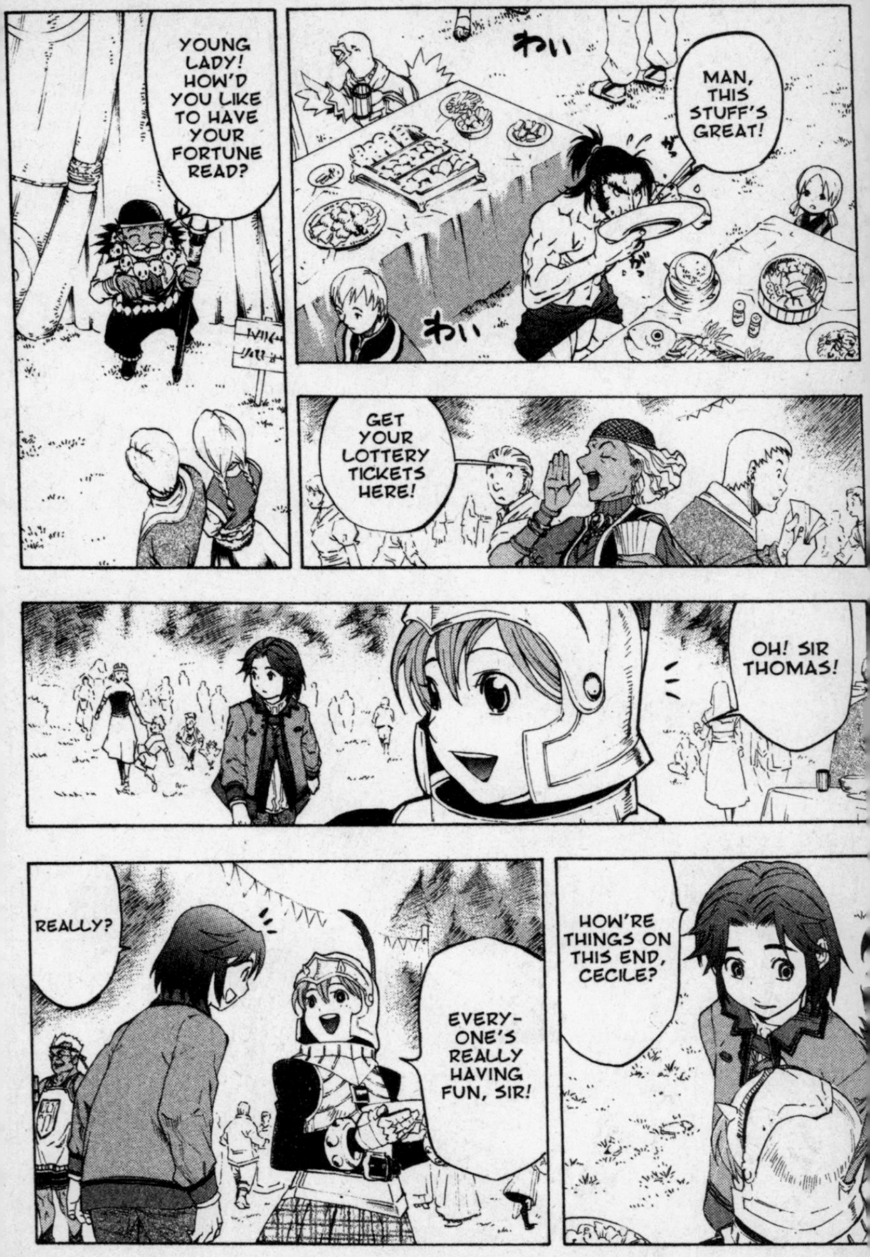
わい
MAN, THIS STUFF'S GREAT!
わい
GET YOUR LOTTERY TICKETS HERE!
YOUNG LADY! HOW'D YOU LIKE TO HAVE YOUR FORTUNE READ?
OH! SIR THOMAS!
HOW'RE THINGS ON THIS END, CECILE?
EVERY-ONE'S REALLY HAVING FUN, SIR!
REALLY?

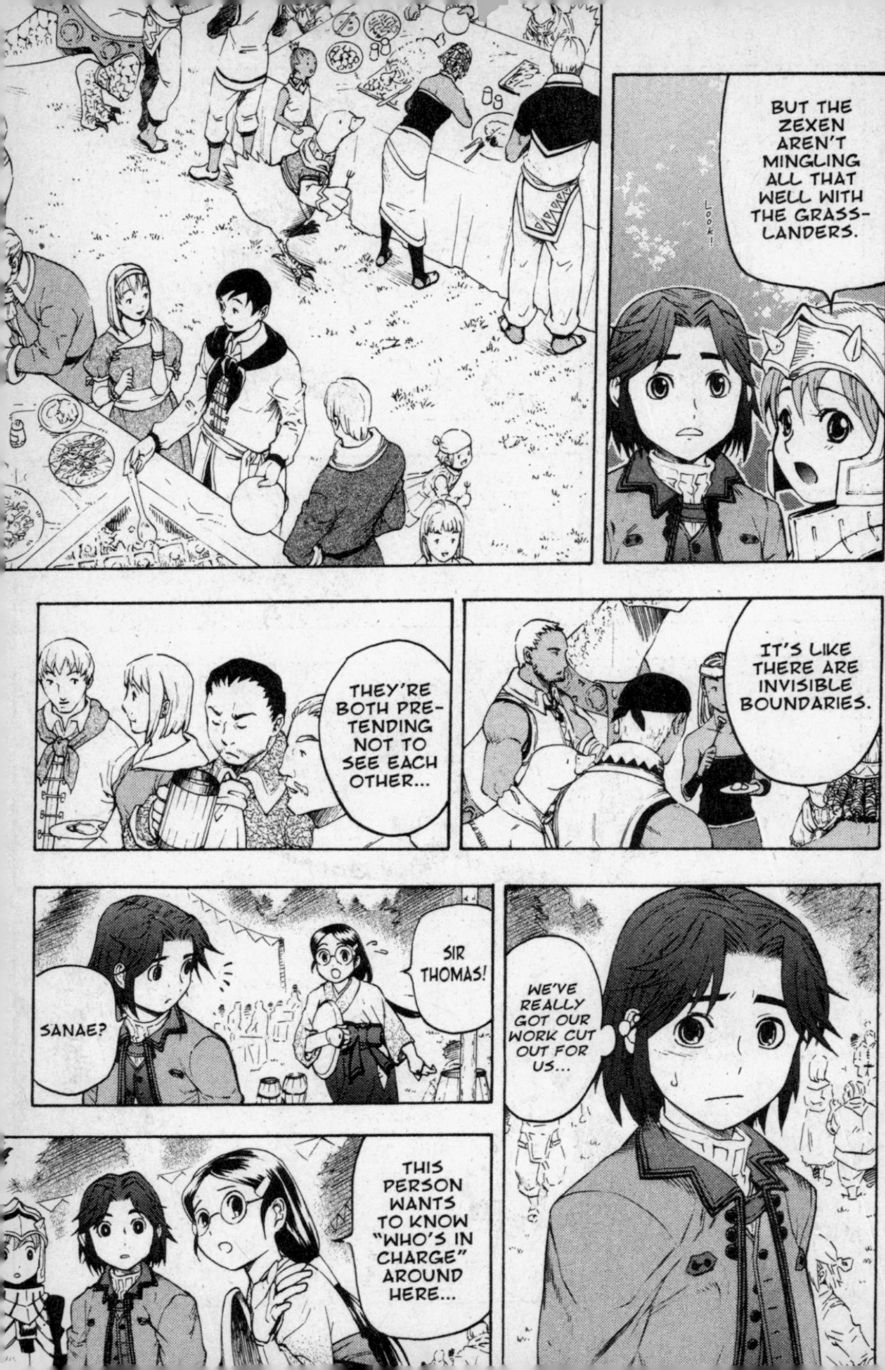
BUT THE ZEXEN AREN'T MINGLING ALL THAT WELL WITH THE GRASS-LANDERS.
Look!
IT'S LIKE THERE ARE INVISIBLE BOUNDARIES.
THEY'RE BOTH PRE-TENDING NOT TO SEE EACH OTHER...
WE'VE REALLY GOT OUR WORK CUT OUT FOR US...
SIR THOMAS!
SANAE?
THIS PERSON WANTS TO KNOW "WHO'S IN CHARGE" AROUND HERE...

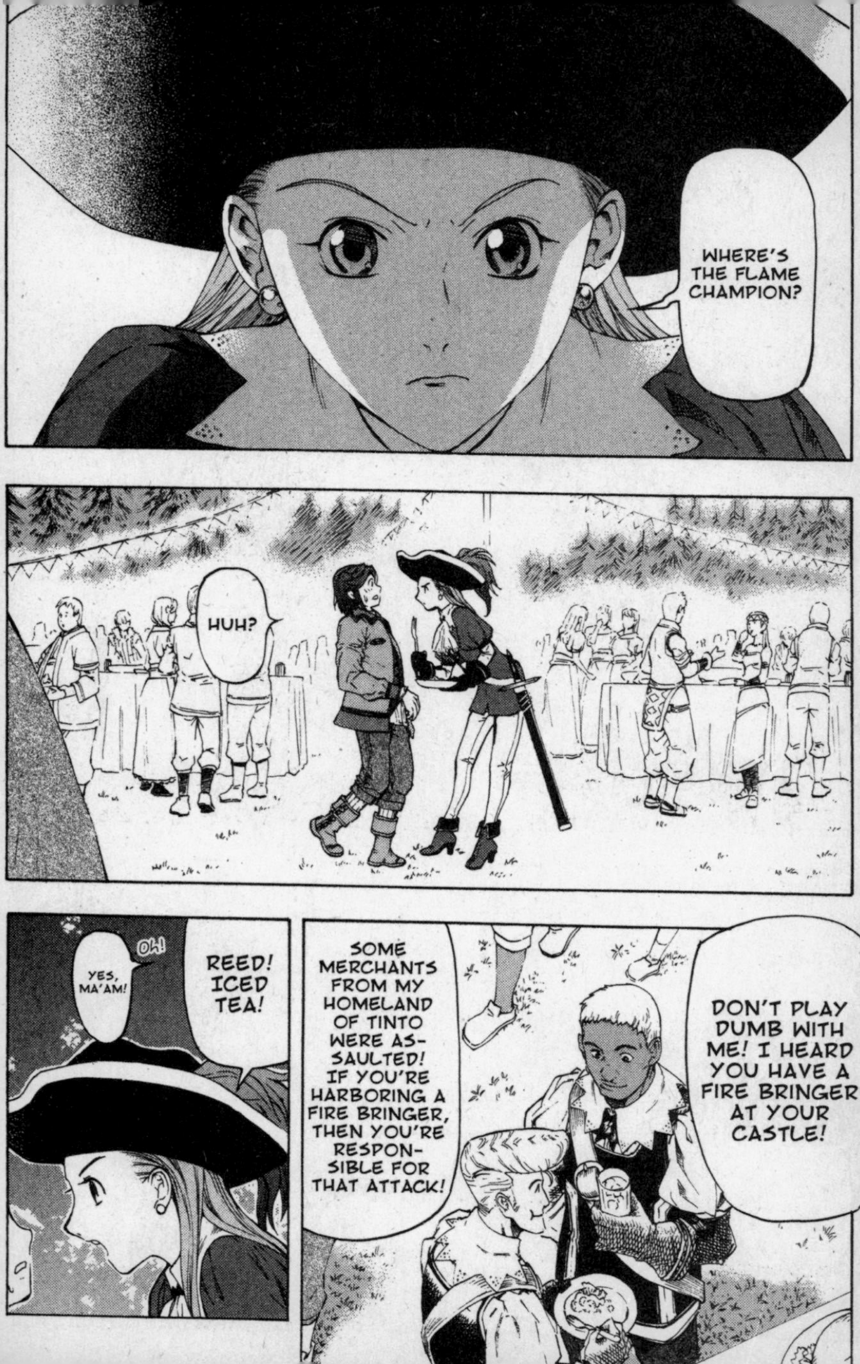
WHERE'S THE FLAME CHAMPION?
HUH?
DON'T PLAY DUMB WITH ME! I HEARD YOU HAVE A FIRE BRINGER AT YOUR CASTLE!
SOME MERCHANTS FROM MY HOMELAND OF TINTO WERE AS-SAULTED! IF YOU'RE HARBORING A FIRE BRINGER, THEN YOU'RE RESPON-SIBLE FOR THAT ATTACK!
REED! ICED TEA!
Oh!
YES, MA'AM!

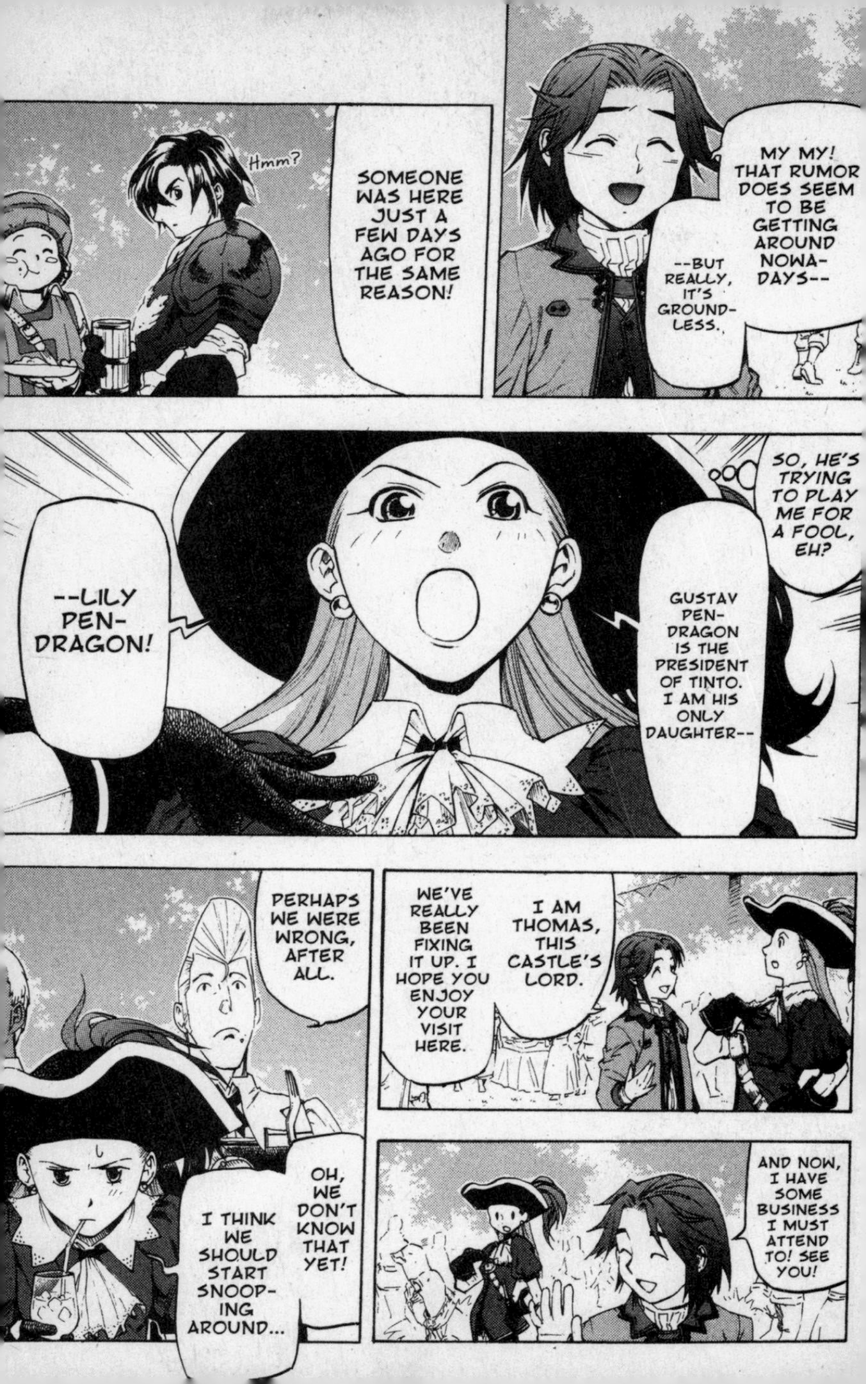
MY MY! THAT RUMOR DOES SEEM TO BE GETTING AROUND NOWADAYS--
--BUT REALLY, IT'S GROUNDLESS.
SOMEONE WAS HERE JUST A FEW DAYS AGO FOR THE SAME REASON!
Hmm?
SO, HE'S TRYING TO PLAY ME FOR A FOOL, EH?
GUSTAV PENDRAGON IS THE PRESIDENT OF TINTO. I AM HIS ONLY DAUGHTER--
--LILY PENDRAGON!
I AM THOMAS, THIS CASTLE'S LORD.
WE'VE REALLY BEEN FIXING IT UP. I HOPE YOU ENJOY YOUR VISIT HERE.
AND NOW, I HAVE SOME BUSINESS I MUST ATTEND TO! SEE YOU!
PERHAPS WE WERE WRONG, AFTER ALL.
OH, WE DON'T KNOW THAT YET!
I THINK WE SHOULD START SNOOPING AROUND...

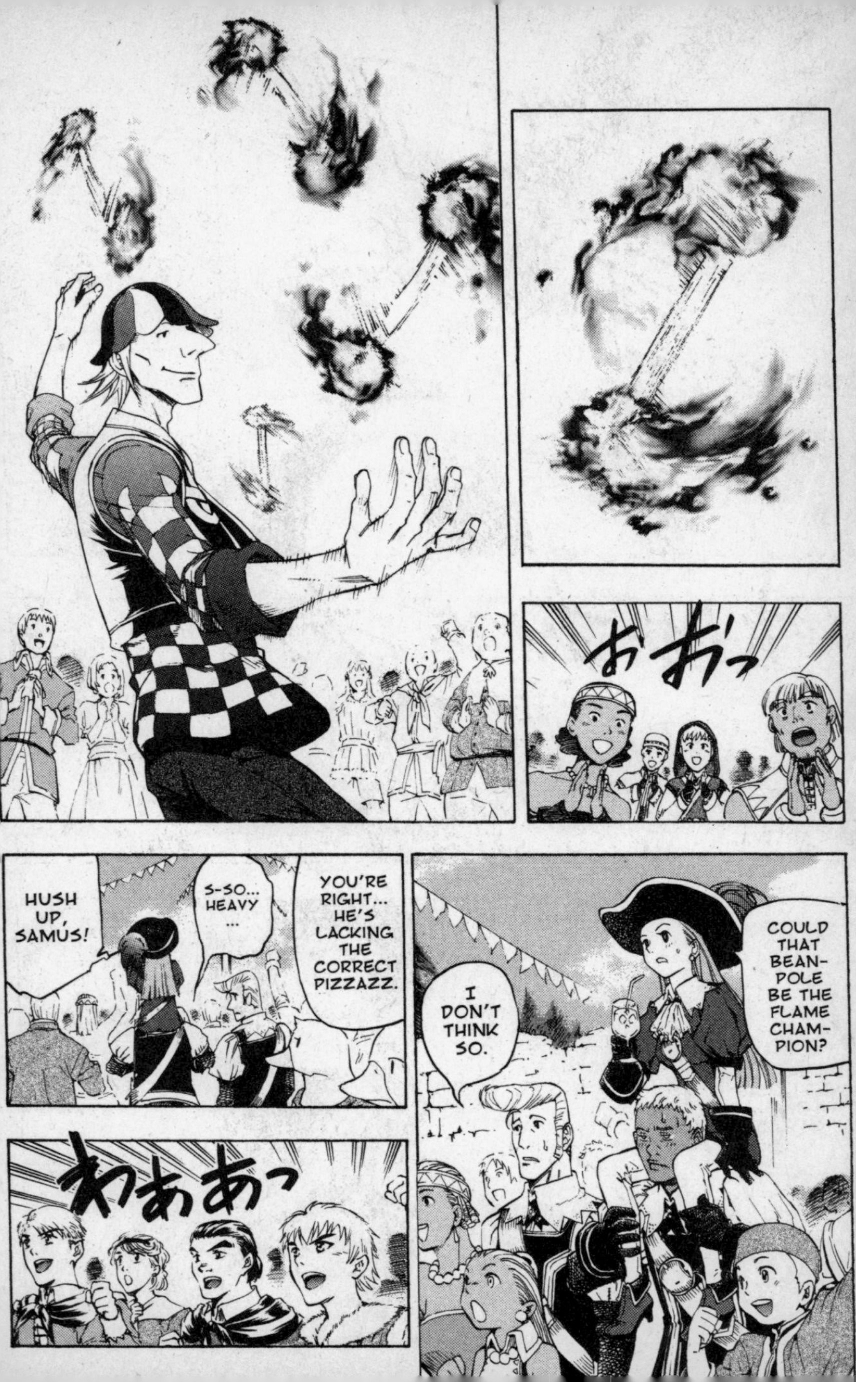
おおっ
COULD THAT BEAN-POLE BE THE FLAME CHAMP-ION?
I DON'T THINK SO.
YOU'RE RIGHT... HE'S LACKING THE CORRECT PIZZAZZ.
S-SO... HEAVY ...
HUSH UP, SAMUS!
わあぁっ

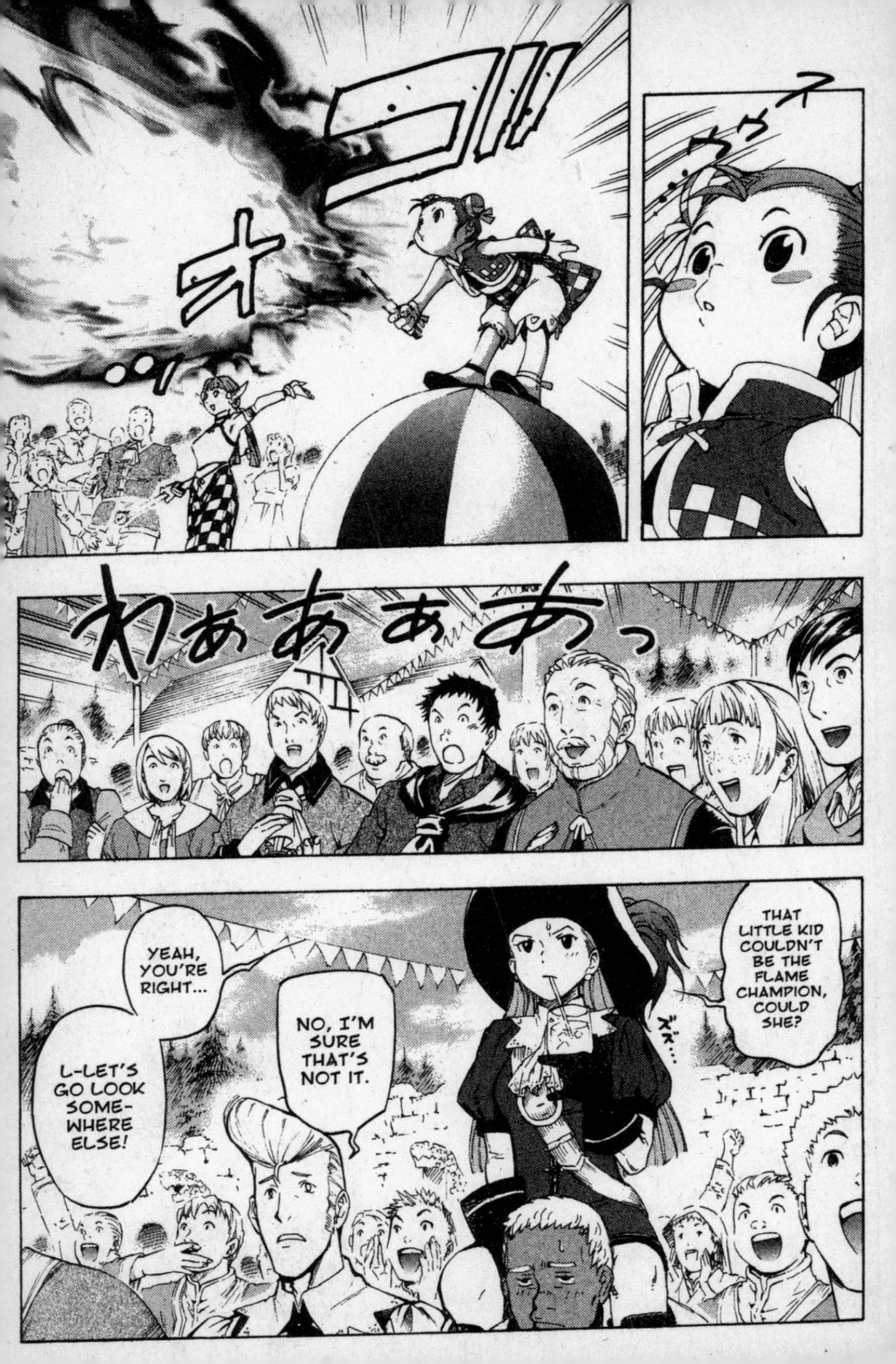
わぁあああっ
THAT LITTLE KID COULDN'T BE THE FLAME CHAMPION, COULD SHE?
ズズ…
NO, I'M SURE THAT'S NOT IT.
YEAH, YOU'RE RIGHT...
L-LET'S GO LOOK SOME-WHERE ELSE!

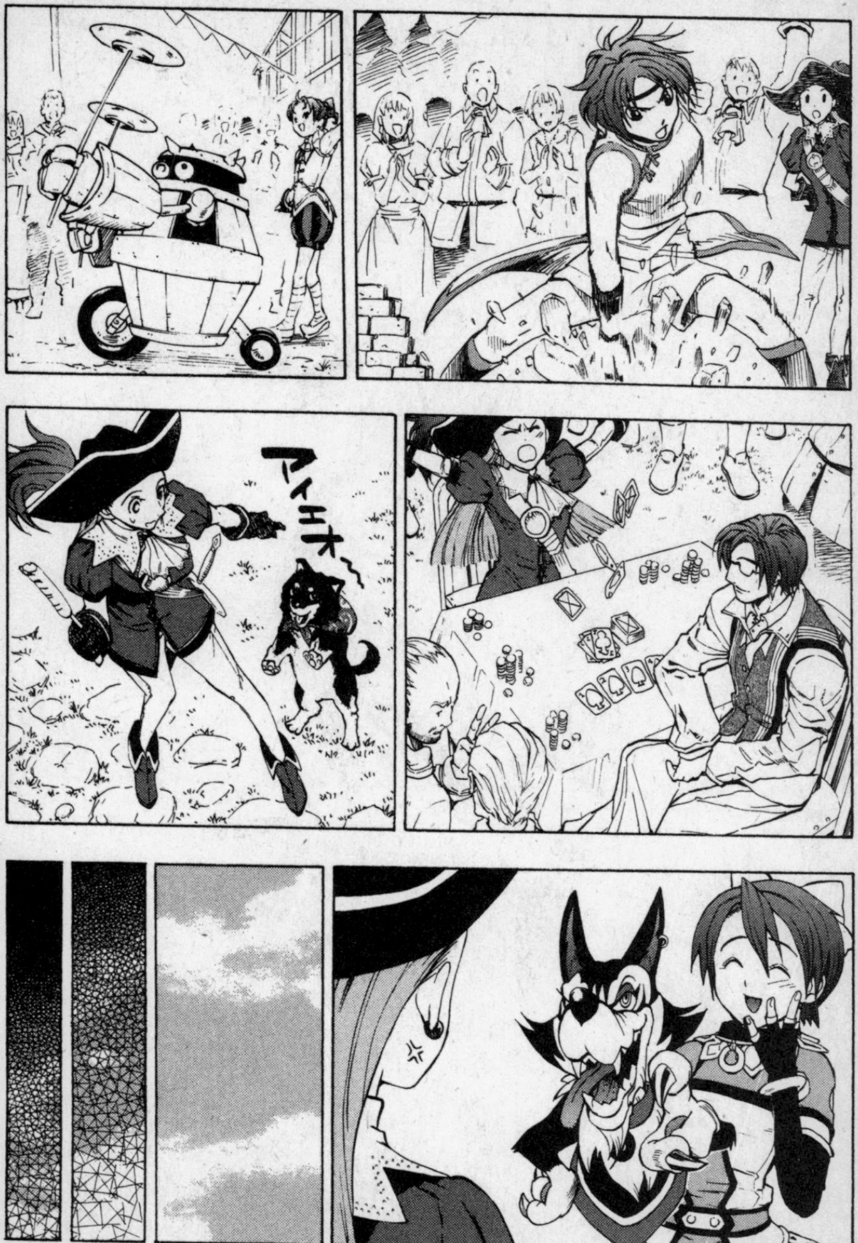
アイエオ〜

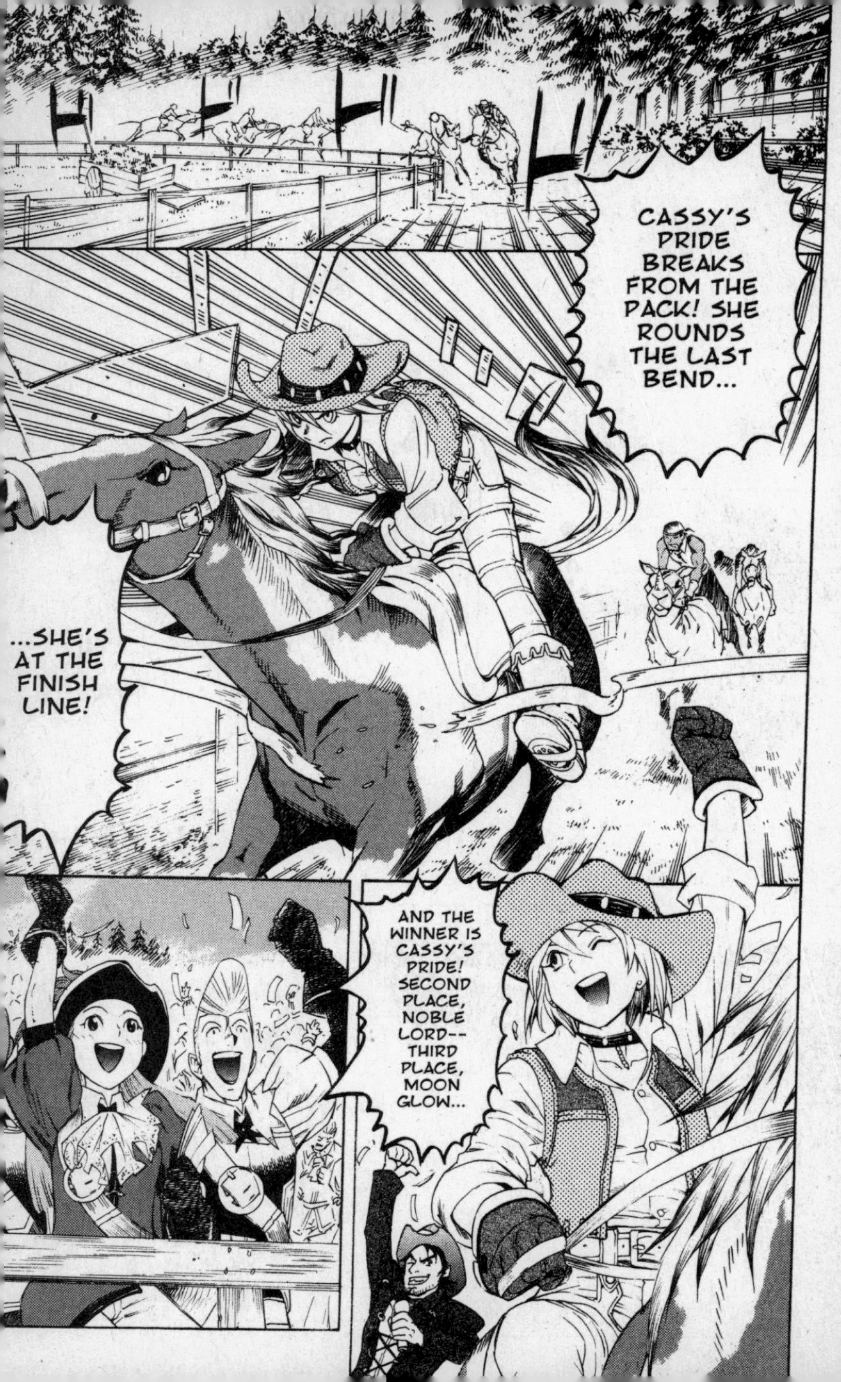
CASSY'S PRIDE BREAKS FROM THE PACK! SHE ROUNDS THE LAST BEND...
...SHE'S AT THE FINISH LINE!
AND THE WINNER IS CASSY'S PRIDE! SECOND PLACE, NOBLE LORD-- THIRD PLACE, MOON GLOW...

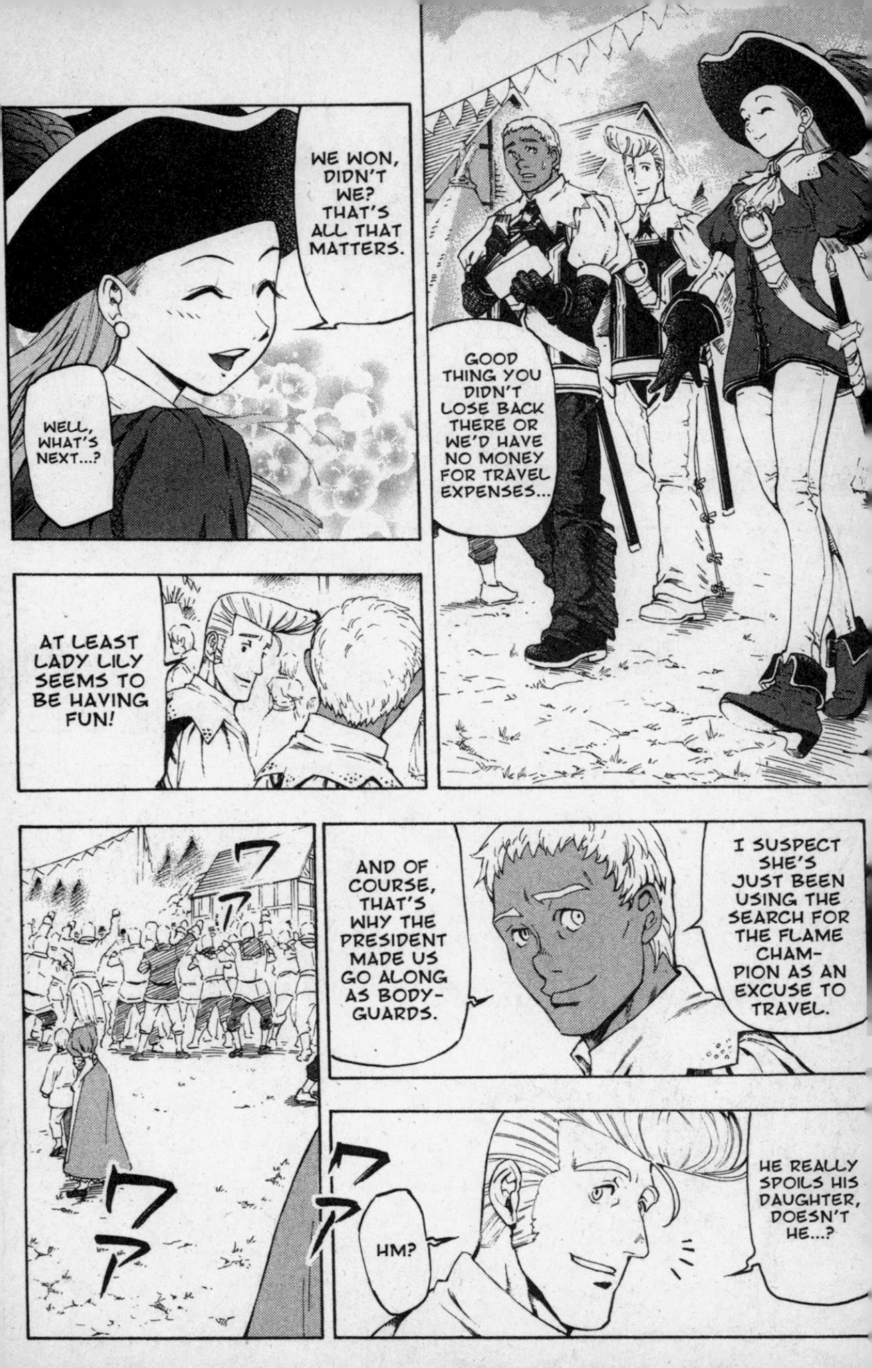
GOOD THING YOU DIDN'T LOSE BACK THERE OR WE'D HAVE NO MONEY FOR TRAVEL EXPENSES...
WE WON, DIDN'T WE? THAT'S ALL THAT MATTERS.
WELL, WHAT'S NEXT...?
AT LEAST LADY LILY SEEMS TO BE HAVING FUN!
I SUSPECT SHE'S JUST BEEN USING THE SEARCH FOR THE FLAME CHAMPION AS AN EXCUSE TO TRAVEL.
AND OF COURSE, THAT'S WHY THE PRESIDENT MADE US GO ALONG AS BODY-GUARDS.
HE REALLY SPOILS HIS DAUGHTER, DOESN'T HE...?
HM?
ワア
ワア
ワア

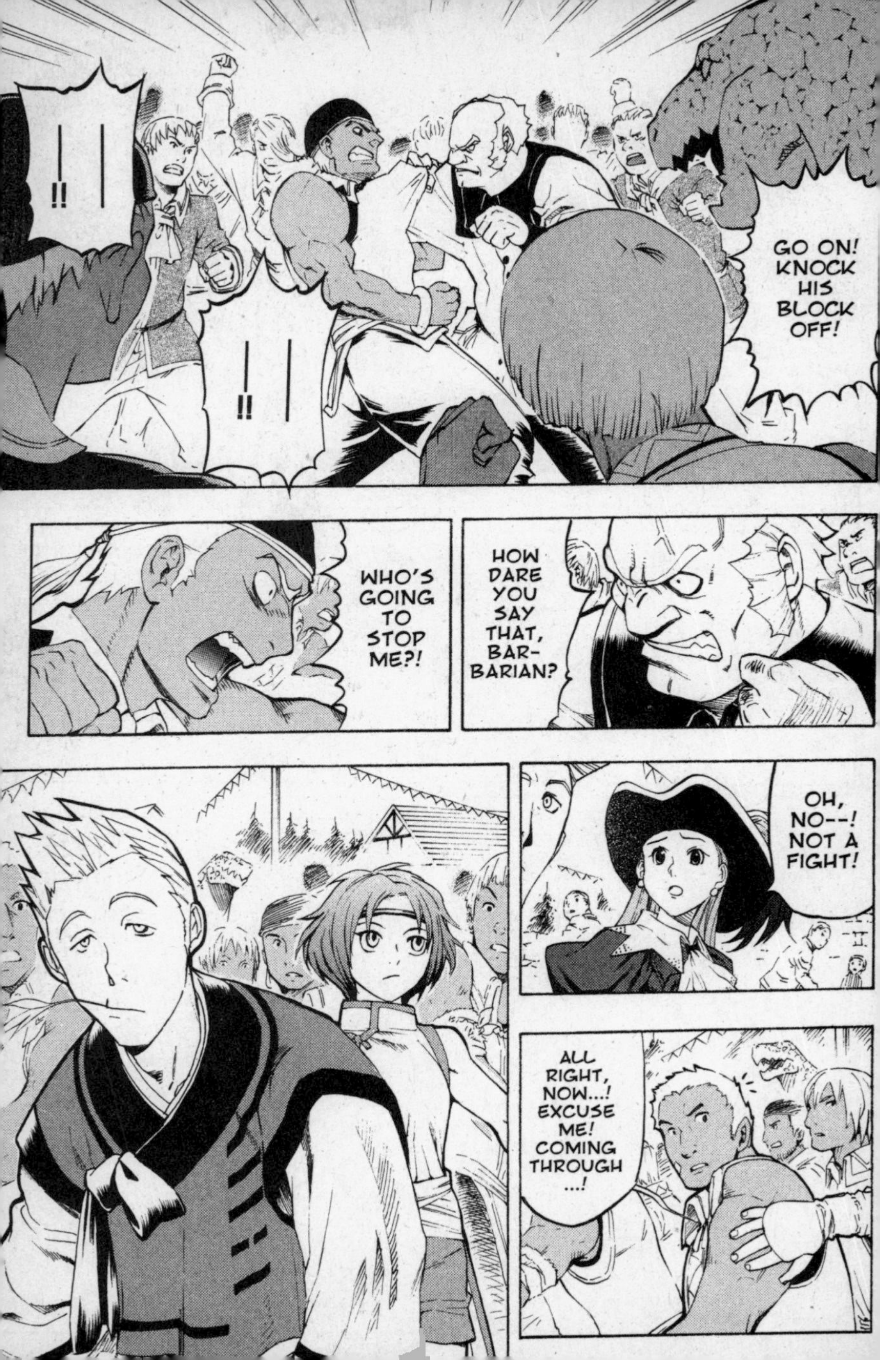
GO ON! KNOCK HIS BLOCK OFF!
!!
!!
HOW DARE YOU SAY THAT, BAR-BARIAN?
WHO'S GOING TO STOP ME?!
OH, NO--! NOT A FIGHT!
ALL RIGHT, NOW...! EXCUSE ME! COMING THROUGH ...!

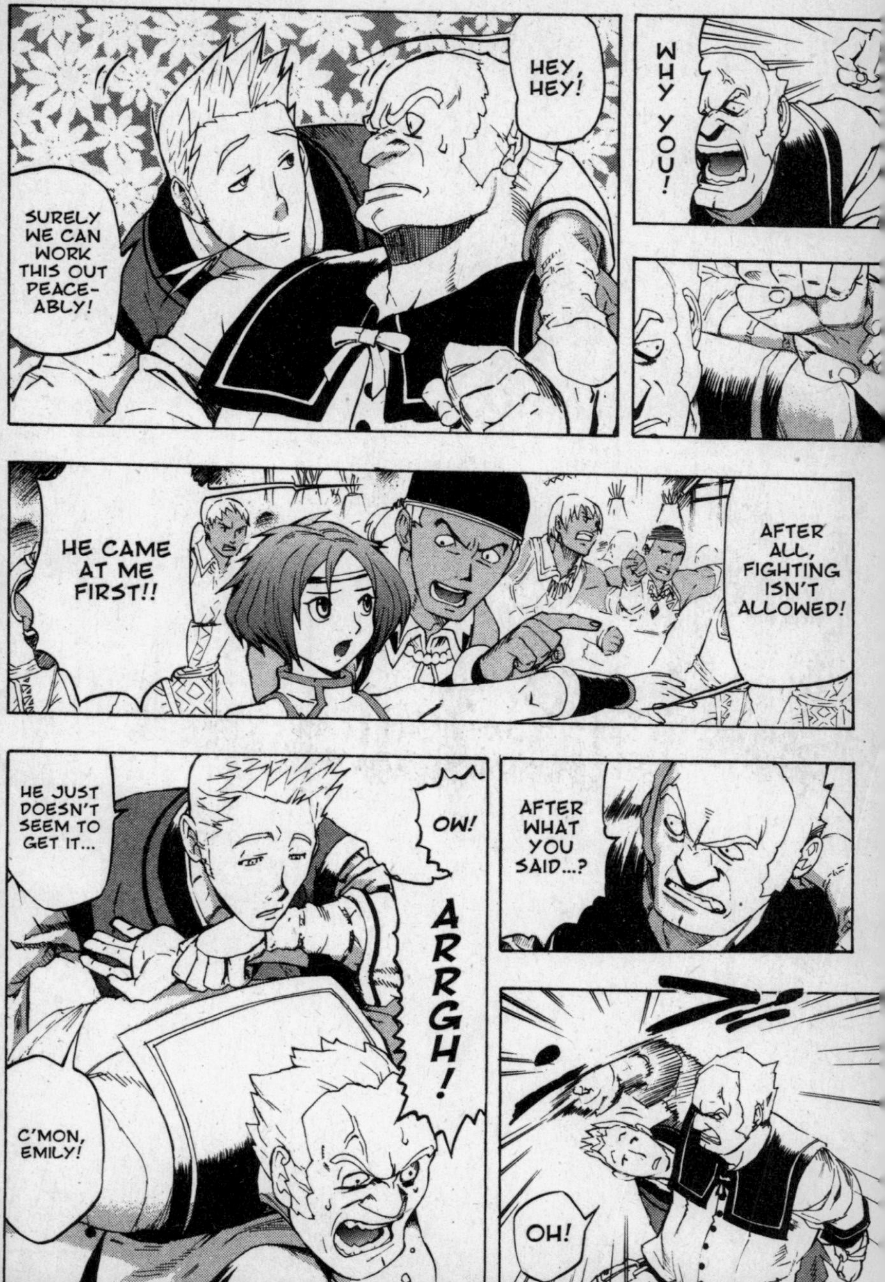
WHY YOU!
HEY, HEY!
SURELY WE CAN WORK THIS OUT PEACE-ABLY!
AFTER ALL, FIGHTING ISN'T ALLOWED!
HE CAME AT ME FIRST!!
AFTER WHAT YOU SAID...?
OH!
OW!
ARRGH!
HE JUST DOESN'T SEEM TO GET IT...
C'MON, EMILY!

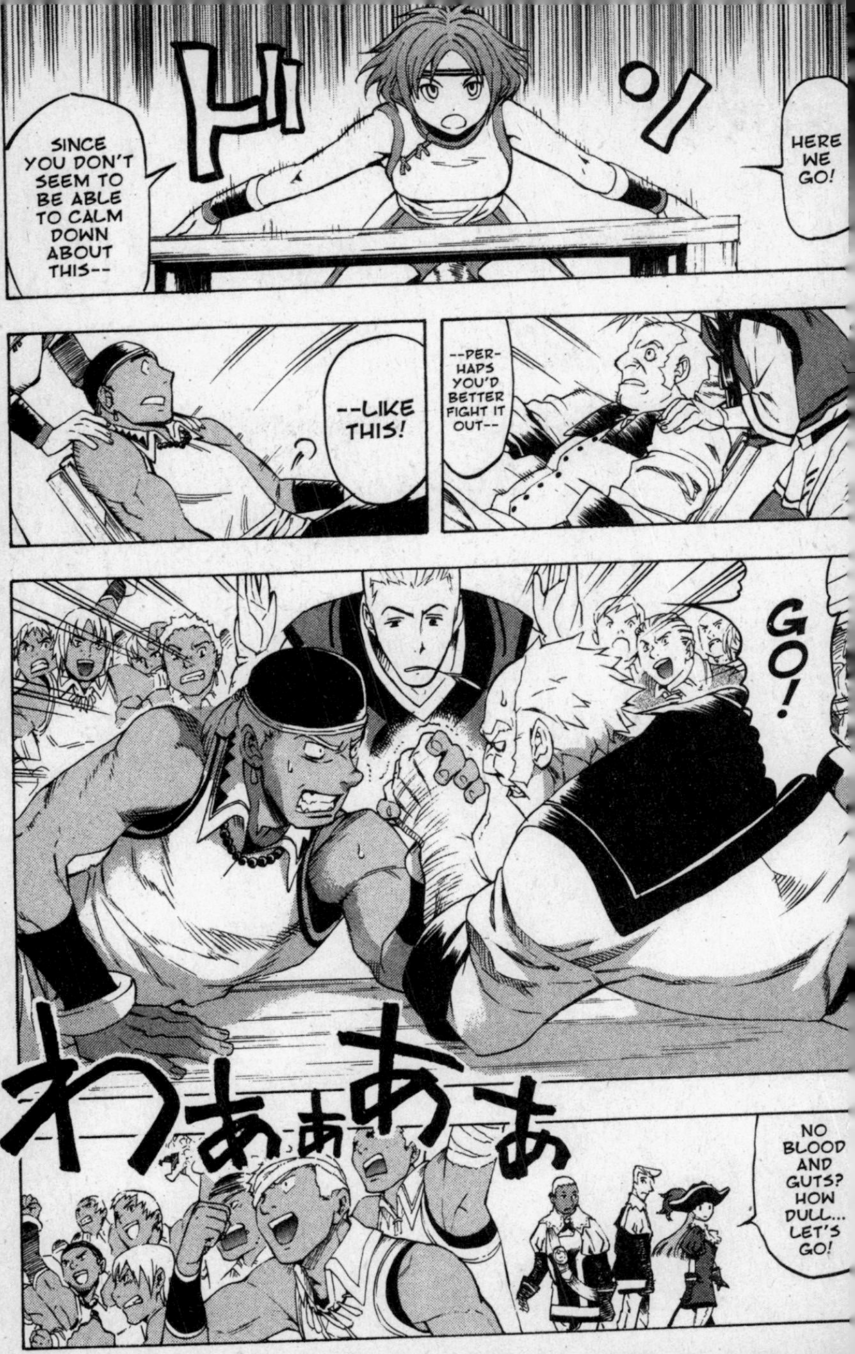

HERE WE GO!
SINCE YOU DON'T SEEM TO BE ABLE TO CALM DOWN ABOUT THIS--
--PER-HAPS YOU'D BETTER FIGHT IT OUT--
--LIKE THIS!
GO!
わあぁああ
NO BLOOD AND GUTS? HOW DULL... LET'S GO!

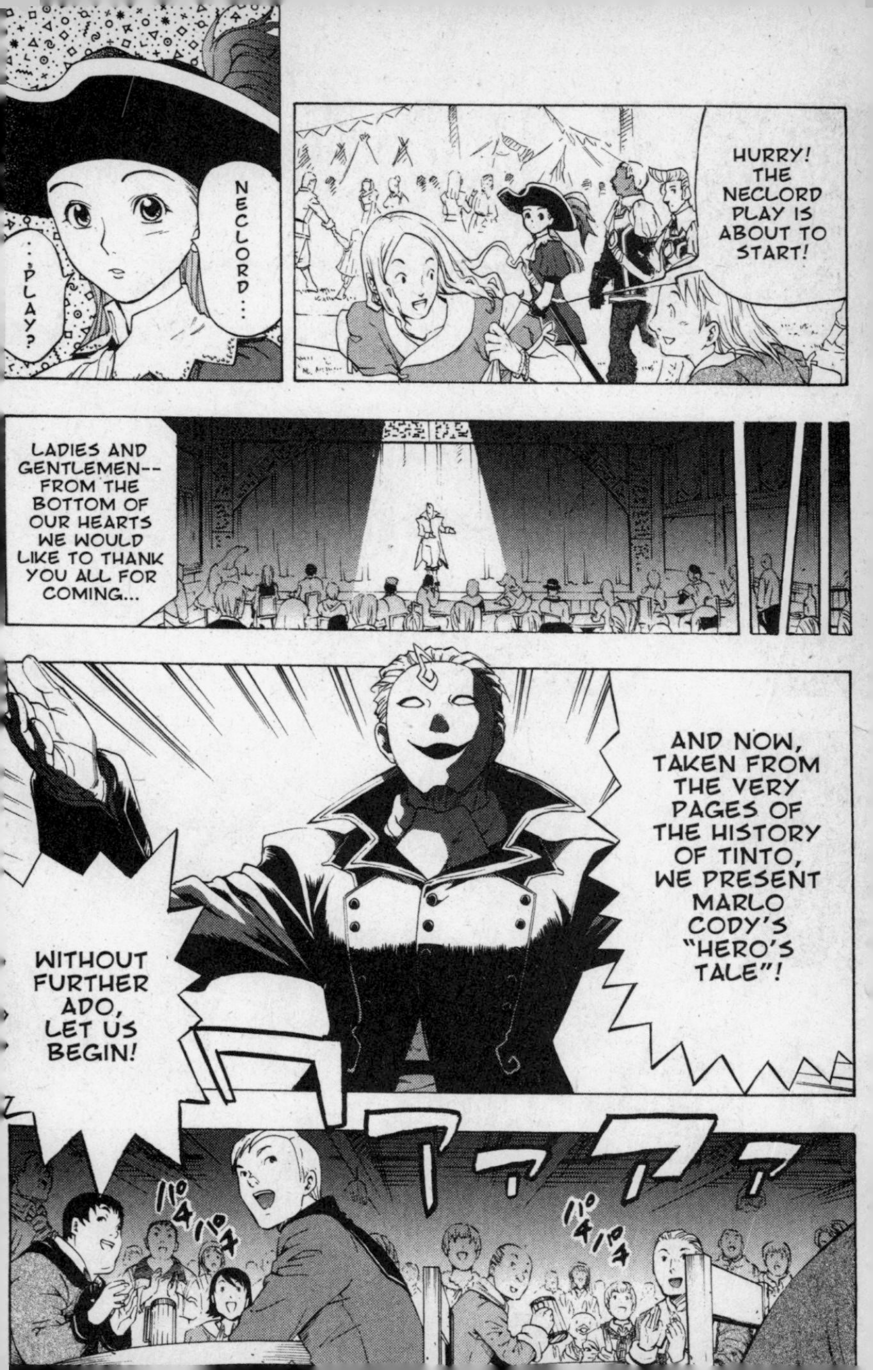
HURRY! THE NECLORD PLAY IS ABOUT TO START!
NECLORD...
...PLAY?
LADIES AND GENTLEMEN-- FROM THE BOTTOM OF OUR HEARTS WE WOULD LIKE TO THANK YOU ALL FOR COMING...
AND NOW, TAKEN FROM THE VERY PAGES OF THE HISTORY OF TINTO, WE PRESENT MARLO CODY'S "HERO'S TALE"!
WITHOUT FURTHER ADO, LET US BEGIN!
ワァァァ
パチパチ
パチパチ

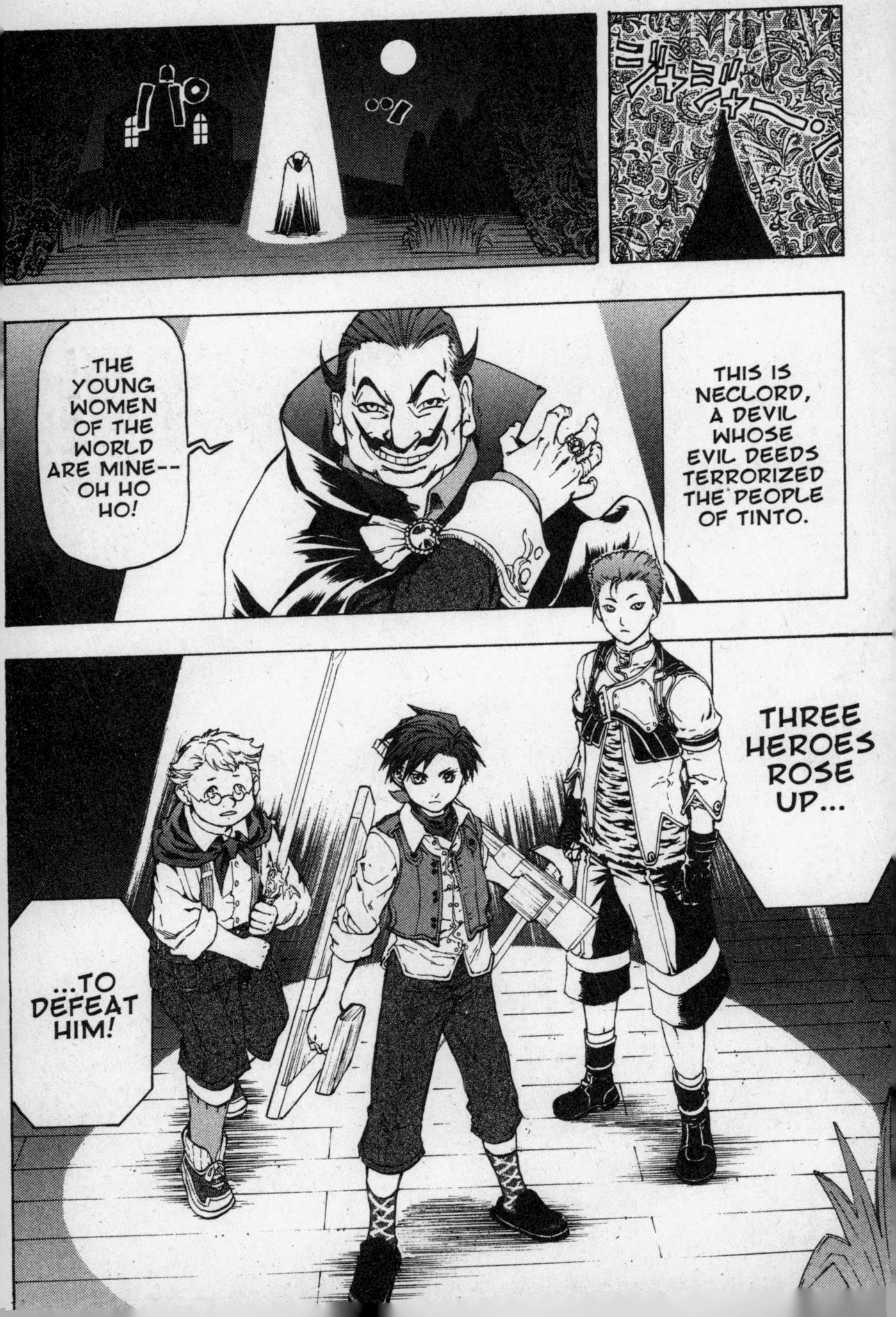
THIS IS NECLORD, A DEVIL WHOSE EVIL DEEDS TERRORIZED THE PEOPLE OF TINTO.
-THE YOUNG WOMEN OF THE WORLD ARE MINE-- OH HO HO!
THREE HEROES ROSE UP...
...TO DEFEAT HIM!

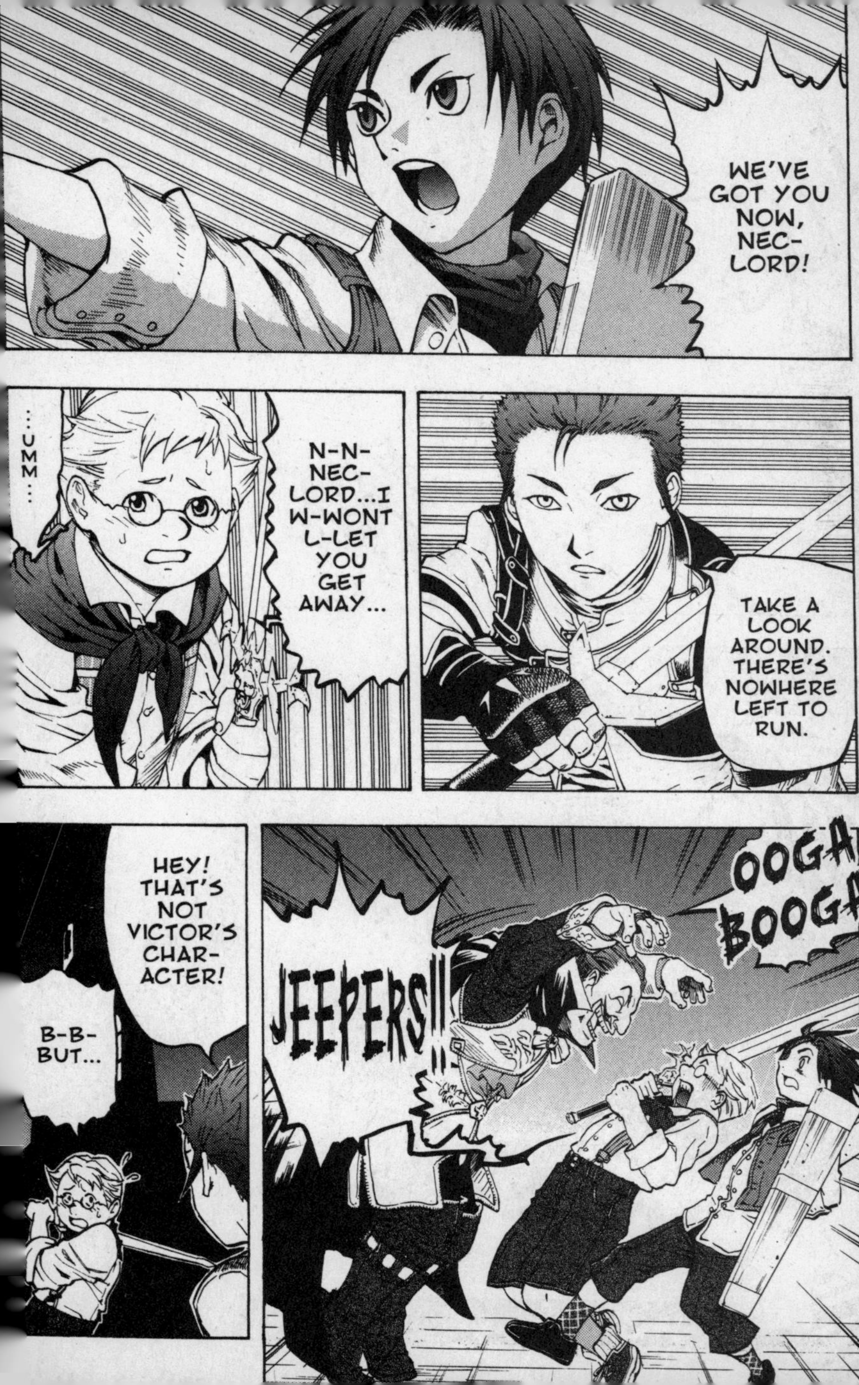
WE'VE GOT YOU NOW, NEC-LORD!
TAKE A LOOK AROUND. THERE'S NOWHERE LEFT TO RUN.
N-N-NEC-LORD...I W-WONT L-LET YOU GET AWAY...
...UMM...
OOGA BOOGA!
JEEPERS!!
HEY! THAT'S NOT VICTOR'S CHAR-ACTER!
B-B-BUT...

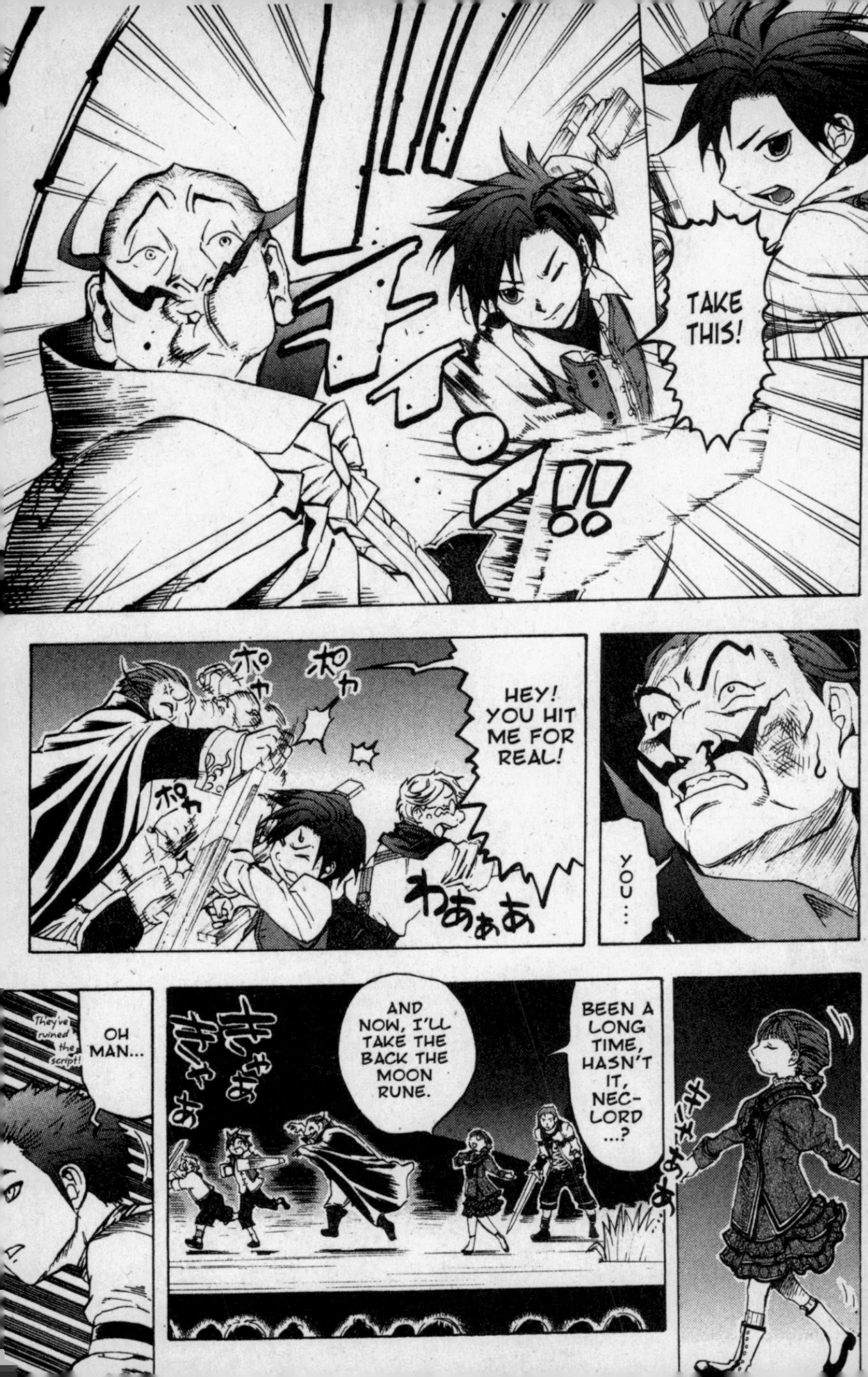
TAKE THIS!
!!
YOU...
HEY! YOU HIT ME FOR REAL!
ポカ
ポカ
ポカ
わあぁあ
BEEN A LONG TIME, HASN'T IT, NEC-LORD...?
AND NOW, I'LL TAKE THE BACK THE MOON RUNE.
OH MAN...
They've ruined the script!

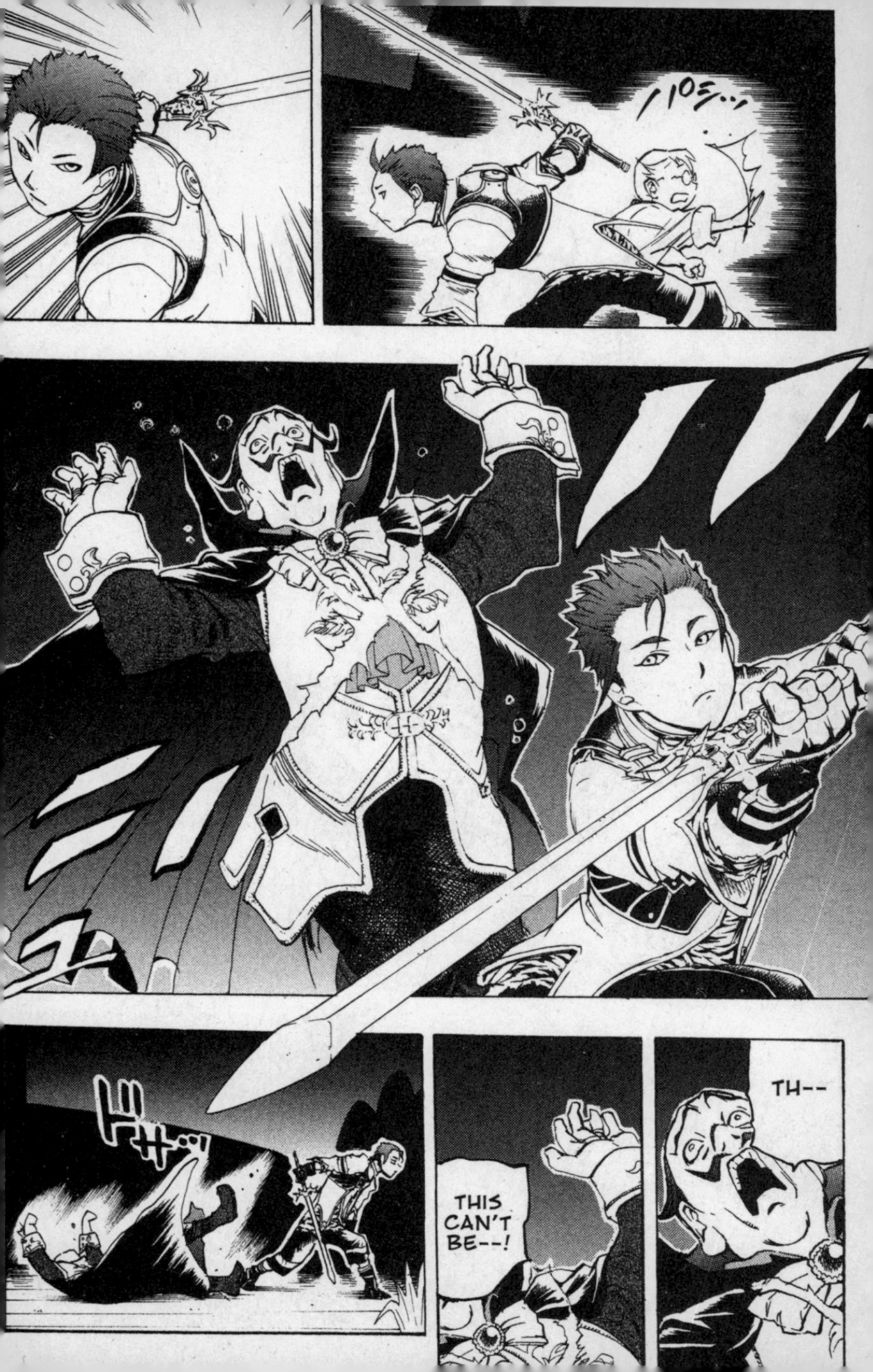
TH--
THIS CAN'T BE--!

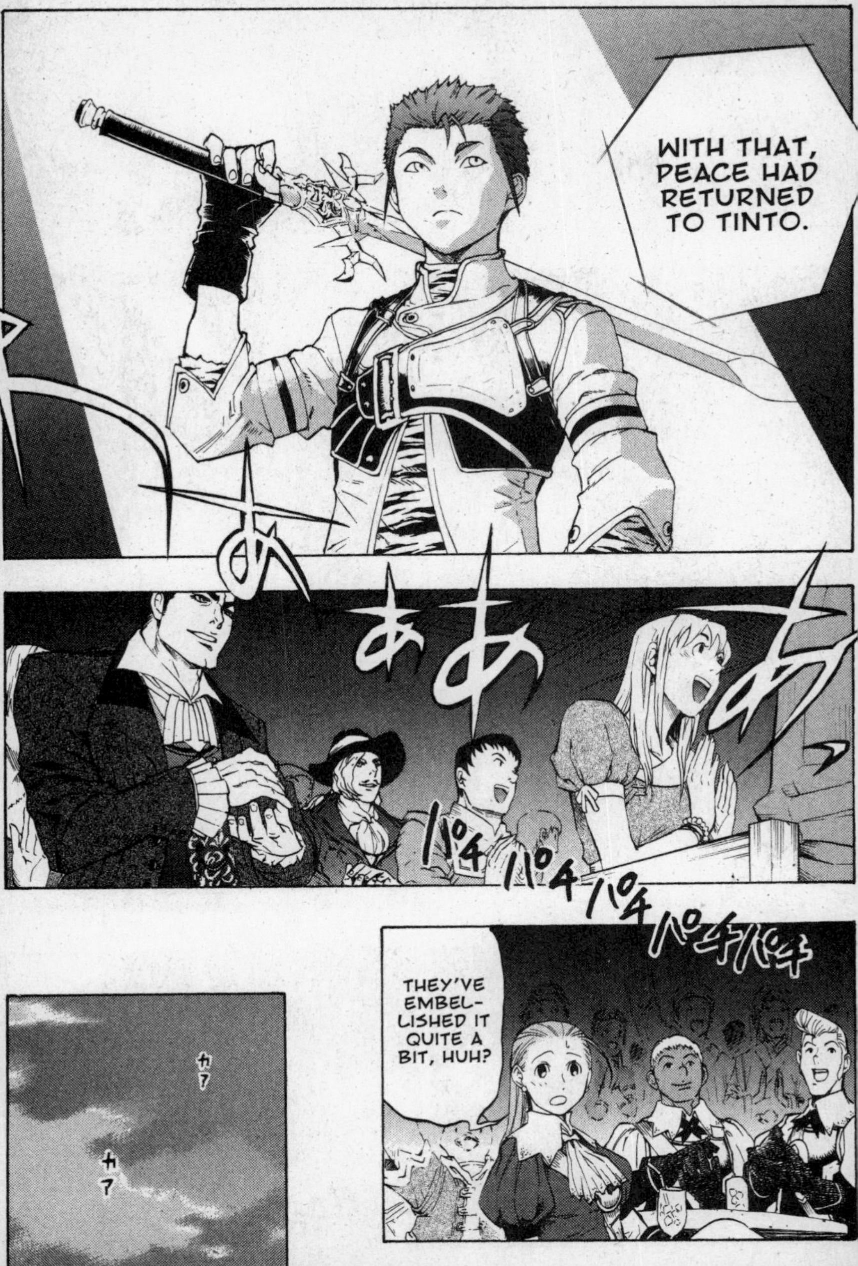
WITH THAT, PEACE HAD RETURNED TO TINTO.
THEY'VE EMBEL-LISHED IT QUITE A BIT, HUH?
カァ
カァ

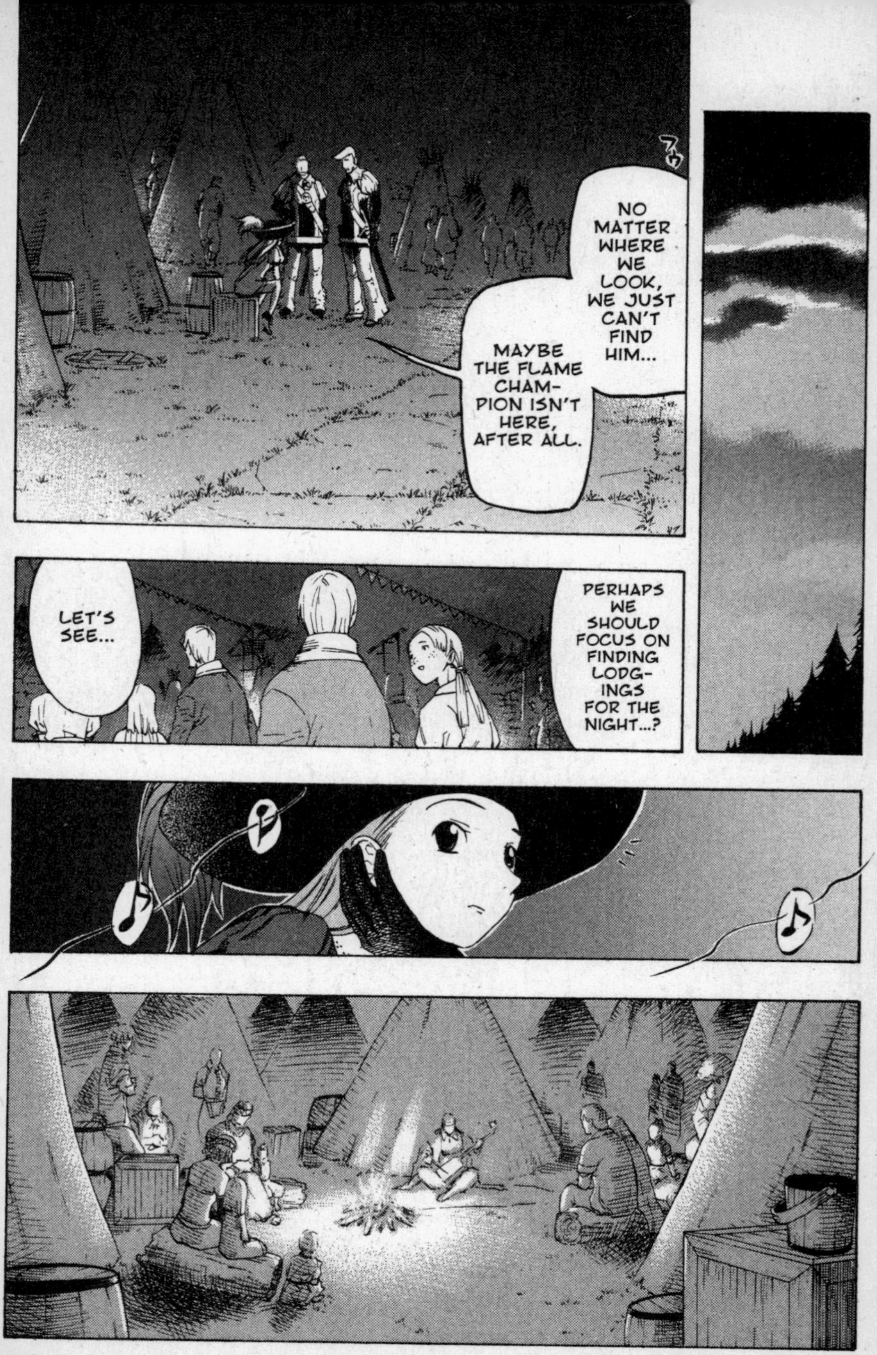

フゥ
NO MATTER WHERE WE LOOK, WE JUST CAN'T FIND HIM...
MAYBE THE FLAME CHAMPION ISN'T HERE, AFTER ALL.
PERHAPS WE SHOULD FOCUS ON FINDING LODGINGS FOR THE NIGHT...?
LET'S SEE...

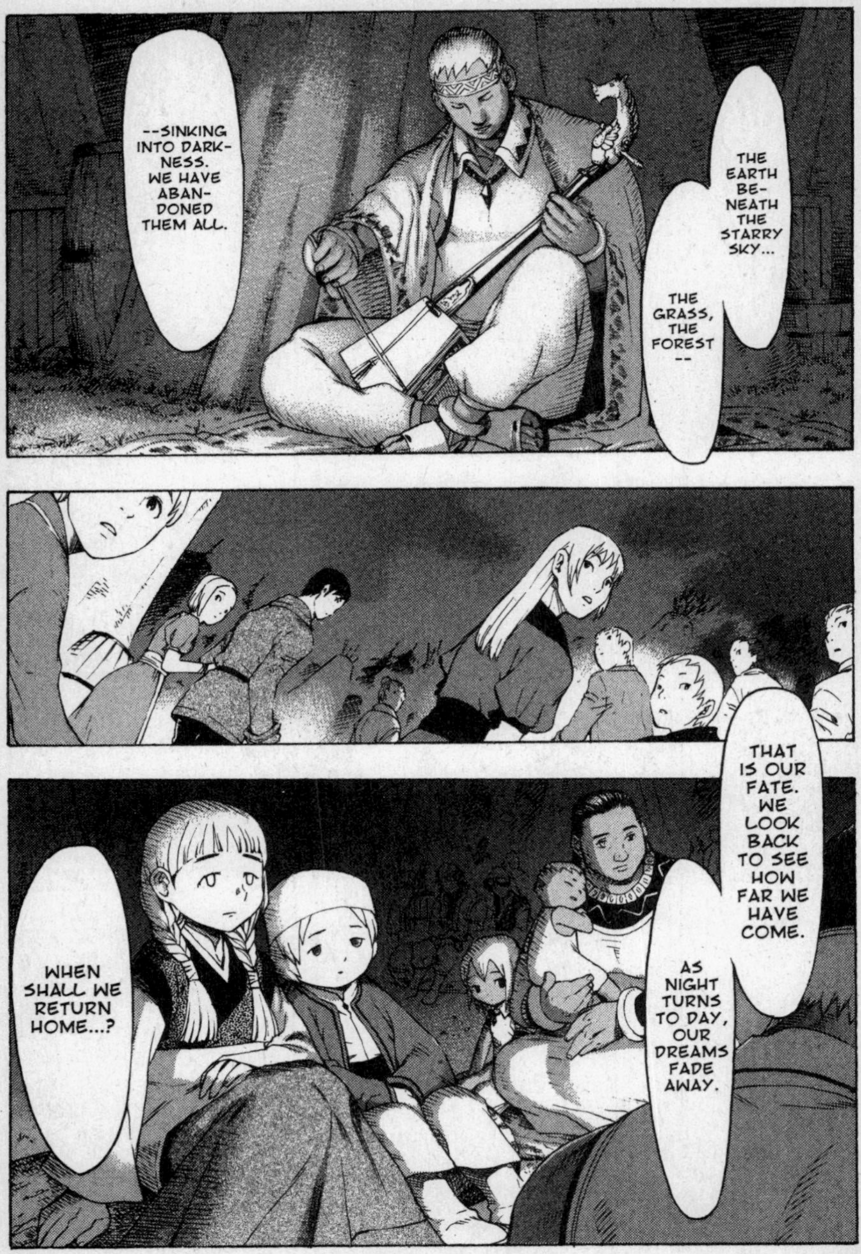
THE EARTH BENEATH THE STARRY SKY...
THE GRASS, THE FOREST --
--SINKING INTO DARKNESS. WE HAVE ABANDONED THEM ALL.
THAT IS OUR FATE. WE LOOK BACK TO SEE HOW FAR WE HAVE COME.
AS NIGHT TURNS TO DAY, OUR DREAMS FADE AWAY.
WHEN SHALL WE RETURN HOME...?

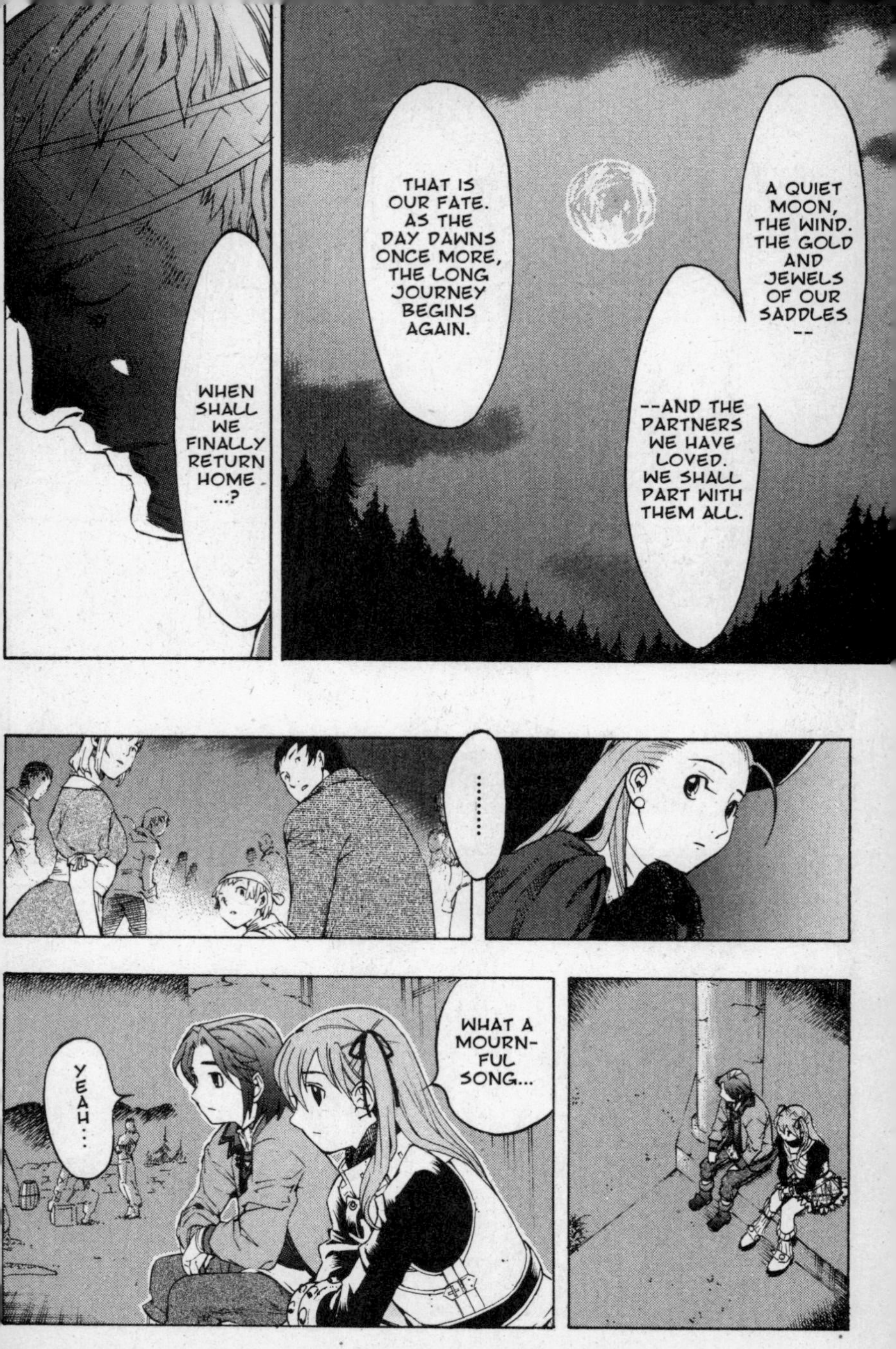
A QUIET MOON, THE WIND. THE GOLD AND JEWELS OF OUR SADDLES --
--AND THE PARTNERS WE HAVE LOVED. WE SHALL PART WITH THEM ALL.
THAT IS OUR FATE. AS THE DAY DAWNS ONCE MORE, THE LONG JOURNEY BEGINS AGAIN.
WHEN SHALL WE FINALLY RETURN HOME ...?
......
WHAT A MOURNFUL SONG...
YEAH...

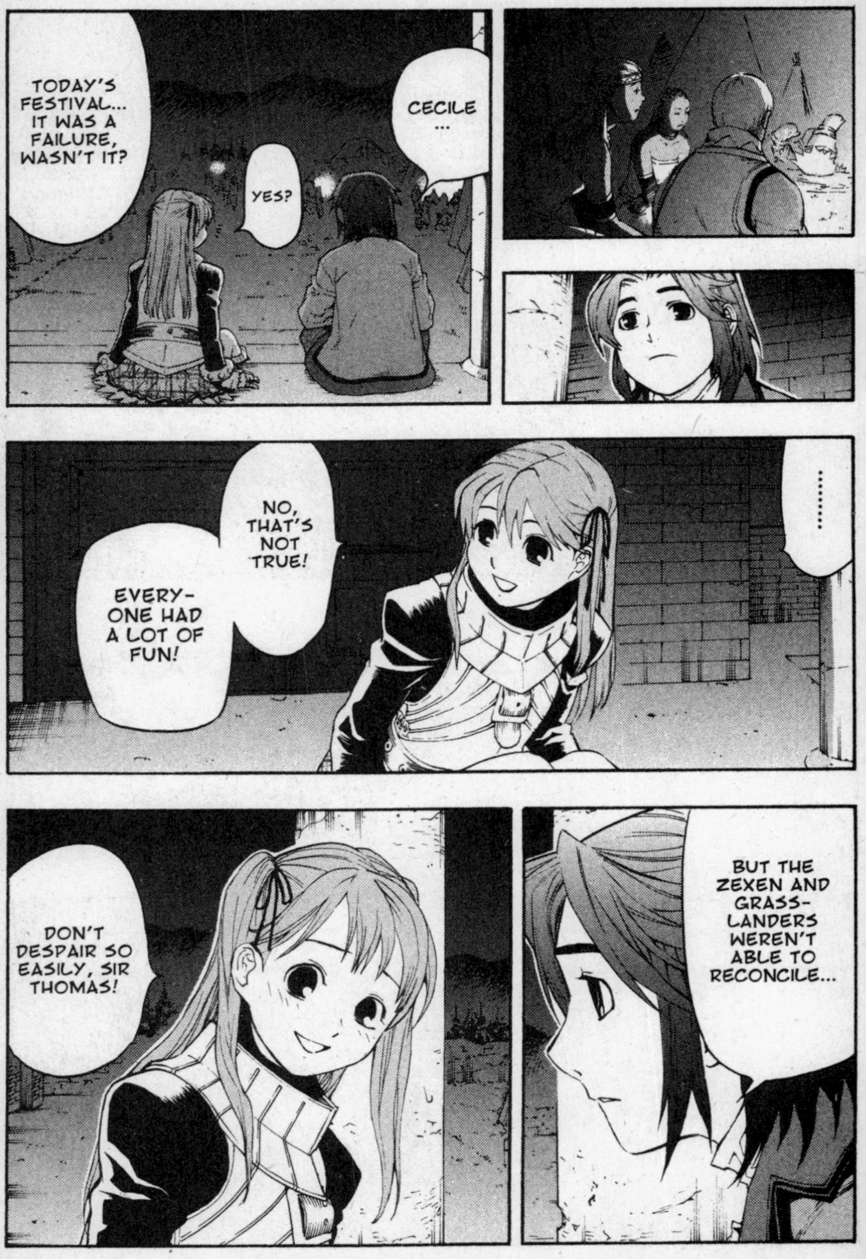
CECILE ...
YES?
TODAY'S FESTIVAL... IT WAS A FAILURE, WASN'T IT?
......
NO, THAT'S NOT TRUE!
EVERY-ONE HAD A LOT OF FUN!
BUT THE ZEXEN AND GRASS-LANDERS WEREN'T ABLE TO RECONCILE...
DON'T DESPAIR SO EASILY, SIR THOMAS!

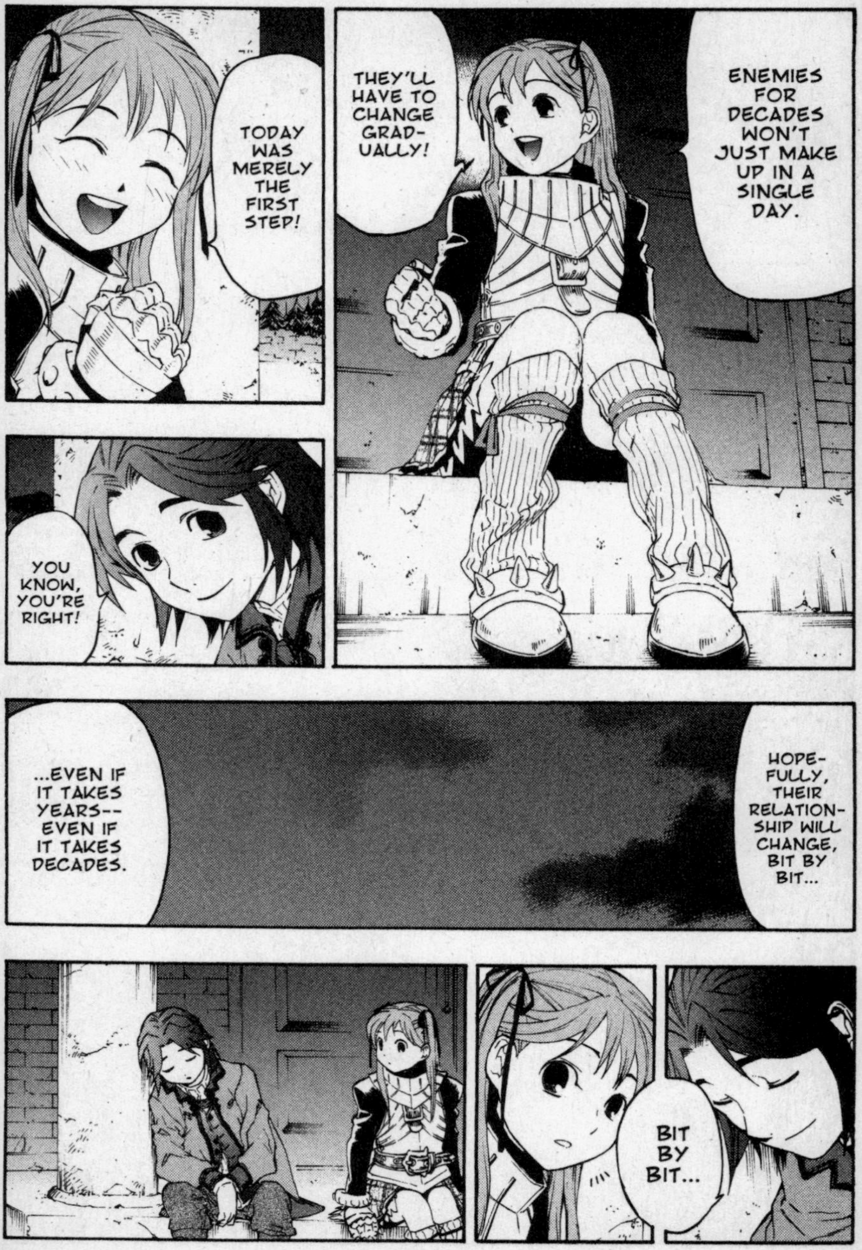
ENEMIES FOR DECADES WON'T JUST MAKE UP IN A SINGLE DAY.
THEY'LL HAVE TO CHANGE GRAD-UALLY!
TODAY WAS MERELY THE FIRST STEP!
YOU KNOW, YOU'RE RIGHT!
HOPE-FULLY, THEIR RELATION-SHIP WILL CHANGE, BIT BY BIT...
...EVEN IF IT TAKES YEARS--EVEN IF IT TAKES DECADES.
BIT BY BIT...

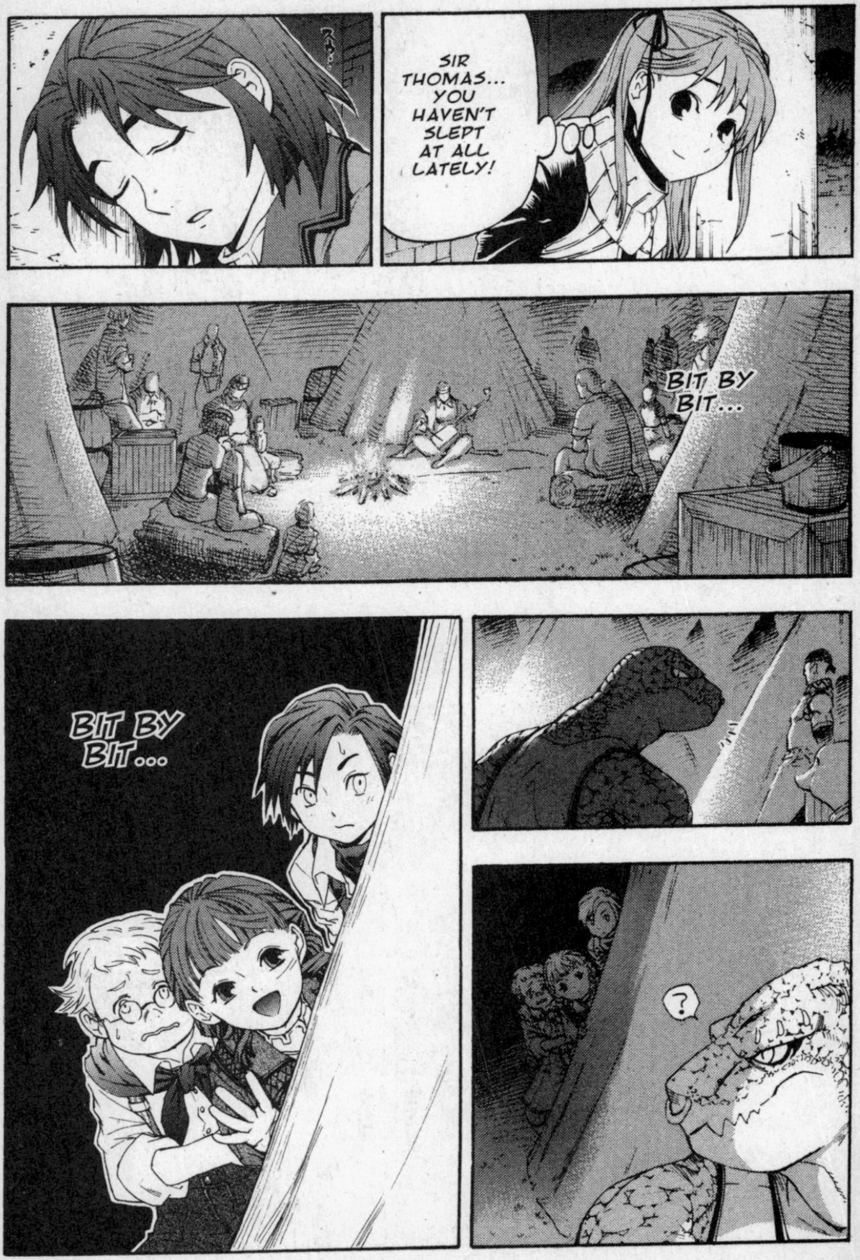
SIR THOMAS... YOU HAVEN'T SLEPT AT ALL LATELY!
BIT BY BIT...
?
BIT BY BIT...

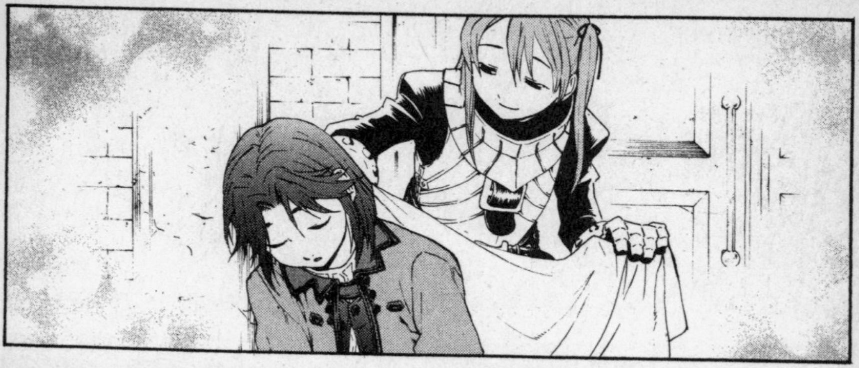
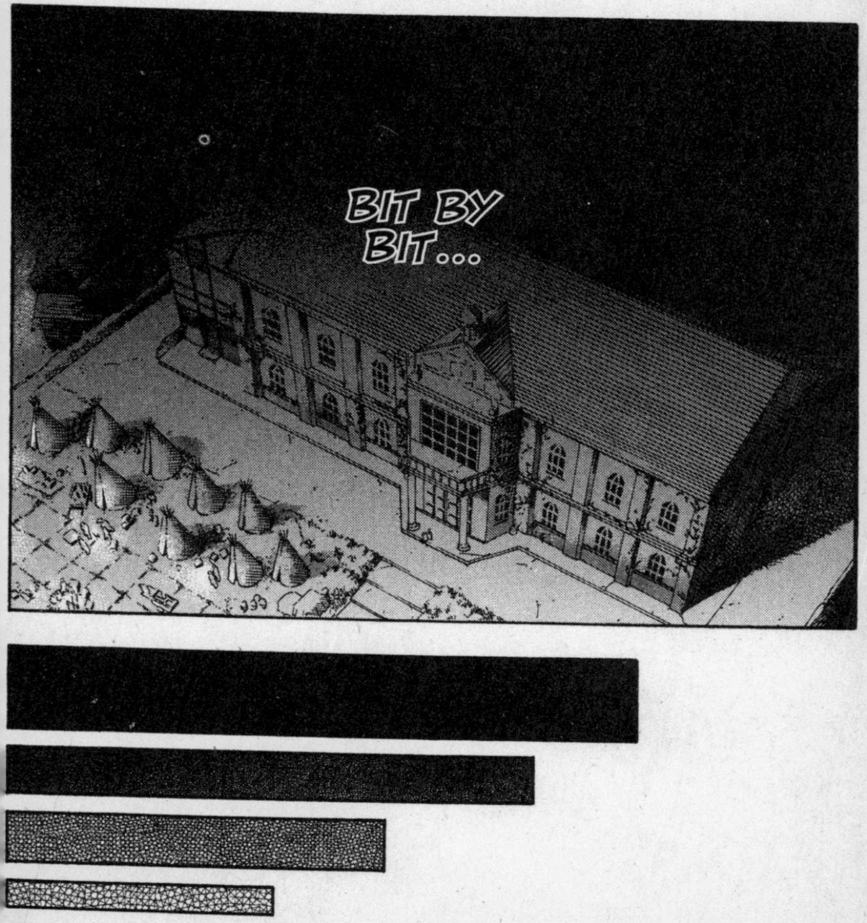
BIT BY BIT...

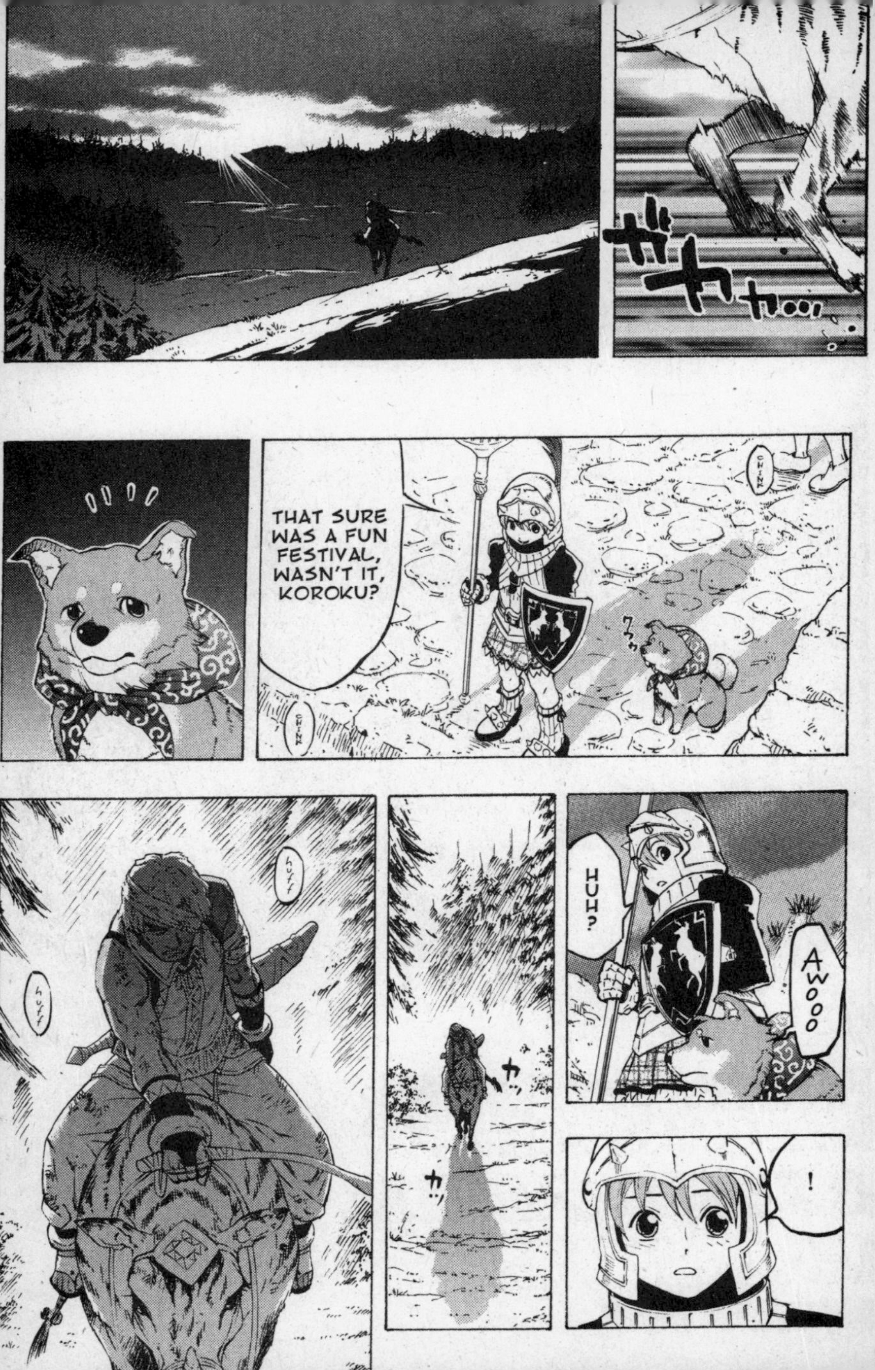

CHINK
THAT SURE WAS A FUN FESTIVAL, WASN'T IT, KOROKU?
CHINK
HUH?
AWOOO
!
HUFF
HUFF

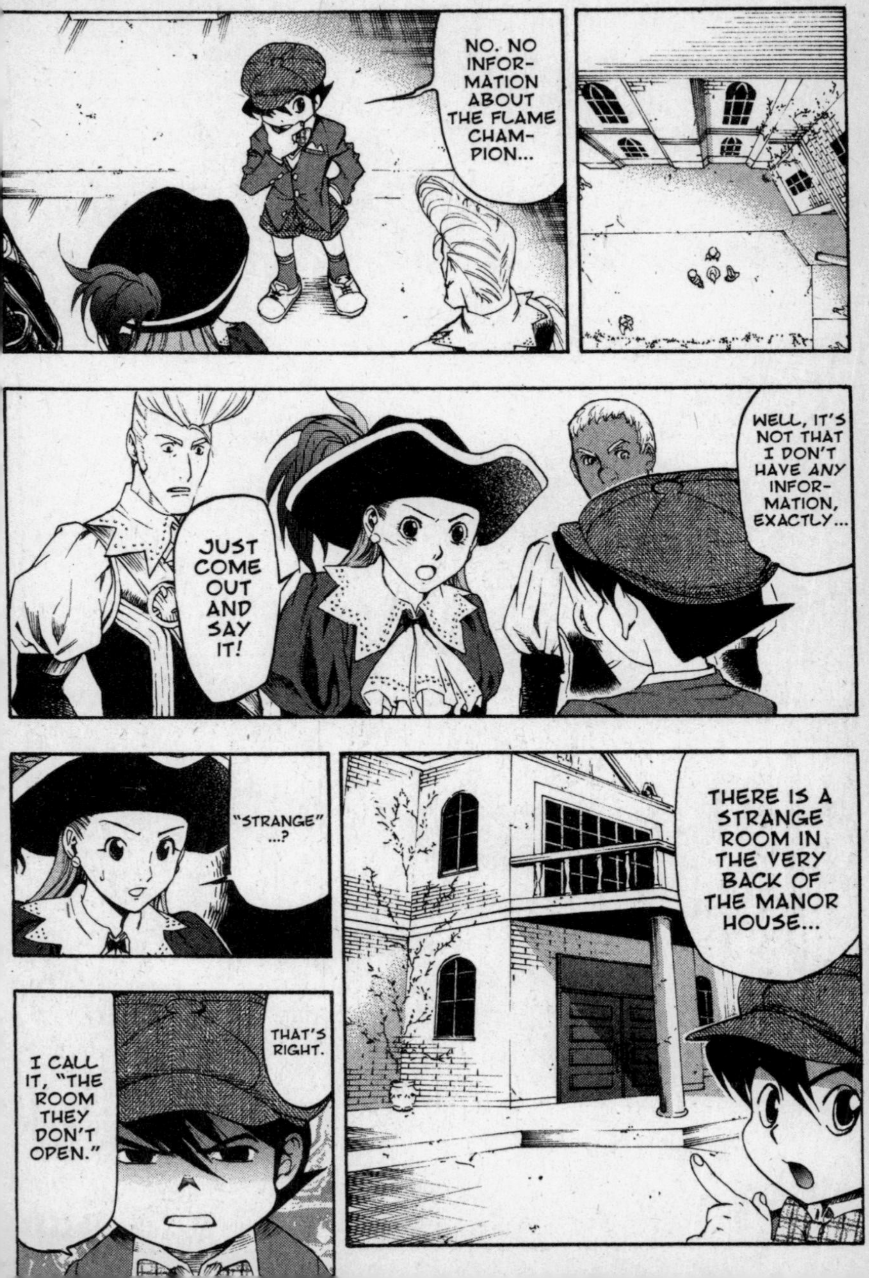
NO. NO INFORMATION ABOUT THE FLAME CHAMPION...
WELL, IT'S NOT THAT I DON'T HAVE ANY INFORMATION, EXACTLY...
JUST COME OUT AND SAY IT!
THERE IS A STRANGE ROOM IN THE VERY BACK OF THE MANOR HOUSE...
"STRANGE" ...?
THAT'S RIGHT.
I CALL IT, "THE ROOM THEY DON'T OPEN."

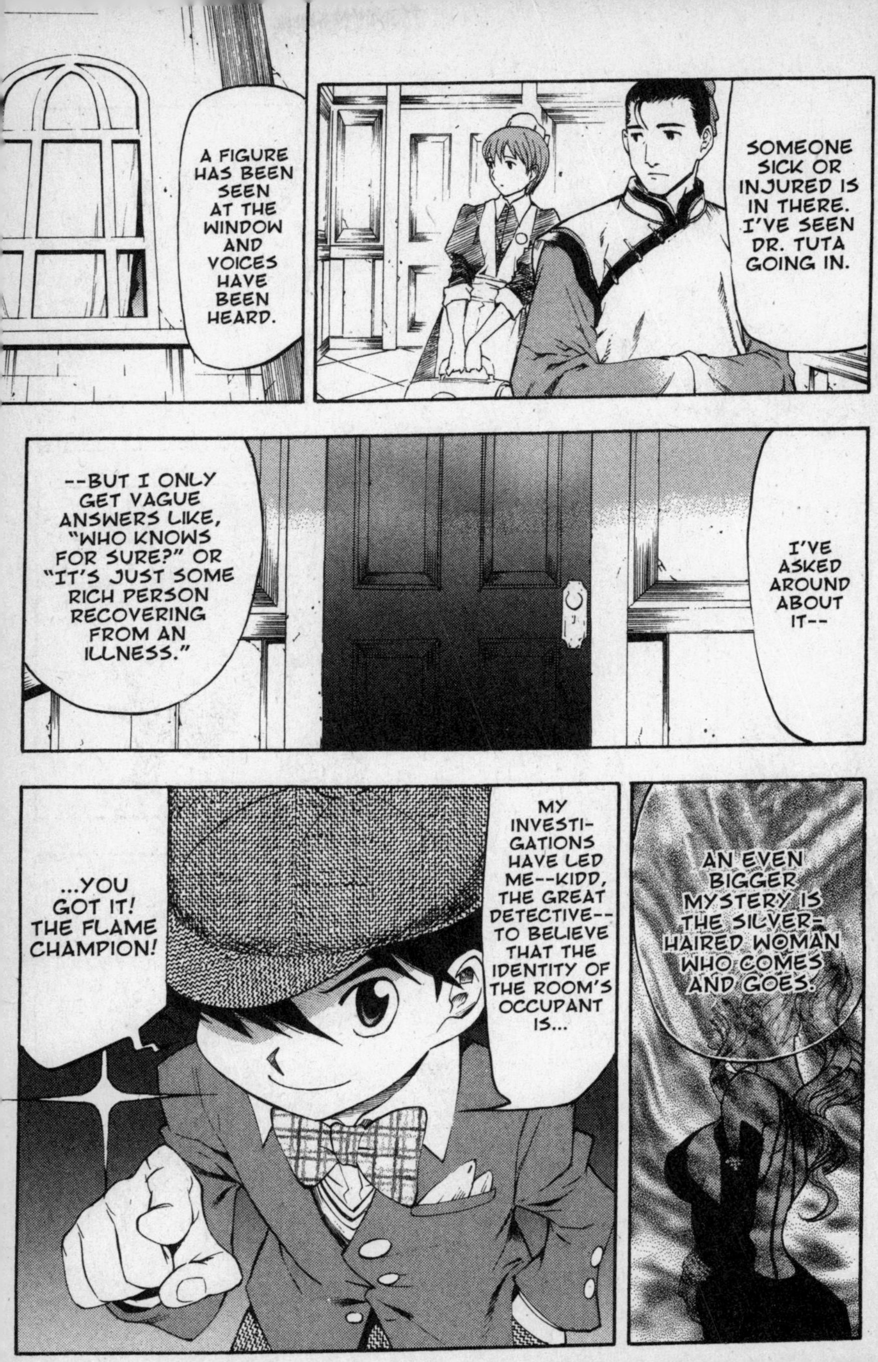
SOMEONE SICK OR INJURED IS IN THERE. I'VE SEEN DR. TUTA GOING IN.
A FIGURE HAS BEEN SEEN AT THE WINDOW AND VOICES HAVE BEEN HEARD.
I'VE ASKED AROUND ABOUT IT--
--BUT I ONLY GET VAGUE ANSWERS LIKE, "WHO KNOWS FOR SURE?" OR "IT'S JUST SOME RICH PERSON RECOVERING FROM AN ILLNESS."
AN EVEN BIGGER MYSTERY IS THE SILVER-HAIRED WOMAN WHO COMES AND GOES.
MY INVESTIGATIONS HAVE LED ME--KIDD, THE GREAT DETECTIVE--TO BELIEVE THAT THE IDENTITY OF THE ROOM'S OCCUPANT IS...
...YOU GOT IT! THE FLAME CHAMPION!

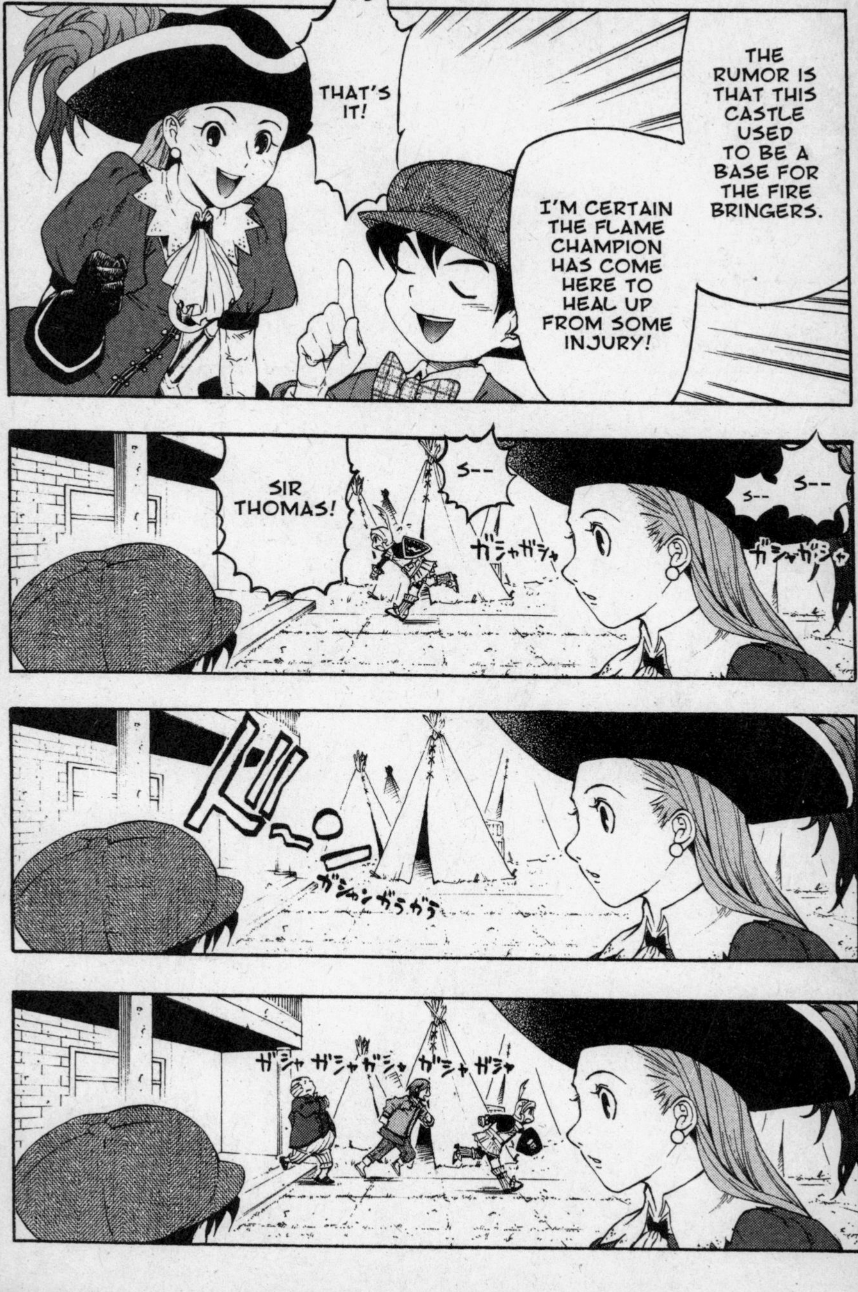
THE RUMOR IS THAT THIS CASTLE USED TO BE A BASE FOR THE FIRE BRINGERS.
I'M CERTAIN THE FLAME CHAMPION HAS COME HERE TO HEAL UP FROM SOME INJURY!
THAT'S IT!
S-- S--
ガシャガシャ
S--
SIR THOMAS!
ガシャガシャ
ガシャンガラガラ
ガシャ ガシャガシャ ガシャ ガシャ

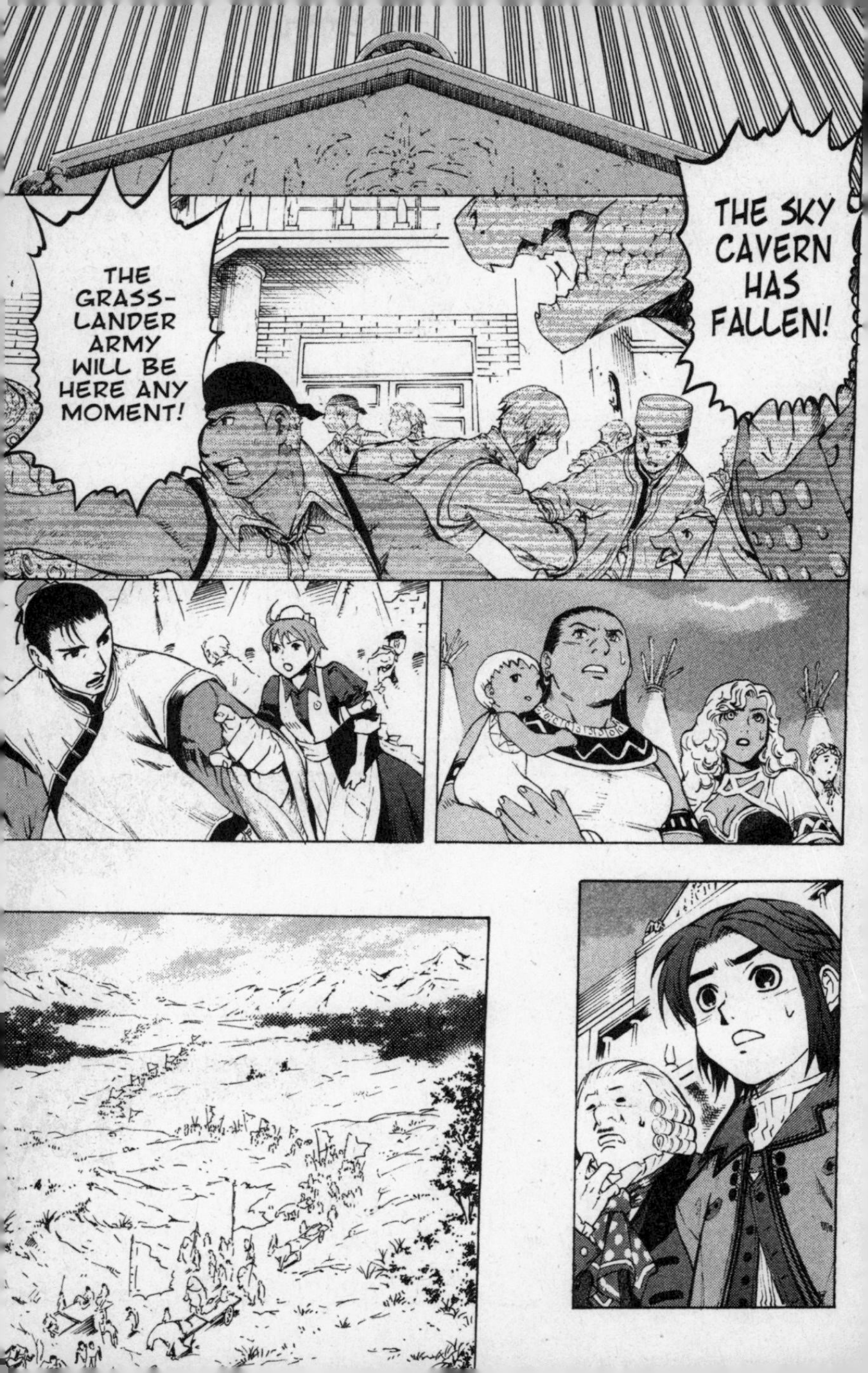
THE SKY CAVERN HAS FALLEN!
THE GRASS-LANDER ARMY WILL BE HERE ANY MOMENT!

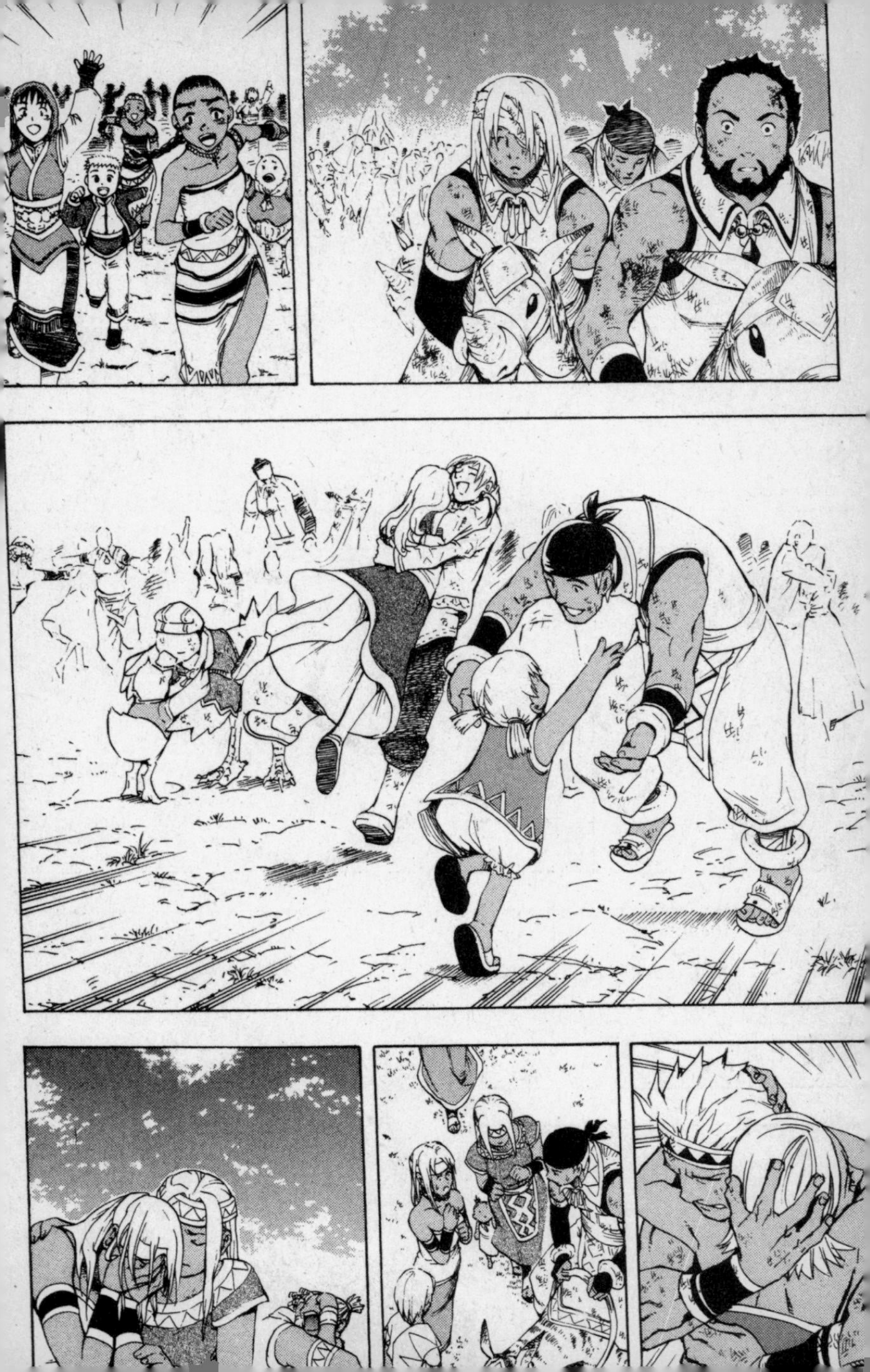

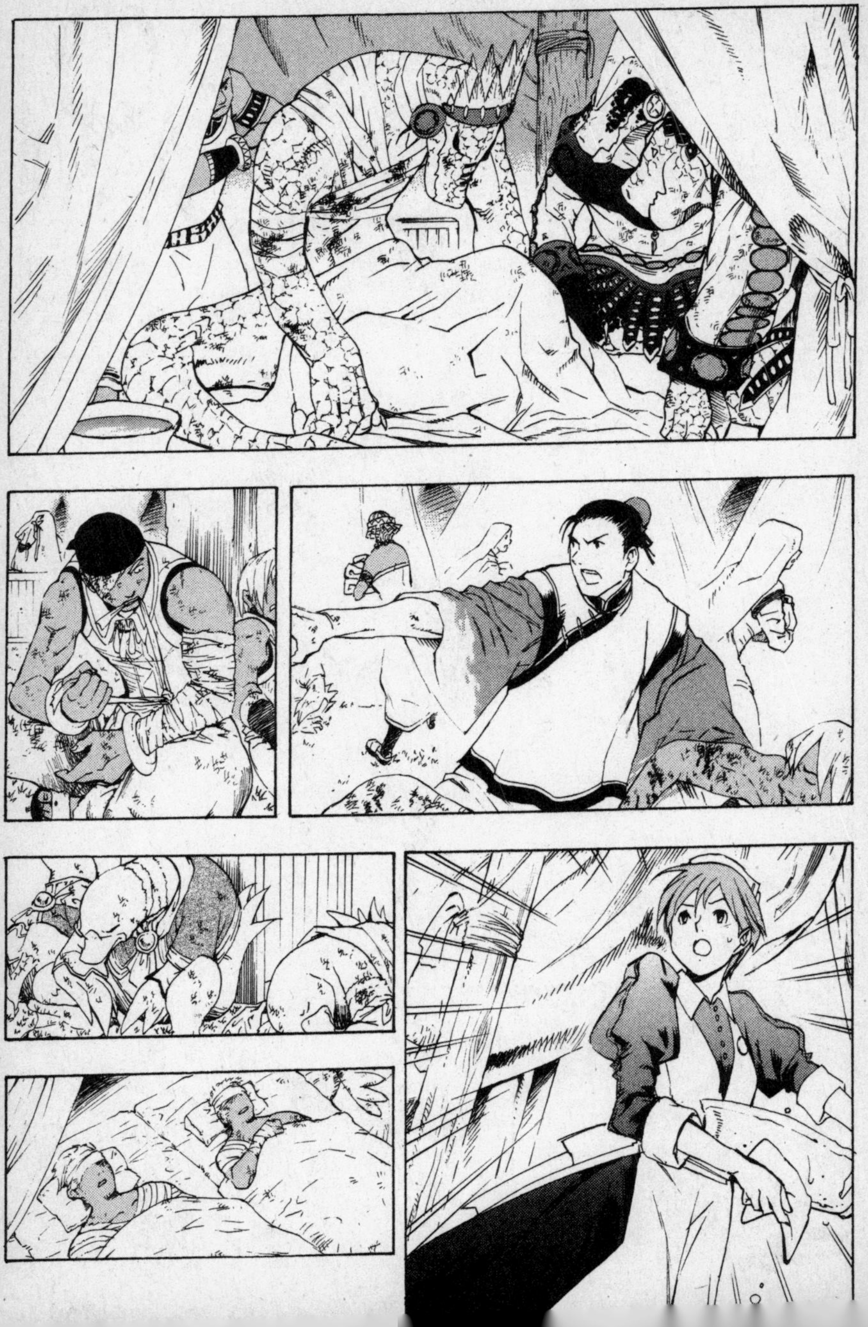

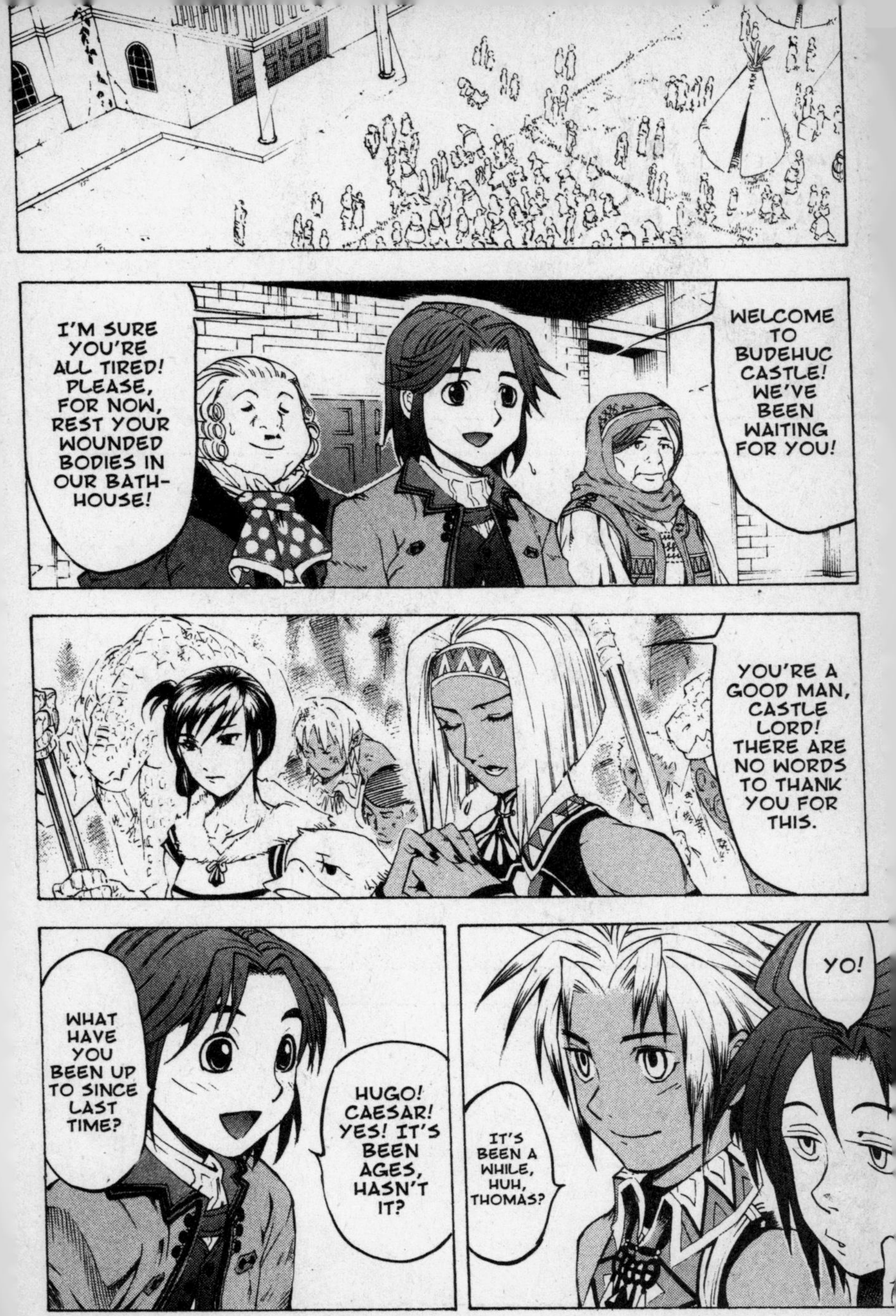
WELCOME TO BUDEHUC CASTLE! WE'VE BEEN WAITING FOR YOU!
I'M SURE YOU'RE ALL TIRED! PLEASE, FOR NOW, REST YOUR WOUNDED BODIES IN OUR BATH-HOUSE!
YOU'RE A GOOD MAN, CASTLE LORD! THERE ARE NO WORDS TO THANK YOU FOR THIS.
YO!
IT'S BEEN A WHILE, HUH, THOMAS?
HUGO! CAESAR! YES! IT'S BEEN AGES, HASN'T IT?
WHAT HAVE YOU BEEN UP TO SINCE LAST TIME?

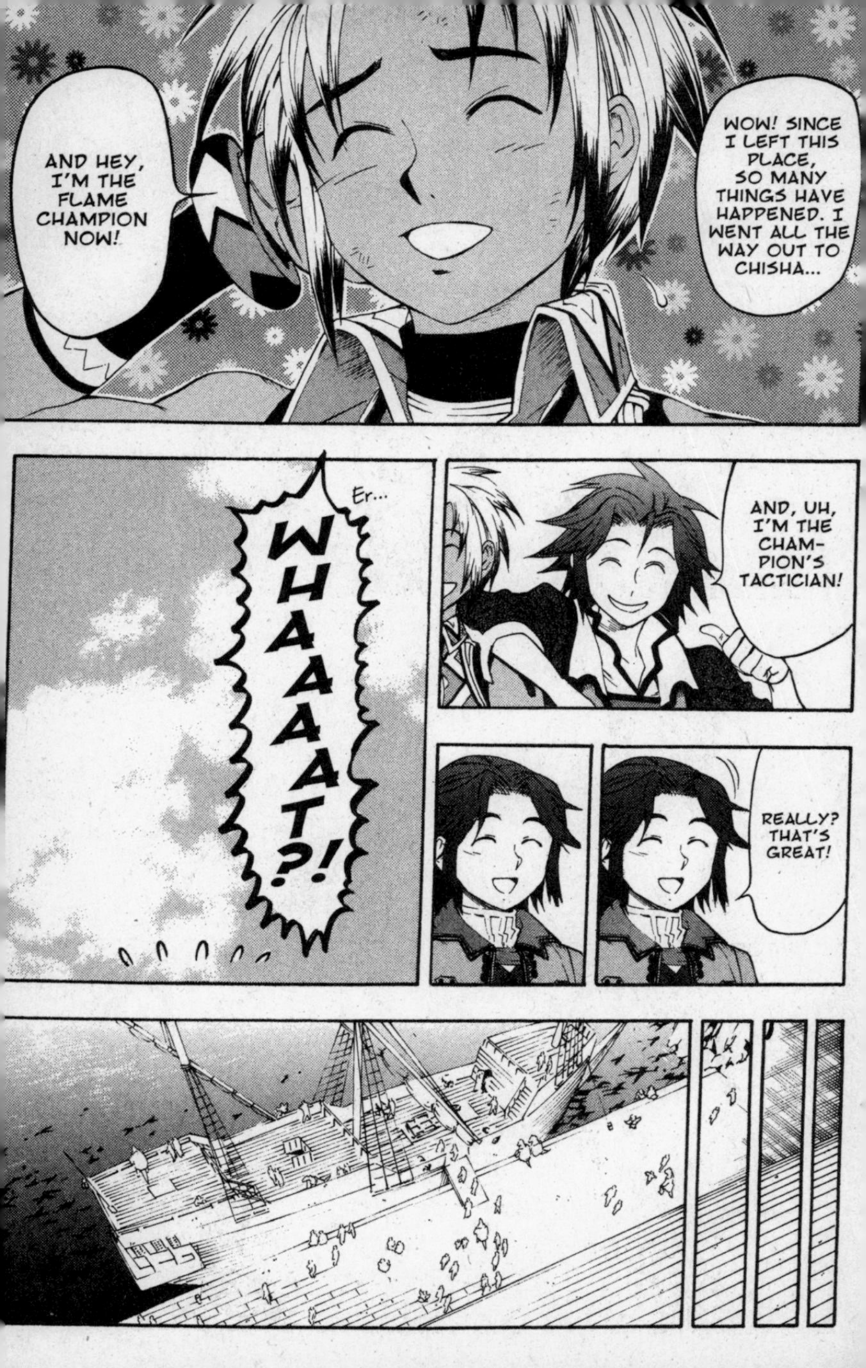
WOW! SINCE I LEFT THIS PLACE, SO MANY THINGS HAVE HAPPENED. I WENT ALL THE WAY OUT TO CHISHA...
AND HEY, I'M THE FLAME CHAMPION NOW!
AND, UH, I'M THE CHAMPION'S TACTICIAN!
REALLY? THAT'S GREAT!
Er...
WHAAAAT?!

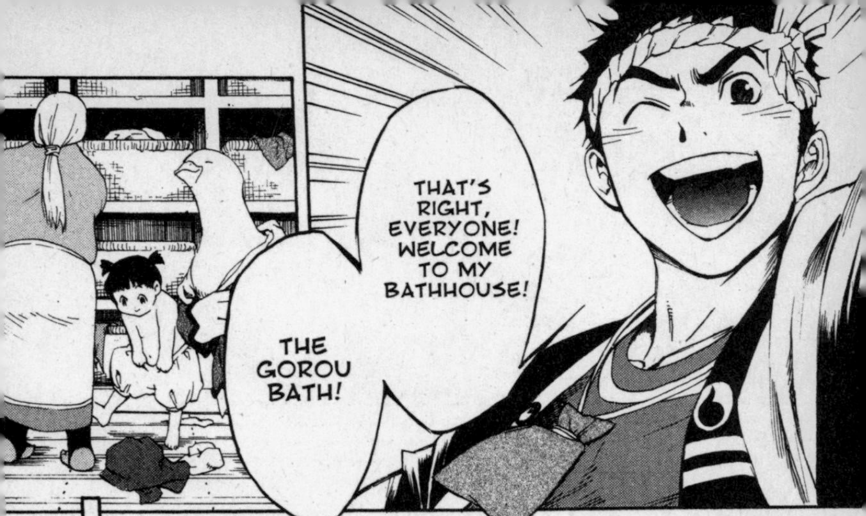
THAT'S RIGHT, EVERYONE! WELCOME TO MY BATHHOUSE!
THE GOROU BATH!
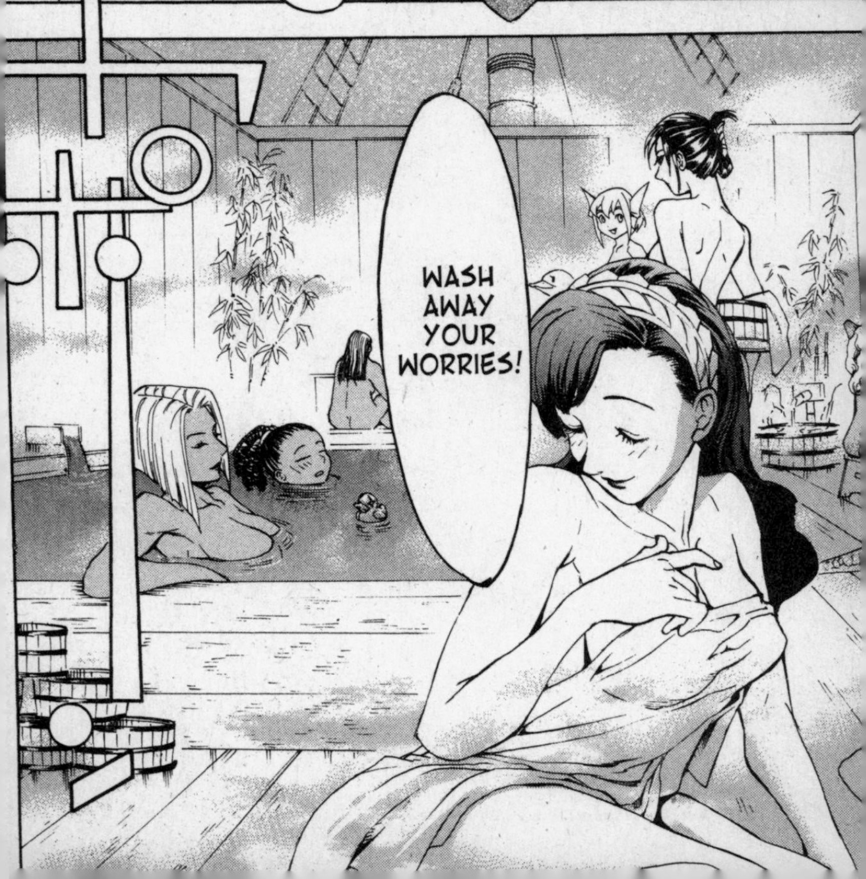
WASH AWAY YOUR WORRIES!

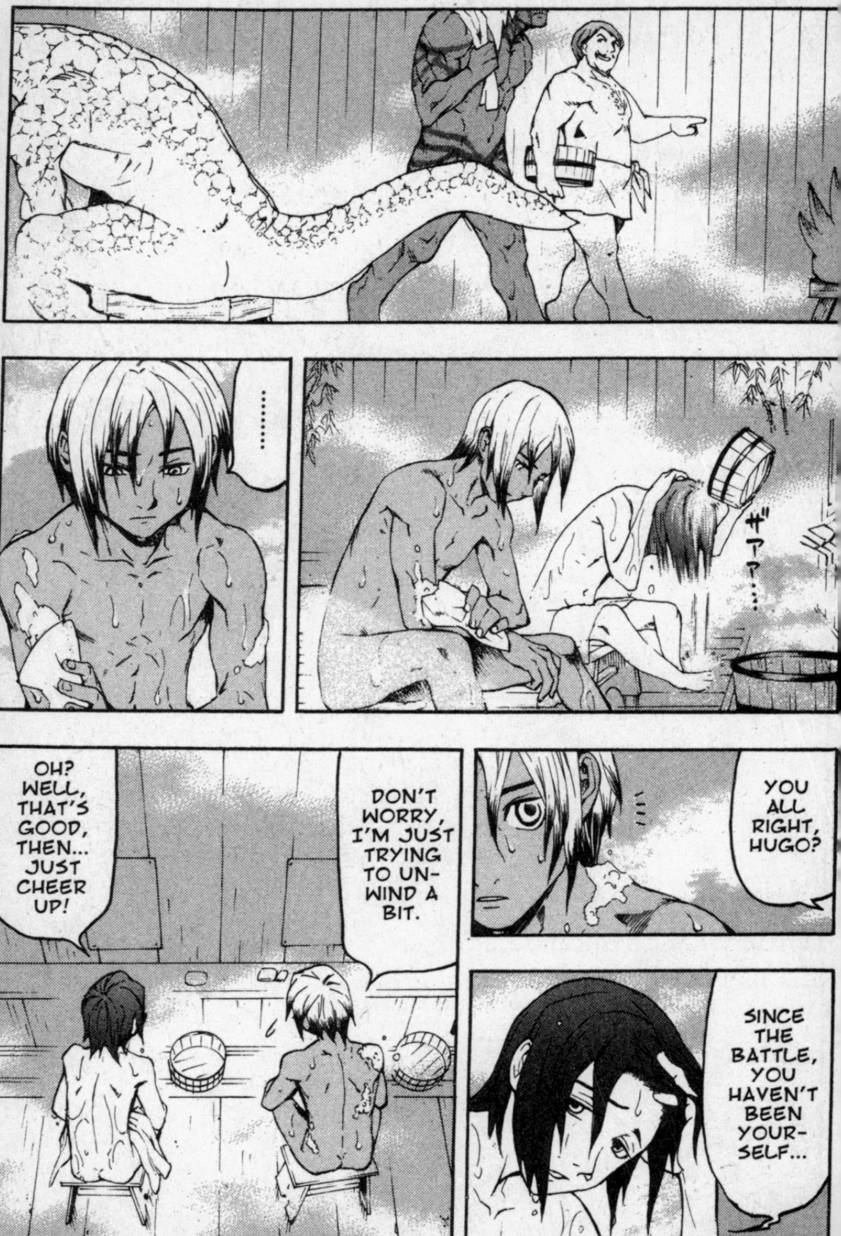
ザアア…
……
YOU ALL RIGHT, HUGO?
SINCE THE BATTLE, YOU HAVEN'T BEEN YOURSELF...
DON'T WORRY, I'M JUST TRYING TO UN-WIND A BIT.
OH? WELL, THAT'S GOOD, THEN... JUST CHEER UP!

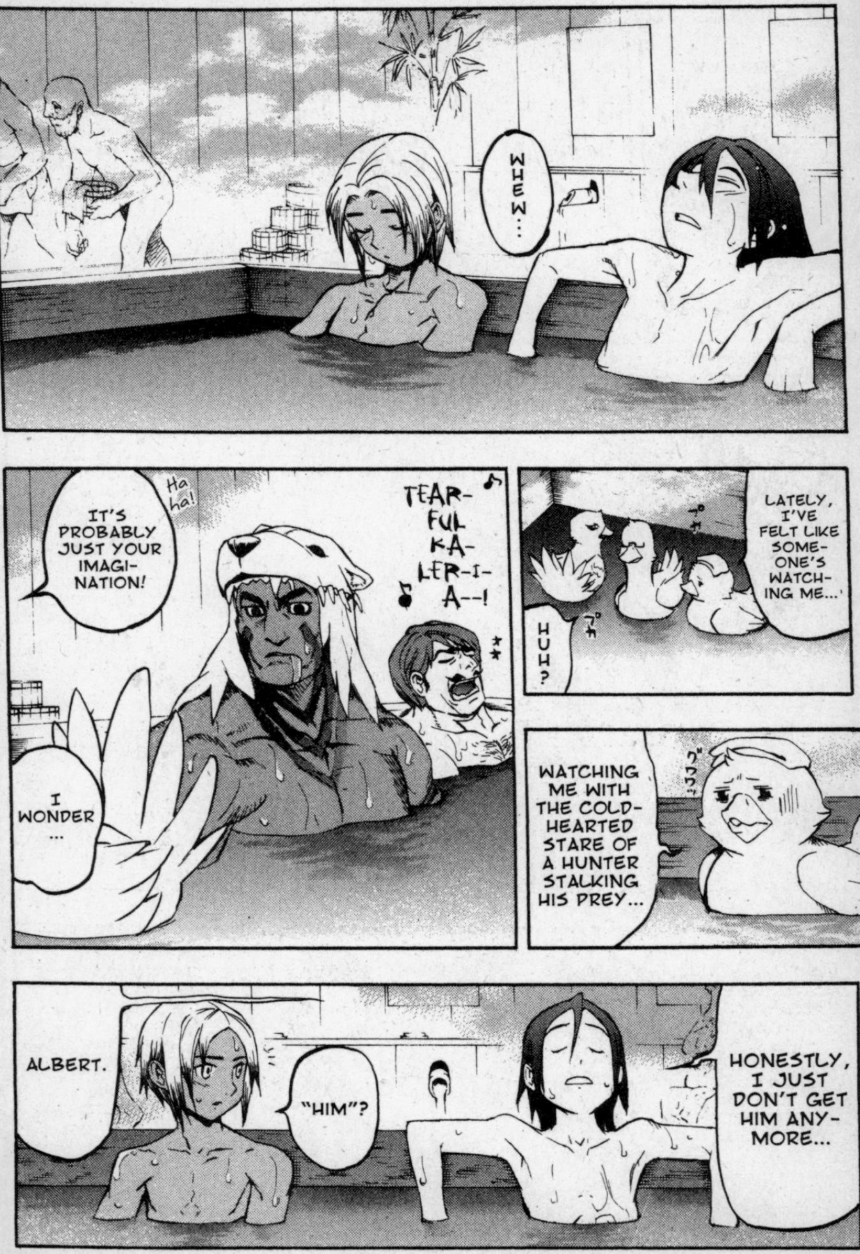
WHEW...
LATELY, I'VE FELT LIKE SOME-ONE'S WATCHING ME...
HUH?
WATCHING ME WITH THE COLD-HEARTED STARE OF A HUNTER STALKING HIS PREY...
TEAR-FUL KA-LER-I-A--!
Ha ha!
IT'S PROBABLY JUST YOUR IMAGI-NATION!
I WONDER...
HONESTLY, I JUST DON'T GET HIM ANY-MORE...
"HIM"?
ALBERT.

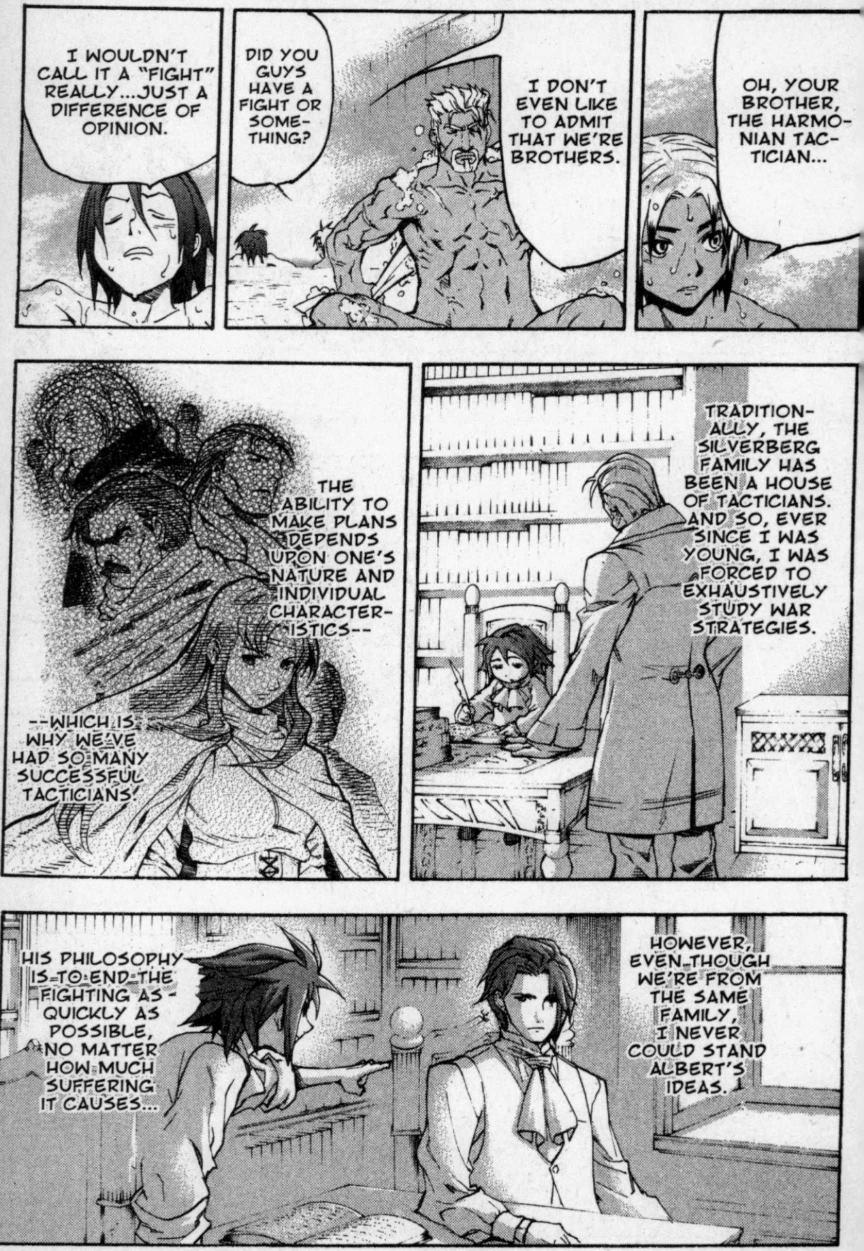
OH, YOUR BROTHER, THE HARMONIAN TACTICIAN...
I DON'T EVEN LIKE TO ADMIT THAT WE'RE BROTHERS.
DID YOU GUYS HAVE A FIGHT OR SOMETHING?
I WOULDN'T CALL IT A "FIGHT" REALLY...JUST A DIFFERENCE OF OPINION.
TRADITIONALLY, THE SILVERBERG FAMILY HAS BEEN A HOUSE OF TACTICIANS. AND SO, EVER SINCE I WAS YOUNG, I WAS FORCED TO EXHAUSTIVELY STUDY WAR STRATEGIES.
THE ABILITY TO MAKE PLANS DEPENDS UPON ONE'S NATURE AND INDIVIDUAL CHARACTERISTICS--
--WHICH IS WHY WE'VE HAD SO MANY SUCCESSFUL TACTICIANS!
HOWEVER, EVEN THOUGH WE'RE FROM THE SAME FAMILY, I NEVER COULD STAND ALBERT'S IDEAS.
HIS PHILOSOPHY IS TO END THE FIGHTING AS QUICKLY AS POSSIBLE, NO MATTER HOW MUCH SUFFERING IT CAUSES...

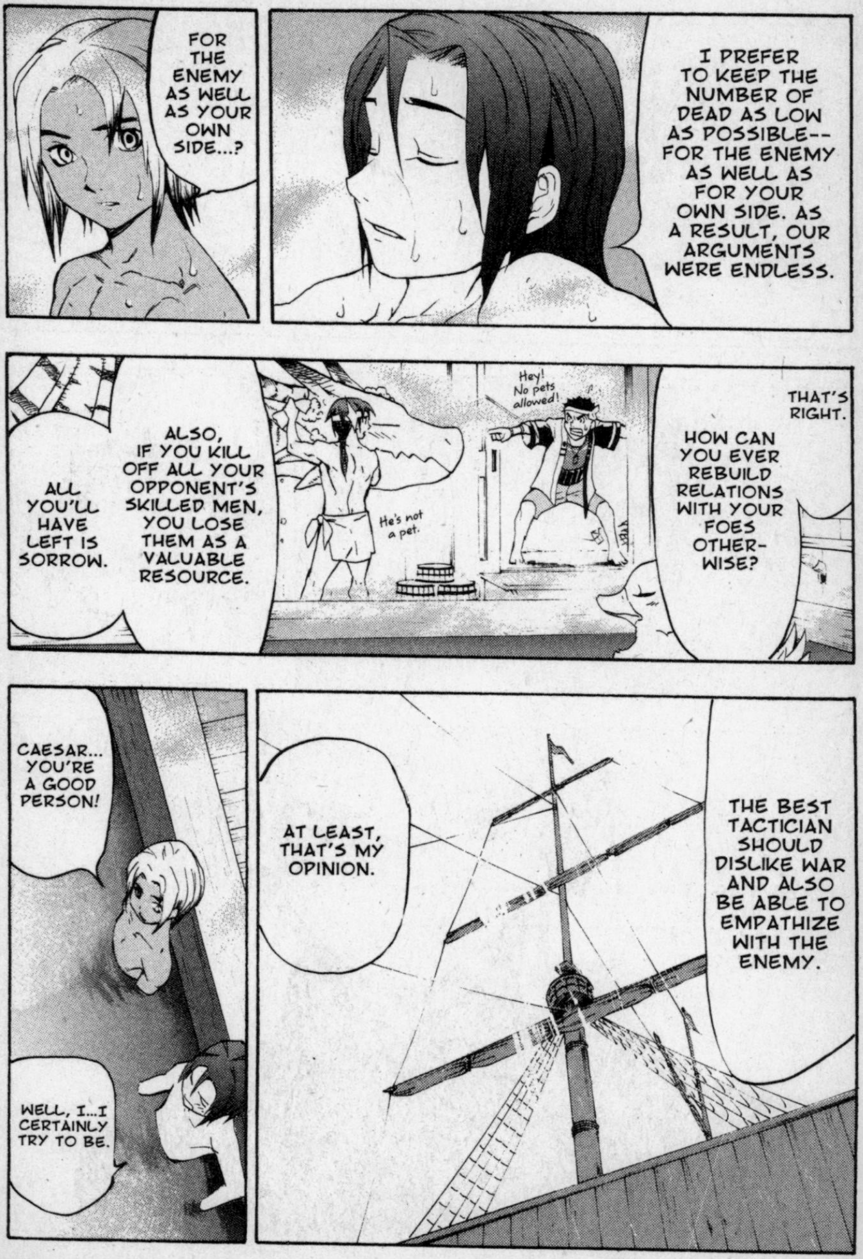
I PREFER TO KEEP THE NUMBER OF DEAD AS LOW AS POSSIBLE-- FOR THE ENEMY AS WELL AS FOR YOUR OWN SIDE. AS A RESULT, OUR ARGUMENTS WERE ENDLESS.
FOR THE ENEMY AS WELL AS YOUR OWN SIDE...?
THAT'S RIGHT.
HOW CAN YOU EVER REBUILD RELATIONS WITH YOUR FOES OTHER-WISE?
Hey! No pets allowed!
He's not a pet.
ALSO, IF YOU KILL OFF ALL YOUR OPPONENT'S SKILLED MEN, YOU LOSE THEM AS A VALUABLE RESOURCE.
ALL YOU'LL HAVE LEFT IS SORROW.
THE BEST TACTICIAN SHOULD DISLIKE WAR AND ALSO BE ABLE TO EMPATHIZE WITH THE ENEMY.
AT LEAST, THAT'S MY OPINION.
CAESAR... YOU'RE A GOOD PERSON!
WELL, I...I CERTAINLY TRY TO BE.

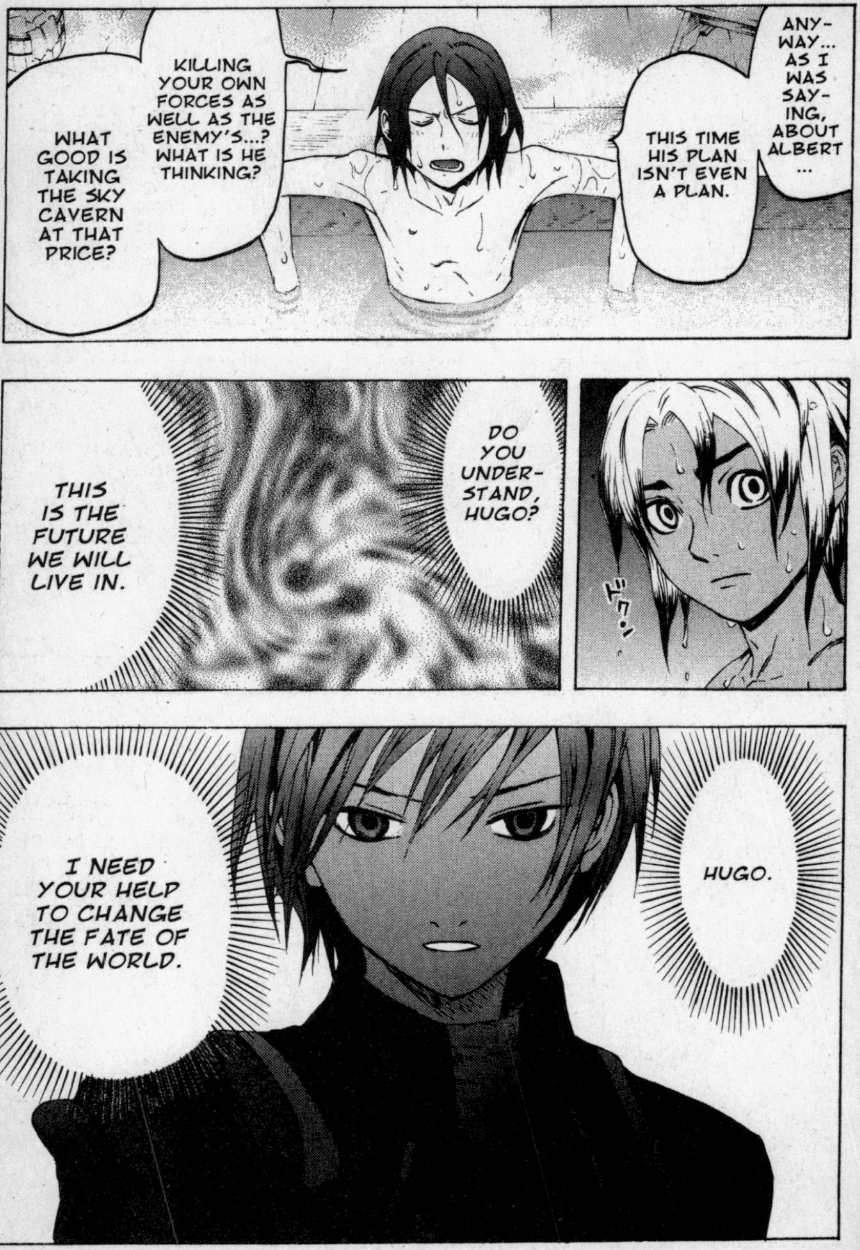
ANY-WAY... AS I WAS SAY-ING, ABOUT ALBERT ...
THIS TIME HIS PLAN ISN'T EVEN A PLAN.
KILLING YOUR OWN FORCES AS WELL AS THE ENEMY'S...? WHAT IS HE THINKING?
WHAT GOOD IS TAKING THE SKY CAVERN AT THAT PRICE?
ドクッ
DO YOU UNDER-STAND, HUGO?
THIS IS THE FUTURE WE WILL LIVE IN.
HUGO.
I NEED YOUR HELP TO CHANGE THE FATE OF THE WORLD.

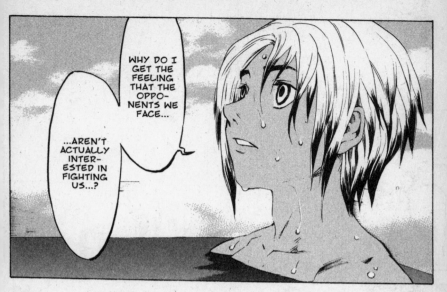

WHY DO I GET THE FEELING THAT THE OPPONENTS WE FACE...
...AREN'T ACTUALLY INTERESTED IN FIGHTING US...?
You're breaking my neck!
Stop whining!
ARE YOU OKAY, HUGO?
キャあああ
PEEPING TOMS!

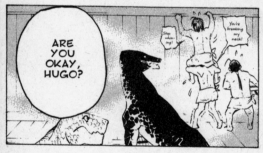

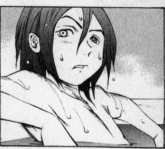

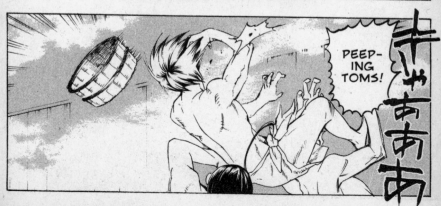

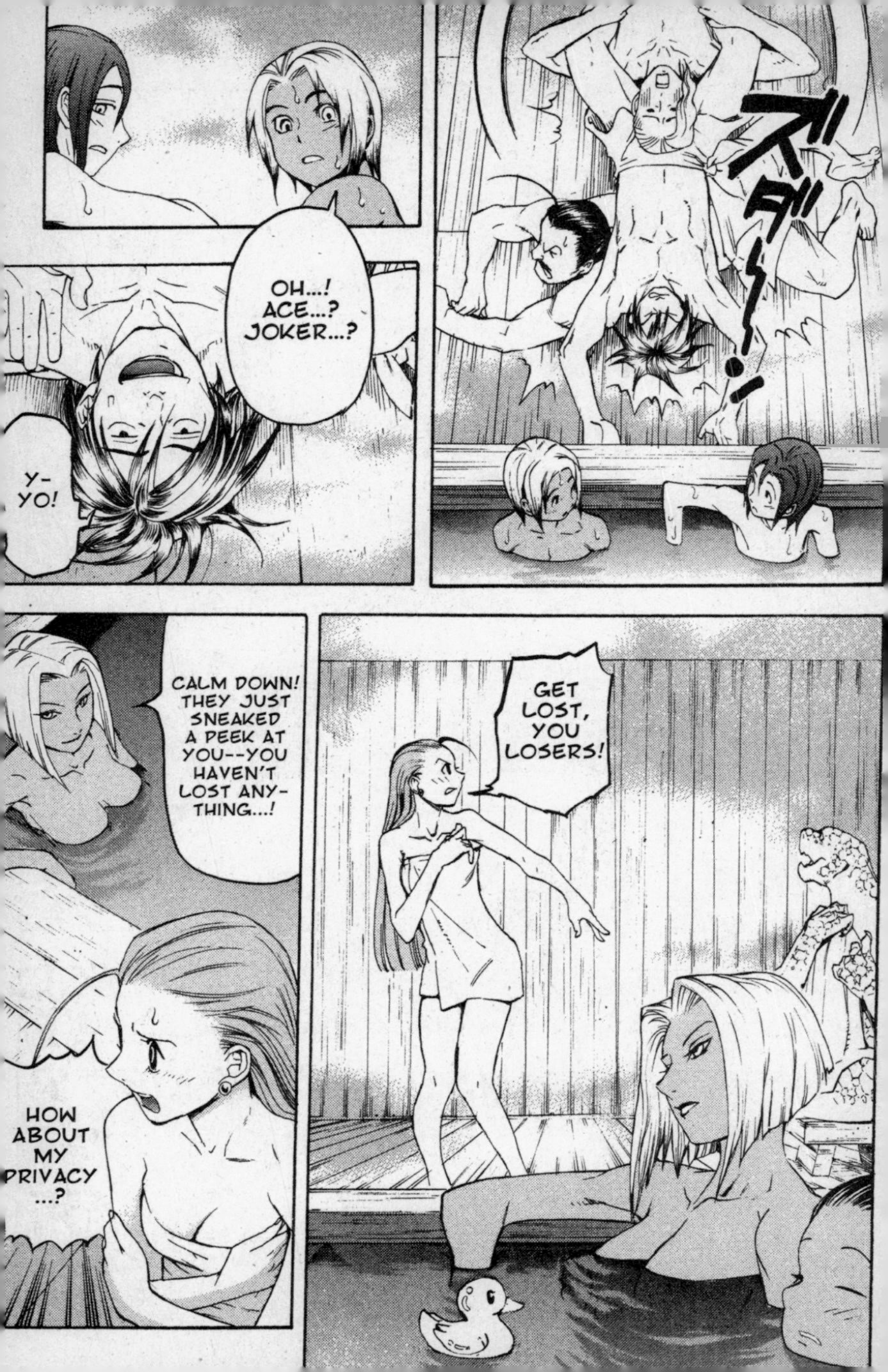
OH...! ACE...? JOKER...?
Y-YO!
GET LOST, YOU LOSERS!
CALM DOWN! THEY JUST SNEAKED A PEEK AT YOU--YOU HAVEN'T LOST ANY-THING...!
HOW ABOUT MY PRIVACY ...?

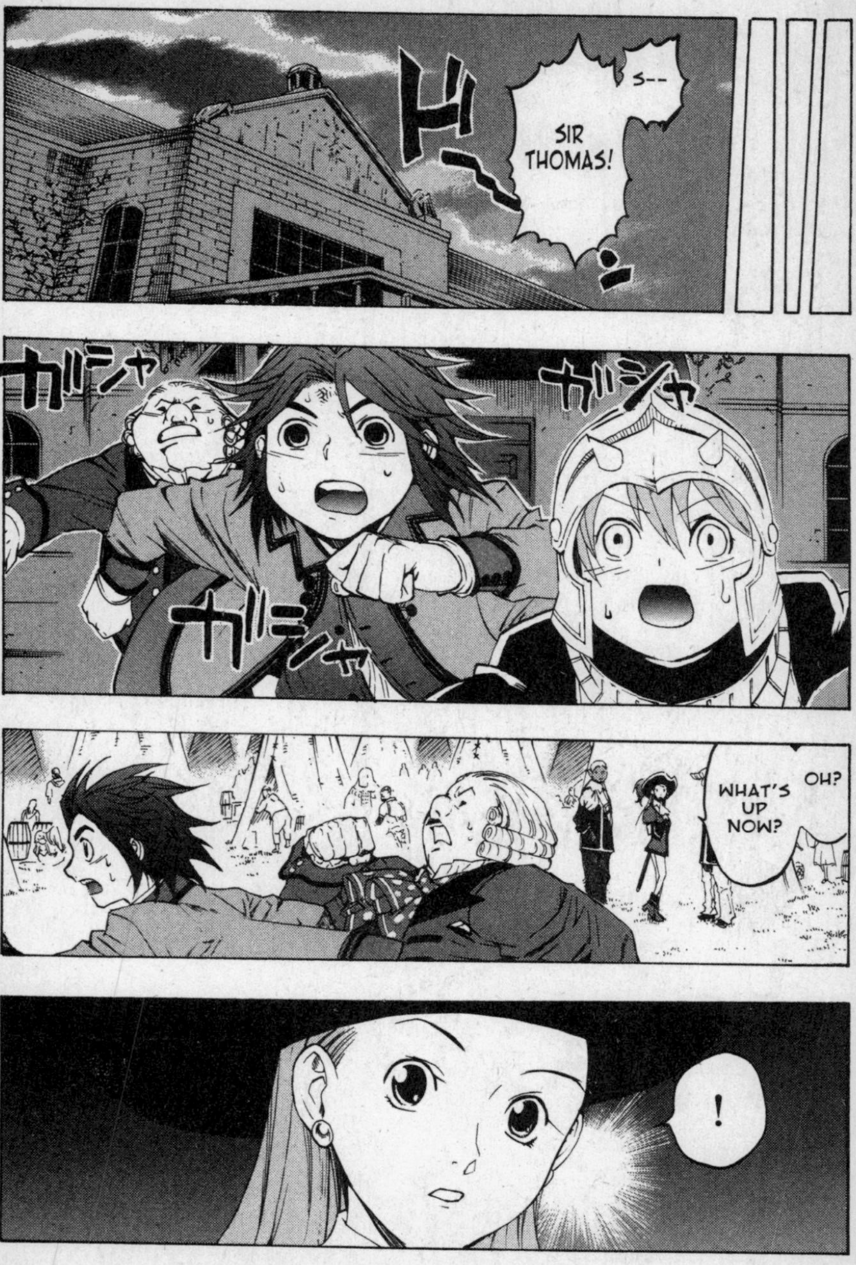
S--
SIR THOMAS!
ドーン
ガシャ
ガシャ
ガシャ
OH?
WHAT'S UP NOW?
!

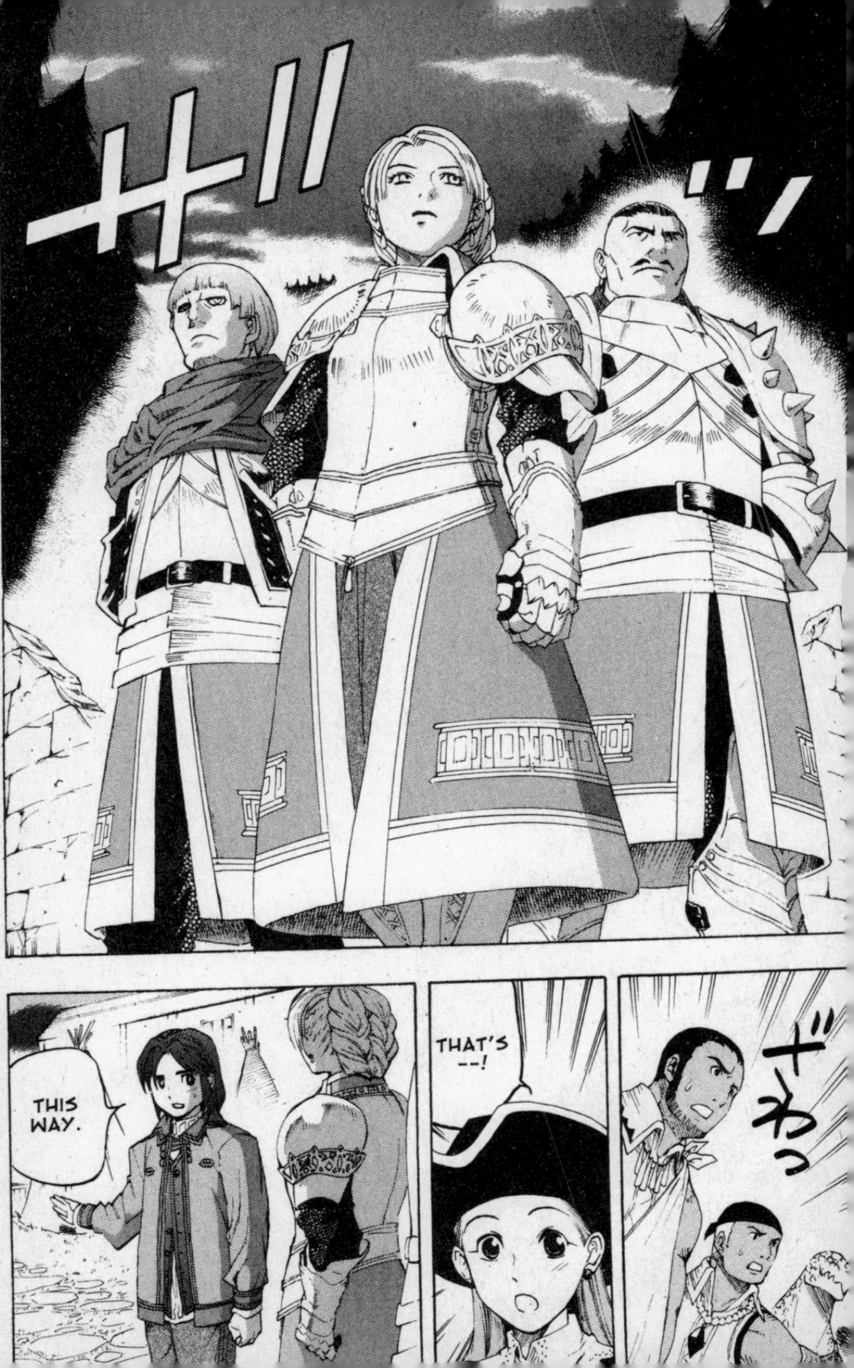
ざわっ
THAT'S --!
THIS WAY.

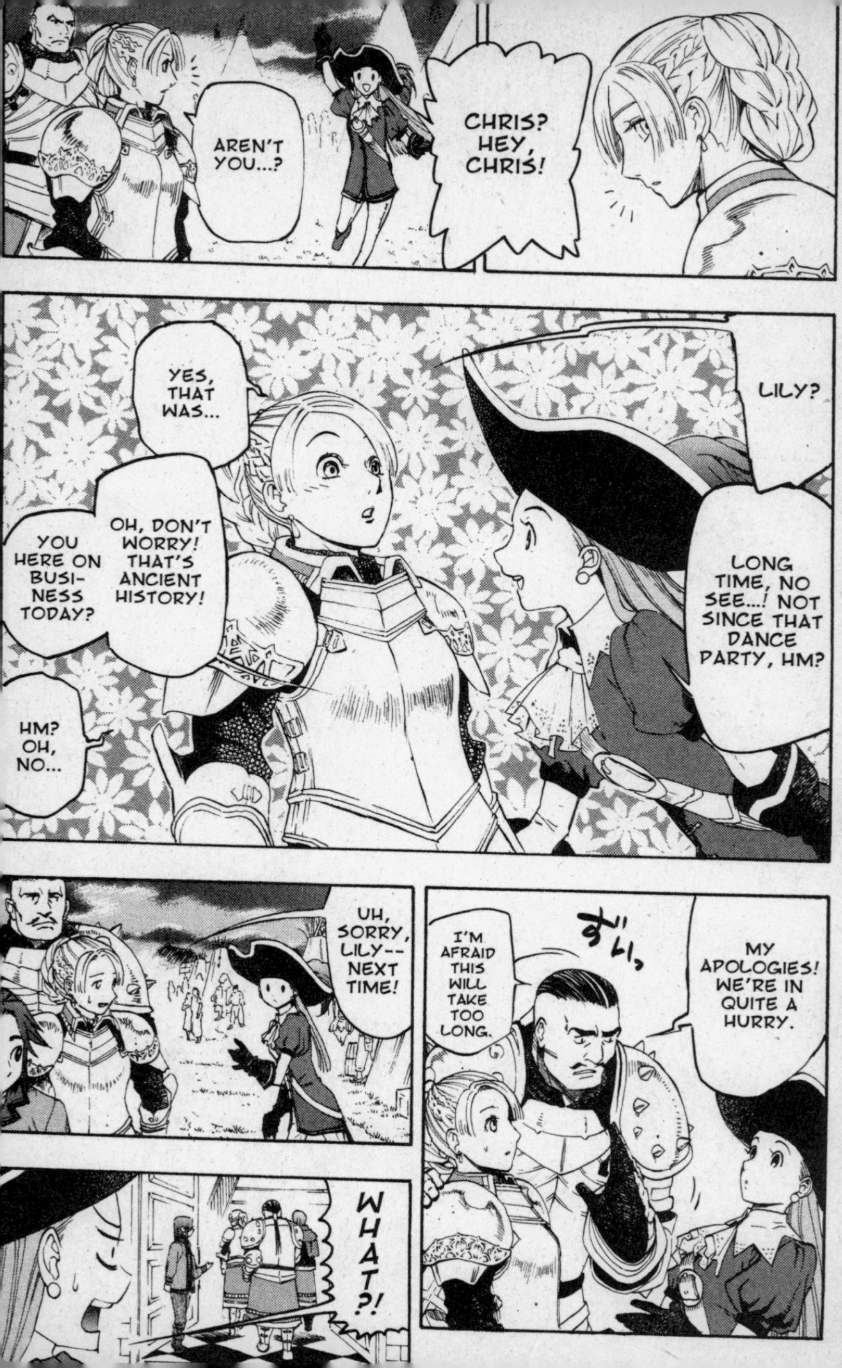

CHRIS? HEY, CHRIS!
AREN'T YOU...?
LILY?
LONG TIME, NO SEE...! NOT SINCE THAT DANCE PARTY, HM?
YES, THAT WAS...
OH, DON'T WORRY! THAT'S ANCIENT HISTORY!
YOU HERE ON BUSI-NESS TODAY?
HM? OH, NO...
MY APOLOGIES! WE'RE IN QUITE A HURRY.
ずいっ
I'M AFRAID THIS WILL TAKE TOO LONG.
UH, SORRY, LILY-- NEXT TIME!
WHAT?!

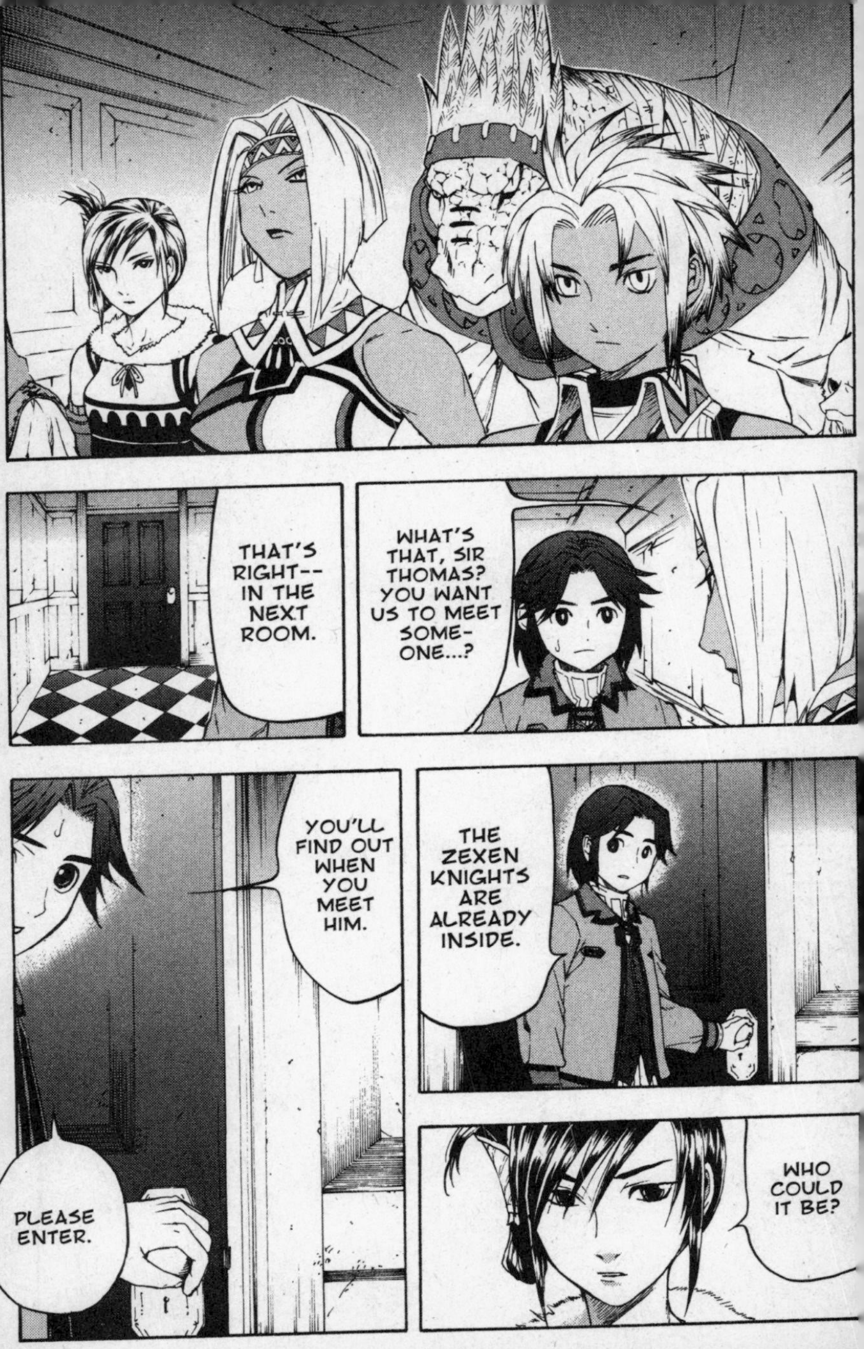
WHAT'S THAT, SIR THOMAS? YOU WANT US TO MEET SOME-ONE...?
THAT'S RIGHT-- IN THE NEXT ROOM.
THE ZEXEN KNIGHTS ARE ALREADY INSIDE.
WHO COULD IT BE?
YOU'LL FIND OUT WHEN YOU MEET HIM.
PLEASE ENTER.

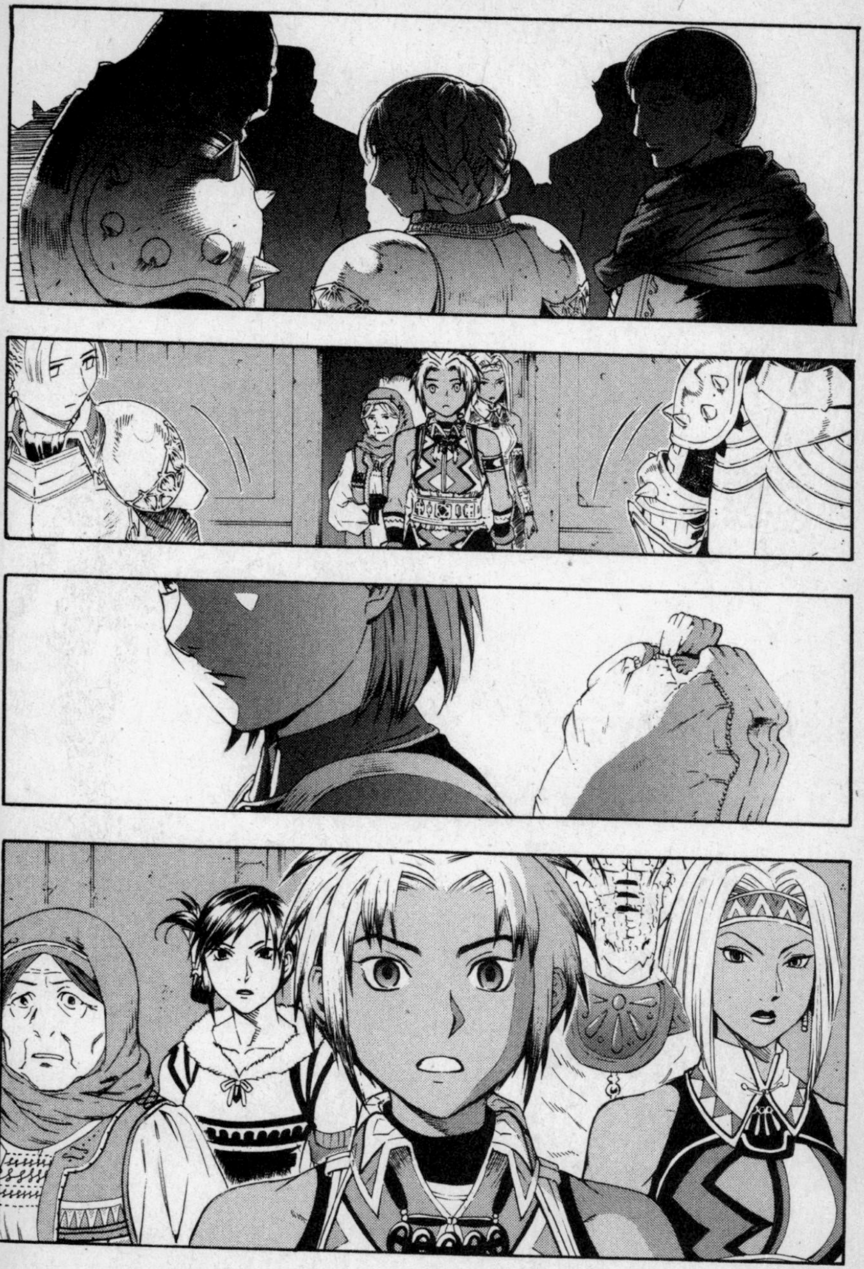

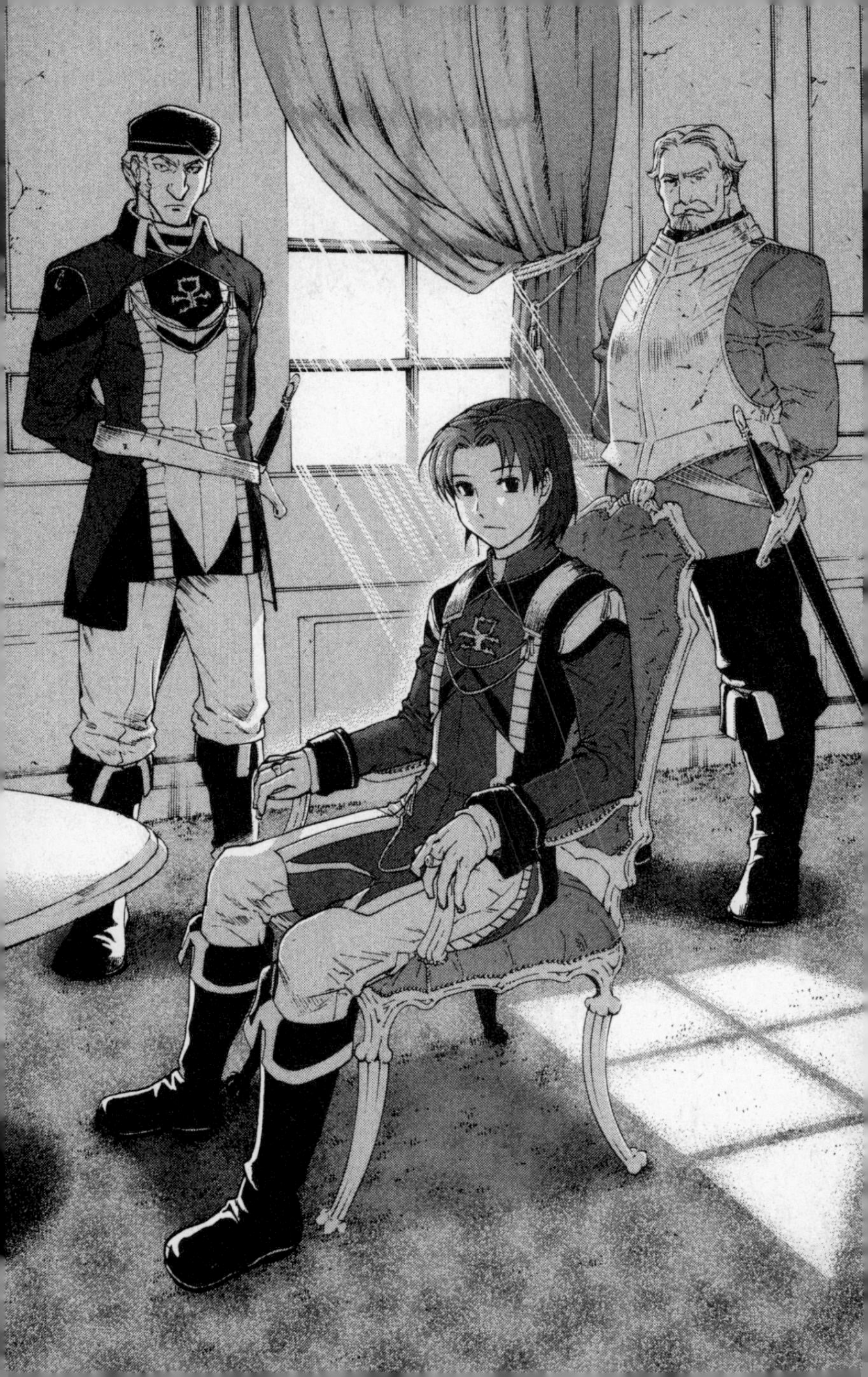

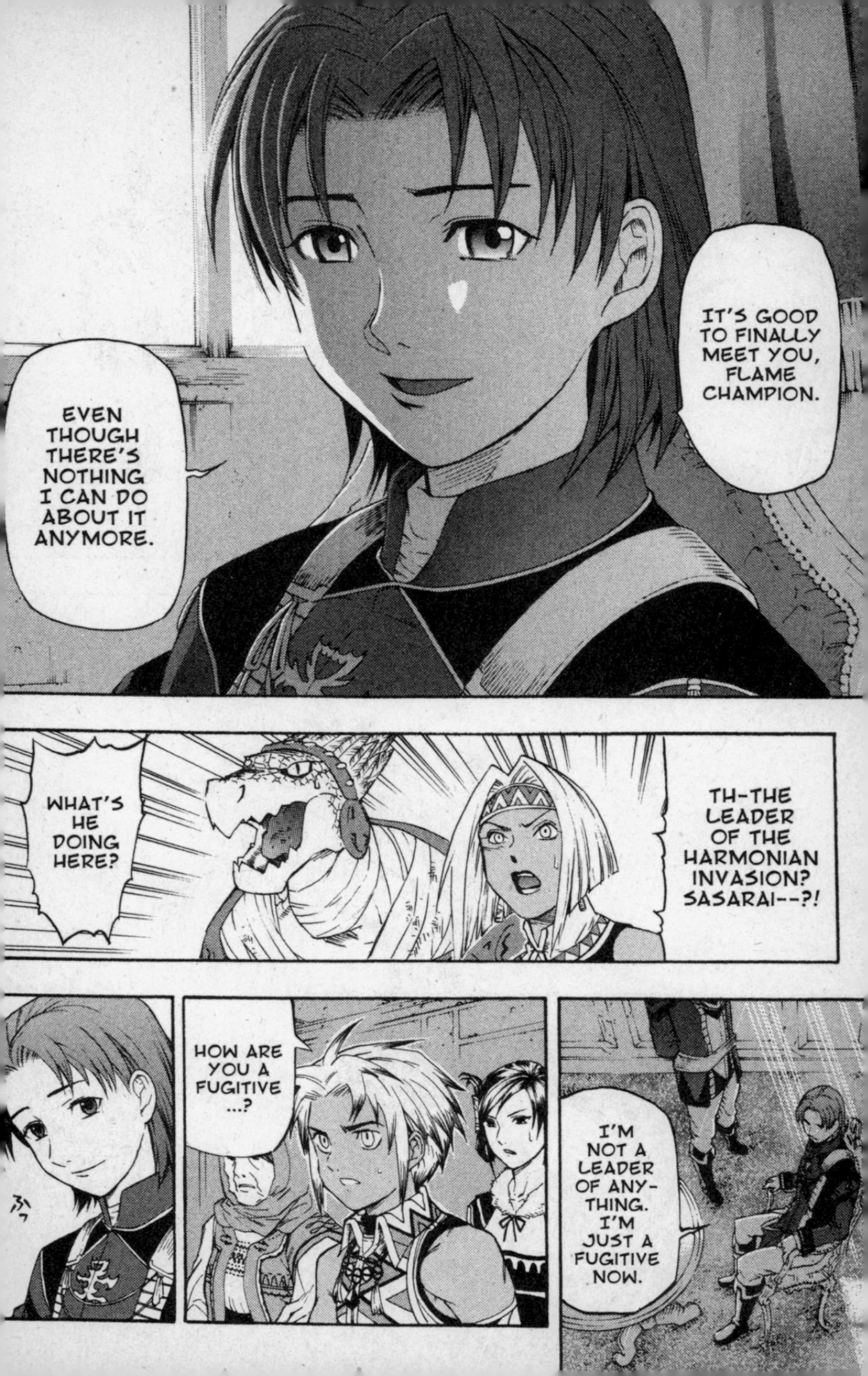
IT'S GOOD TO FINALLY MEET YOU, FLAME CHAMPION.
EVEN THOUGH THERE'S NOTHING I CAN DO ABOUT IT ANYMORE.
TH-THE LEADER OF THE HARMONIAN INVASION? SASARAI--?!
WHAT'S HE DOING HERE?
I'M NOT A LEADER OF ANYTHING. I'M JUST A FUGITIVE NOW.
HOW ARE YOU A FUGITIVE ...?
ふっ

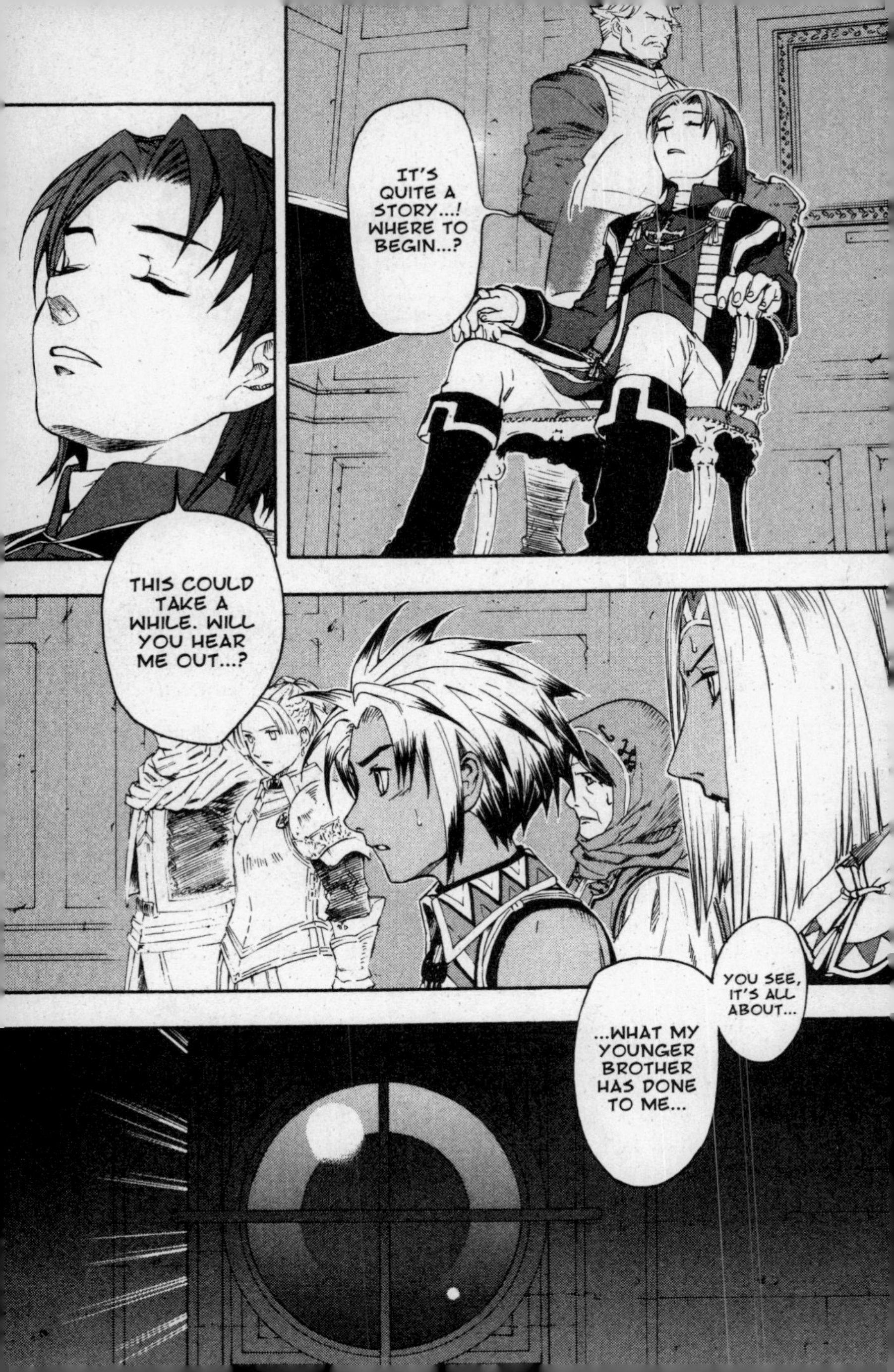
IT'S QUITE A STORY...! WHERE TO BEGIN...?
THIS COULD TAKE A WHILE. WILL YOU HEAR ME OUT...?
YOU SEE, IT'S ALL ABOUT...
...WHAT MY YOUNGER BROTHER HAS DONE TO ME...

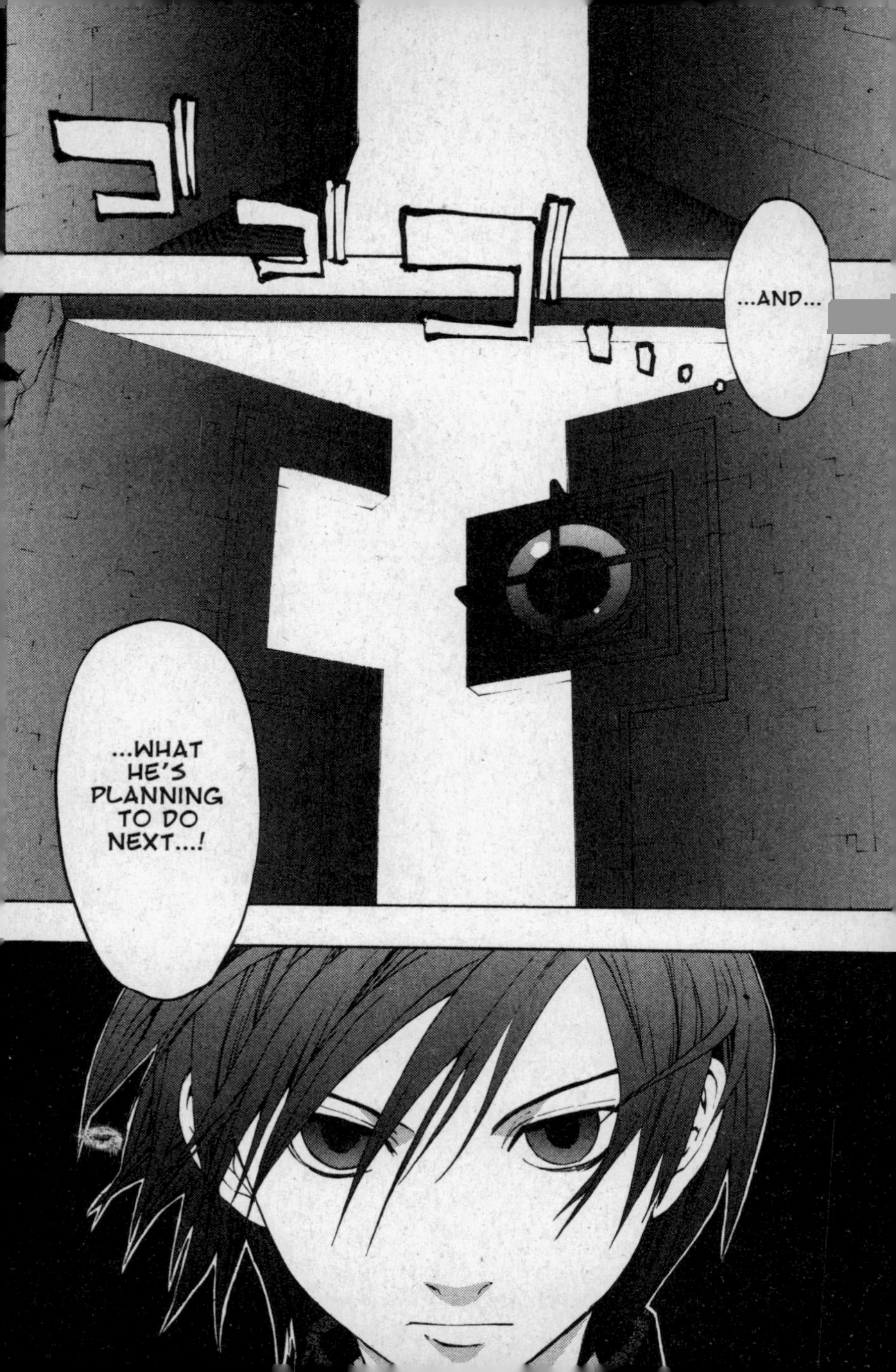
ゴゴゴ
...AND...
...WHAT HE'S PLANNING TO DO NEXT...!

Suikoden III
The Successor of Fate

continued in Volume 10

What was really difficult this time was the scene between Queen and the bug soldiers. In the end, she convinced them to make the choice, but you can't say they completely decided to rebel. It's as if you don't know if Queen's words really did the trick. I think it's interesting to wonder what you would have done had you been a bug soldier--and what would have led to such a choice.

Anyway, as to the characters of the 108 Stars, I've been drawing them in the background bit by bit and it looks like, thankfully, I'll be able to get all 108 (I've gotten 103 at present)! I think that finding all the characters of the 108 Stars is fun, so to those of you who haven't played it yet, please do!

Well now, we've finally gotten to the climax. I know how I want to draw it, but I don't know if I'll be able to convey it right...

At any rate, I'll give it my best! See ya later.

In Volume 10 of

Suikoden III
幻想水滸伝

Sasarai, now recuperating at Budehuc Castle, reveals to the Zexen and Grasslanders what he knows of Luc's shocking plans of destruction.

For the people of Zexen, the Grasslands and Harmonia, stopping this unstoppable enemy is their only chance at survival.

But will their desire to live today create a desolate tomorrow? Don't miss next volume!

ATTENTION FANS OF *SUIKODEN III* AND AKI SHIMIZU!

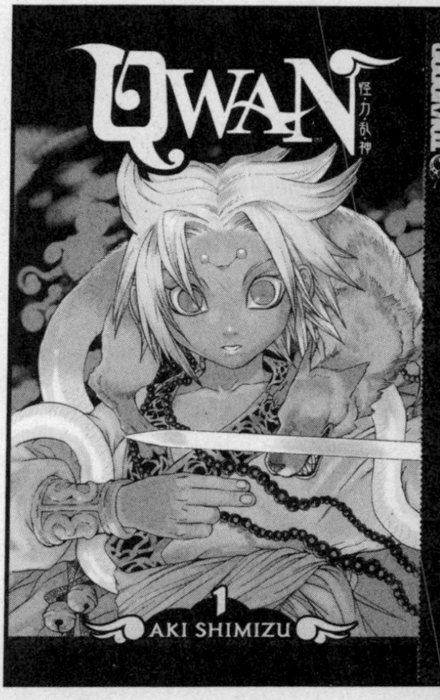

QWAN
1
AKI SHIMIZU

If you can't get enough of Aki Shimizu's fantastic artwork and storytelling, be sure to check out the following sneek peek at ***Qwan,*** another TOKYOPOP manga by the writer / artist of *Suikoden III!*

Chikei, a lowlife, has eaten the offerings the villagers left out for their god. Chikei also took something from the strange child named Qwan and refused to return it. In retaliation, Qwan ratted Chikei out to the villagers, who tied him to a tree as demon bait. Though Chikei doesn't believe in demons, they certainly seem to believe in him...

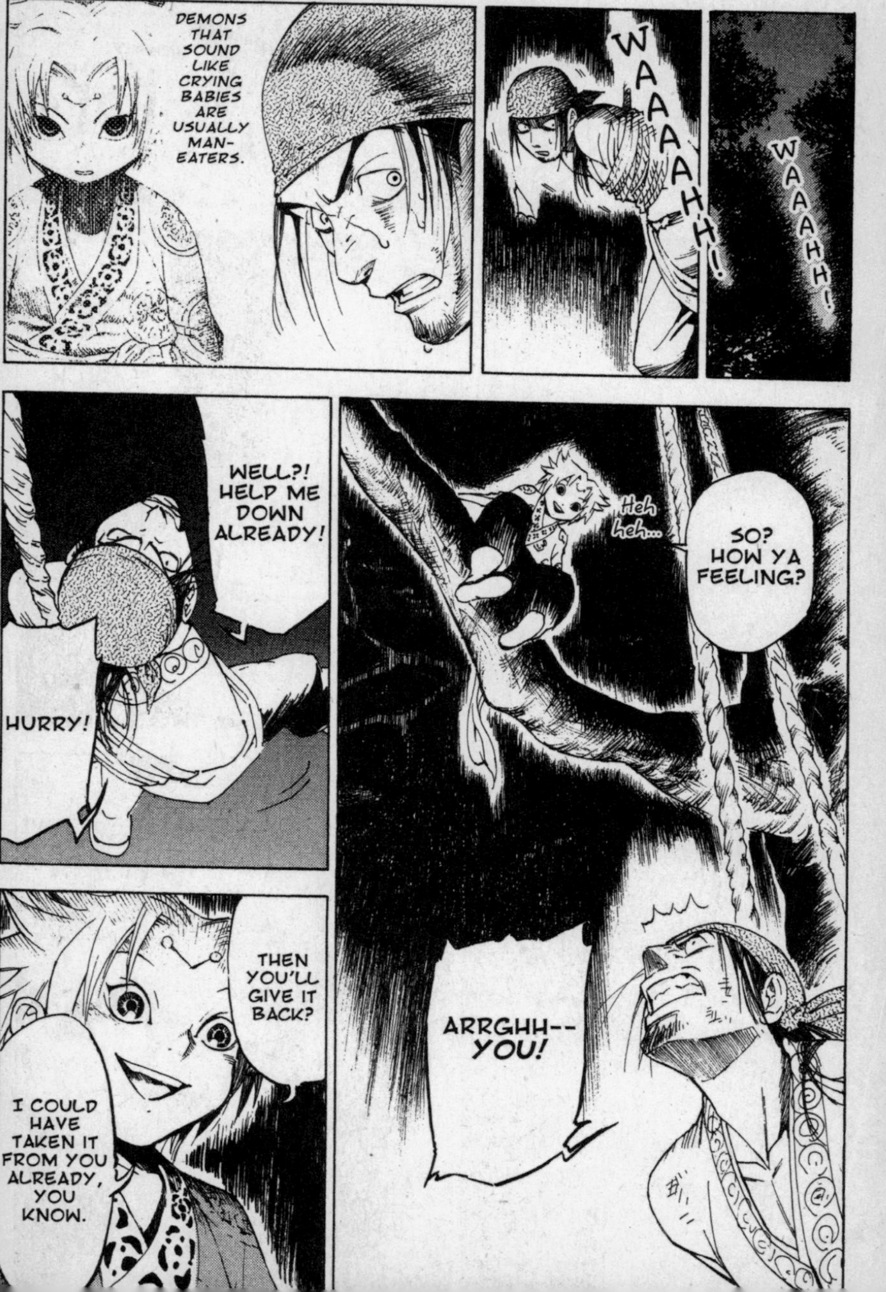
WAAAAHH!
WAAAAHH!
DEMONS THAT SOUND LIKE CRYING BABIES ARE USUALLY MAN-EATERS.
Heh heh...
SO? HOW YA FEELING?
ARRGHH-- YOU!
WELL?! HELP ME DOWN ALREADY!
HURRY!
THEN YOU'LL GIVE IT BACK?
I COULD HAVE TAKEN IT FROM YOU ALREADY, YOU KNOW.

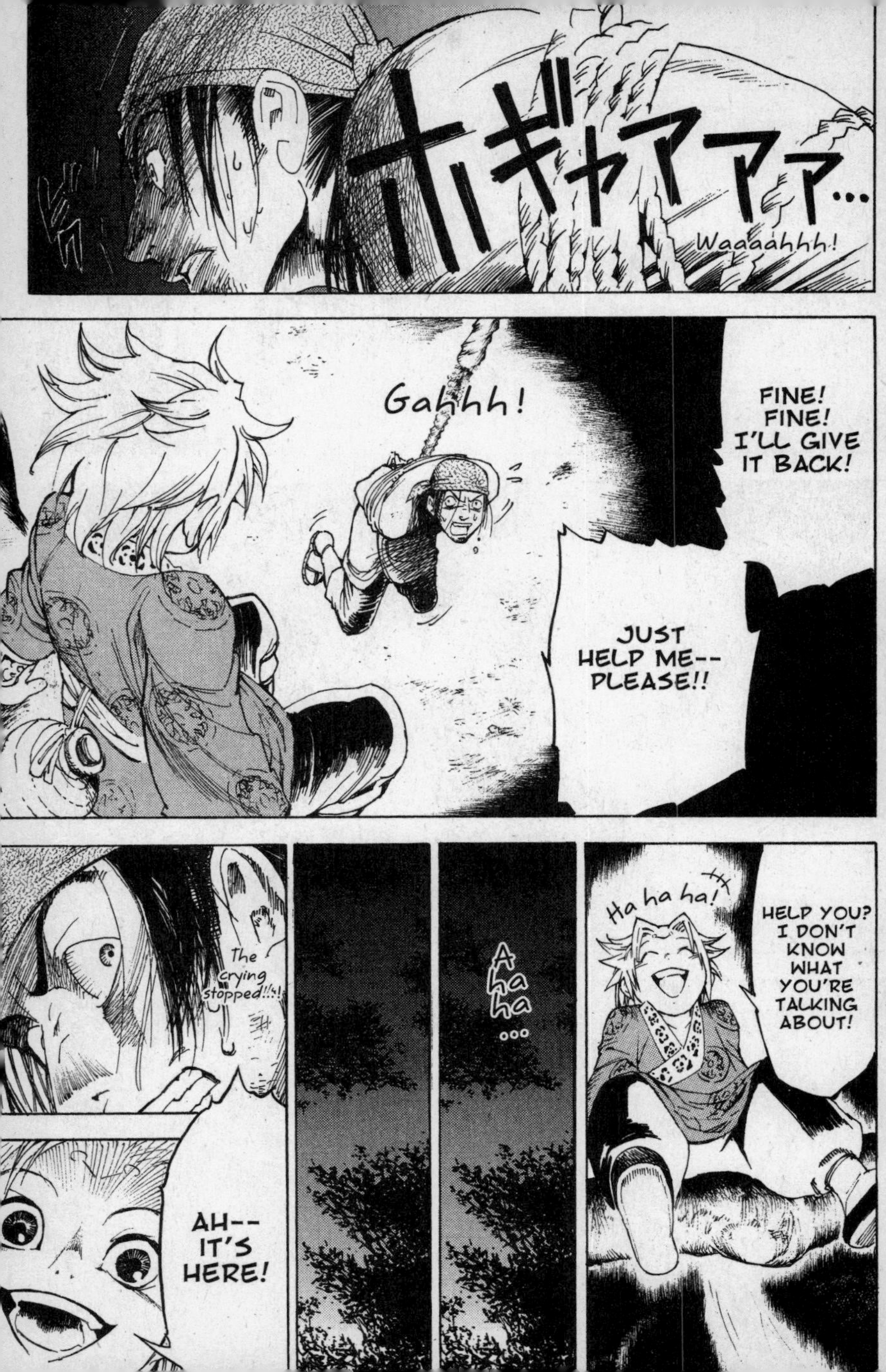
ホギャアァァ…
Waaaahhh!
FINE! FINE! I'LL GIVE IT BACK!
JUST HELP ME-- PLEASE!!
Gahhh!
HELP YOU? I DON'T KNOW WHAT YOU'RE TALKING ABOUT!
Ha ha ha!
A ha ha…
The crying stopped!!
AH-- IT'S HERE!

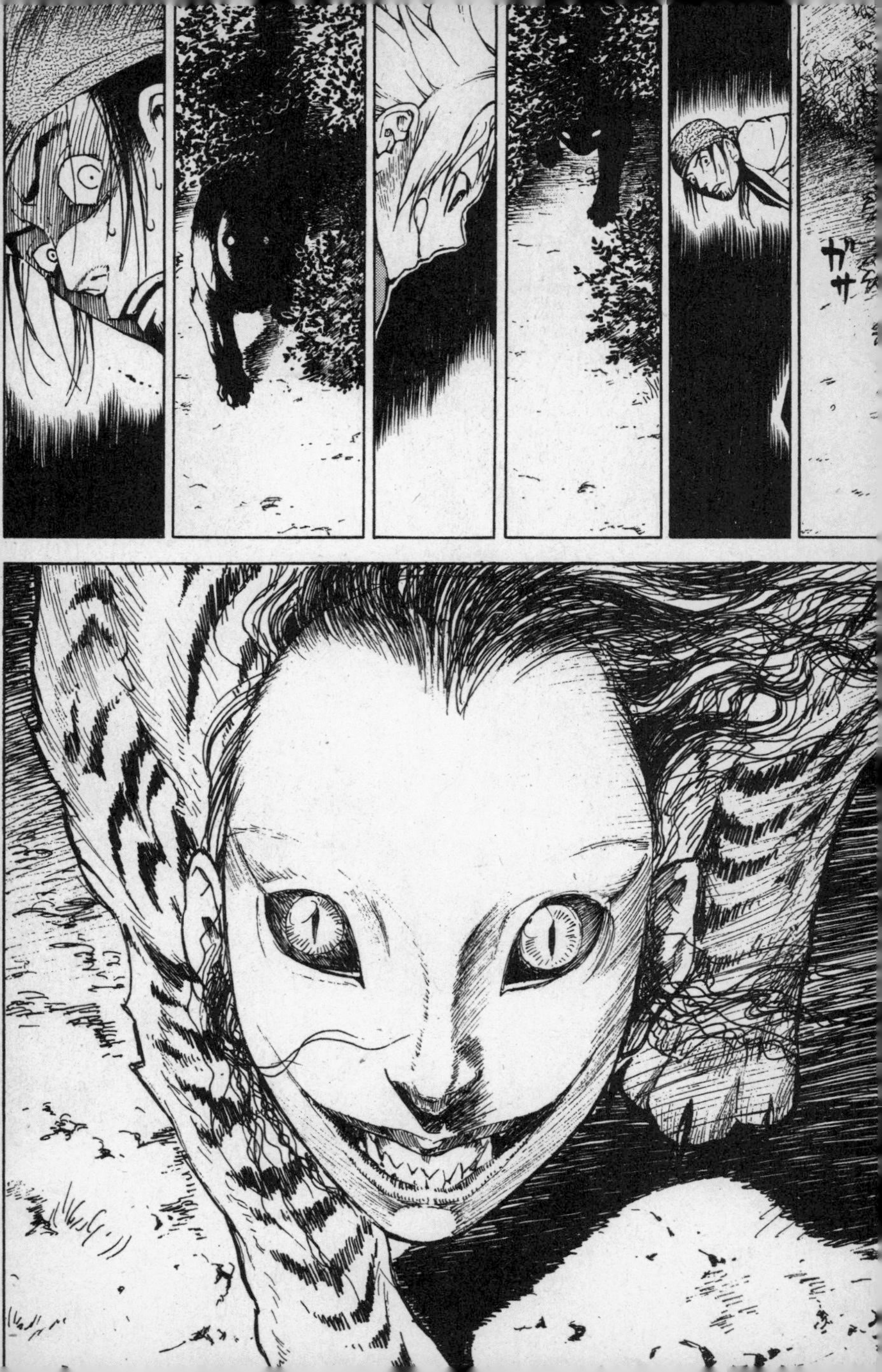
ガサ

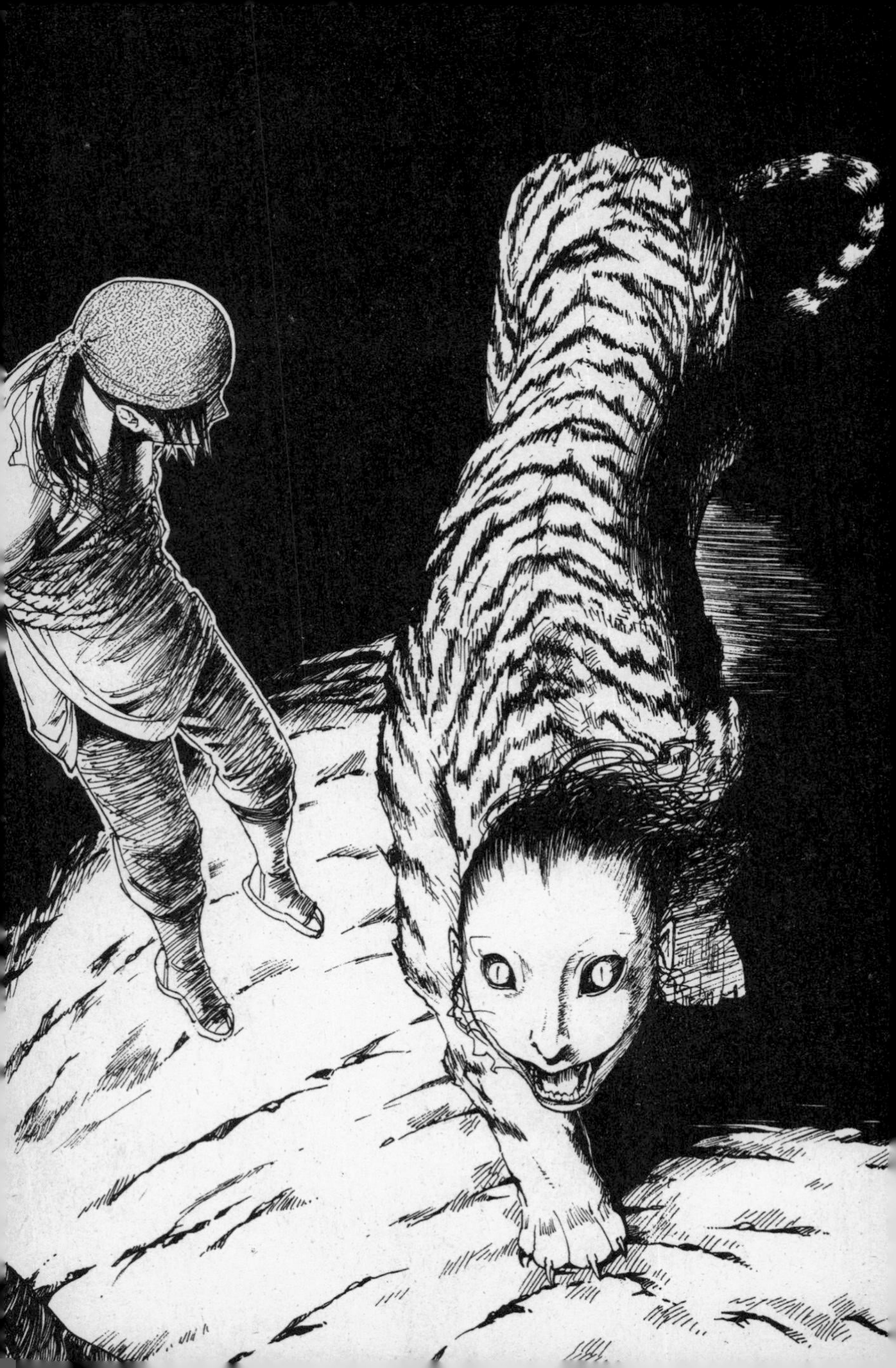

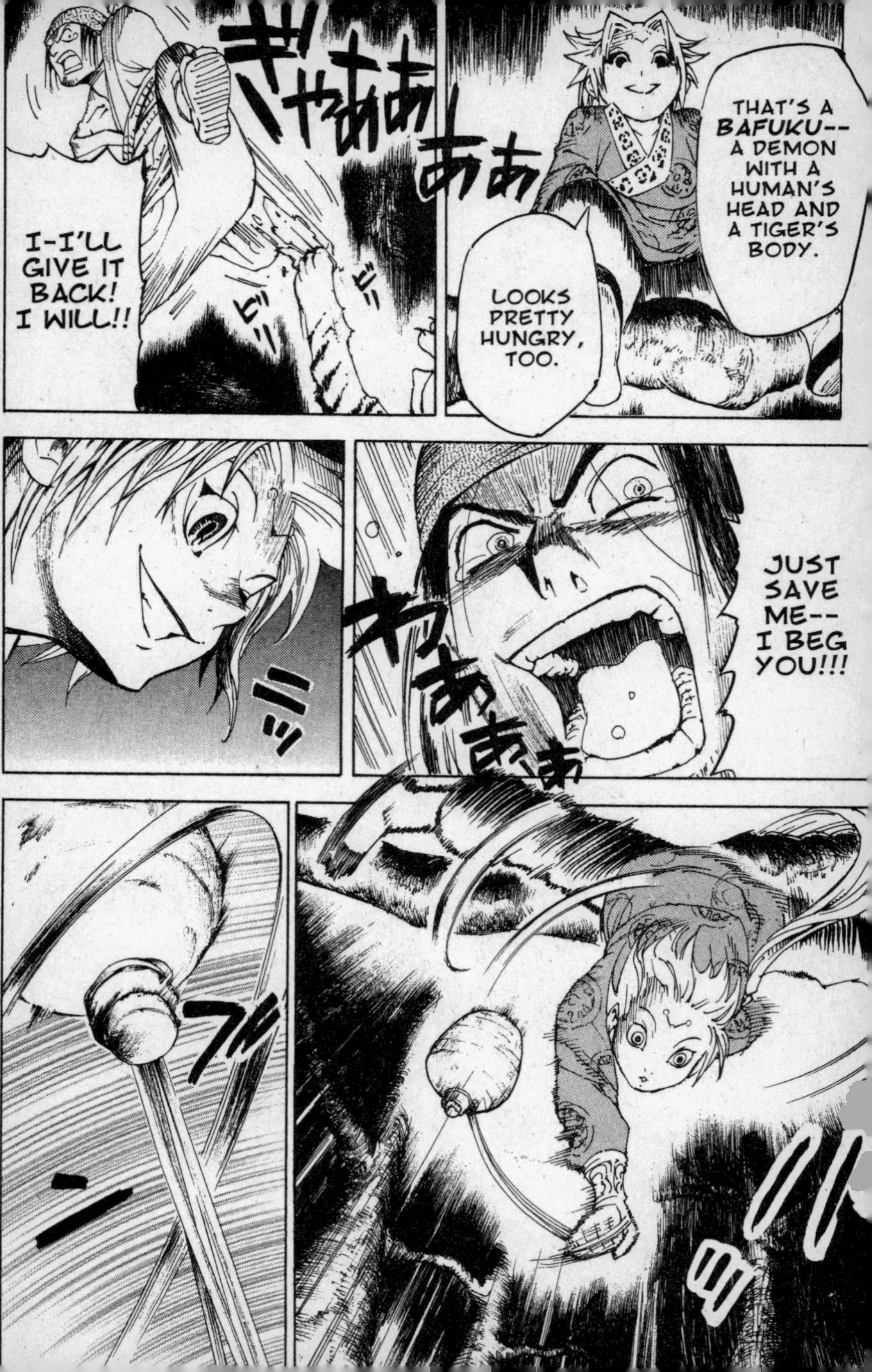
THAT'S A BAFUKU-- A DEMON WITH A HUMAN'S HEAD AND A TIGER'S BODY.
LOOKS PRETTY HUNGRY, TOO.
I-I'LL GIVE IT BACK! I WILL!!
JUST SAVE ME-- I BEG YOU!!!

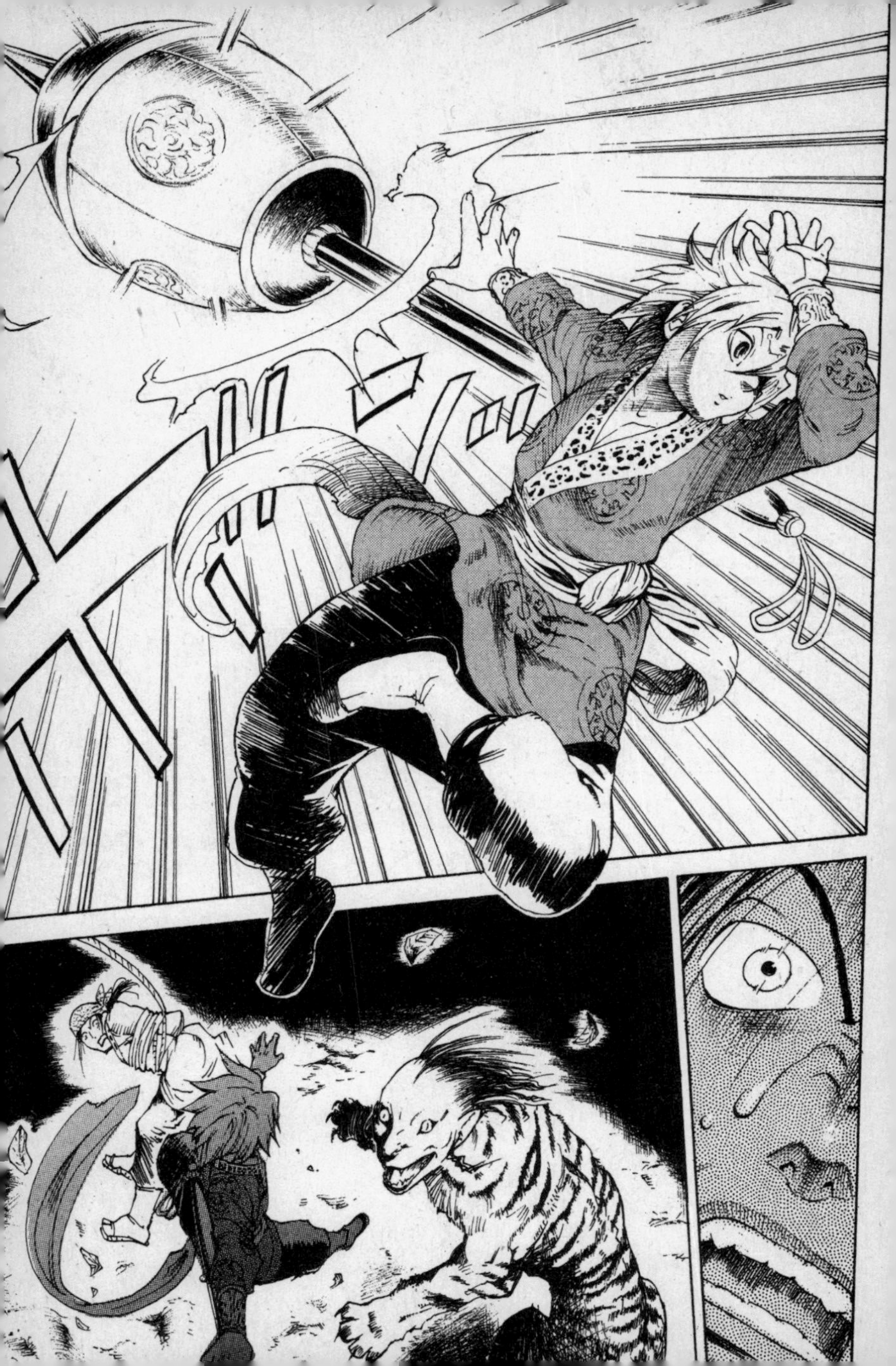

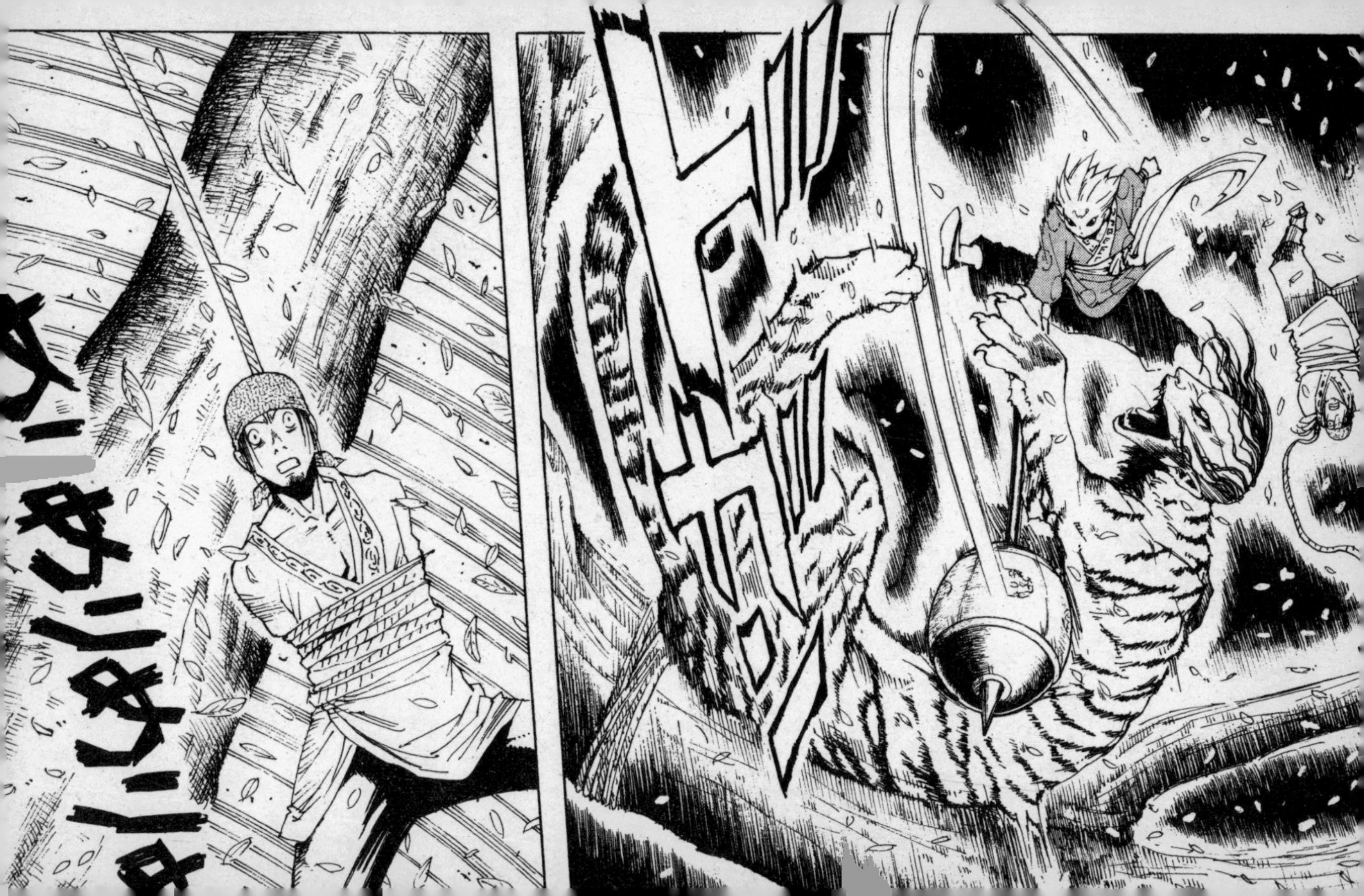
めりめり

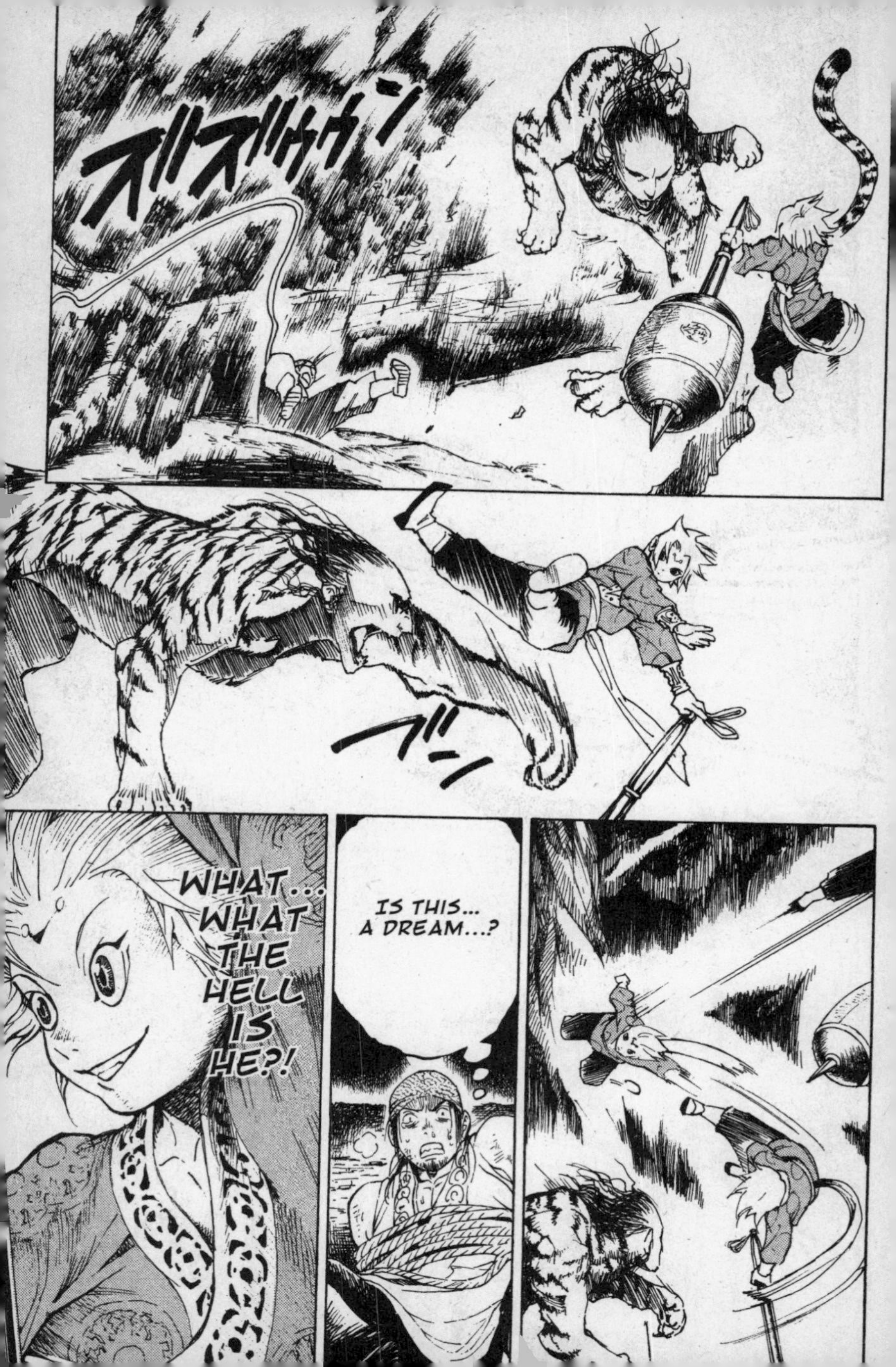
ブン
IS THIS... A DREAM...?
WHAT... WHAT THE HELL IS HE?!

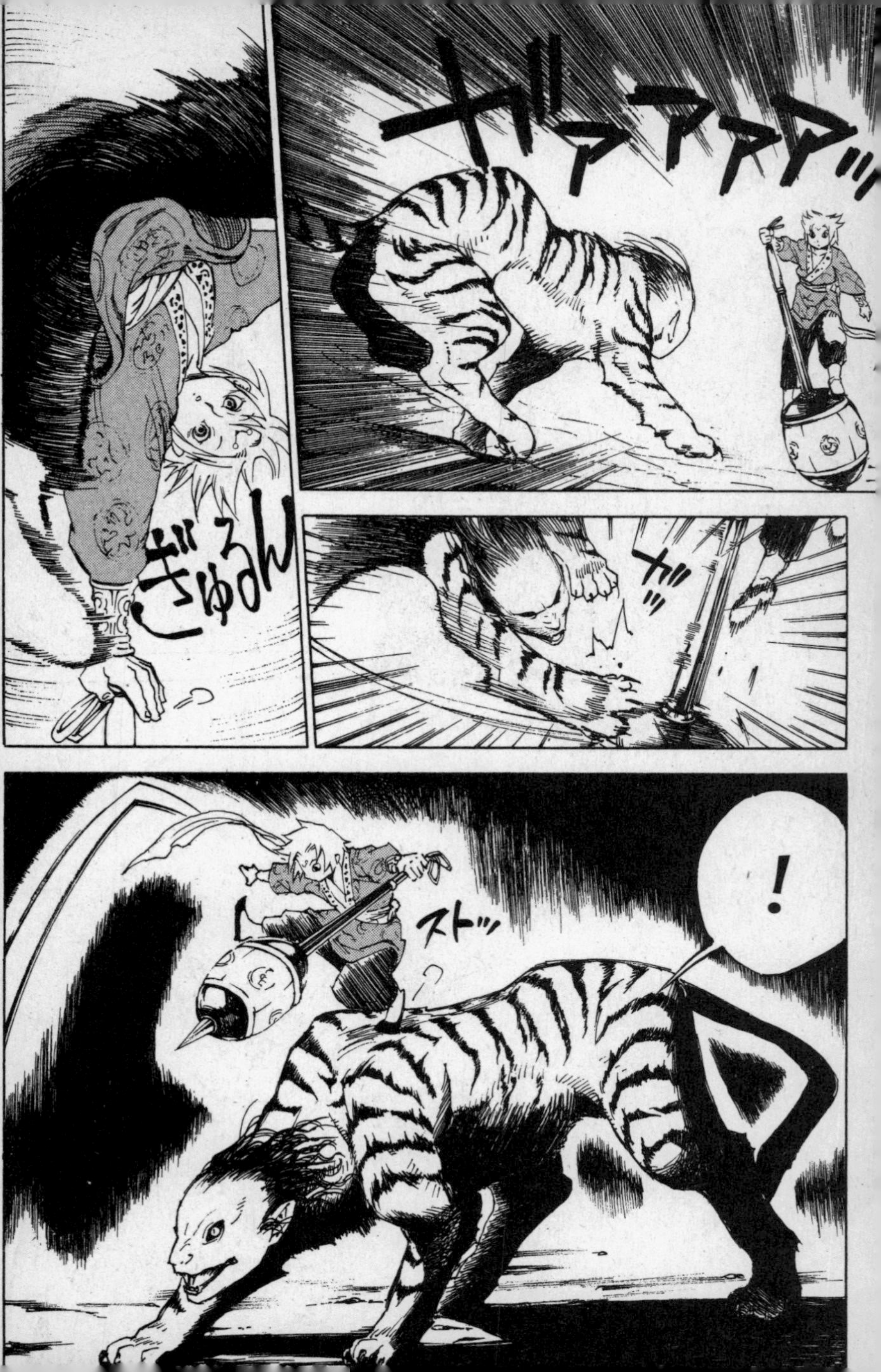
ガァアアアッ
ガッ
ぎゅるん
!
ストッ

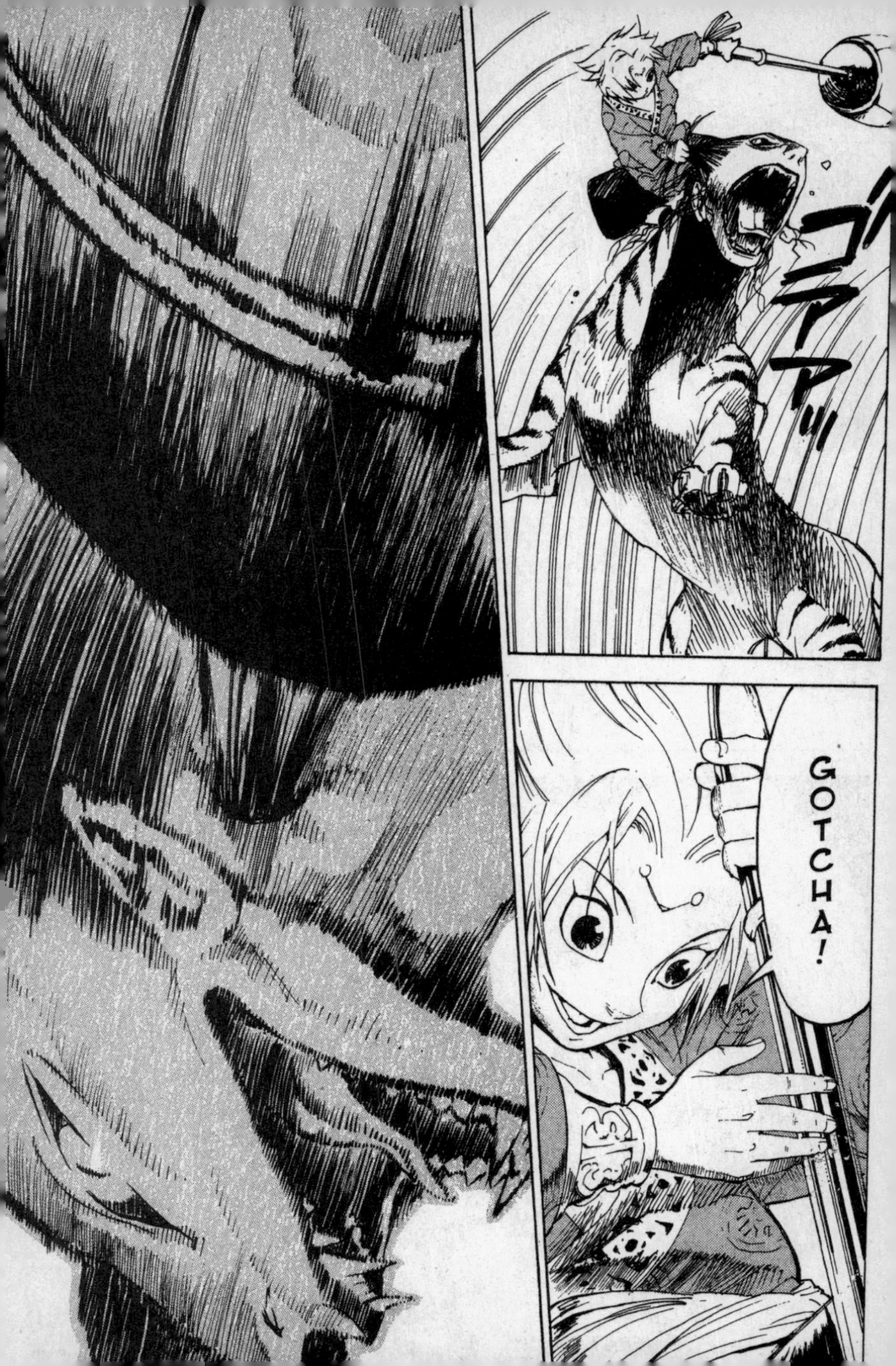
ゴアアッ
GOTCHA!

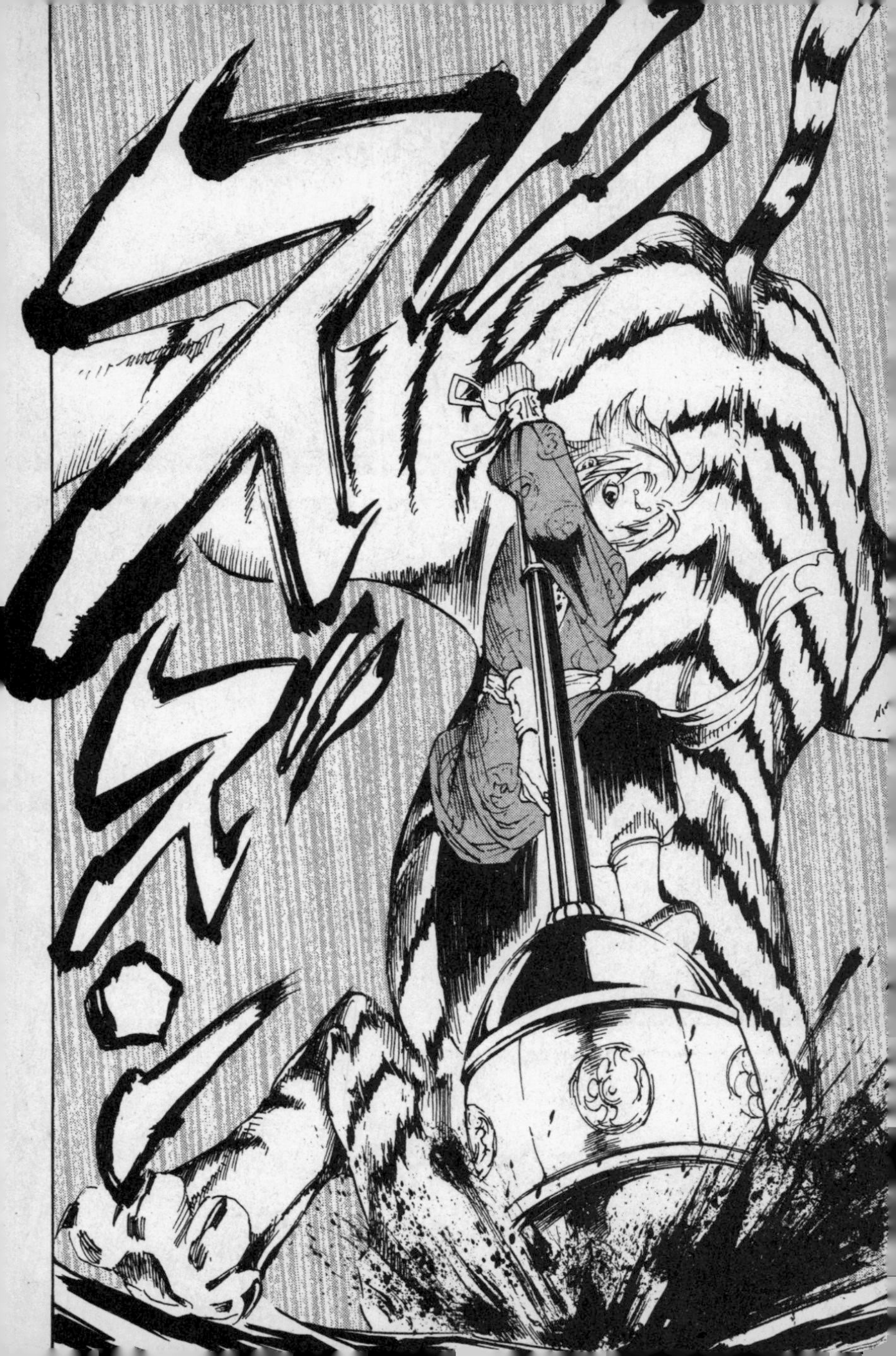

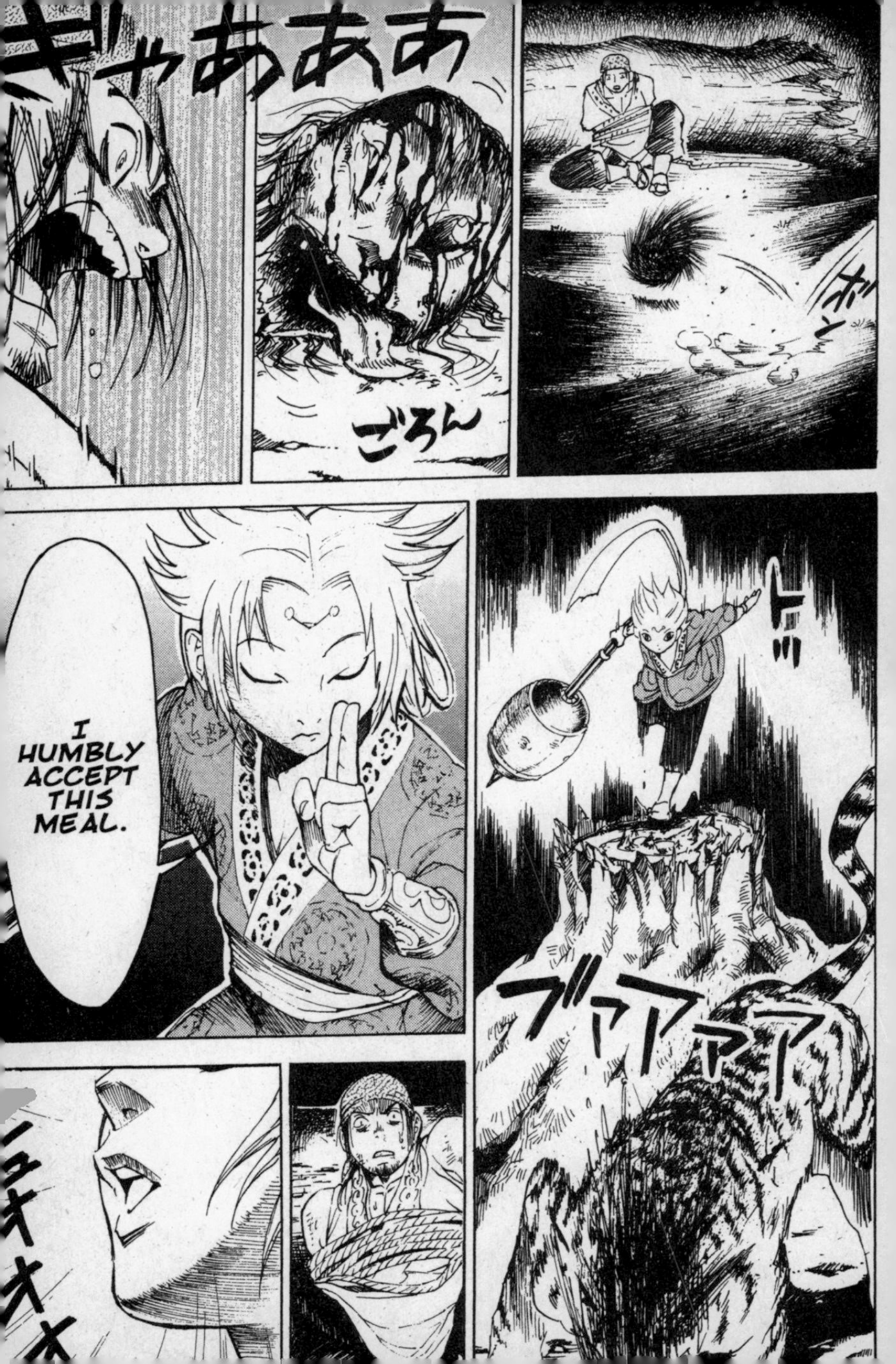
ボン
ぎゃあああ
ごろん
ドッ
ブァアアア
I HUMBLY ACCEPT THIS MEAL.

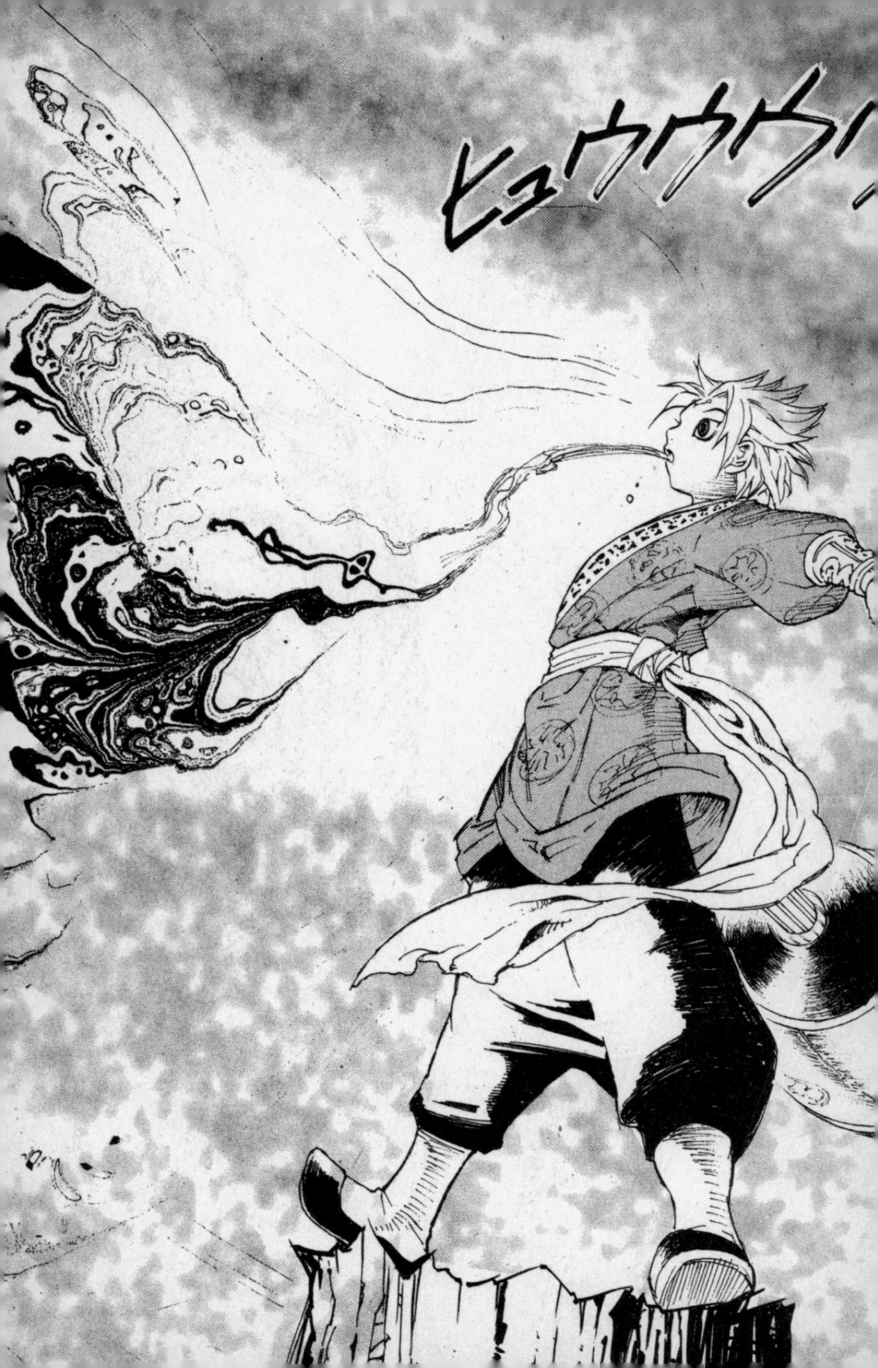
ヒュウウウ!

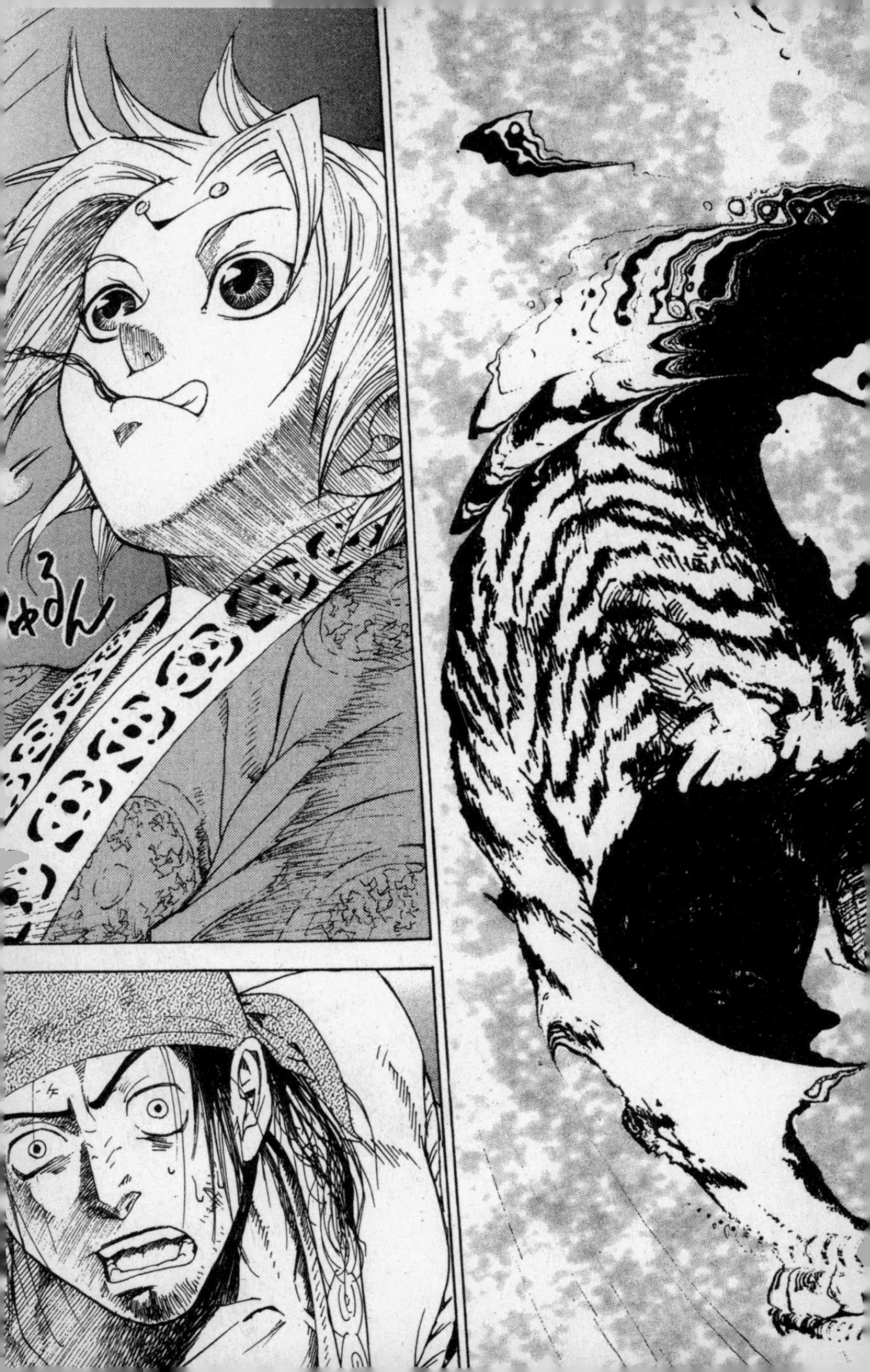
ゃるん

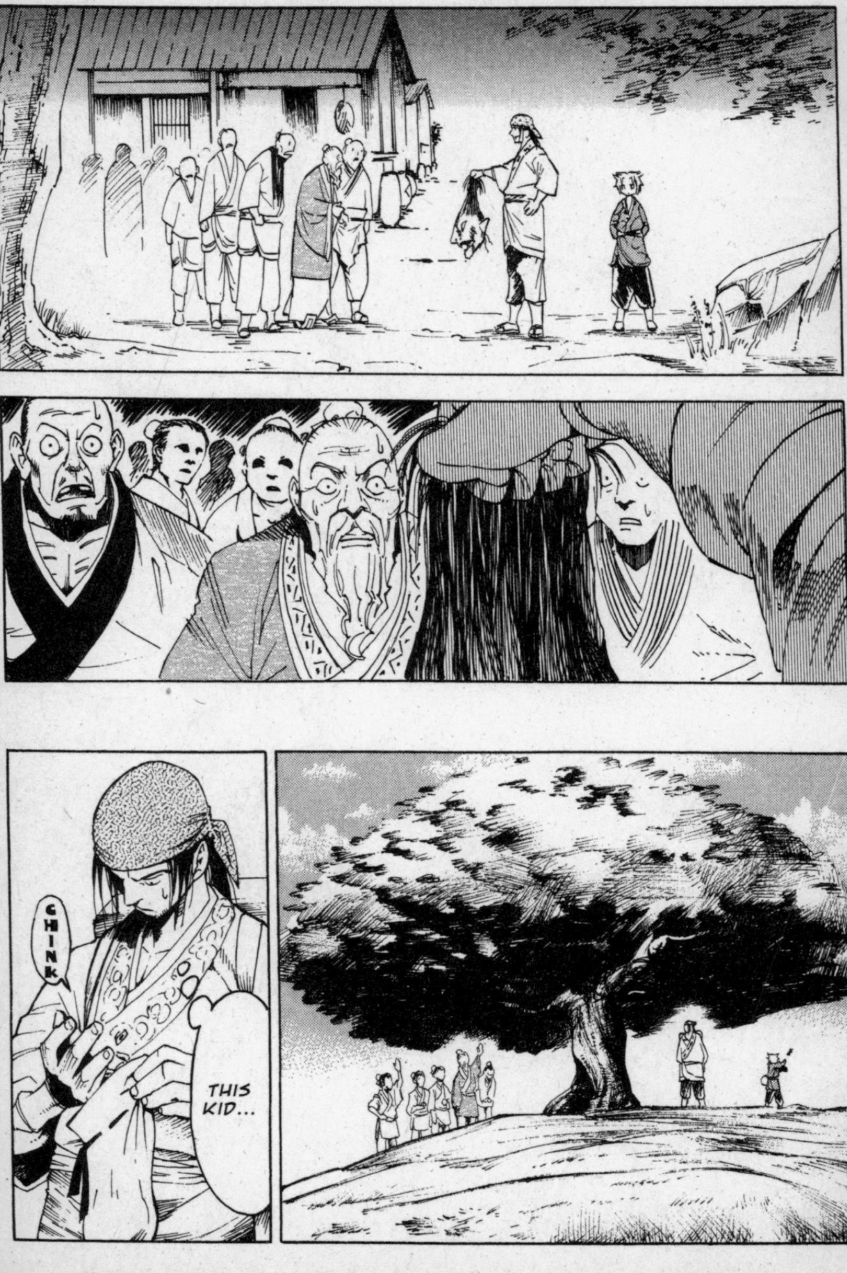
CHINK
THIS KID...

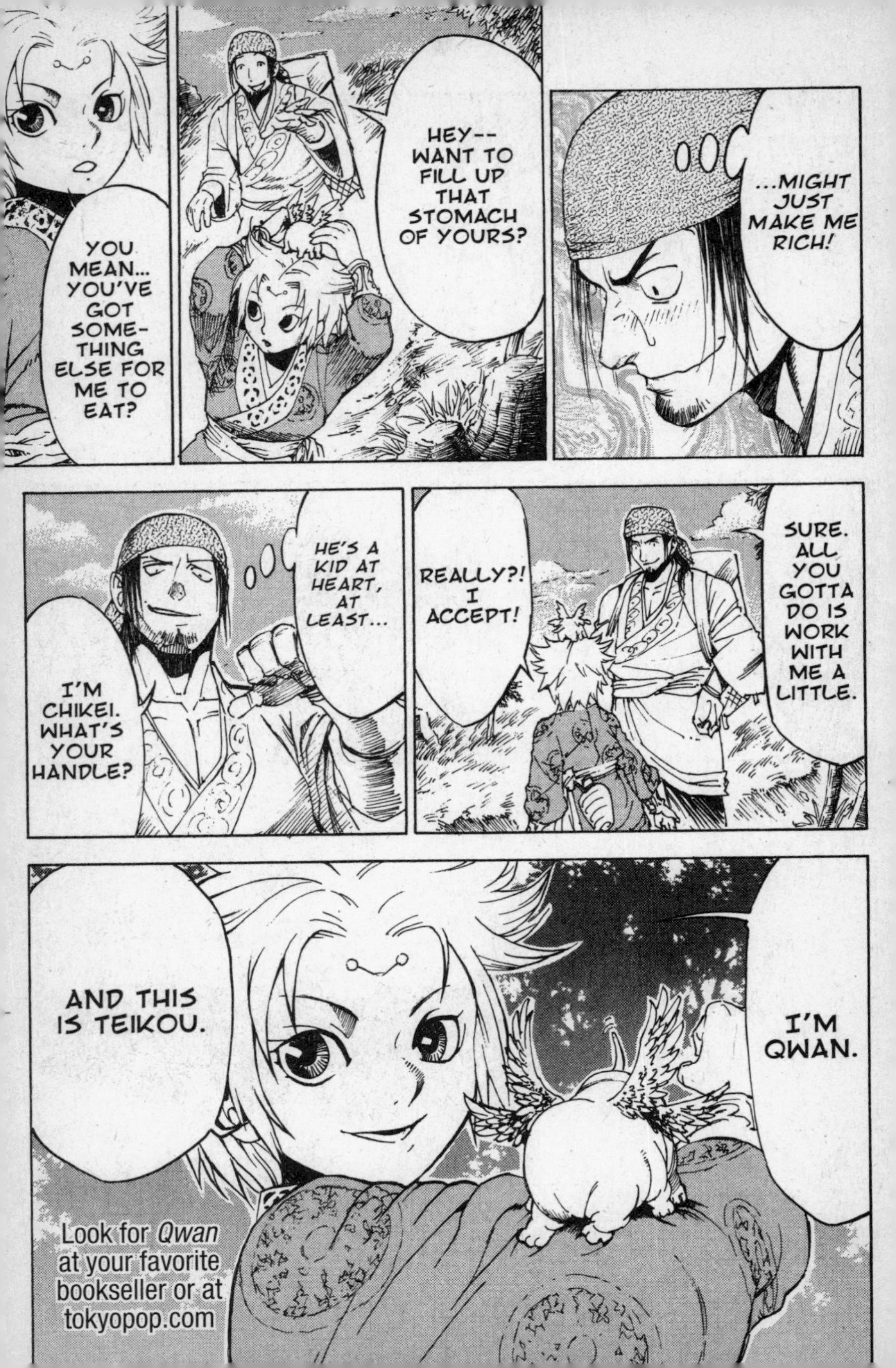
...MIGHT JUST MAKE ME RICH!
HEY-- WANT TO FILL UP THAT STOMACH OF YOURS?
YOU MEAN... YOU'VE GOT SOME-THING ELSE FOR ME TO EAT?
SURE. ALL YOU GOTTA DO IS WORK WITH ME A LITTLE.
REALLY?! I ACCEPT!
HE'S A KID AT HEART, AT LEAST...
I'M CHIKEI. WHAT'S YOUR HANDLE?
I'M QWAN.
AND THIS IS TEIKOU.

TOKYOPOP SHOP

WWW.TOKYOPOP.COM/SHOP

Check out all the sizzling hot merchandise and your favorite manga at the shop!

HOT NEWS!
Check out the TOKYOPOP SHOP! The world's best collection of manga in English is now available online in one place!

BIZENGHAST POSTER

PRINCESS AI POSTCARDS

I Luv Halloween Glow-in-the-Dark STICKERS!

I LUV HALLOWEEN BUTTONS & STICKERS

- LOOK FOR SPECIAL OFFERS
- PRE-ORDER UPCOMING RELEASES
- COMPLETE YOUR COLLECTIONS

Ayumu struggles with her studies, and the all-important high school entrance exams are approaching. Fortunately, she has help from her best bud Shii-chan, who is at the top of the class. But when the test results come back, the friends are surprised: Ayumu surpasses Shii-chan's scores and gets into the school of her choice—without Shii-chan! Losing her friend is so painful for Ayumu that she starts cutting herself to ease her sorrow. Finally, Ayumu seeks comfort in a new friend, Manami. But will Manami prove to be the friend that Ayumu truly needs? Or will Ayumu continue down a dark path?

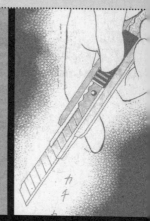

Volume 1

LIFE

Keiko Suenobu

It's about real teenagers...

It's about real high school...

It's about real life.

LIFE
BY KEIKO SUENOBU

LIFE™

OT
OLDER TEEN
AGE 16+

© Keiko Suenobu

STOP!

This is the back of the book.
You wouldn't want to spoil a great ending!

This book is printed "manga-style," in the authentic Japanese right-to-left format. Since none of the artwork has been flipped or altered, readers get to experience the story just as the creator intended. You've been asking for it, so TOKYOPOP® delivered: authentic, hot-off-the-press, and far more fun!

DIRECTIONS

If this is your first time reading manga-style, here's a quick guide to help you understand how it works.

It's easy... just start in the top right panel and follow the numbers. Have fun, and look for more 100% authentic manga from TOKYOPOP®!